# Alive
## The Final Evolution

4

**Story by Tadashi Kawashima**
**Art by Adachitoka**

Translated and adapted by
**Anastasia Moreno**

Lettered by
**North Market Street Graphics**

Ballantine Books • New York

*Alive* volume 4 is a work of fiction. Names, characters, places, and incidents are the products of the author's imagination or are used fictitiously. Any resemblance to actual events, locales, or persons, living or dead, is entirely coincidental.

A Del Rey Manga/Kodansha Trade Paperback Original



Published in the United States by Del Rey Books, an imprint of The Random House Publishing Group, a division of Random House, Inc., New York.



Publication rights arranged through Kodansha Ltd.

First published in Japan in 2004 by Kodansha Ltd., Tokyo

ISBN 978-0-345-49938-7

Printed in the United States of America

www.delreymanga.com

9 8 7 6 5 4 3 2 1

Translator/Adapter—Anastasia Moreno
Lettering—North Market Street Graphics

# Contents

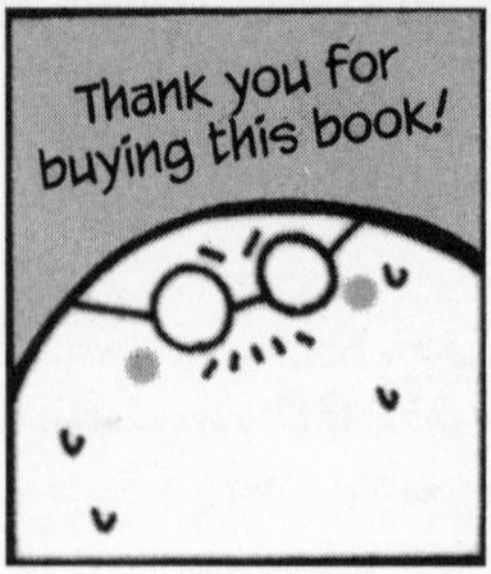
Thank you for buying this book!

**Tadashi Kawashima**

I borrowed the name "Nami" from a friend. Same with "Okada," who looks like me.

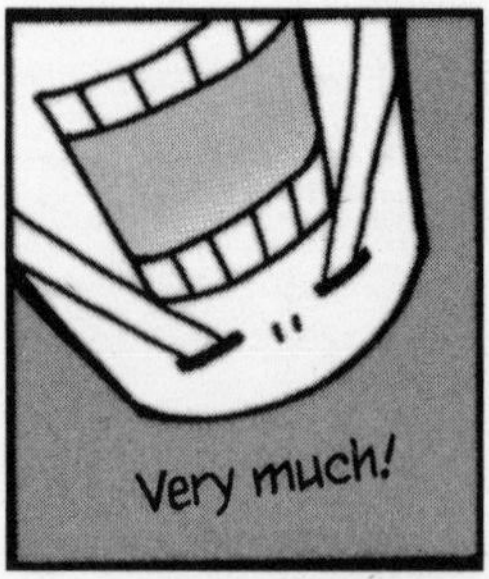
Very much!

**Adachitoka**

This series has lasted a year so far, thanks to readers like you.

# Honorifics Explained

Throughout the Del Rey Manga books, you will find Japanese honorifics left intact in the translations. For those not familiar with how the Japanese use honorifics and, more important, how they differ from American honorifics, we present this brief overview.

Politeness has always been a critical facet of Japanese culture. Ever since the feudal era, when Japan was a highly stratified society, use of honorifics—which can be defined as polite speech that indicates relationship or status—has played an essential role in the Japanese language. When addressing someone in Japanese, an honorific usually takes the form of a suffix attached to one's name (example: "Asuna-san"), is used as a title at the end of one's name, or appears in place of the name itself (example: "Negi-sensei," or simply "Sensei").

Honorifics can be expressions of respect or endearment. In the context of manga and anime, honorifics give insight into the nature of the relationship between characters. Many English translations leave out these important honorifics and therefore distort the feel of the original Japanese. Because Japanese honorifics contain nuances that English honorifics lack, it is our policy at Del Rey not to translate them. Here, instead, is a guide to some of the honorifics you may encounter in Del Rey Manga.

**-san:**  This is the most common honorific and is equivalent to Mr., Miss, Ms., or Mrs. It is the all-purpose honorific and can be used in any situation where politeness is required.

**-sama:**  This is one level higher than "-san" and is used to confer great respect.

**-dono:**  This comes from the word "tono," which means "lord." It is an even higher level than "-sama" and confers utmost respect.

**-kun:** This suffix is used at the end of boys' names to express familiarity or endearment. It is also sometimes used by men among friends, or when addressing someone younger or of a lower station.

**-chan:** This is used to express endearment, mostly toward girls. It is also used for little boys, pets, and even among lovers. It gives a sense of childish cuteness.

**Bozu:** This is an informal way to refer to a boy, similar to the English terms "kid" and "squirt."

**Sempai/ Senpai:** This title suggests that the addressee is one's senior in a group or organization. It is most often used in a school setting, where underclassmen refer to their upperclassmen as "sempai." It can also be used in the workplace, such as when a newer employee addresses an employee who has seniority in the company.

**Kohai:** This is the opposite of "sempai" and is used toward underclassmen in school or newcomers in the workplace. It connotes that the addressee is of a lower station.

**Sensei:** Literally meaning "one who has come before," this title is used for teachers, doctors, or masters of any profession or art.

**-[blank]:** This is usually forgotten in these lists, but it is perhaps the most significant difference between Japanese and English. The lack of honorific means that the speaker has permission to address the person in a very intimate way. Usually, only family, spouses, or very close friends have this kind of permission. Known as *yobisute,* it can be gratifying when someone who has earned the intimacy starts to call one by one's name without an honorific. But when that intimacy hasn't been earned, it can be very insulting.

# Alive

4

Writer / Tadashi Kawashima
Artist / Adachitoka

## contents



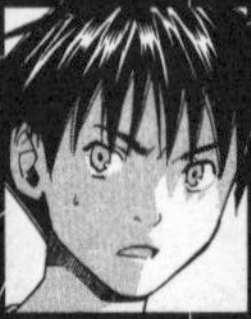

### Taisuke Kanou

High school student weak in fights, but has a strong sense of justice. During "Nightmare Week," acquired a supernatural power to control heat. Currently on a journey to find Hirose and Megumi.

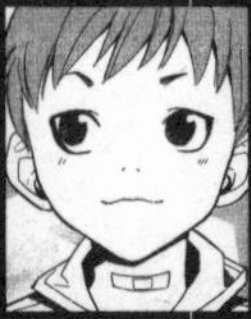

### Yuta Takizawa

Little boy traveling with Taisuke. Has a deep emotional scar resulting from witnessing his mother's suicide. Has ability to isolate space and has saved Taisuke several times already.

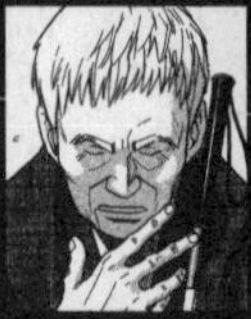

### Kiyomitsu Misaki

Old man blind from birth. Can see a person's past and future by touching them. Saw Taisuke's future by accident.

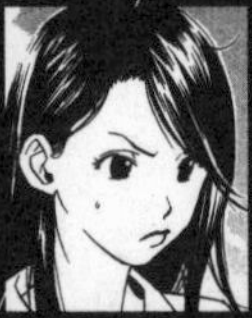

### Youko Kanou

Taisuke's older sister and also school nurse. Strong- willed woman who raised Taisuke after their parents died.

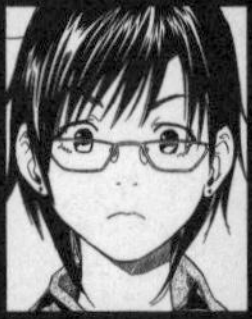

### Kyouko Amamiya

Passionate reporter of a weekly gossip magazine. Opposes the editorial policy of focusing on gossip and far-fetched occult material, and investigates the string of incidents related to the mass suicides.

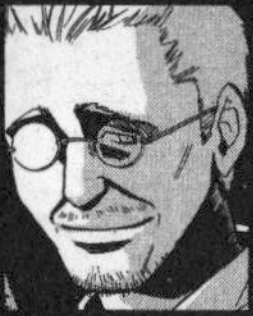

### Shigeki Katsumata

Former detective, and a leader type amongst the "comrades" with supernatural powers. Received orders from "the One" and plans to start a world revolution.

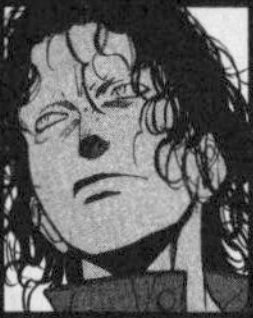

### Takumi Yura

One of Katsumata's "comrades." Controls highly pressurized air bubbles, and claims to be a leader of humans, but slaughters people mercilessly. Has frizzy hair and wears coveralls.

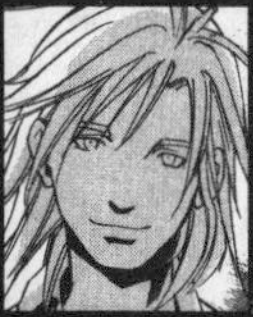

### Kenichirou Morio

One of Katsumata's "comrades." Controls wind to create sharp blades of air like a *kamaitachi* to slice humans. Hates Taisuke for burning a permanent scar on his face.

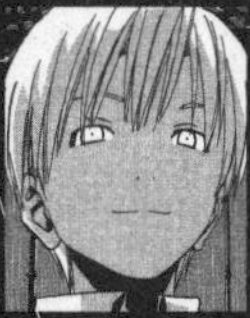

### Yuichi Hirose

Taisuke's close friend. He used to be weak and shy, but changed personalities after he acquired supernatural powers, and kidnapped Megumi. Accompanies Katsumata.

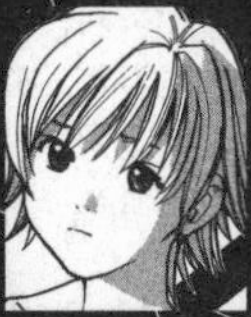

### Megumi Ochiai

Taisuke's childhood girlfriend. She always ends up arguing with Taisuke because she worries about him so much. Kidnapped by Hirose and confined to the house.

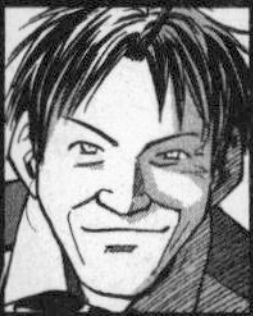

### Yoshikatsu Utsunomiya

Katsumata's police academy classmate, who has abilities to create illusions. Didn't join Katsumata's group, tried to kill his whole family, but was stopped by Taisuke, and so he committed suicide.

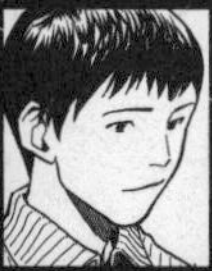

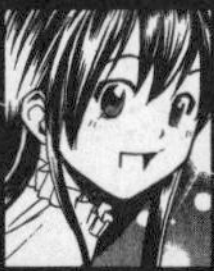

### Yoshiteru & Rin

Siblings running away from their father who was trying to kill them. They almost died inside their father's illusion, but Taisuke and Yuta saved them.

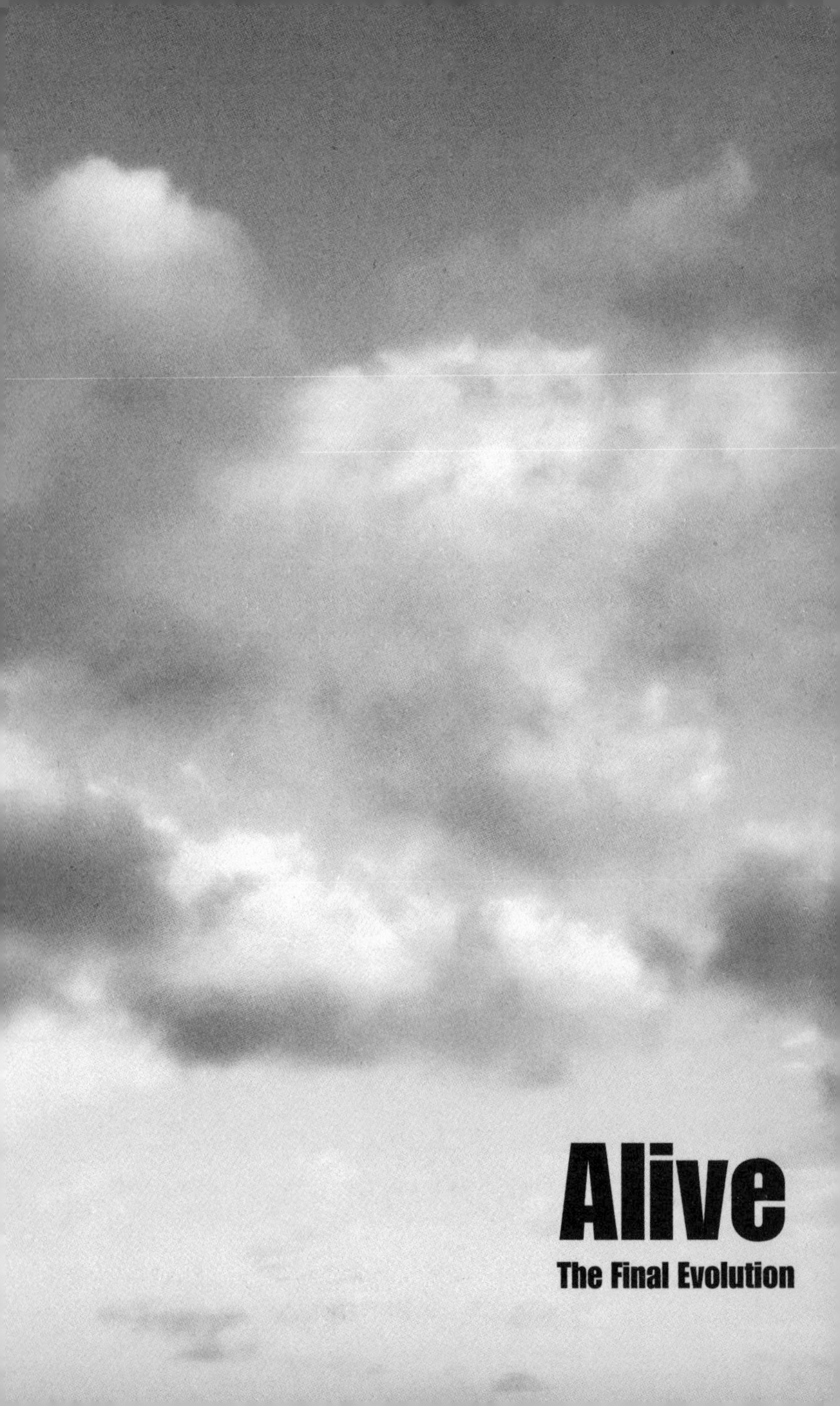

# Alive

## The Final Evolution

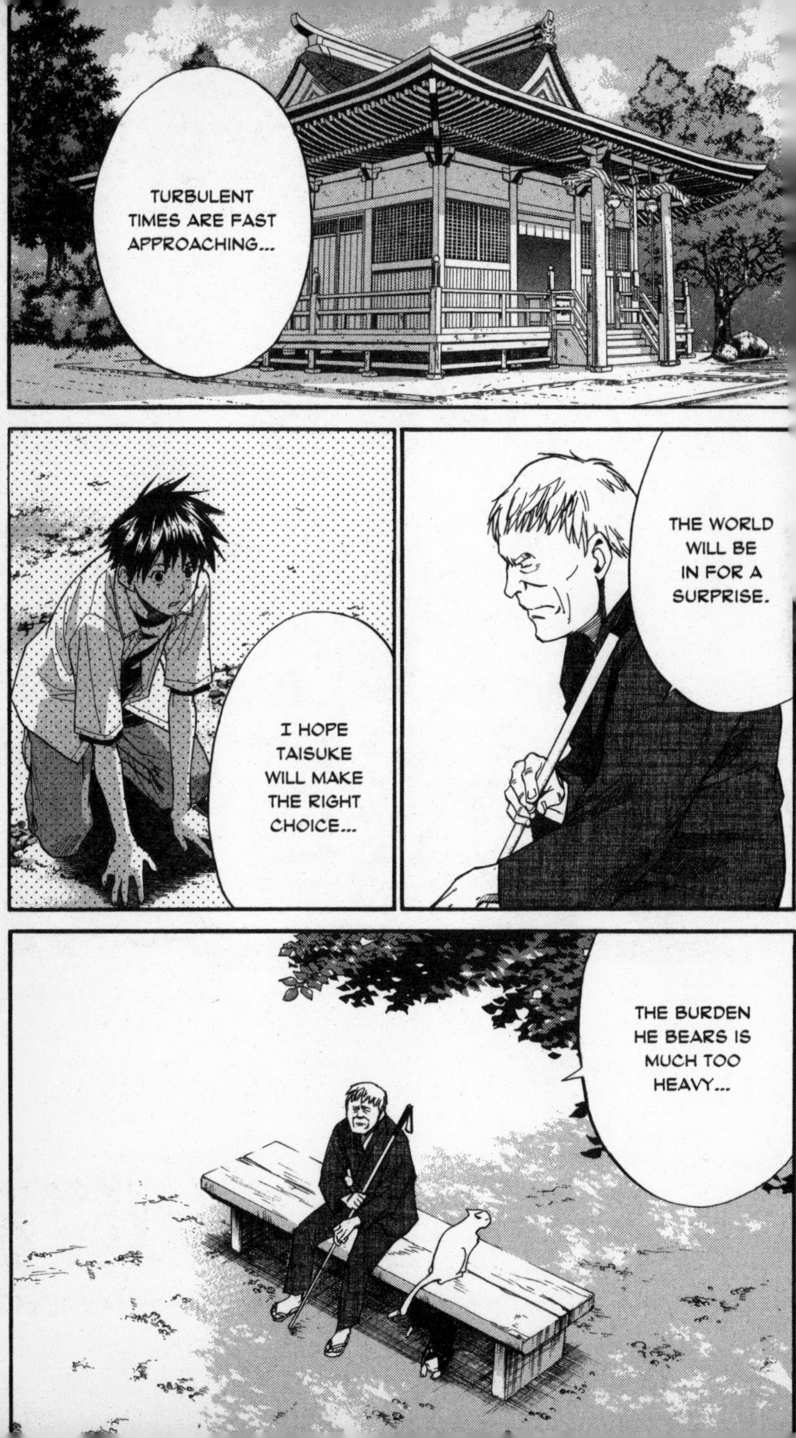
TURBULENT TIMES ARE FAST APPROACHING...
THE WORLD WILL BE IN FOR A SURPRISE.
I HOPE TAISUKE WILL MAKE THE RIGHT CHOICE...
THE BURDEN HE BEARS IS MUCH TOO HEAVY...

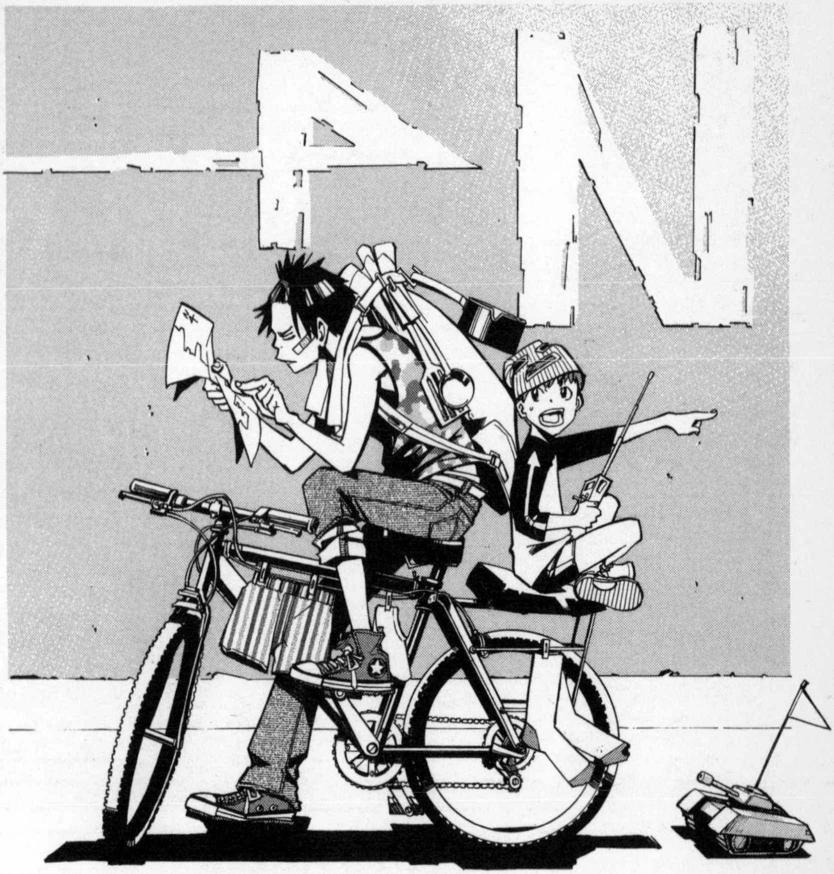

## Chapter 12

# Obviously

*Wisely, and slow; they stumble who run fast.*

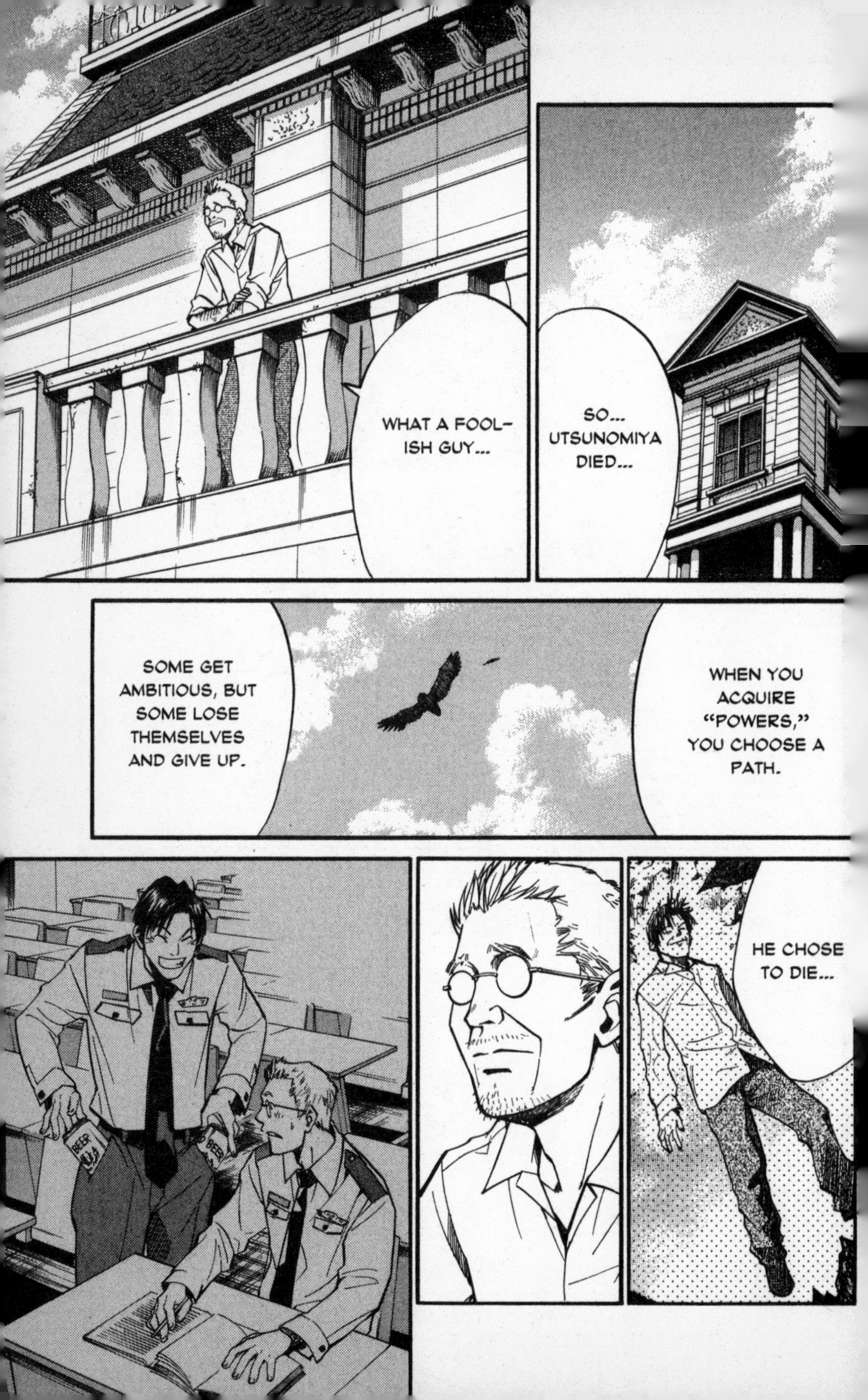
SO... UTSUNOMIYA DIED...
WHAT A FOOL-ISH GUY...
WHEN YOU ACQUIRE "POWERS," YOU CHOOSE A PATH.
SOME GET AMBITIOUS, BUT SOME LOSE THEMSELVES AND GIVE UP.
HE CHOSE TO DIE...

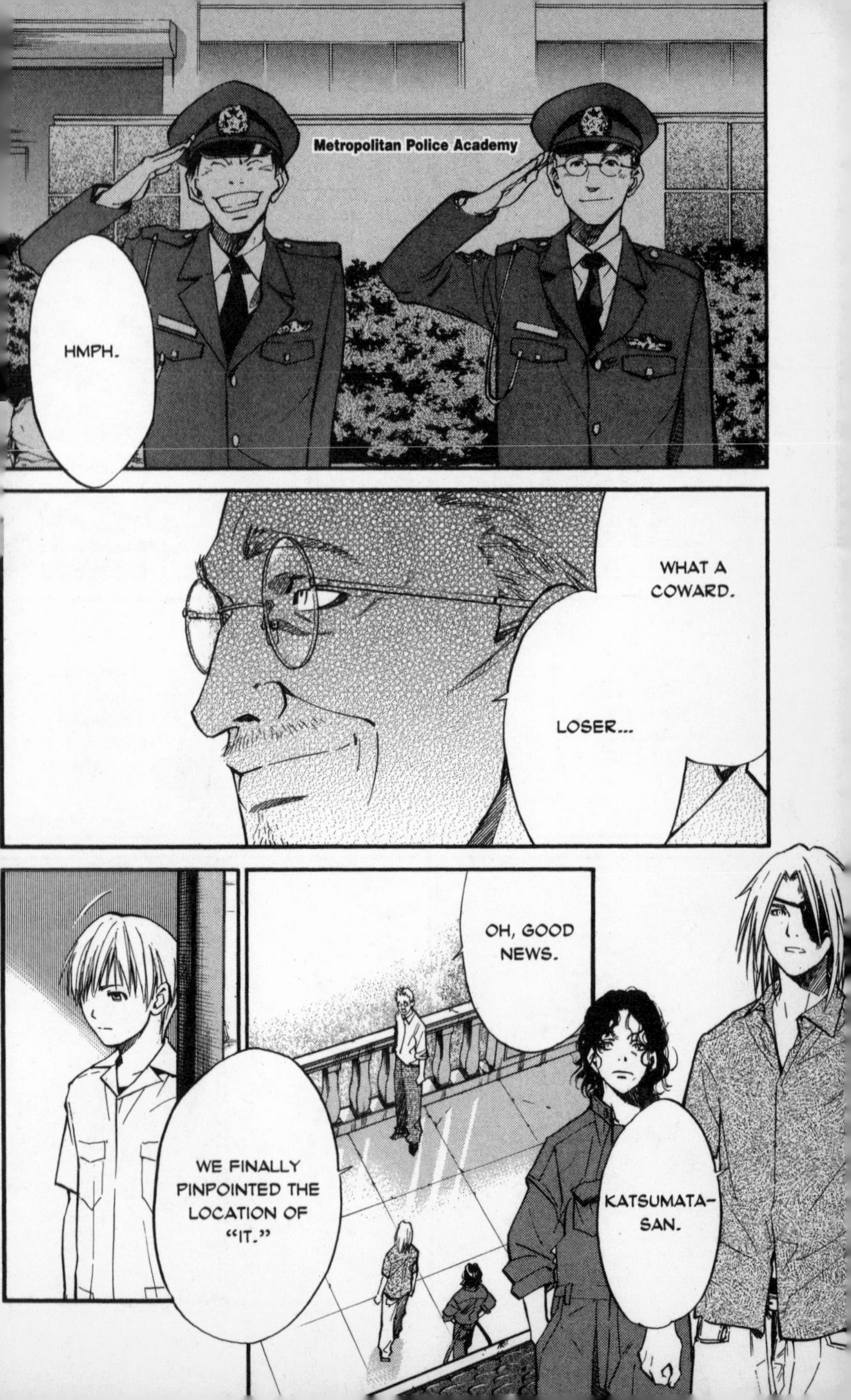
Metropolitan Police Academy
HMPH.
WHAT A COWARD.
LOSER...
OH, GOOD NEWS.
KATSUMATA-SAN.
WE FINALLY PINPOINTED THE LOCATION OF "IT."

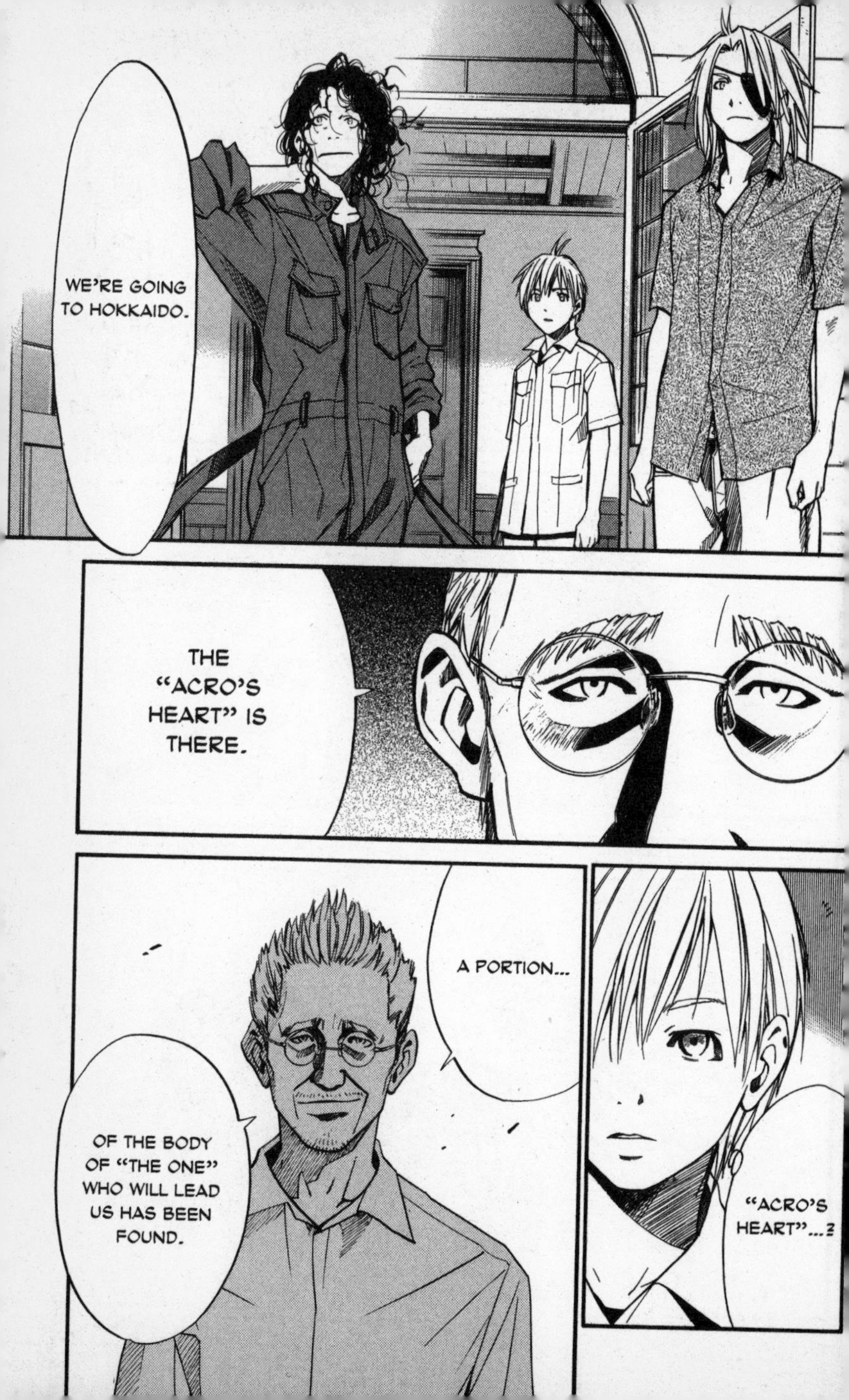
WE'RE GOING TO HOKKAIDO.
THE "ACRO'S HEART" IS THERE.
"ACRO'S HEART"...?
A PORTION...
OF THE BODY OF "THE ONE" WHO WILL LEAD US HAS BEEN FOUND.

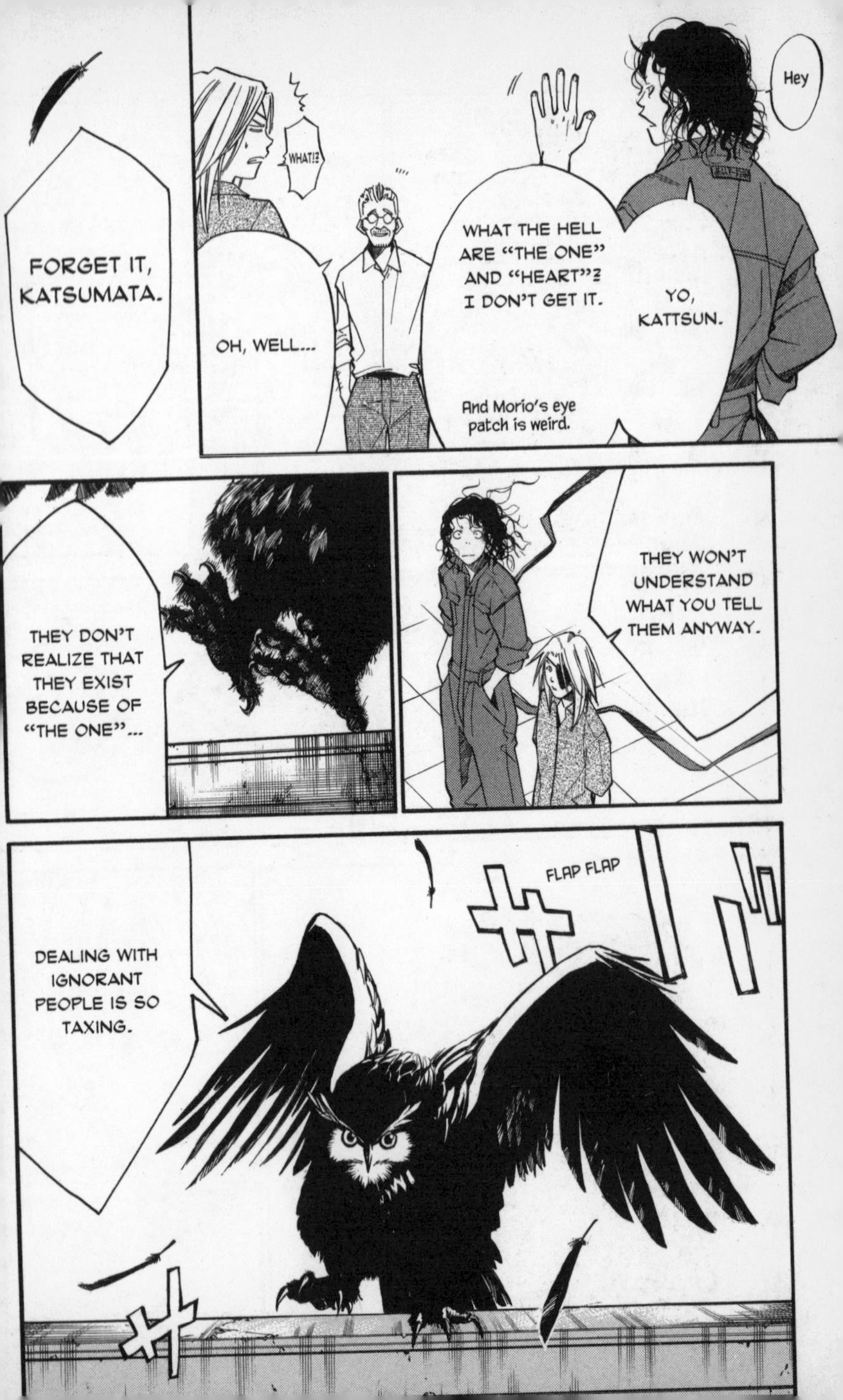
Hey
YO, KATTSUN.
WHAT THE HELL ARE "THE ONE" AND "HEART"? I DON'T GET IT.
And Morio's eye patch is weird.
WHAT!?
OH, WELL...
FORGET IT, KATSUMATA.
THEY WON'T UNDERSTAND WHAT YOU TELL THEM ANYWAY.
THEY DON'T REALIZE THAT THEY EXIST BECAUSE OF "THE ONE"...
FLAP FLAP
DEALING WITH IGNORANT PEOPLE IS SO TAXING.

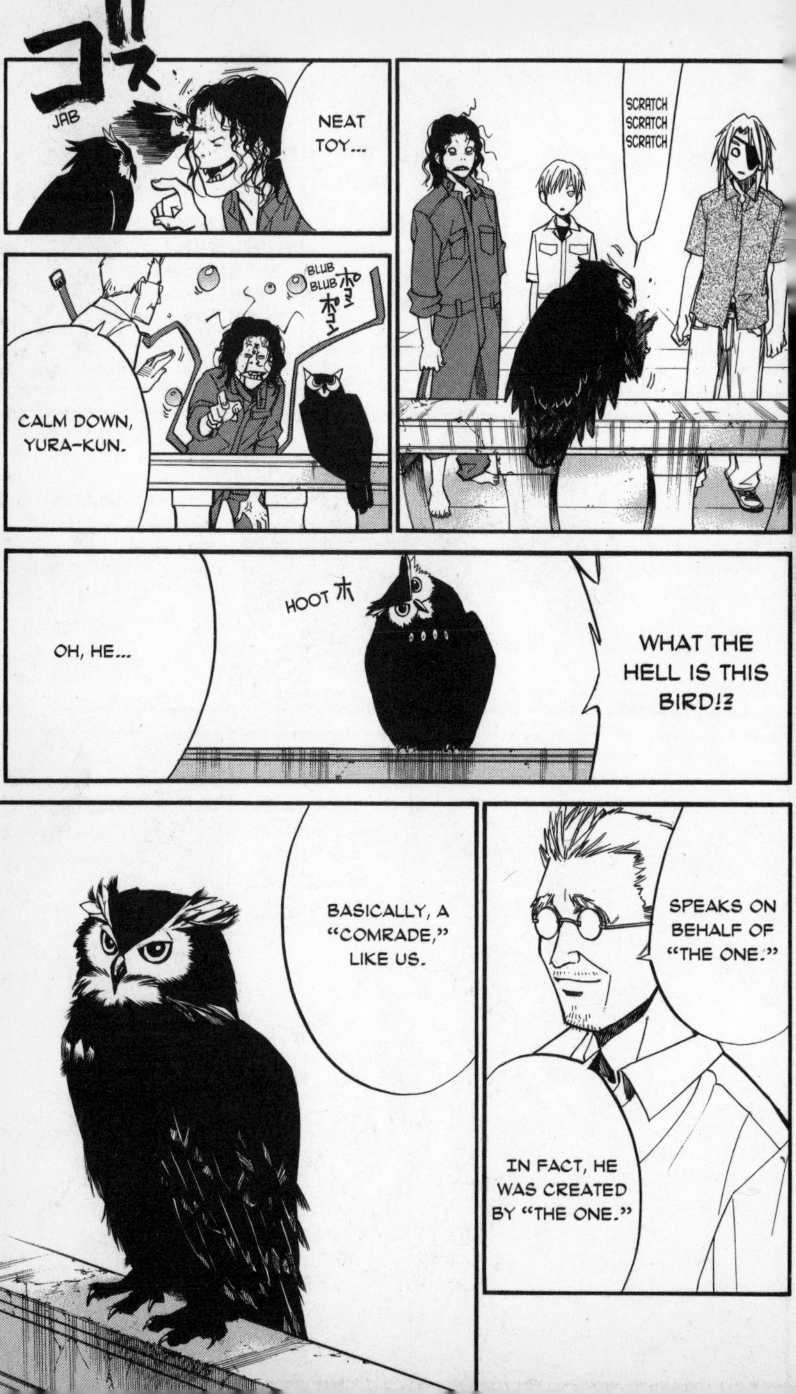
SCRATCH SCRATCH SCRATCH
JAB
NEAT TOY...
CALM DOWN, YURA-KUN.
BLUB BLUB
WHAT THE HELL IS THIS BIRD!?
HOOT
OH, HE...
SPEAKS ON BEHALF OF "THE ONE."
IN FACT, HE WAS CREATED BY "THE ONE."
BASICALLY, A "COMRADE," LIKE US.

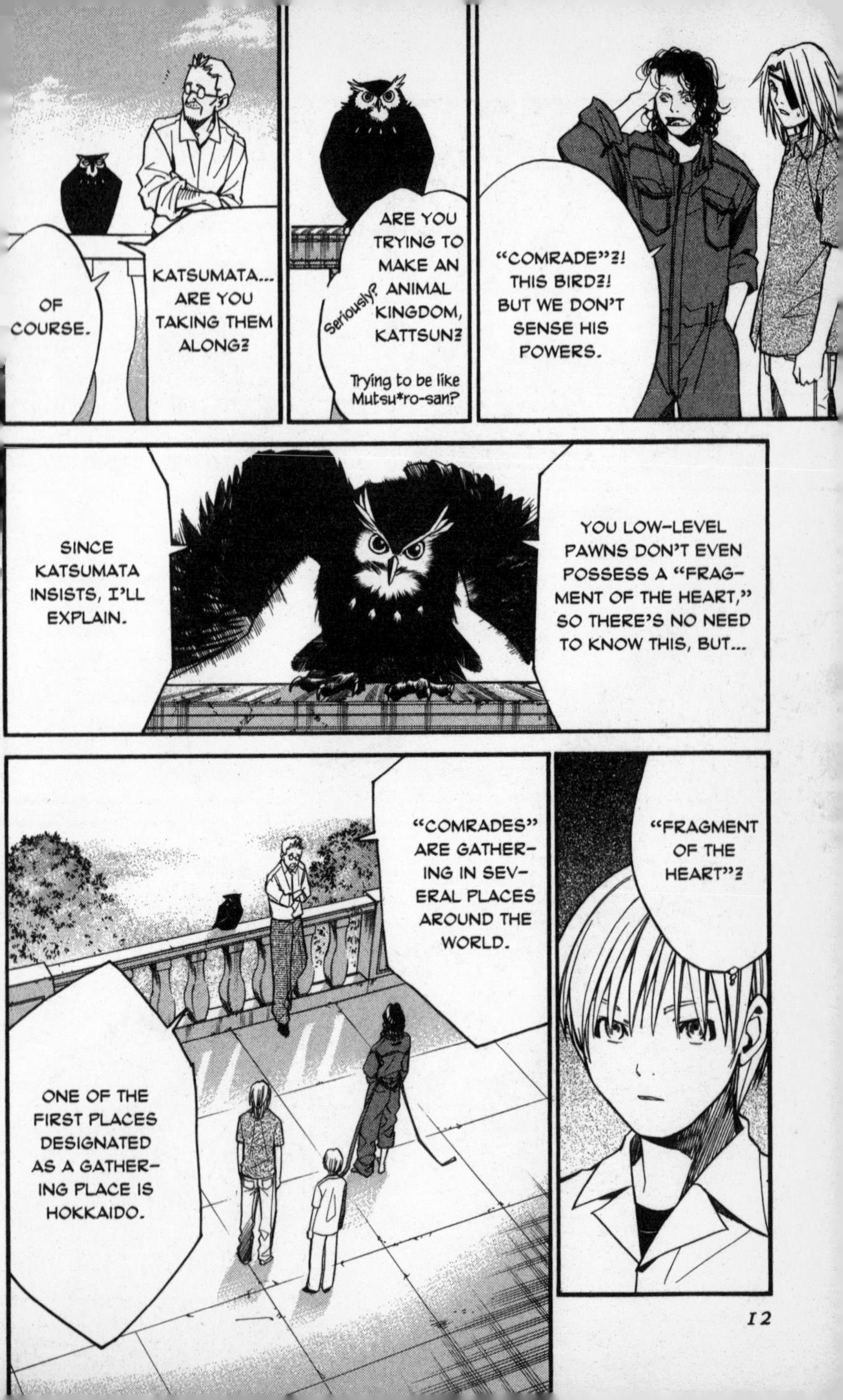
"COMRADE"?! THIS BIRD?! BUT WE DON'T SENSE HIS POWERS.
ARE YOU TRYING TO MAKE AN ANIMAL KINGDOM, KATTSUN?
Seriously?
Trying to be like Mutsu*ro-san?
KATSUMATA... ARE YOU TAKING THEM ALONG?
OF COURSE.
YOU LOW-LEVEL PAWNS DON'T EVEN POSSESS A "FRAGMENT OF THE HEART," SO THERE'S NO NEED TO KNOW THIS, BUT...
SINCE KATSUMATA INSISTS, I'LL EXPLAIN.
"FRAGMENT OF THE HEART"?
"COMRADES" ARE GATHERING IN SEVERAL PLACES AROUND THE WORLD.
ONE OF THE FIRST PLACES DESIGNATED AS A GATHERING PLACE IS HOKKAIDO.

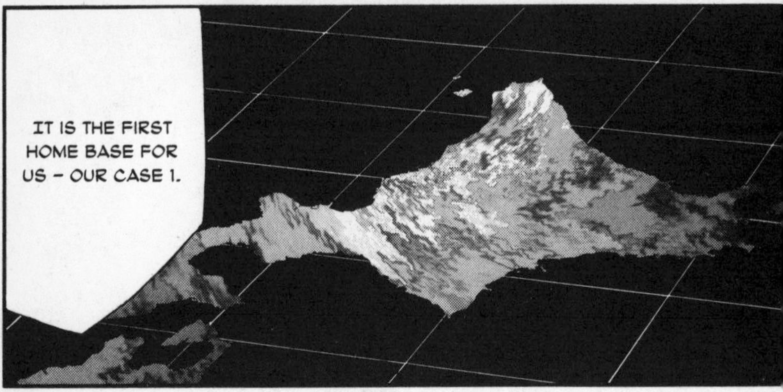
IT IS THE FIRST HOME BASE FOR US – OUR CASE 1.
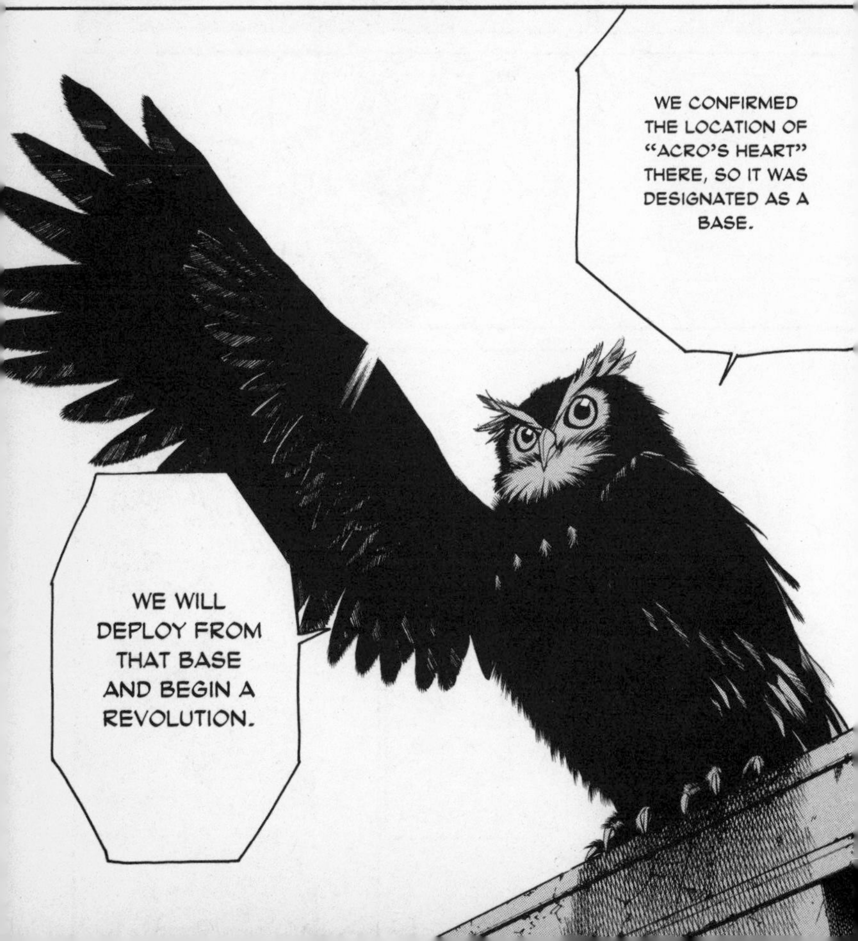
WE CONFIRMED THE LOCATION OF "ACRO'S HEART" THERE, SO IT WAS DESIGNATED AS A BASE.
WE WILL DEPLOY FROM THAT BASE AND BEGIN A REVOLUTION.

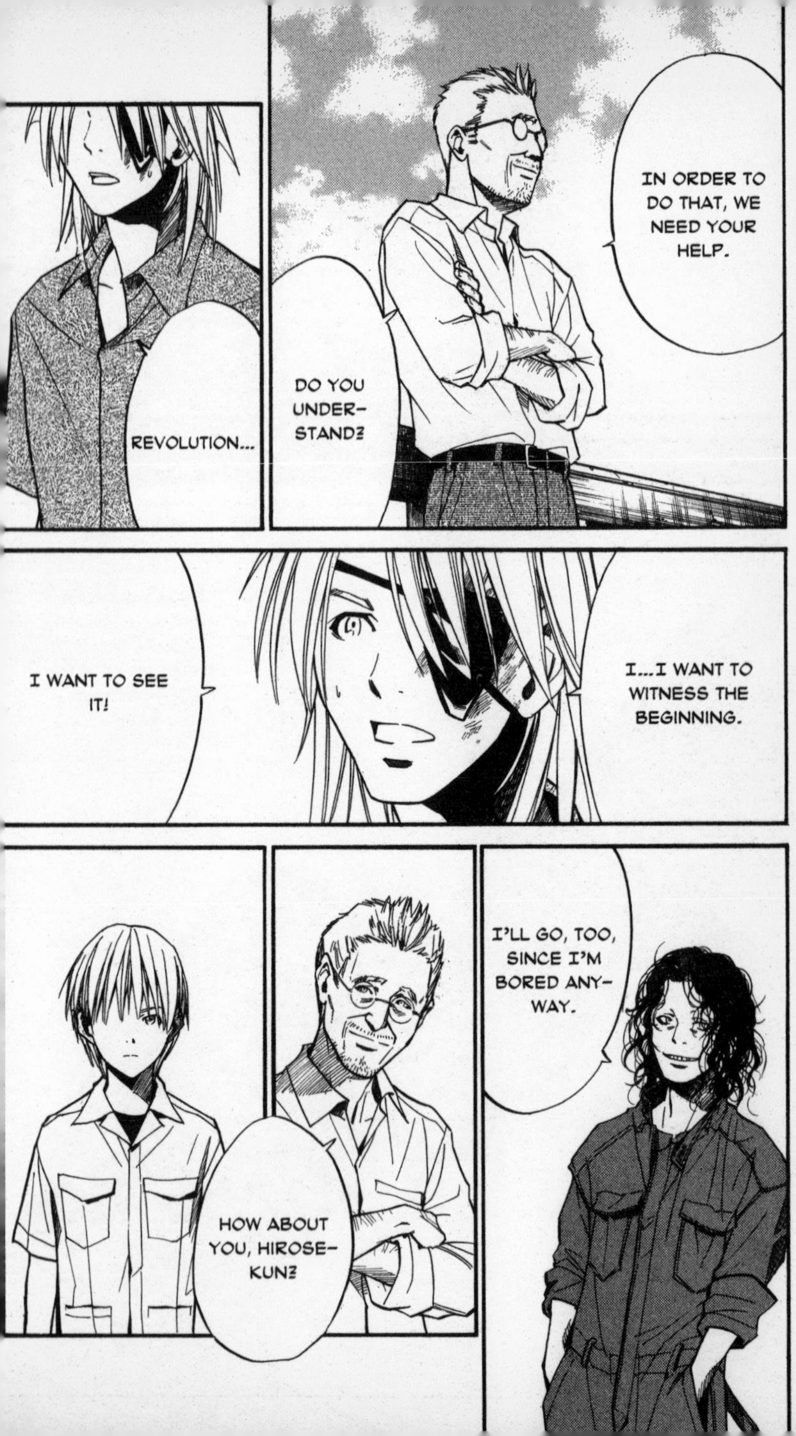
IN ORDER TO DO THAT, WE NEED YOUR HELP.
DO YOU UNDER-STAND?
REVOLUTION...
I...I WANT TO WITNESS THE BEGINNING.
I WANT TO SEE IT!
I'LL GO, TOO, SINCE I'M BORED ANY-WAY.
HOW ABOUT YOU, HIROSE-KUN?

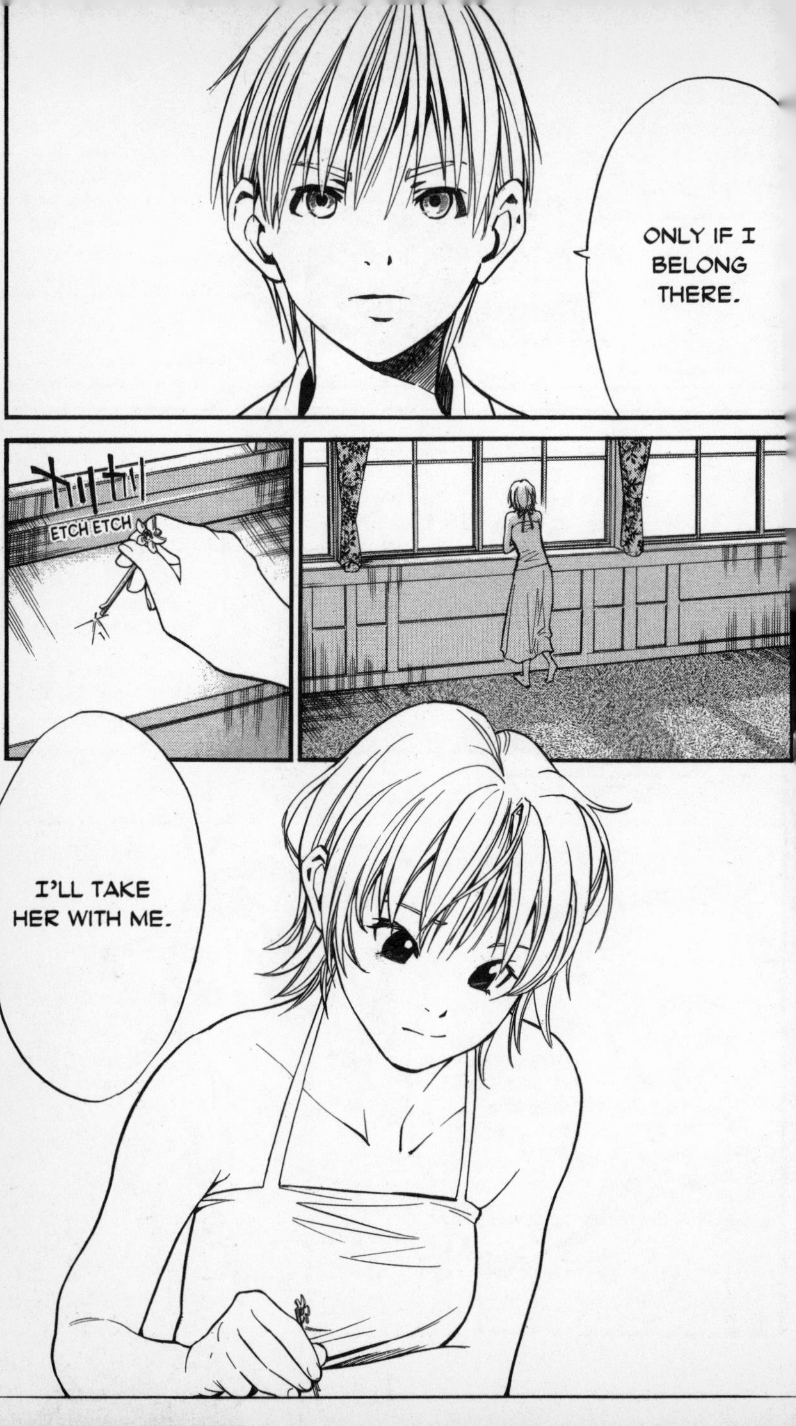
ONLY IF I BELONG THERE.
カリカリ
ETCH ETCH
I'LL TAKE HER WITH ME.

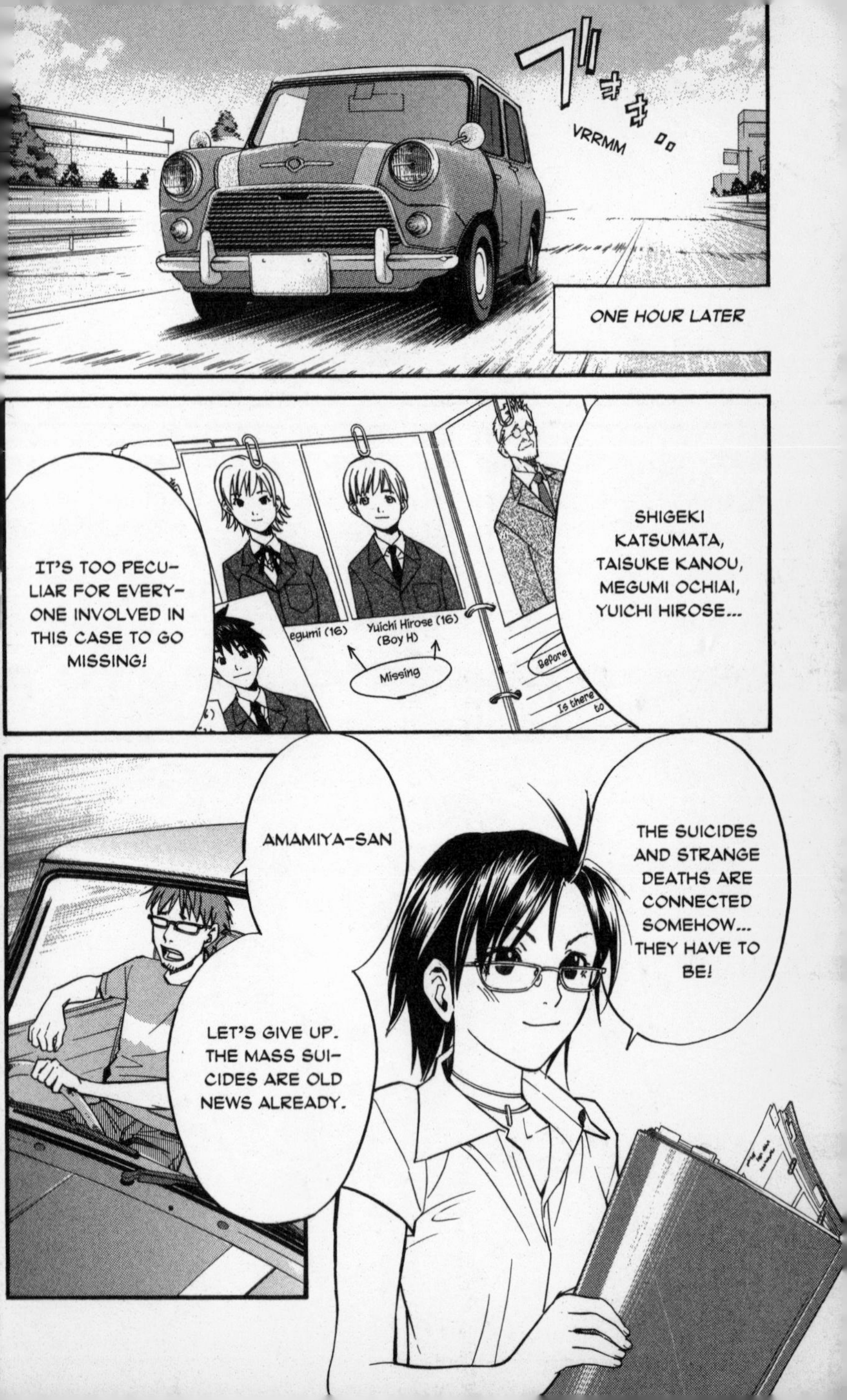
VRRMM
ONE HOUR LATER
SHIGEKI KATSUMATA, TAISUKE KANOU, MEGUMI OCHIAI, YUICHI HIROSE...
Yuichi Hirose (16)
(Boy H)
Missing
IT'S TOO PECULIAR FOR EVERYONE INVOLVED IN THIS CASE TO GO MISSING!
THE SUICIDES AND STRANGE DEATHS ARE CONNECTED SOMEHOW... THEY HAVE TO BE!
AMAMIYA-SAN
LET'S GIVE UP. THE MASS SUICIDES ARE OLD NEWS ALREADY.

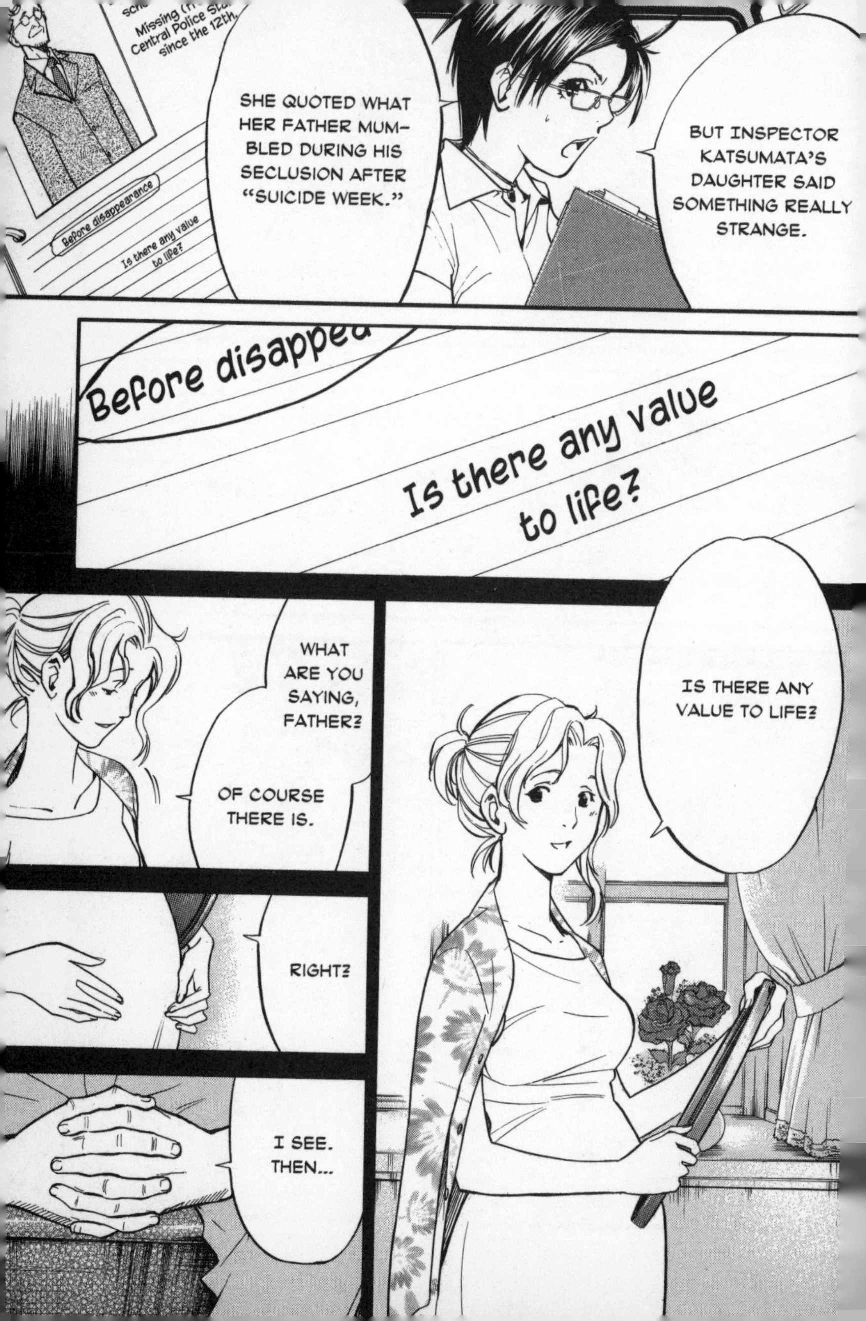
BUT INSPECTOR KATSUMATA'S DAUGHTER SAID SOMETHING REALLY STRANGE.
SHE QUOTED WHAT HER FATHER MUMBLED DURING HIS SECLUSION AFTER "SUICIDE WEEK."
since the 12th,
Before disappearance
Is there any value to life?
Is there any value to life?
IS THERE ANY VALUE TO LIFE?
WHAT ARE YOU SAYING, FATHER?
OF COURSE THERE IS.
RIGHT?
I SEE. THEN...

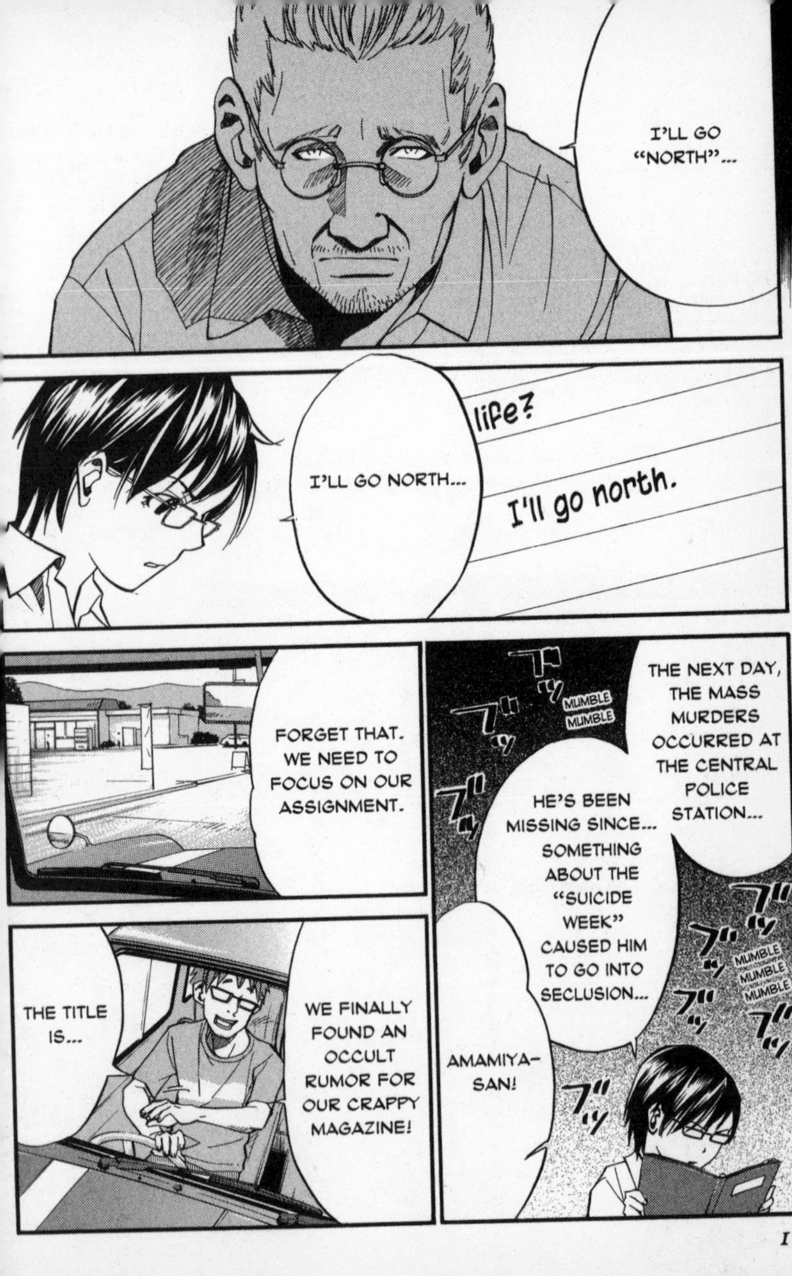
I'LL GO "NORTH"...
life?
I'll go north.
I'LL GO NORTH...
THE NEXT DAY, THE MASS MURDERS OCCURRED AT THE CENTRAL POLICE STATION...
MUMBLE MUMBLE
HE'S BEEN MISSING SINCE... SOMETHING ABOUT THE "SUICIDE WEEK" CAUSED HIM TO GO INTO SECLUSION...
MUMBLE MUMBLE MUMBLE
AMAMIYA-SAN!
FORGET THAT. WE NEED TO FOCUS ON OUR ASSIGNMENT.
WE FINALLY FOUND AN OCCULT RUMOR FOR OUR CRAPPY MAGAZINE!
THE TITLE IS...

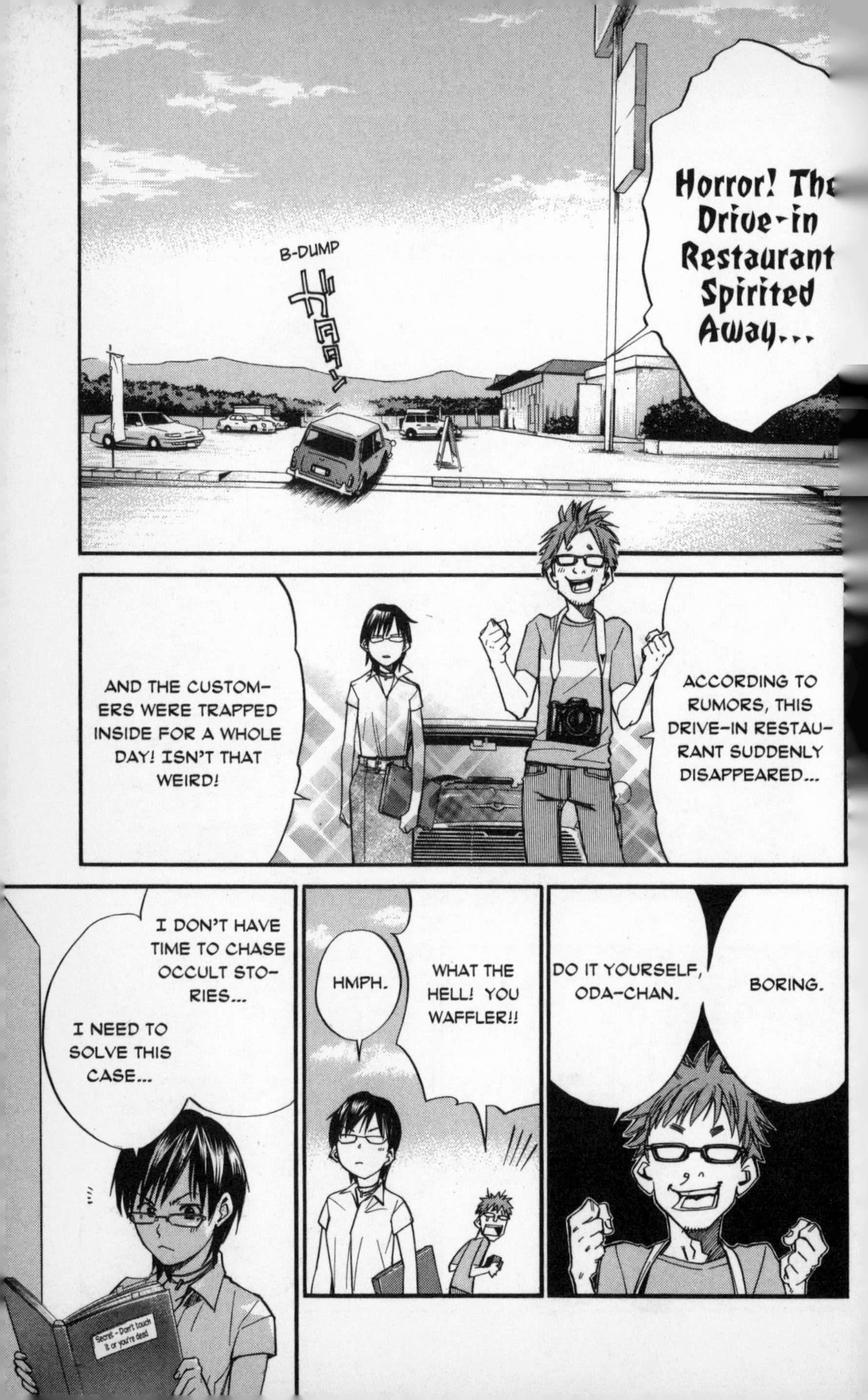
Horror! The Drive-in Restaurant Spirited Away...
B-DUMP
ACCORDING TO RUMORS, THIS DRIVE-IN RESTAURANT SUDDENLY DISAPPEARED...
AND THE CUSTOMERS WERE TRAPPED INSIDE FOR A WHOLE DAY! ISN'T THAT WEIRD!
BORING.
DO IT YOURSELF, ODA-CHAN.
WHAT THE HELL! YOU WAFFLER!!
HMPH.
I DON'T HAVE TIME TO CHASE OCCULT STORIES...
I NEED TO SOLVE THIS CASE...
Secret - Don't touch it or you're dead

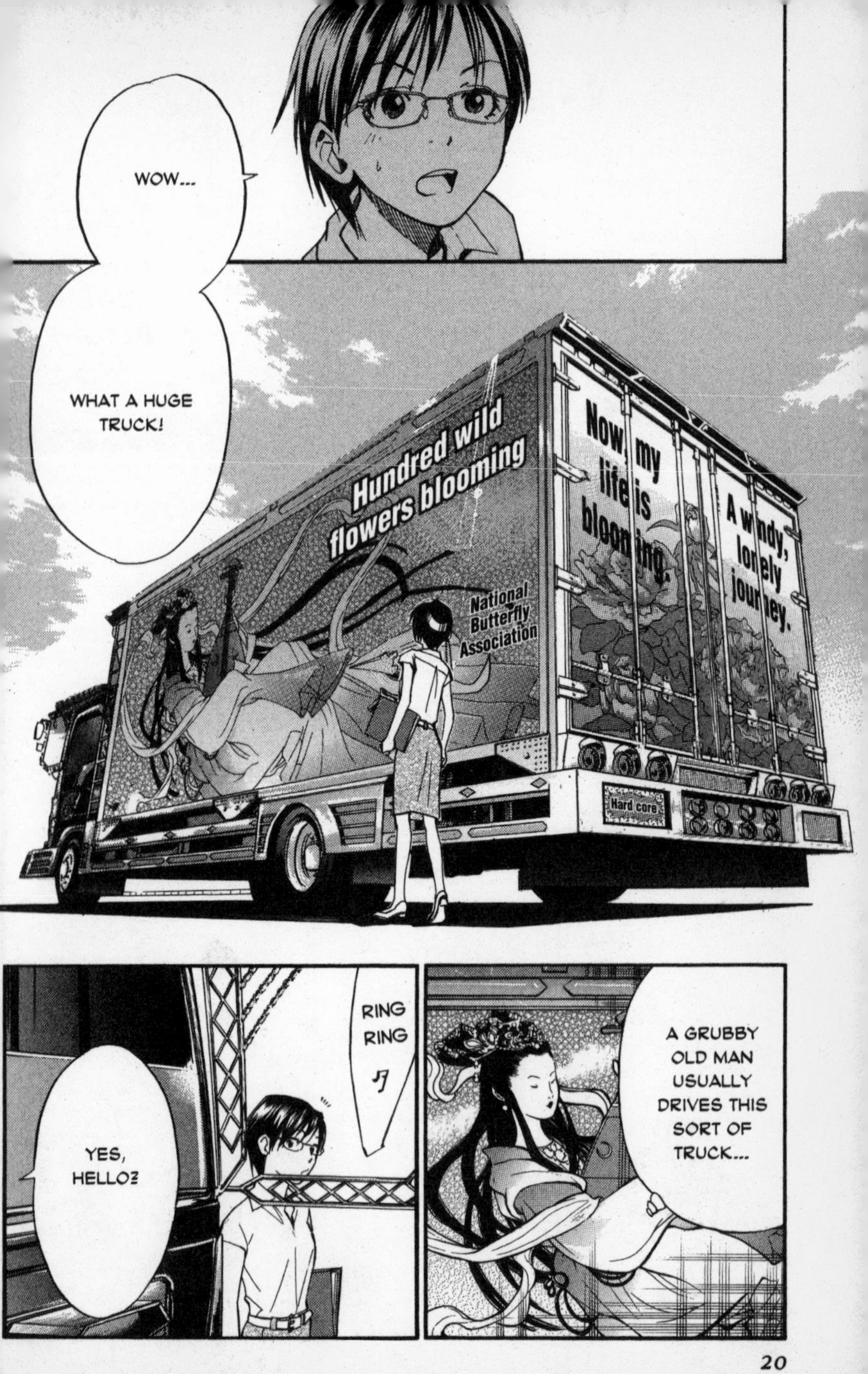
WOW...
WHAT A HUGE TRUCK!
Now, my life is blooming.
A windy, lonely journey.
Hundred wild flowers blooming
National Butterfly Association
Hard core
A GRUBBY OLD MAN USUALLY DRIVES THIS SORT OF TRUCK...
RING RING
YES, HELLO?

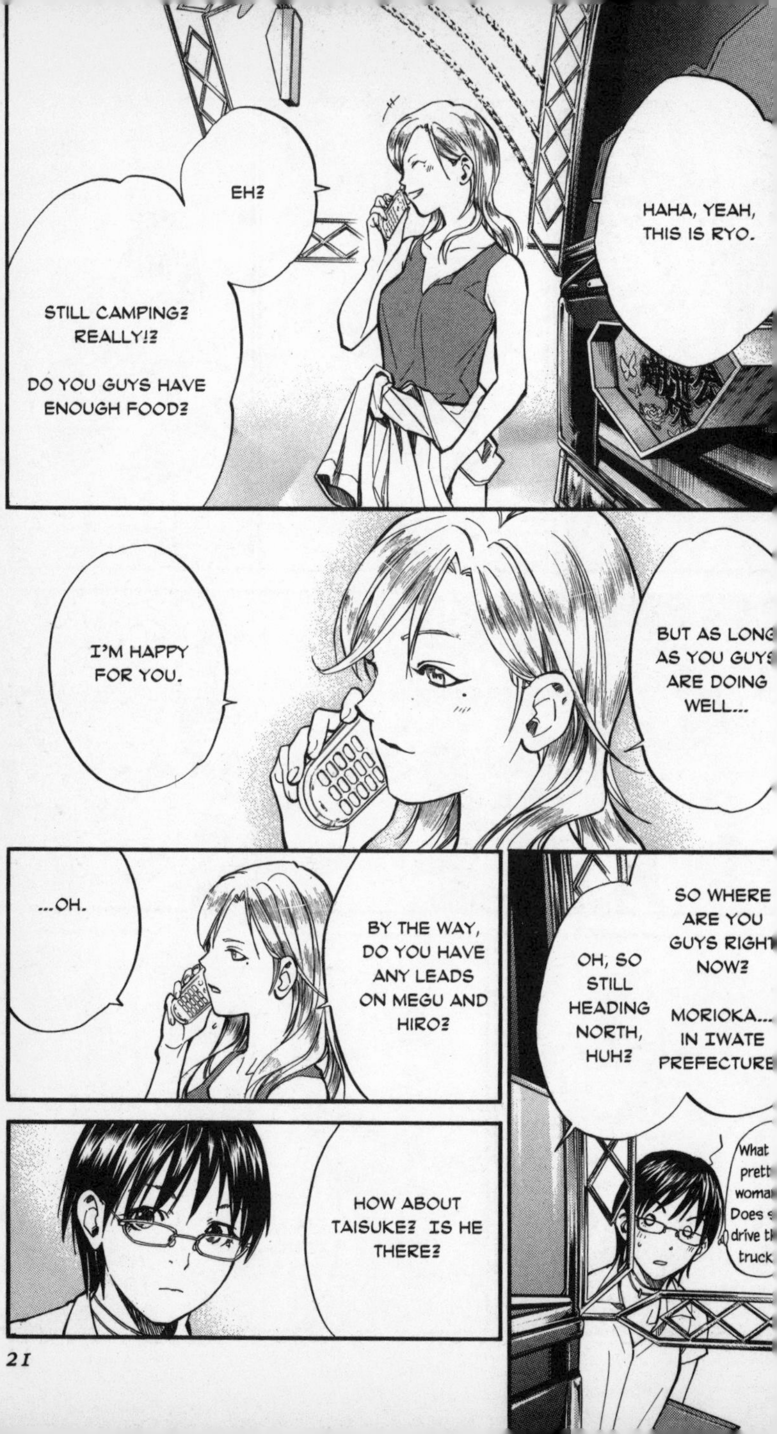
HAHA, YEAH, THIS IS RYO.
EH?
STILL CAMPING? REALLY!?
DO YOU GUYS HAVE ENOUGH FOOD?
BUT AS LONG AS YOU GUYS ARE DOING WELL...
I'M HAPPY FOR YOU.
SO WHERE ARE YOU GUYS RIGHT NOW?
MORIOKA... IN IWATE PREFECTURE
OH, SO STILL HEADING NORTH, HUH?
What prett woma Does s drive t truck
BY THE WAY, DO YOU HAVE ANY LEADS ON MEGU AND HIRO?
...OH.
HOW ABOUT TAISUKE? IS HE THERE?

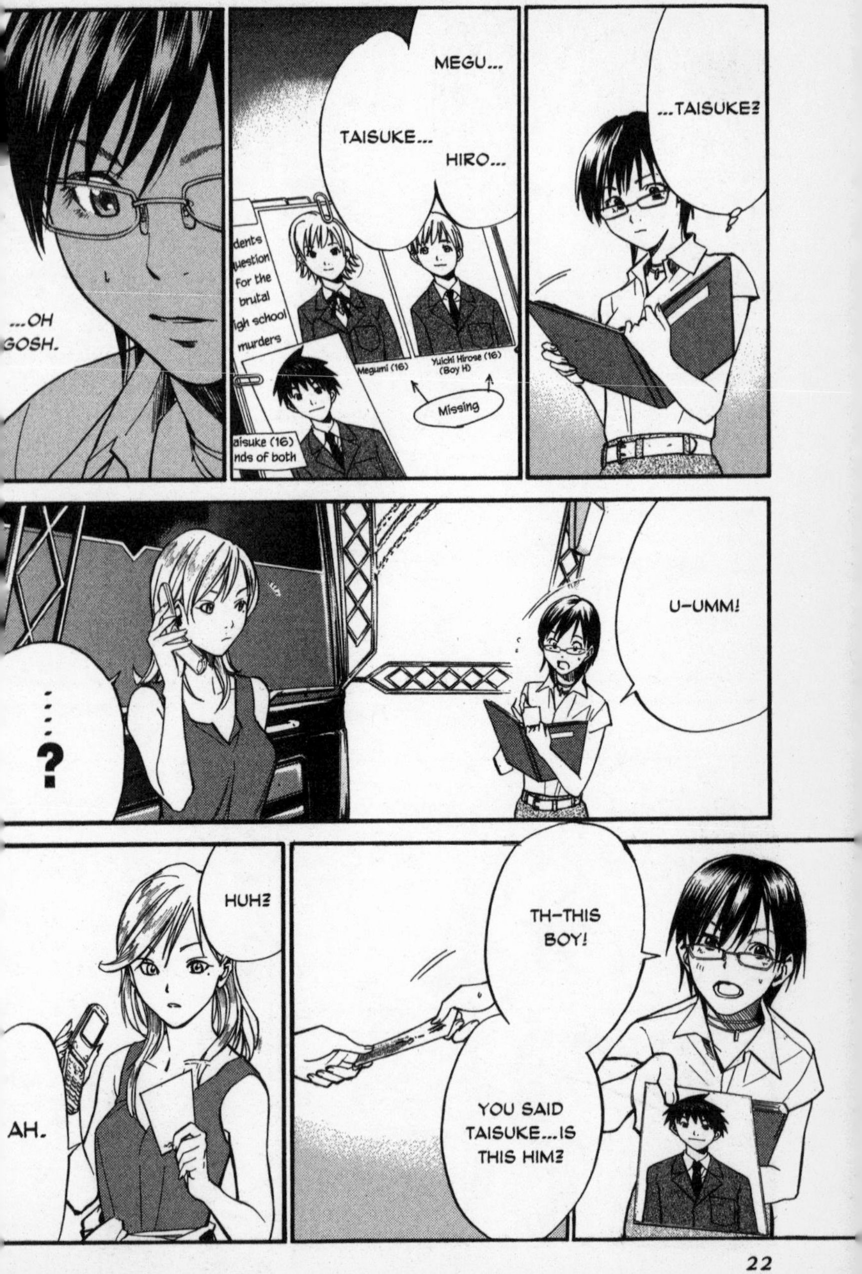
...TAISUKE?
MEGU...
TAISUKE...
HIRO...
dents
uestion
for the
brutal
igh school
murders
Megumi (16)
Yuichi Hirose (16)
(Boy H)
Missing
aisuke (16)
nds of both
...OH GOSH.
U-UMM!
....?
TH-THIS BOY!
YOU SAID TAISUKE...IS THIS HIM?
HUH?
AH.

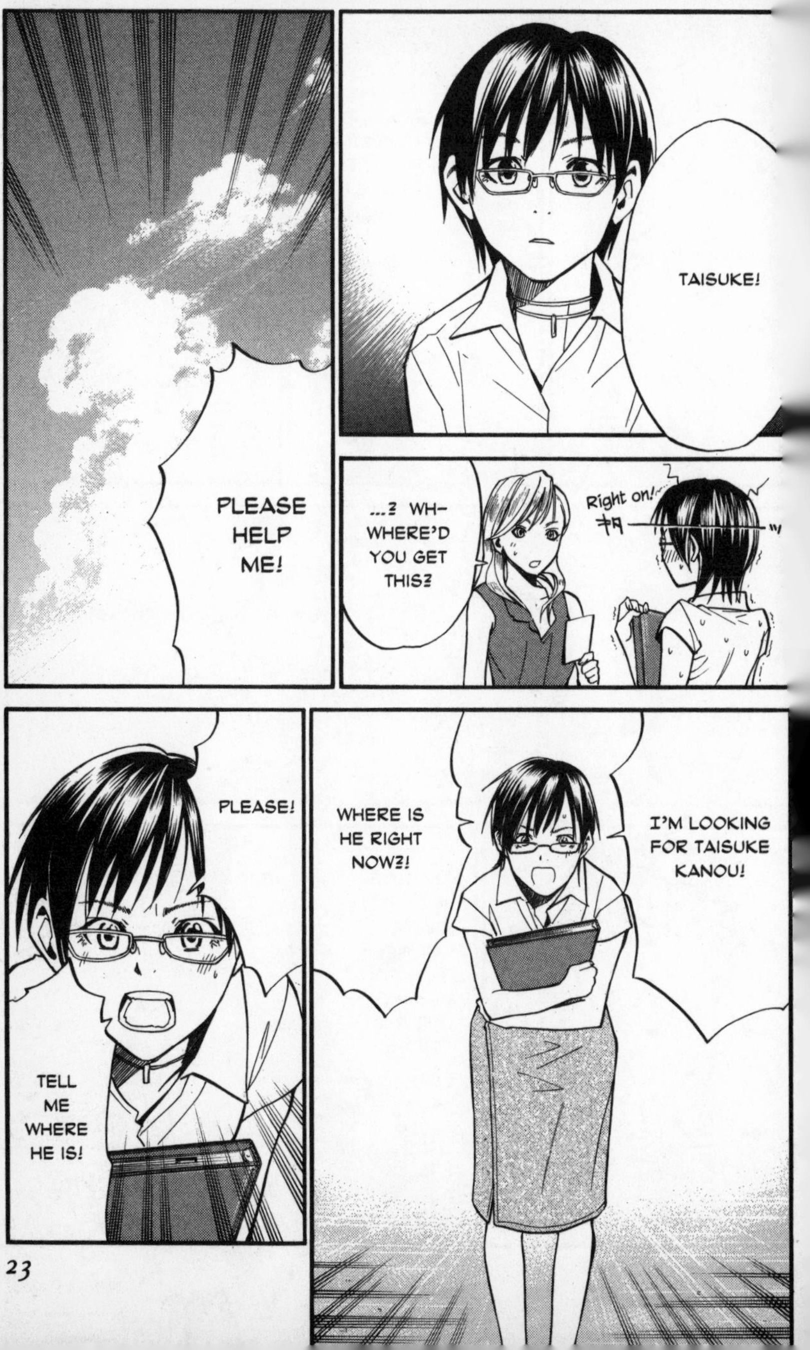
TAISUKE!
Right on!
...? WH- WHERE'D YOU GET THIS?
PLEASE HELP ME!
I'M LOOKING FOR TAISUKE KANOU!
WHERE IS HE RIGHT NOW?!
PLEASE!
TELL ME WHERE HE IS!

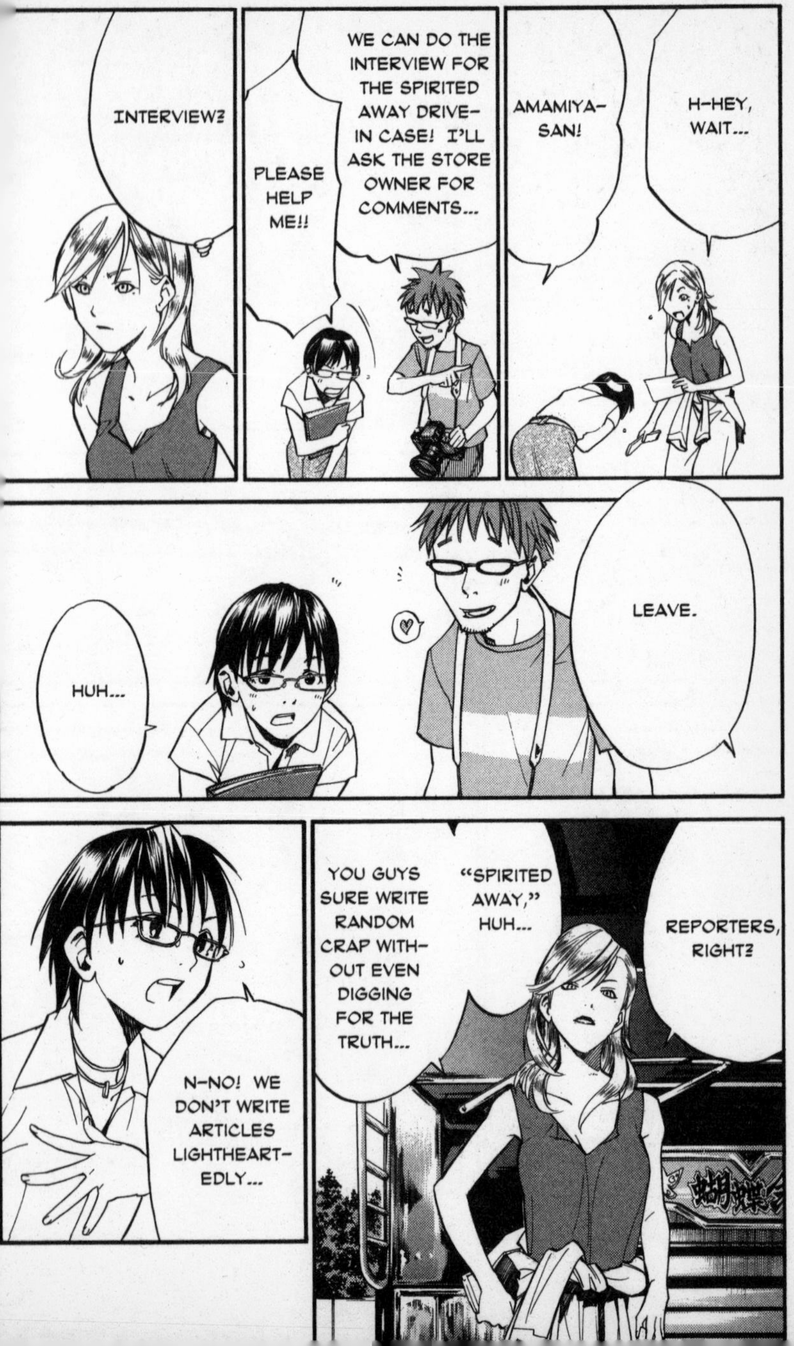
H-HEY, WAIT...
AMAMIYA-SAN!
WE CAN DO THE INTERVIEW FOR THE SPIRITED AWAY DRIVE-IN CASE! I'LL ASK THE STORE OWNER FOR COMMENTS...
PLEASE HELP ME!!
INTERVIEW?
LEAVE.
HUH...
REPORTERS, RIGHT?
"SPIRITED AWAY," HUH...
YOU GUYS SURE WRITE RANDOM CRAP WITHOUT EVEN DIGGING FOR THE TRUTH...
N-NO! WE DON'T WRITE ARTICLES LIGHTHEARTEDLY...

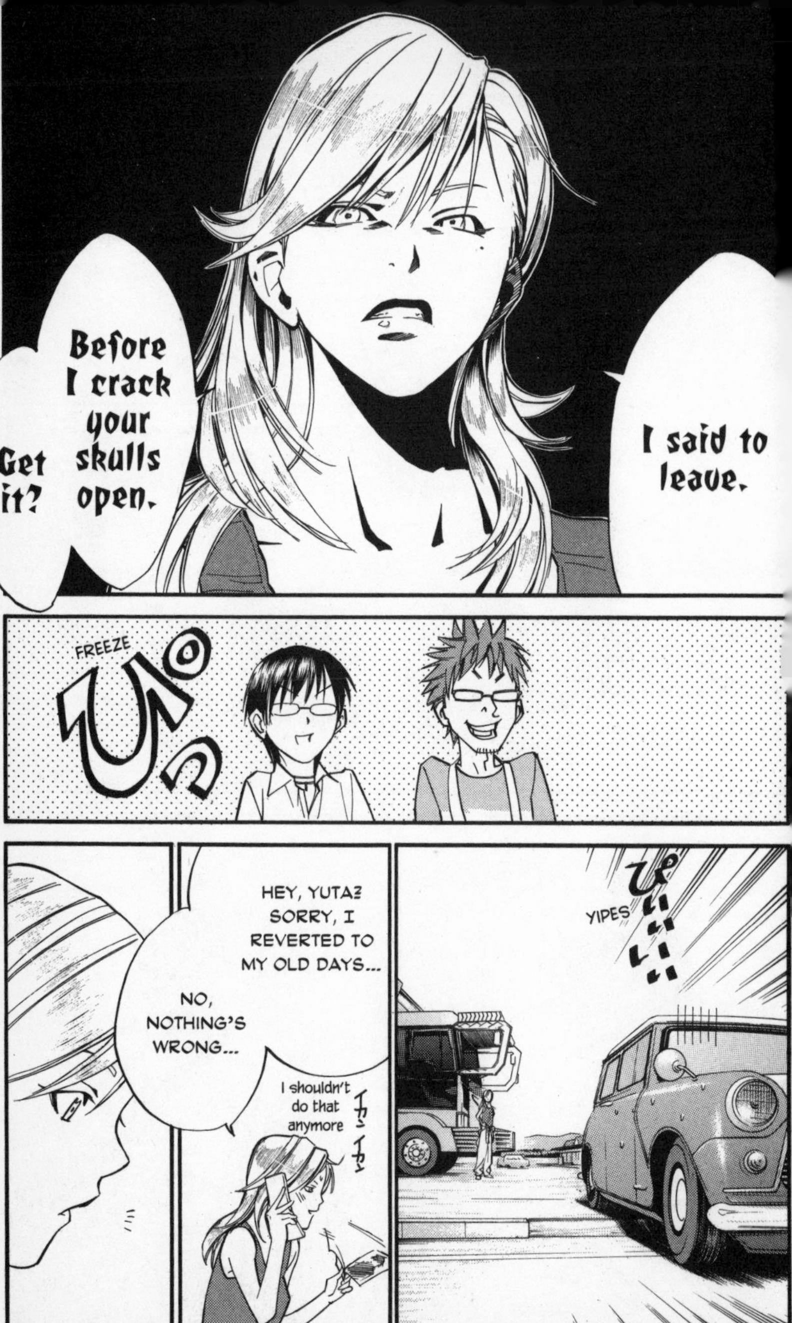

I said to leave.
Before I crack your skulls open.
Get it?
FREEZE
YIPES
HEY, YUTA? SORRY, I REVERTED TO MY OLD DAYS...
NO, NOTHING'S WRONG...
I shouldn't do that anymore

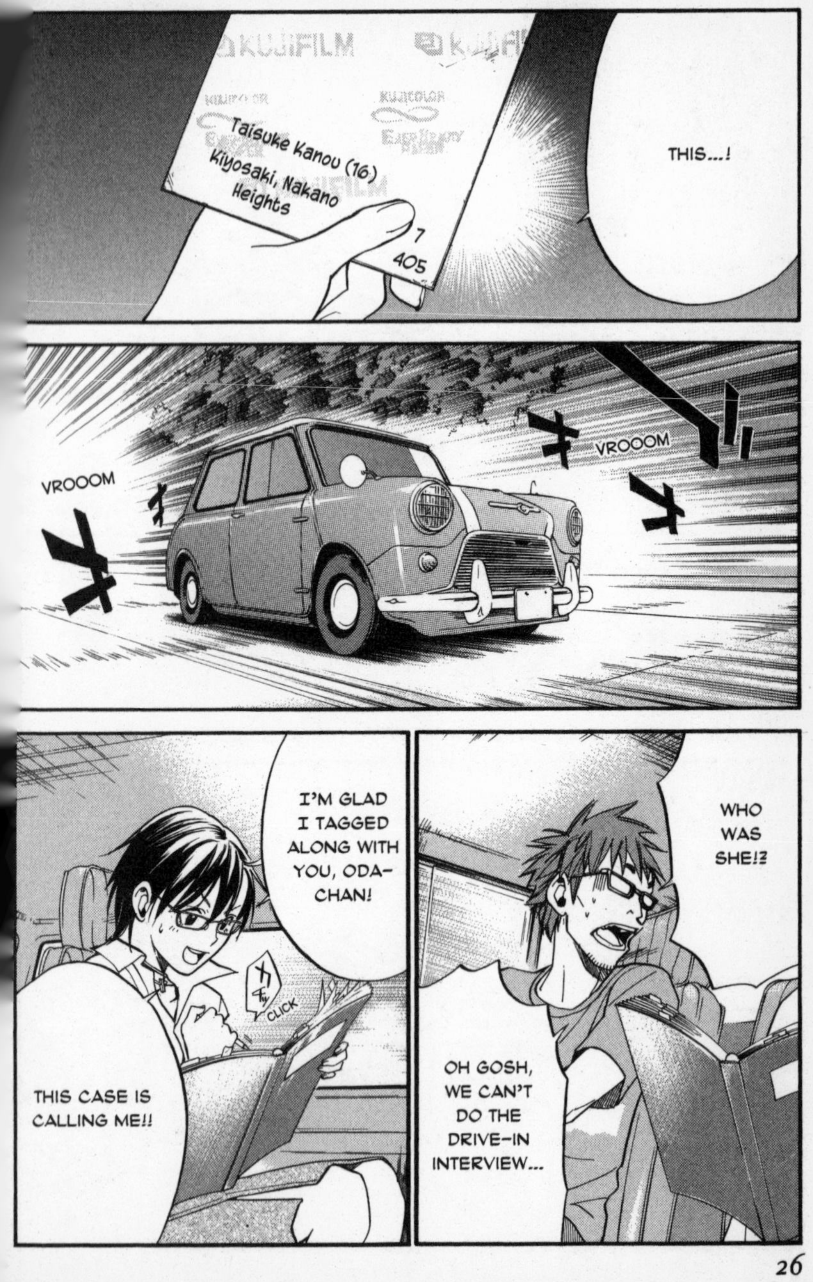
KUJIFILM
KUJIFILM
KUJICOLOR
Taisuke Kanou (16)
Kiyosaki, Nakano Heights
7
405
THIS...!
VROOOM
VROOOM
WHO WAS SHE!?
OH GOSH, WE CAN'T DO THE DRIVE-IN INTERVIEW...
I'M GLAD I TAGGED ALONG WITH YOU, ODA-CHAN!
CLICK
THIS CASE IS CALLING ME!!

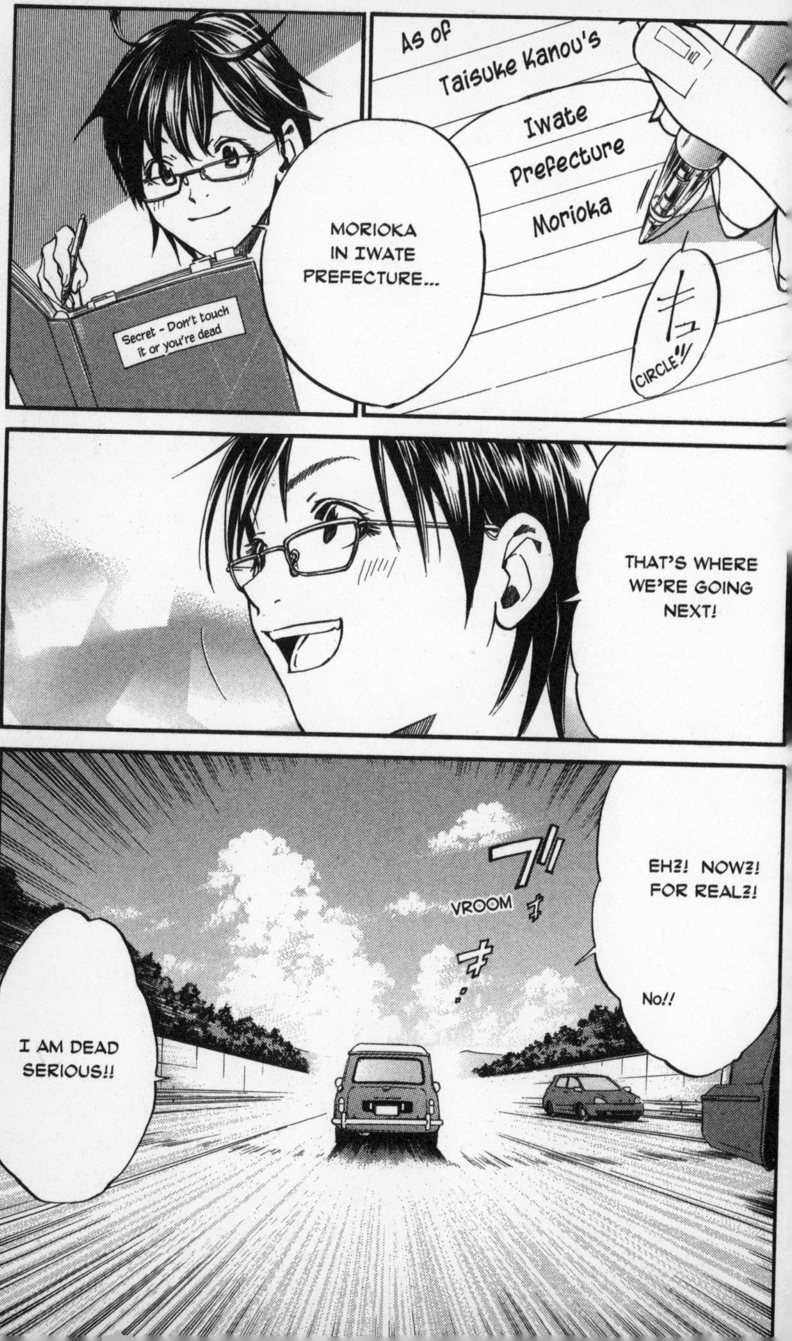
As of
Taisuke Kanou's
Iwate
Prefecture
Morioka
CIRCLE
MORIOKA IN IWATE PREFECTURE...
Secret - Don't touch it or you're dead
THAT'S WHERE WE'RE GOING NEXT!
EH?! NOW?! FOR REAL?!
No!!
VROOM
I AM DEAD SERIOUS!!

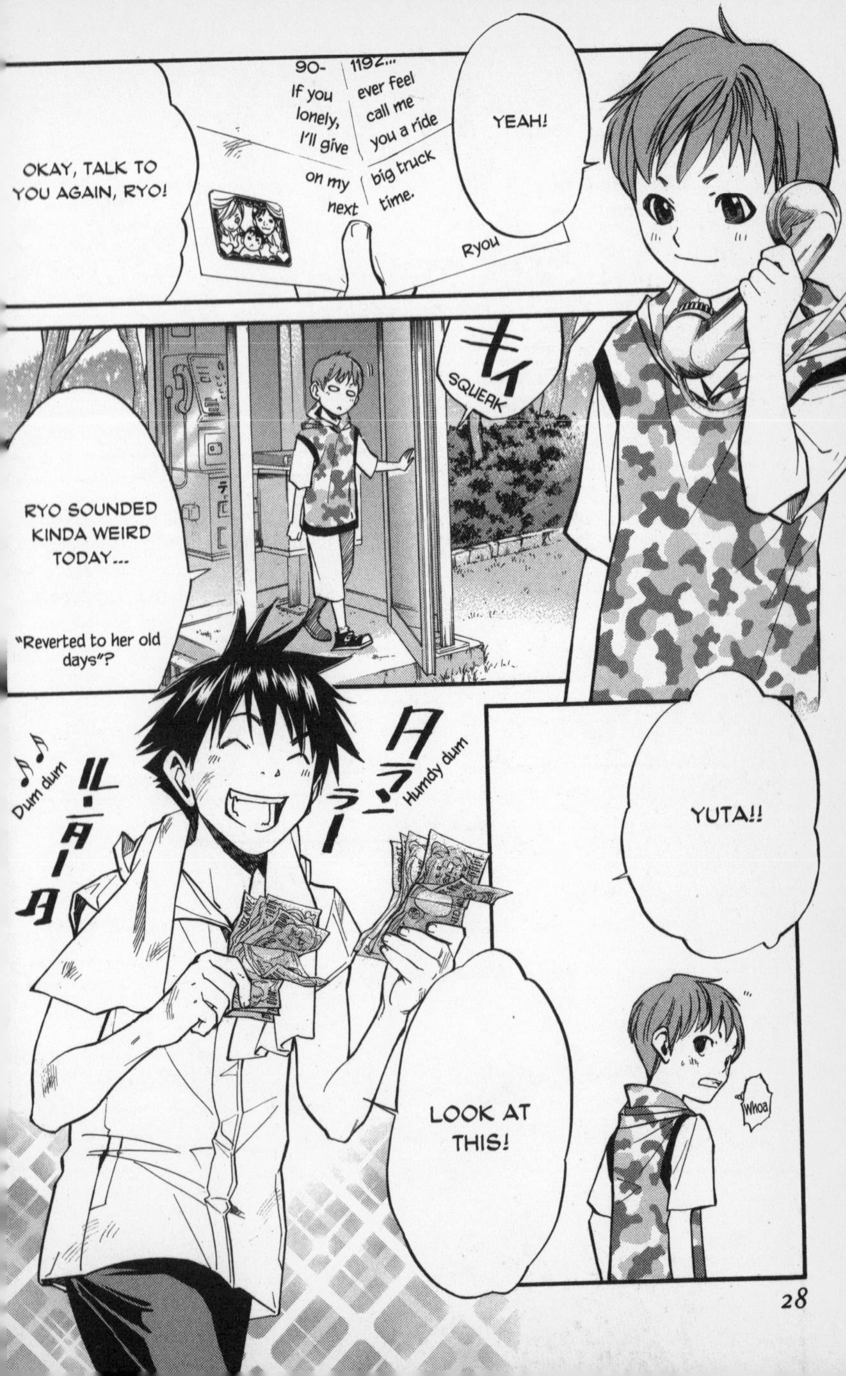
YEAH!
90- 1192...
If you ever feel lonely, call me I'll give you a ride on my big truck next time.
Ryou
OKAY, TALK TO YOU AGAIN, RYO!
SQUEAK
RYO SOUNDED KINDA WEIRD TODAY...
"Reverted to her old days"?
YUTA!!
Whoa
LOOK AT THIS!
Humdy dum
Dum dum

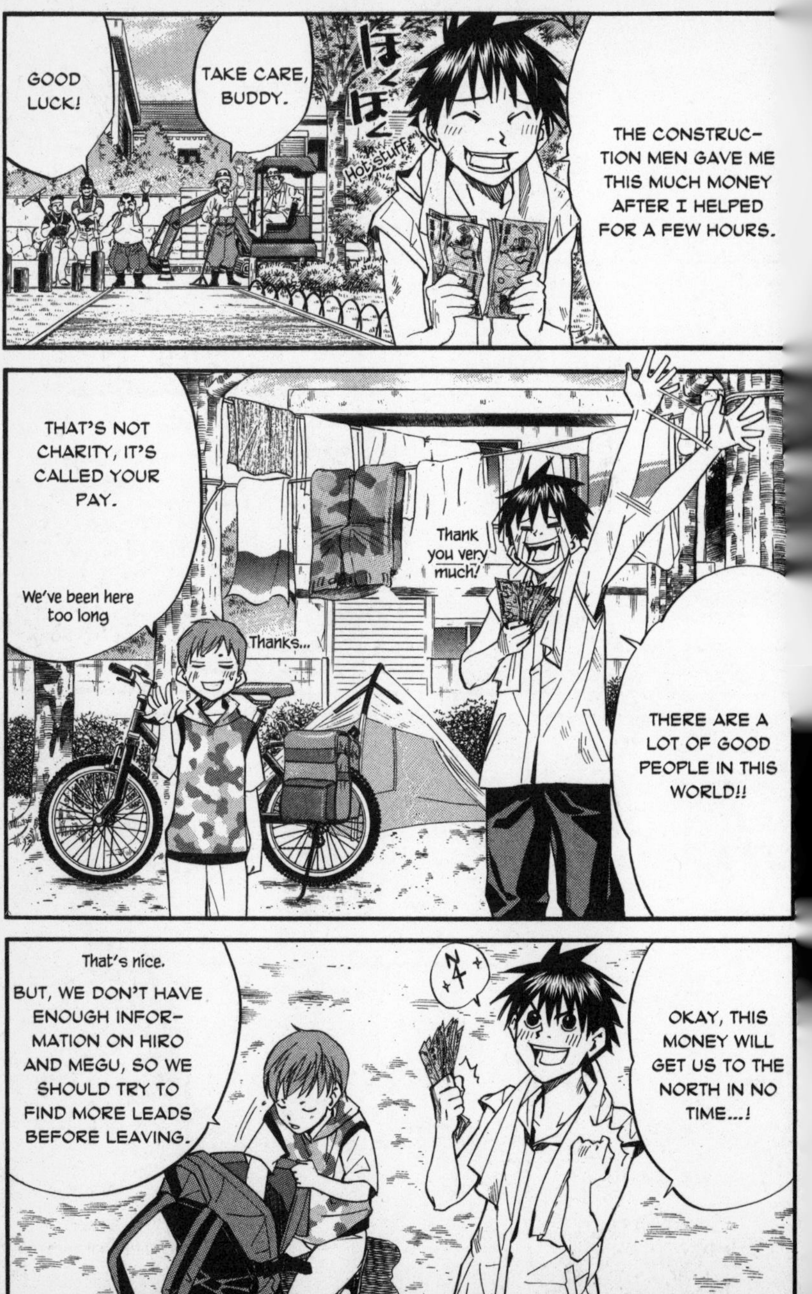
THE CONSTRUCTION MEN GAVE ME THIS MUCH MONEY AFTER I HELPED FOR A FEW HOURS.
ほくほく
Hot stuff
TAKE CARE, BUDDY.
GOOD LUCK!
THERE ARE A LOT OF GOOD PEOPLE IN THIS WORLD!!
Thank you very much!
Thanks...
THAT'S NOT CHARITY, IT'S CALLED YOUR PAY.
We've been here too long
OKAY, THIS MONEY WILL GET US TO THE NORTH IN NO TIME...!
That's nice.
BUT, WE DON'T HAVE ENOUGH INFORMATION ON HIRO AND MEGU, SO WE SHOULD TRY TO FIND MORE LEADS BEFORE LEAVING.

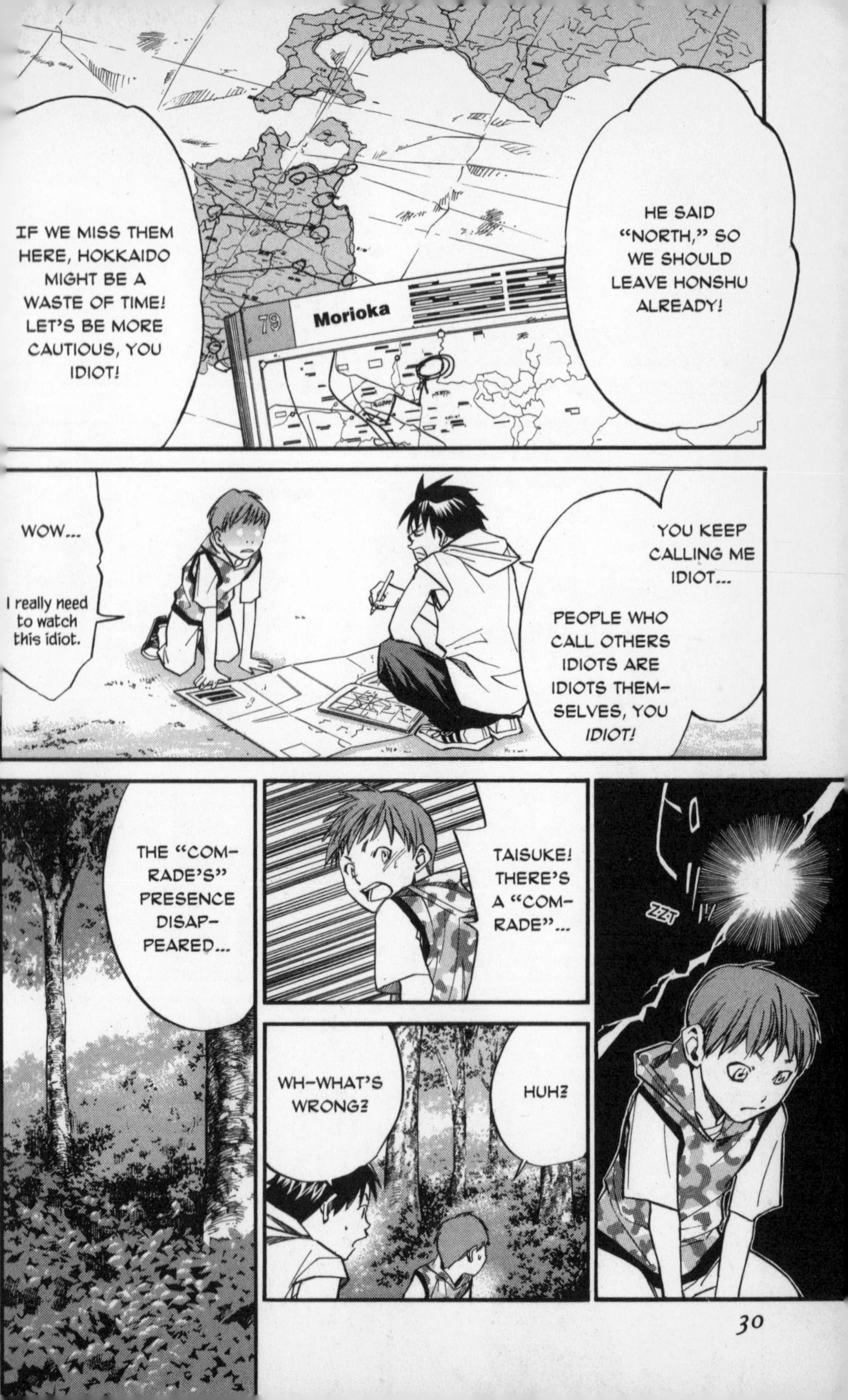

HE SAID "NORTH," SO WE SHOULD LEAVE HONSHU ALREADY!
79
Morioka
IF WE MISS THEM HERE, HOKKAIDO MIGHT BE A WASTE OF TIME! LET'S BE MORE CAUTIOUS, YOU IDIOT!
YOU KEEP CALLING ME IDIOT...
PEOPLE WHO CALL OTHERS IDIOTS ARE IDIOTS THEMSELVES, YOU *IDIOT!*
WOW...
I really need to watch this idiot.
ZZAT
TAISUKE! THERE'S A "COMRADE"...
HUH?
WH-WHAT'S WRONG?
THE "COMRADE'S" PRESENCE DISAPPEARED...

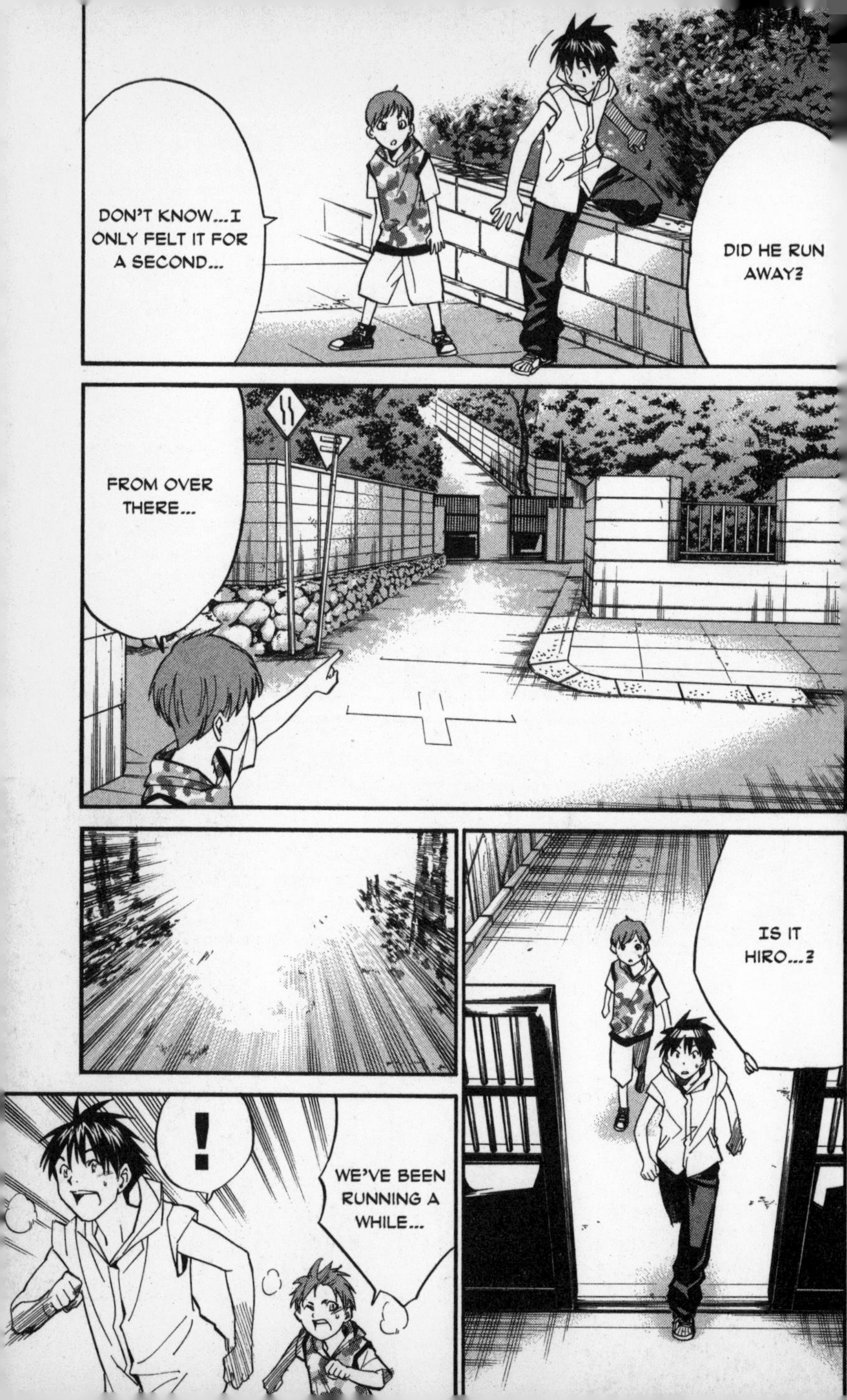
DID HE RUN AWAY?
DON'T KNOW...I ONLY FELT IT FOR A SECOND...
FROM OVER THERE...
IS IT HIRO...?
!
WE'VE BEEN RUNNING A WHILE...

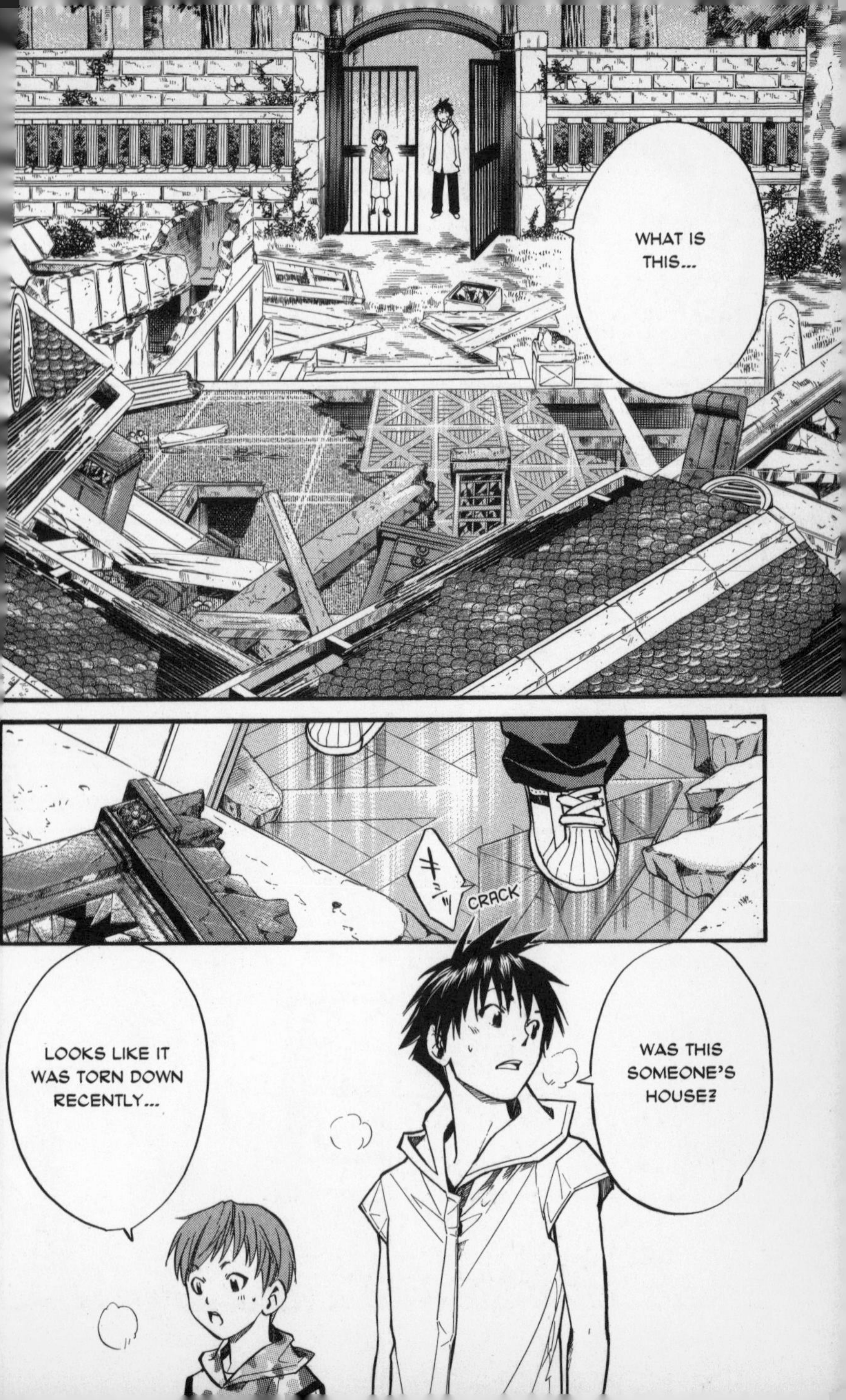

WHAT IS THIS...
キシッ
CRACK
WAS THIS SOMEONE'S HOUSE?
LOOKS LIKE IT WAS TORN DOWN RECENTLY...

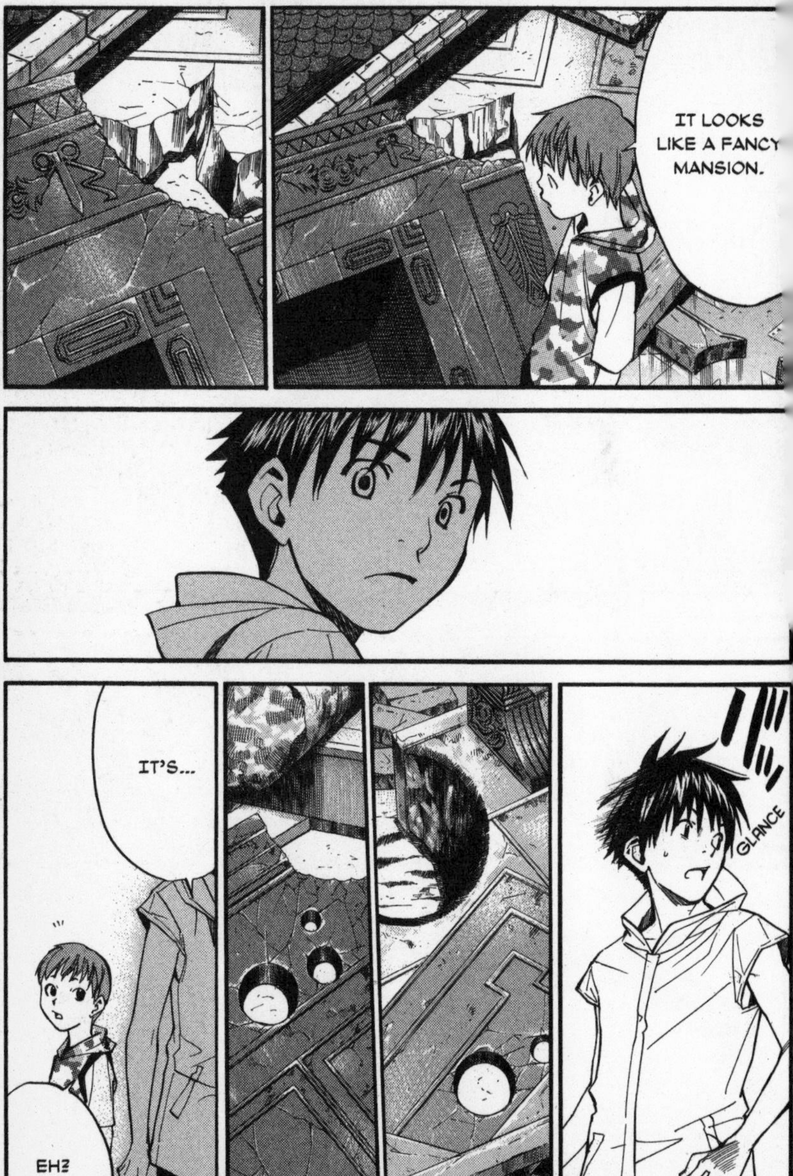
IT LOOKS LIKE A FANCY MANSION.
GLANCE
IT'S...
EH?

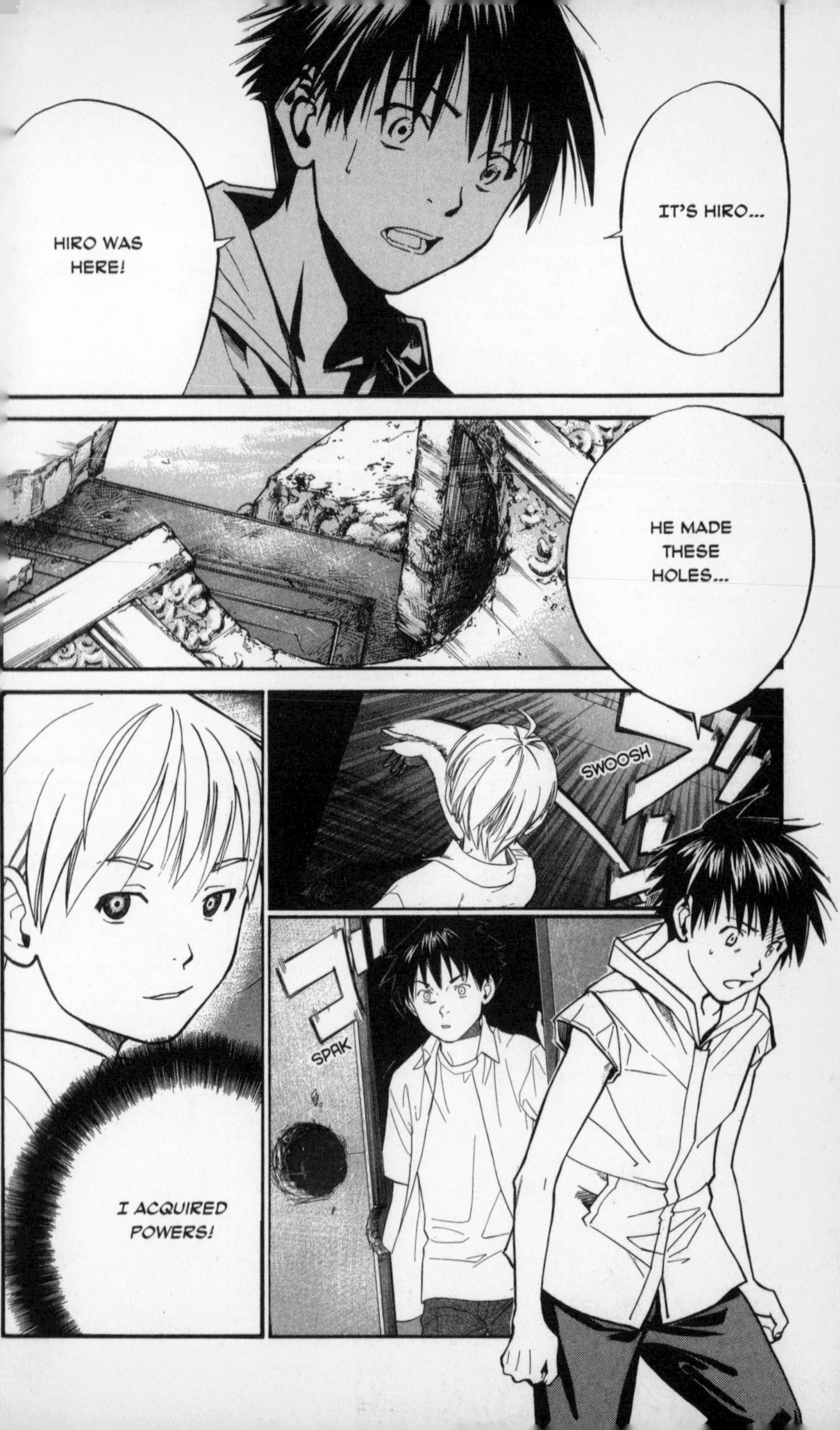
IT'S HIRO...
HIRO WAS HERE!
HE MADE THESE HOLES...
SWOOSH
SPAK
I ACQUIRED POWERS!

MEGU...

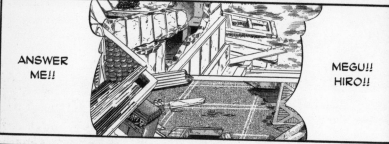

ANSWER ME!!

MEGU!! HIRO!!

H-HEY, MEGU AND HIRO ARE...

MEGU!!

ARE THEY HERE!?

HIRO!

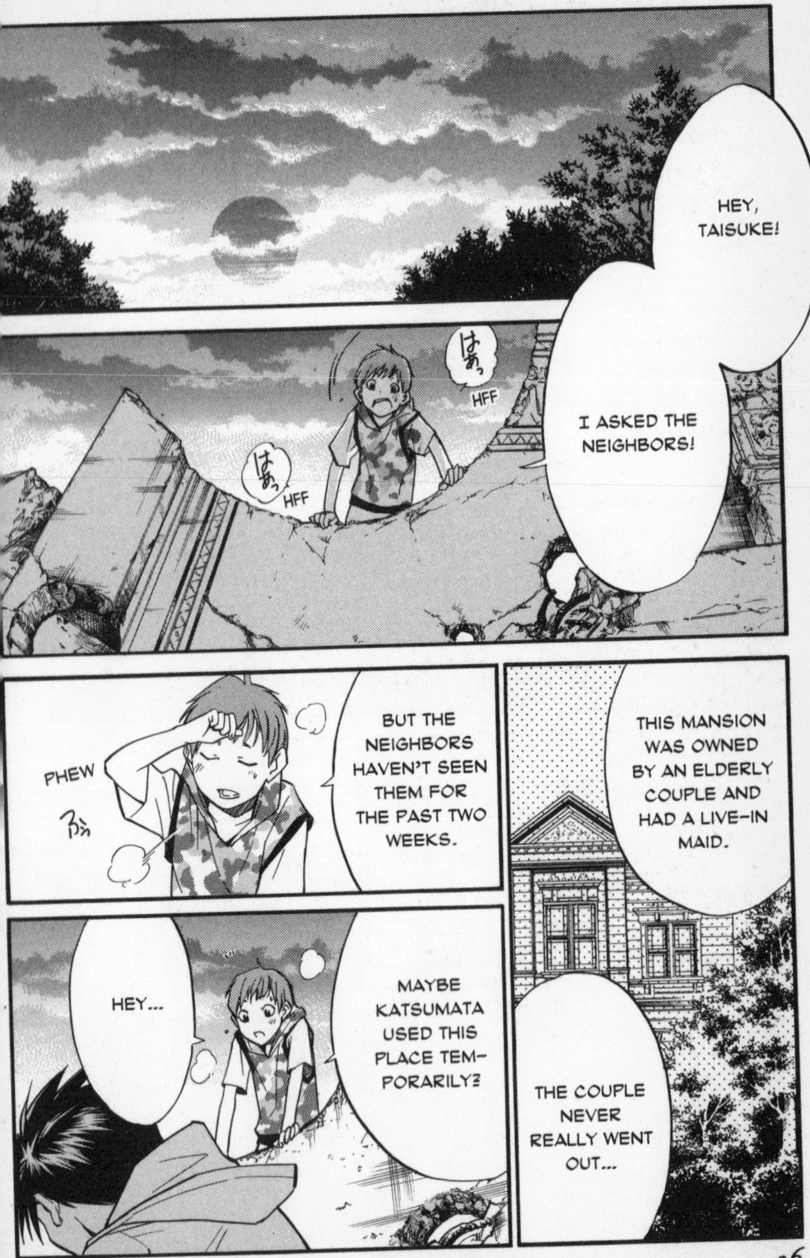
HEY, TAISUKE!
I ASKED THE NEIGHBORS!
はあっ
HFF
はあっ
HFF
THIS MANSION WAS OWNED BY AN ELDERLY COUPLE AND HAD A LIVE-IN MAID.
THE COUPLE NEVER REALLY WENT OUT...
BUT THE NEIGHBORS HAVEN'T SEEN THEM FOR THE PAST TWO WEEKS.
PHEW
MAYBE KATSUMATA USED THIS PLACE TEM-PORARILY?
HEY...

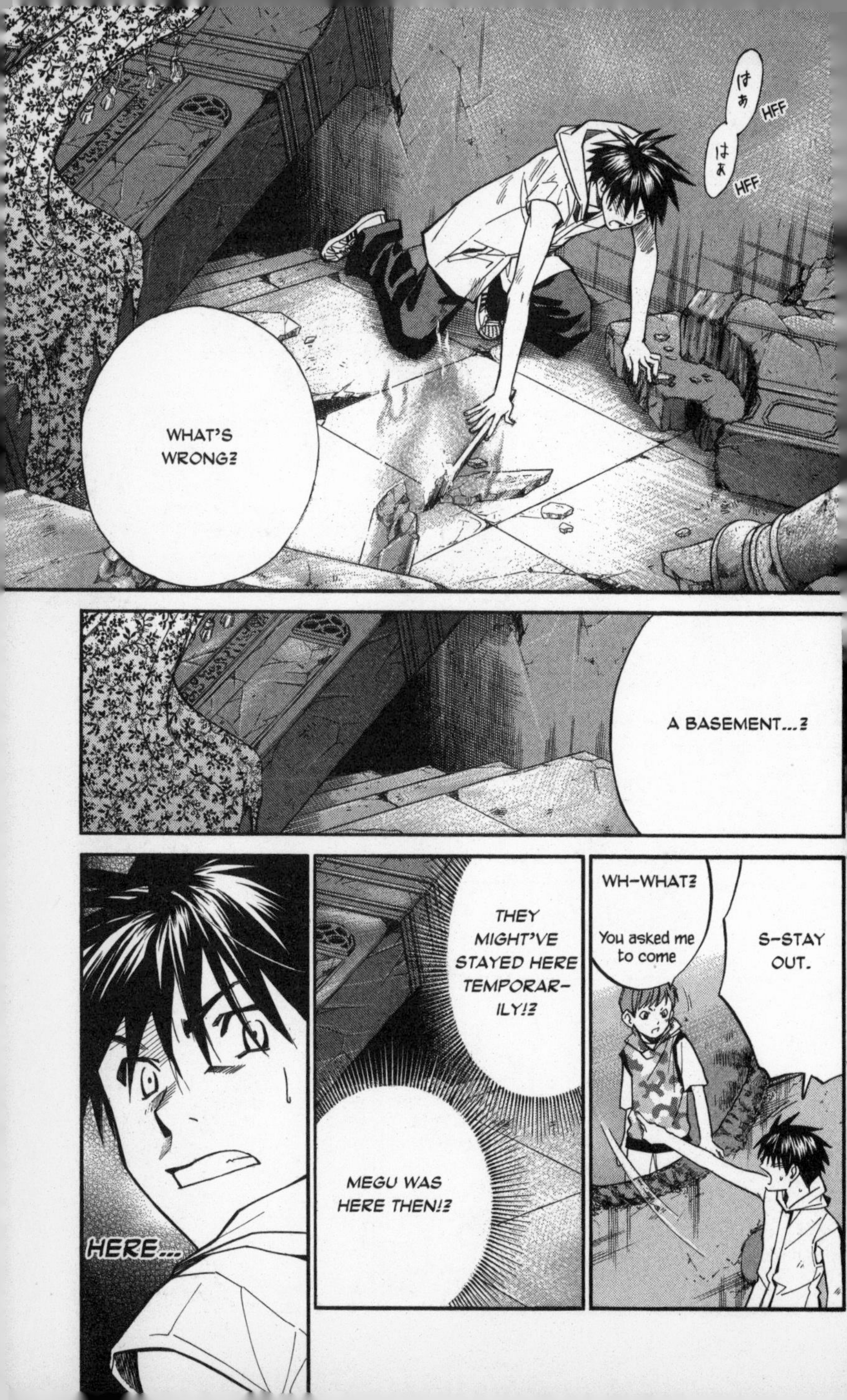
はぁ
HFF
はぁ
HFF
WHAT'S WRONG?
A BASEMENT...?
S-STAY OUT.
WH-WHAT?
You asked me to come
THEY MIGHT'VE STAYED HERE TEMPORAR-ILY!?
MEGU WAS HERE THEN!?
HERE...

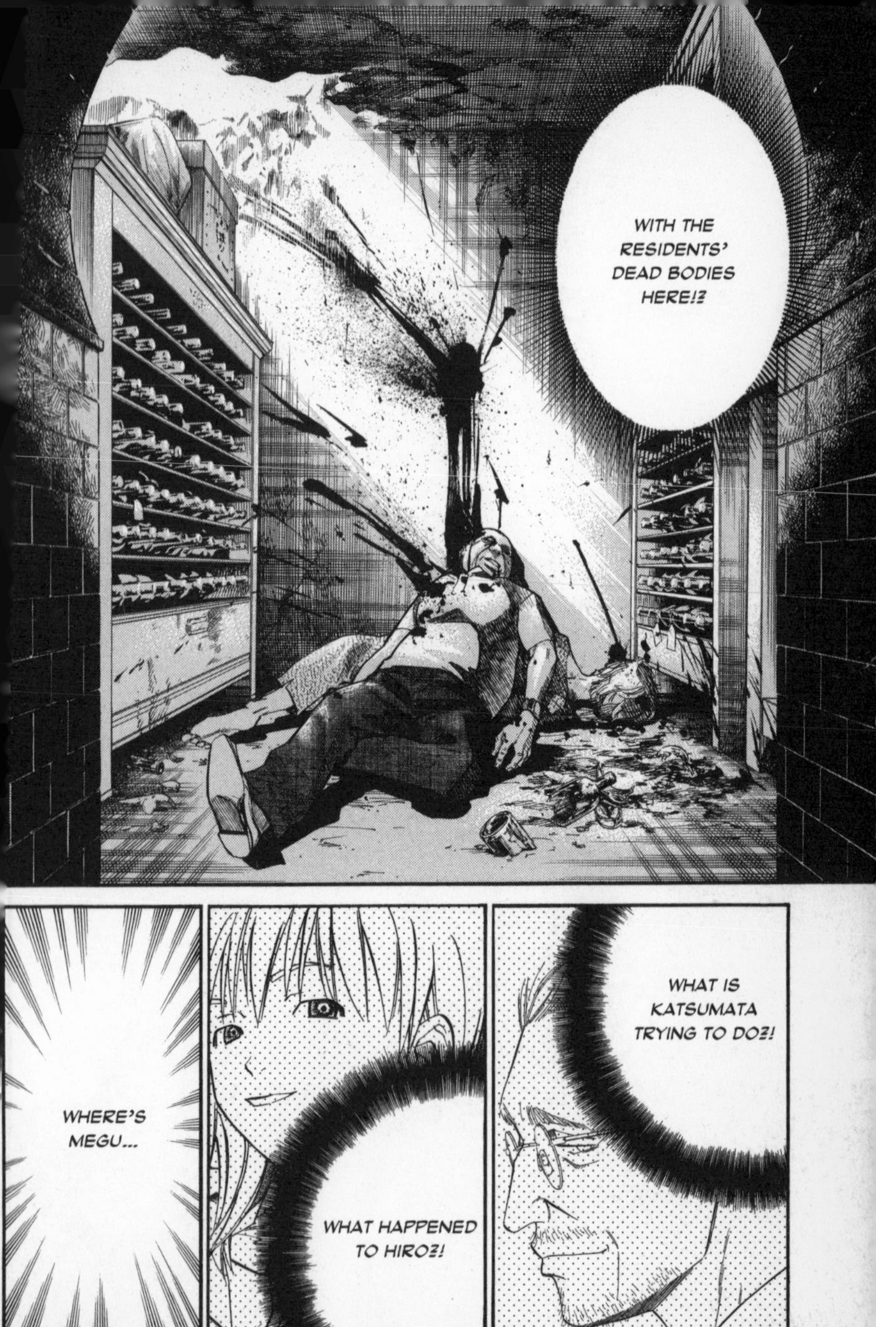
WITH THE RESIDENTS' DEAD BODIES HERE!?
WHAT IS KATSUMATA TRYING TO DO?!
WHAT HAPPENED TO HIRO?!
WHERE'S MEGU...

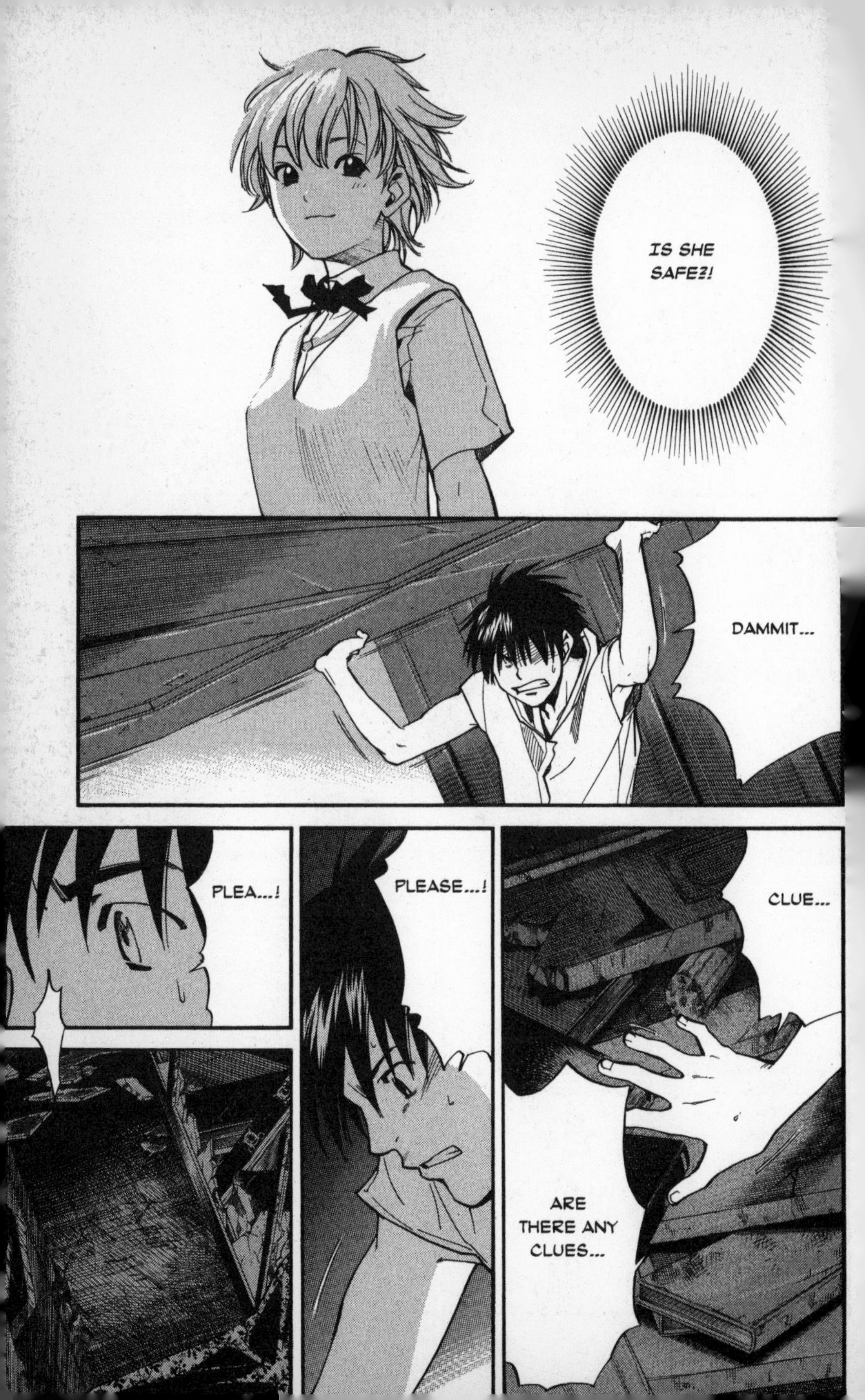
IS SHE SAFE?!
DAMMIT...
CLUE...
ARE THERE ANY CLUES...
PLEASE...!
PLEA...!

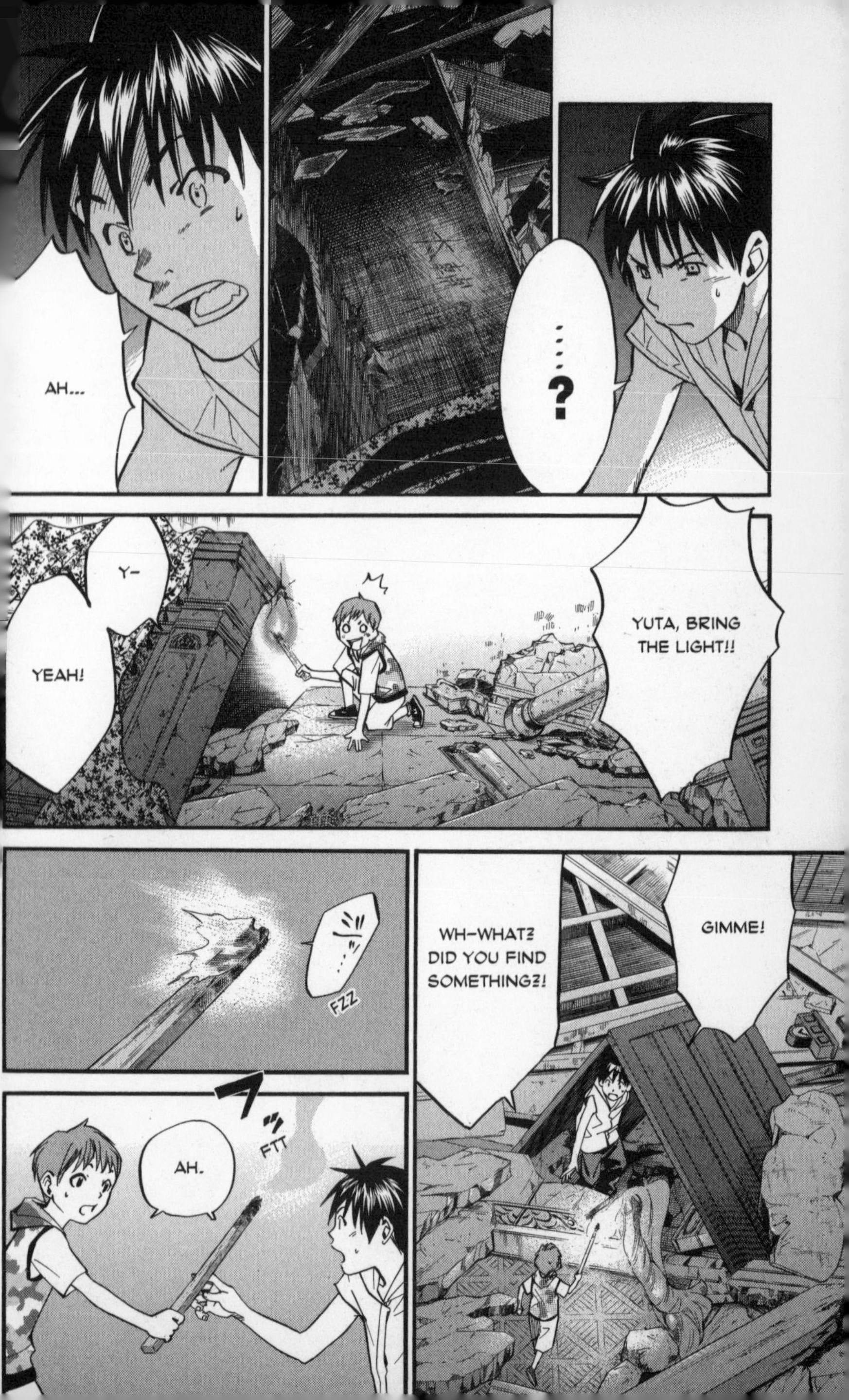
....?
AH...
YUTA, BRING THE LIGHT!!
Y-
YEAH!
GIMME!
WH-WHAT? DID YOU FIND SOMETHING?!
FZZ
FTT
AH.

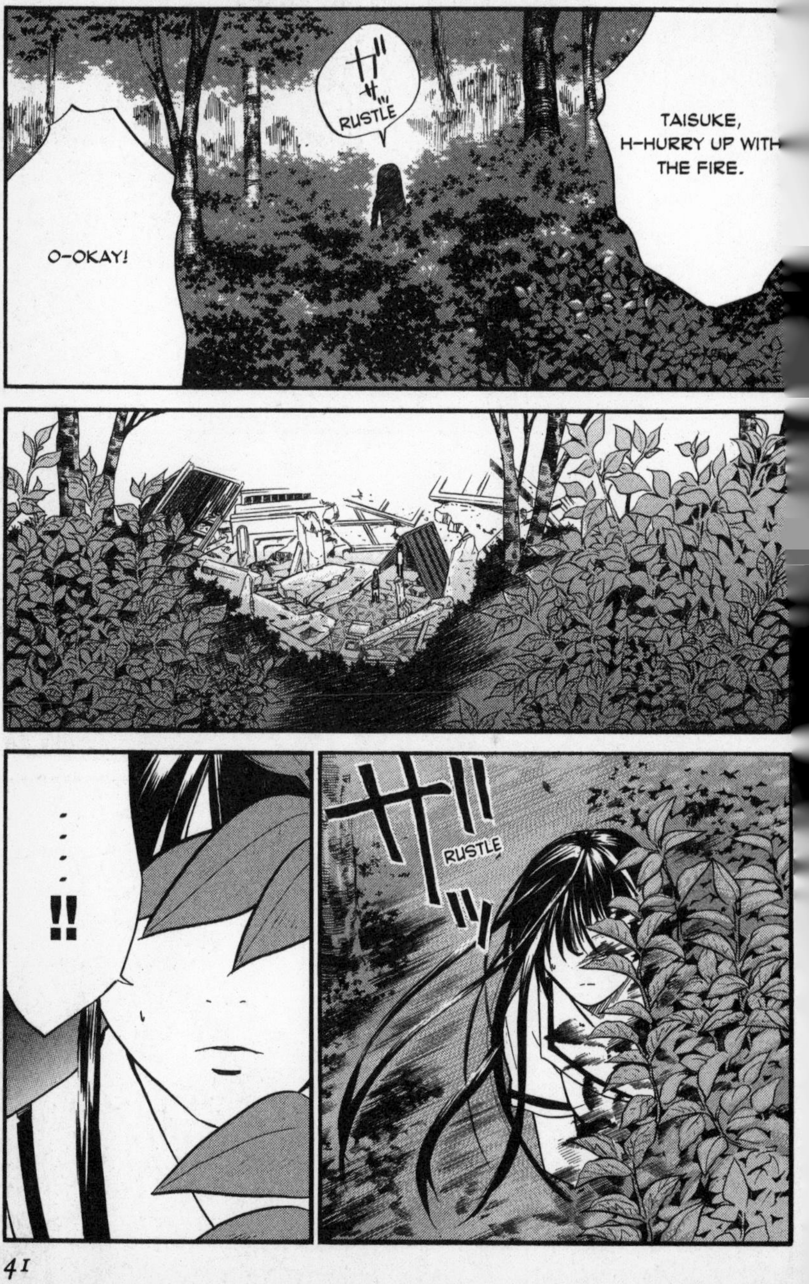

TAISUKE, H-HURRY UP WITH THE FIRE.
RUSTLE
O-OKAY!
RUSTLE
......
!!

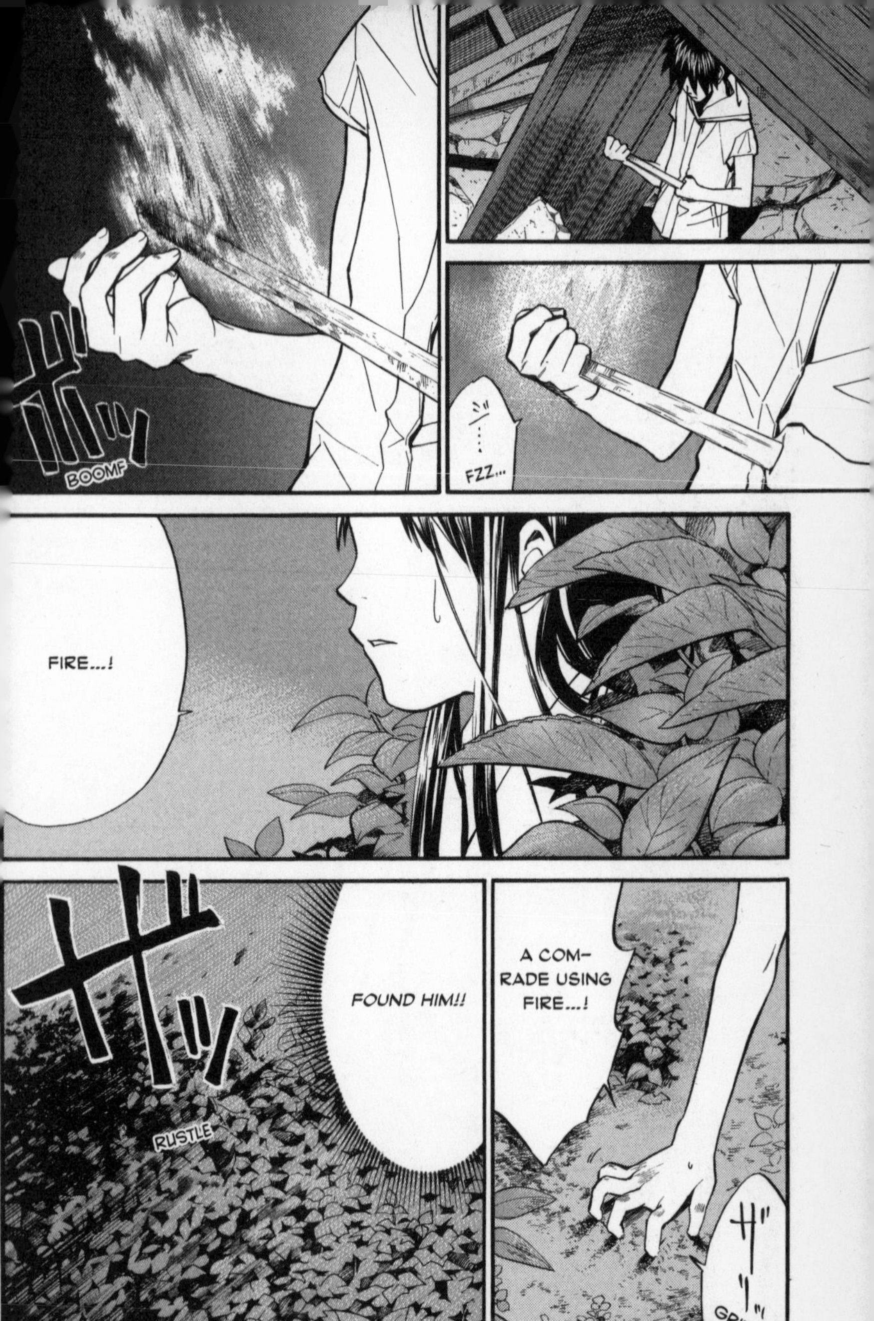
FZZ...
BOOMF
FIRE...!
A COM-
RADE USING
FIRE...!
GRIT
FOUND HIM!!
RUSTLE

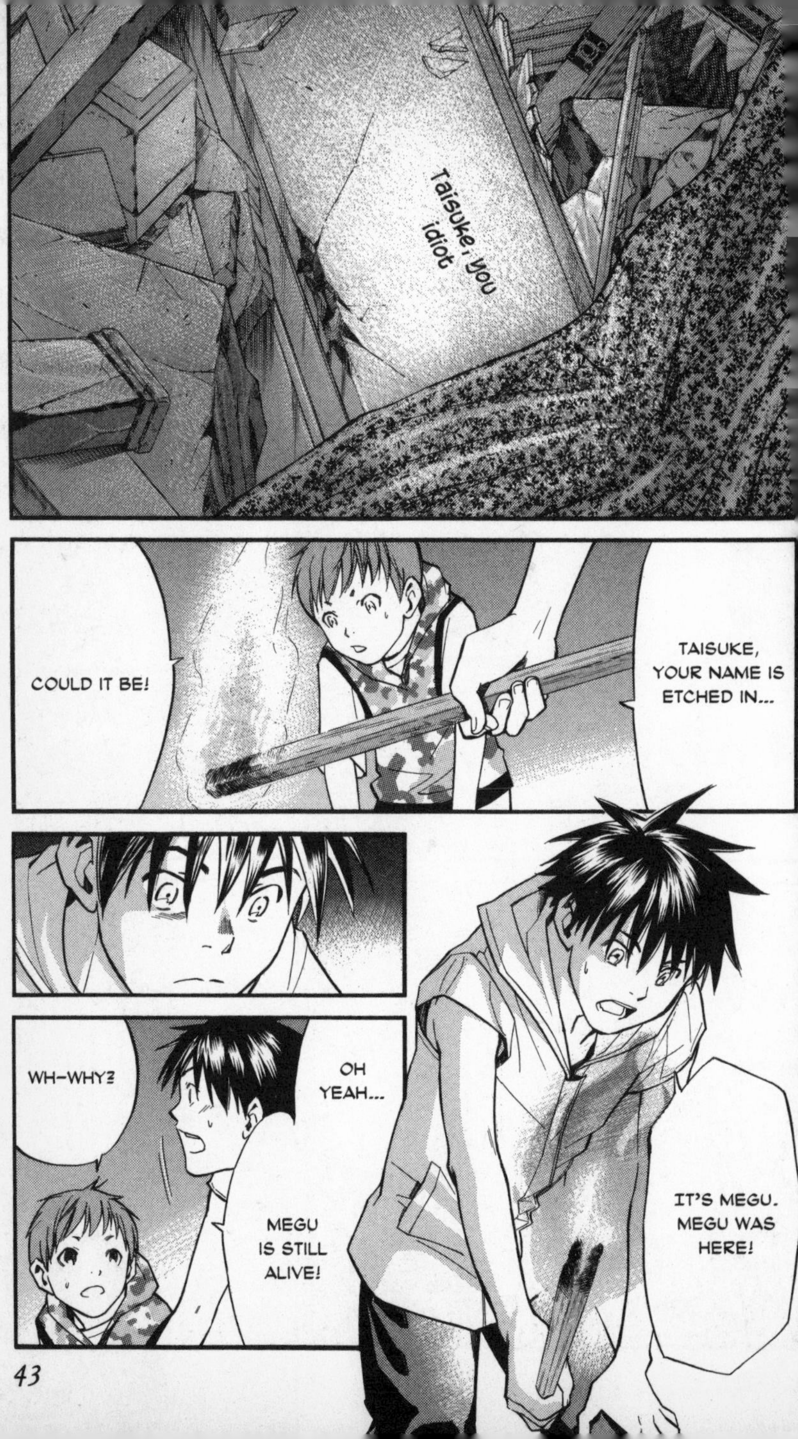
Taisuke, you idiot
TAISUKE, YOUR NAME IS ETCHED IN...
COULD IT BE!
IT'S MEGU. MEGU WAS HERE!
OH YEAH...
WH-WHY?
MEGU IS STILL ALIVE!

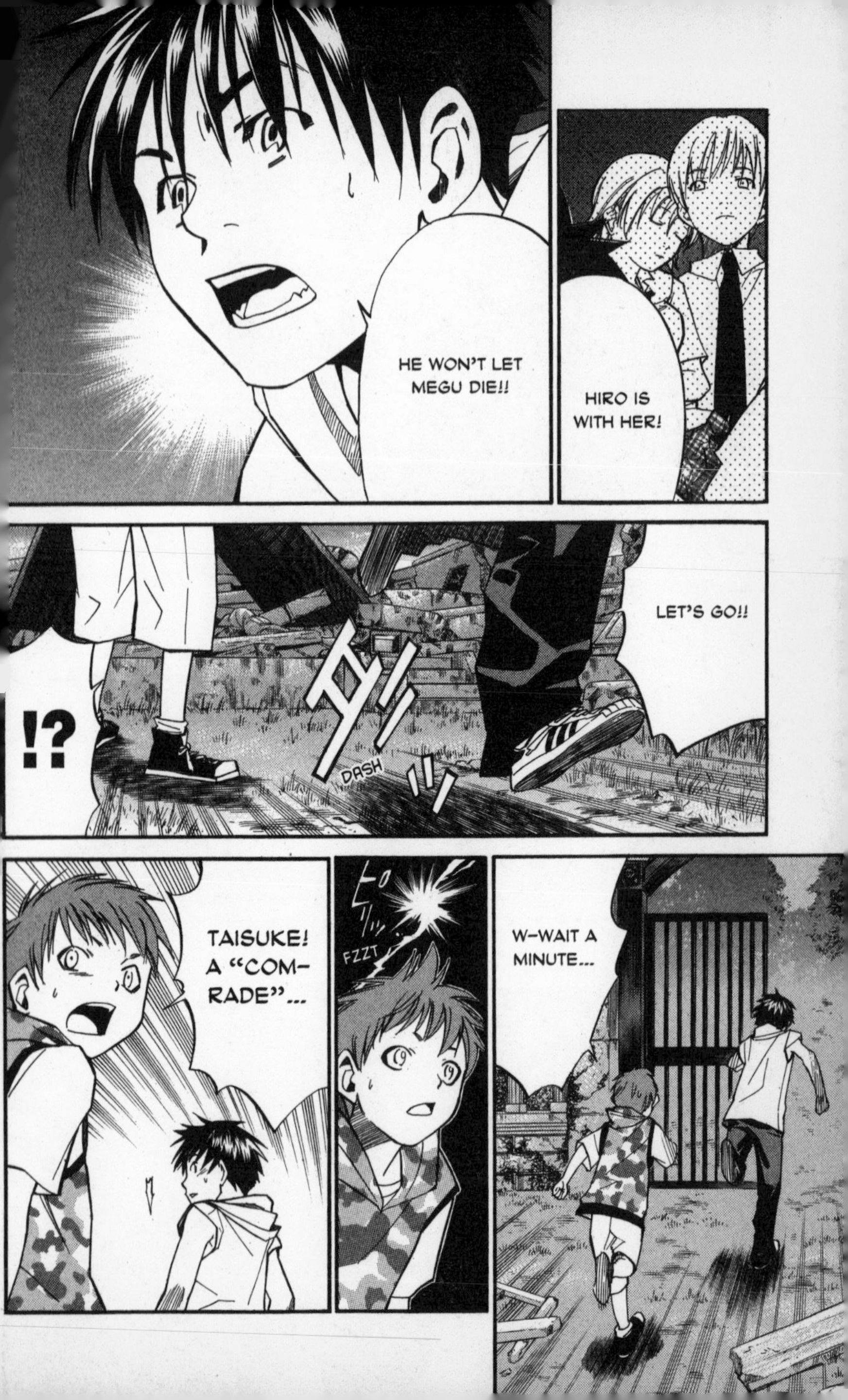
HIRO IS WITH HER!
HE WON'T LET MEGU DIE!!
LET'S GO!!
DASH
!?
W-WAIT A MINUTE...
FZZT
TAISUKE! A "COM-RADE"...

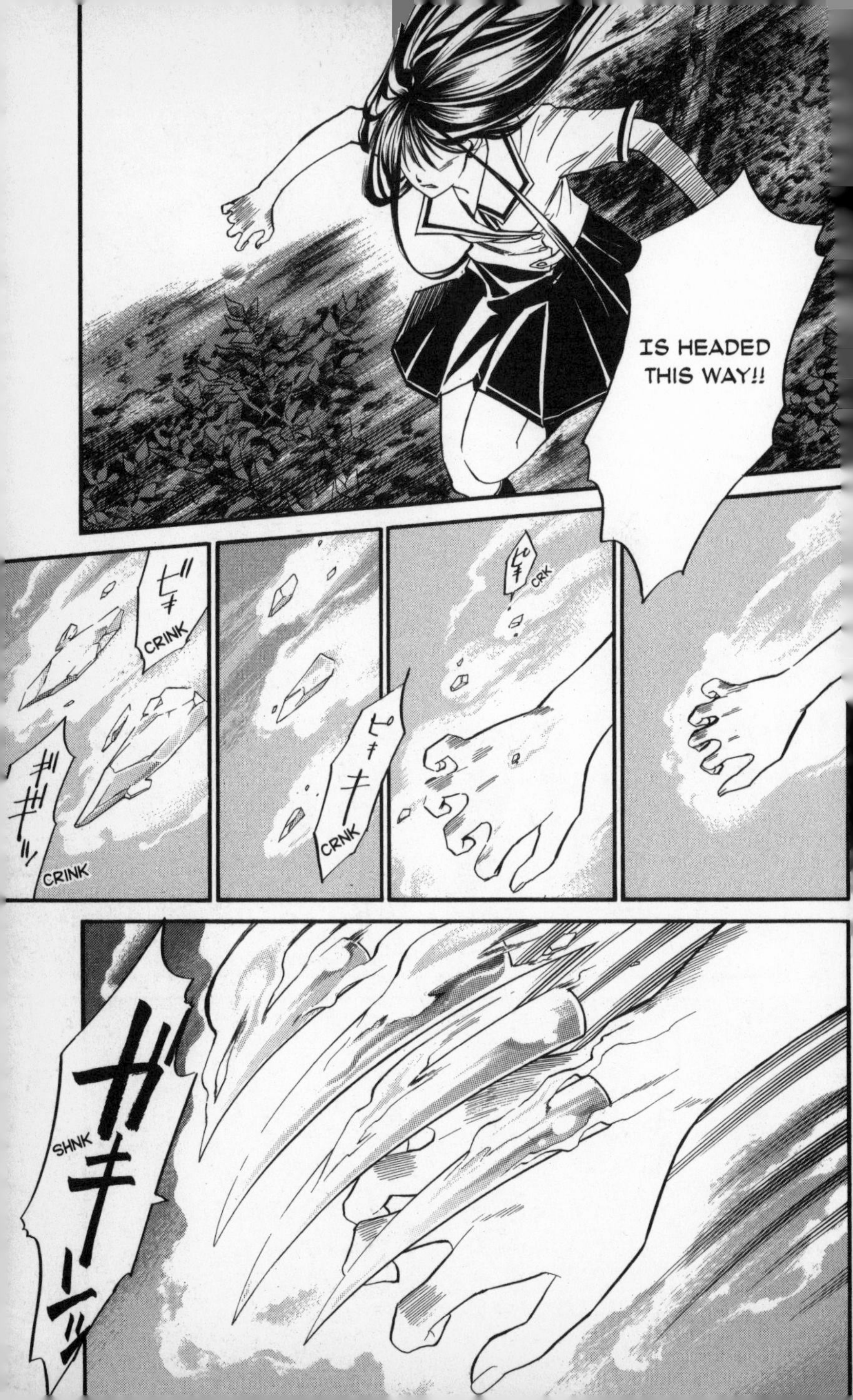
IS HEADED THIS WAY!!
CRK
CRNK
CRINK
CRINK
ガキーンッ
SHNK

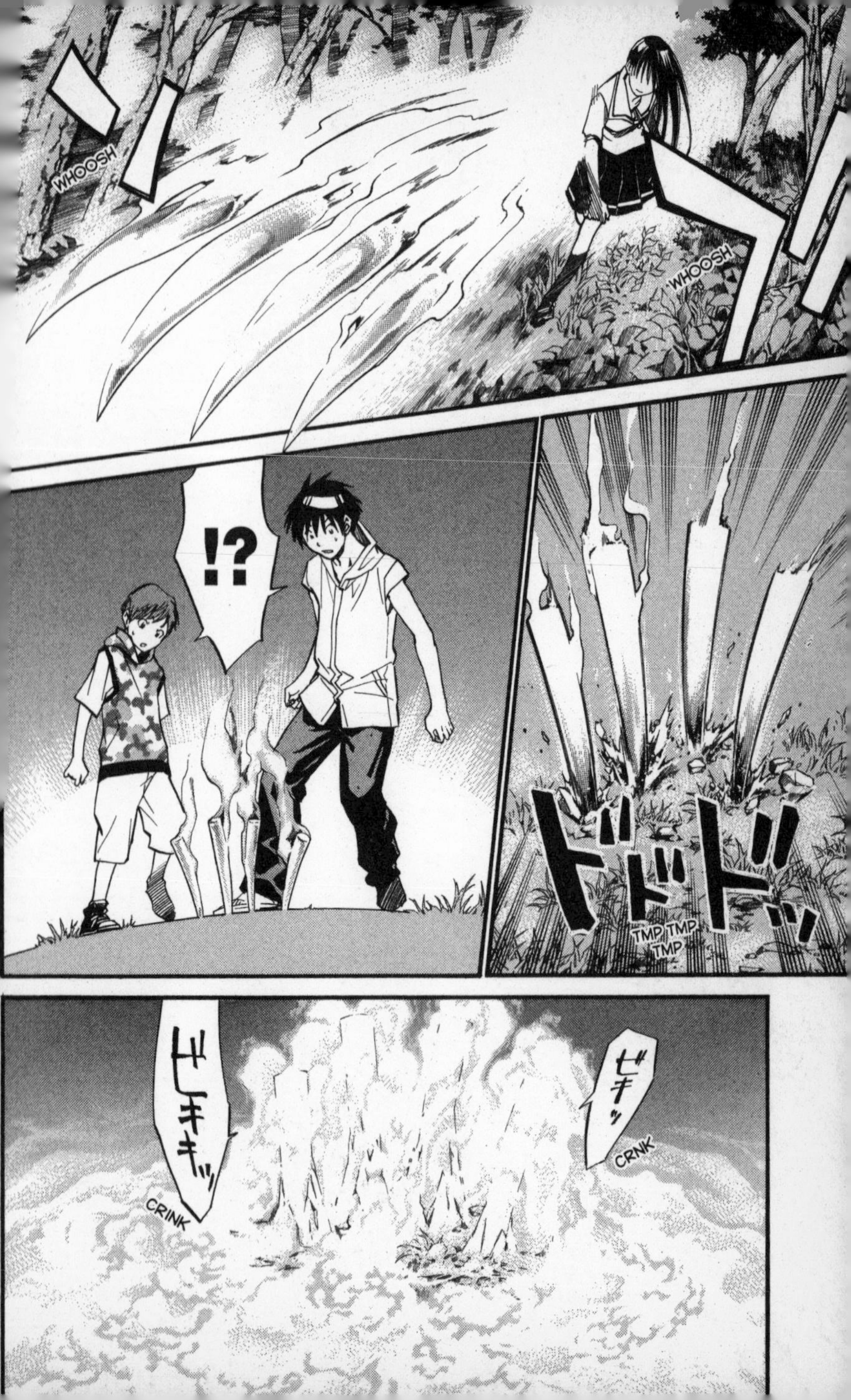
WHOOSH
WHOOSH
ドドドッ
TMP TMP TMP
!?
ビキッ
CRNK
ビキキッ
CRNK

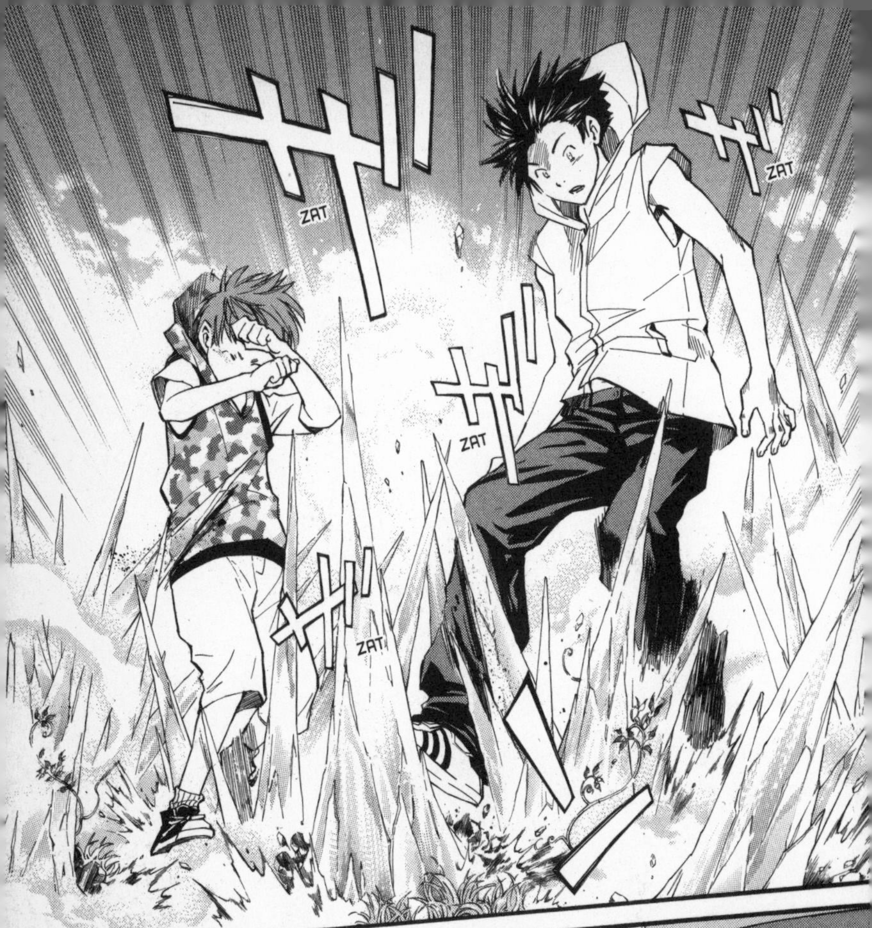
ZAT
ZAT
ZAT
ZAT

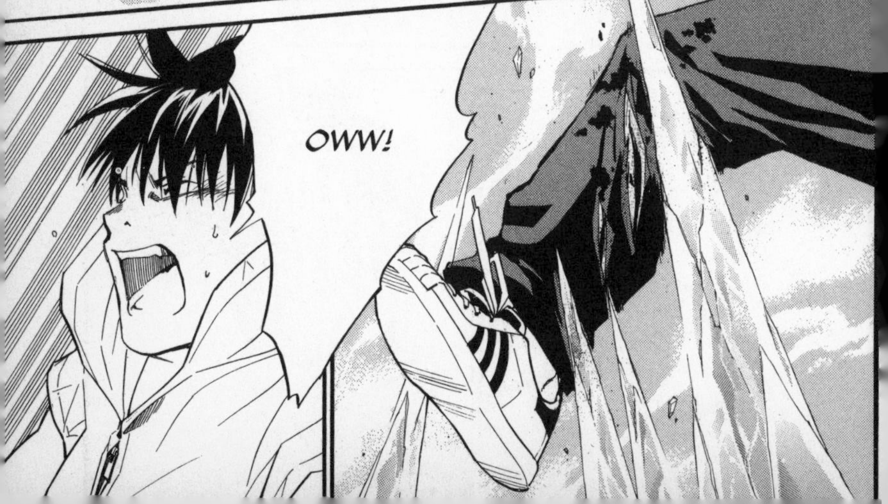
OWW!

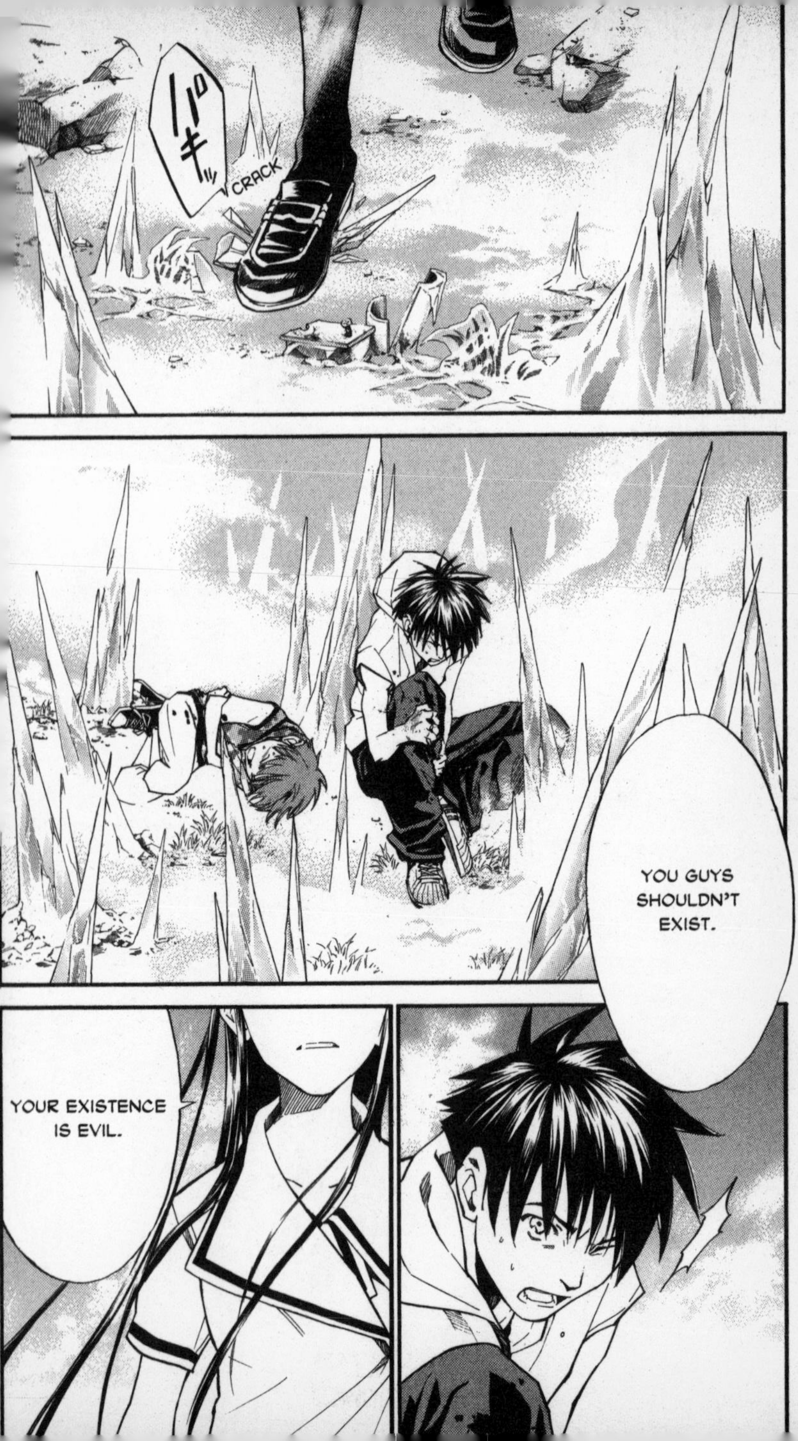
パキッ
CRACK
YOU GUYS SHOULDN'T EXIST.
YOUR EXISTENCE IS EVIL.

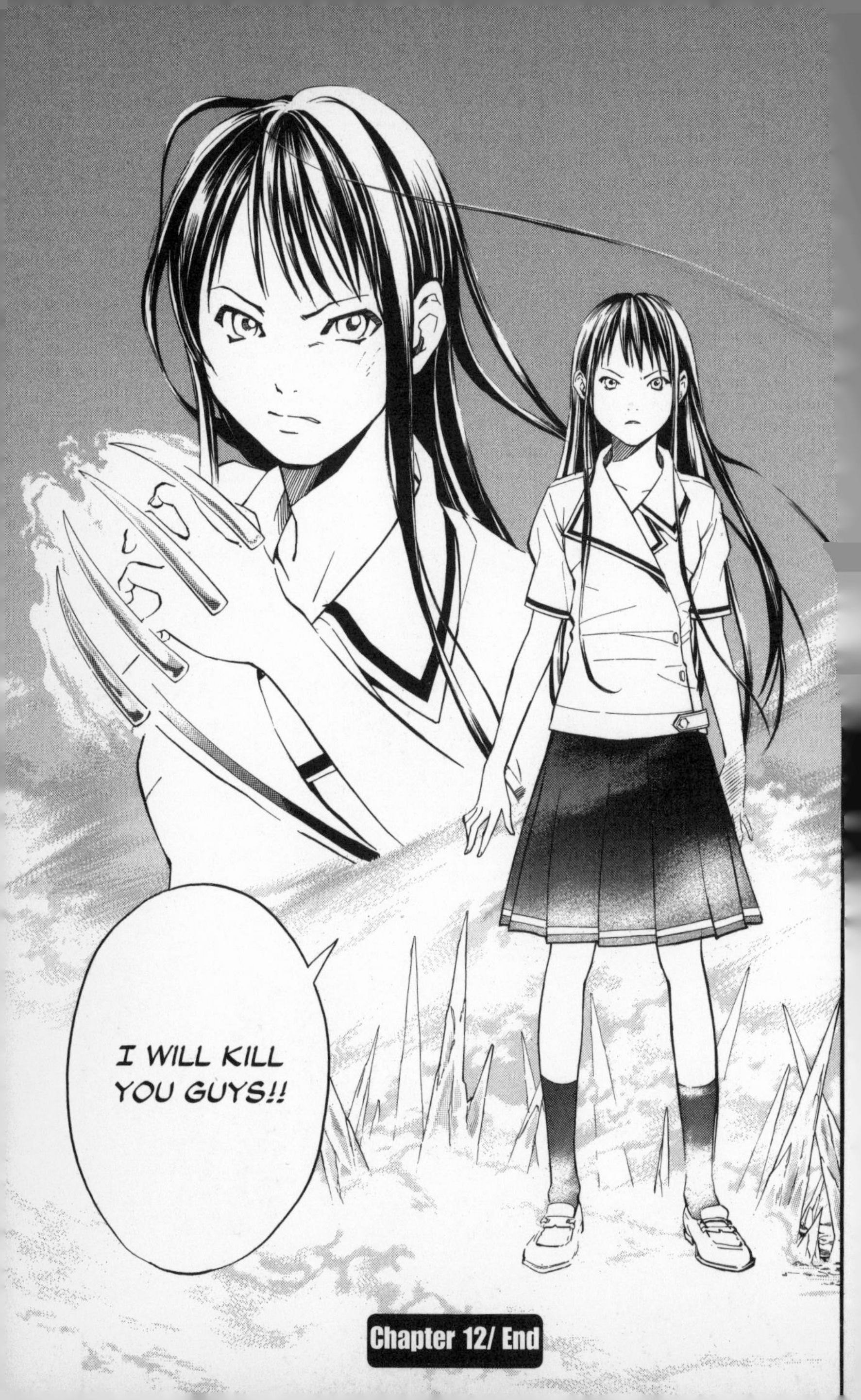
I WILL KILL YOU GUYS!!
Chapter 12/ End

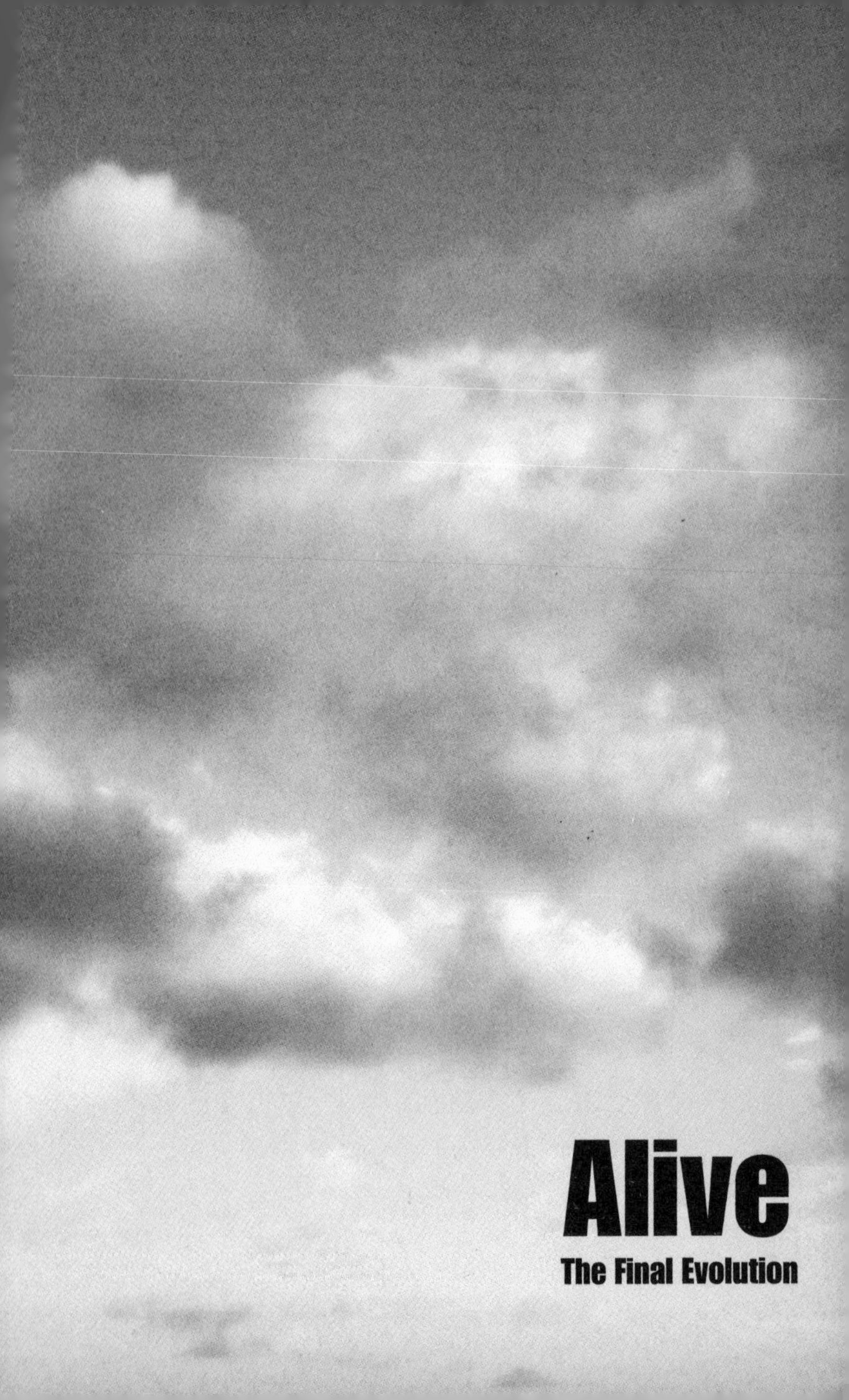
Alive
The Final Evolution

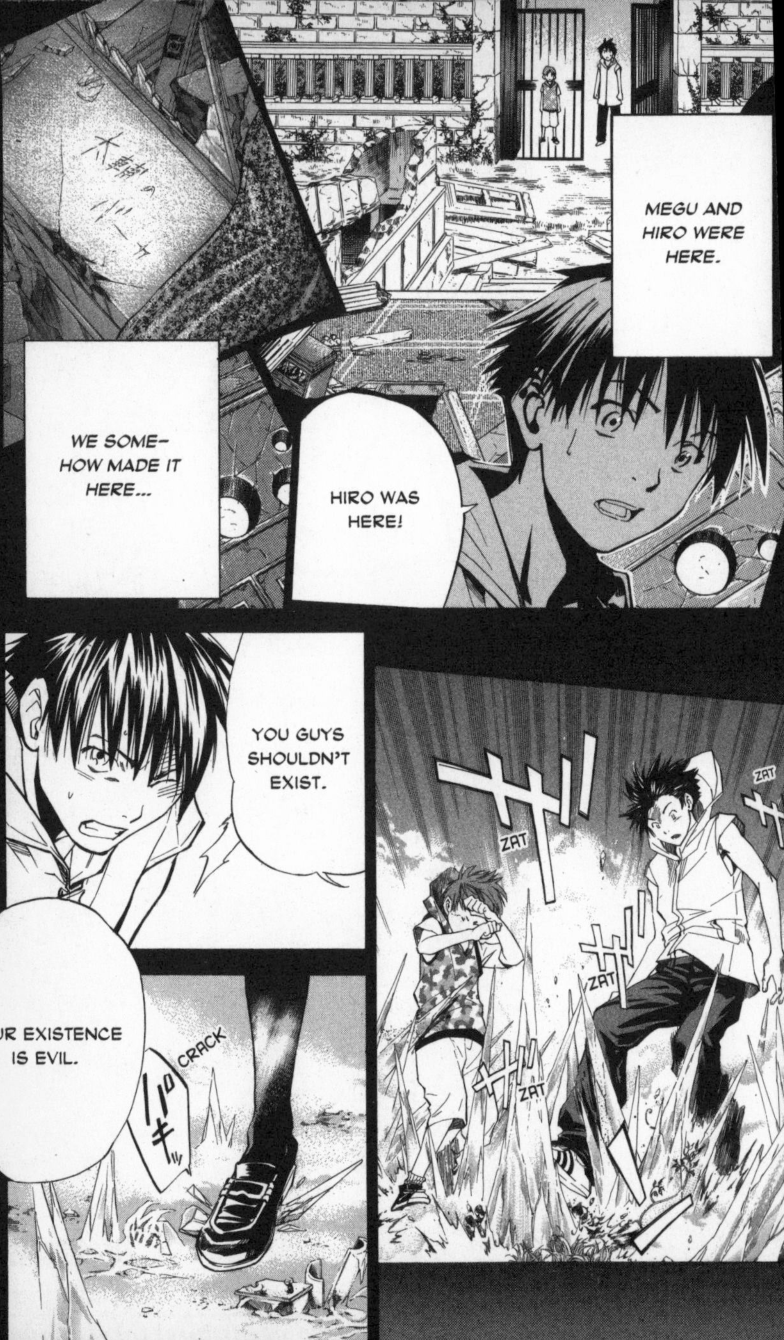
MEGU AND HIRO WERE HERE.
HIRO WAS HERE!
WE SOME-HOW MADE IT HERE...
ZAT
ZAT
ZAT
ZAT
YOU GUYS SHOULDN'T EXIST.
YOUR EXISTENCE IS EVIL.
CRACK

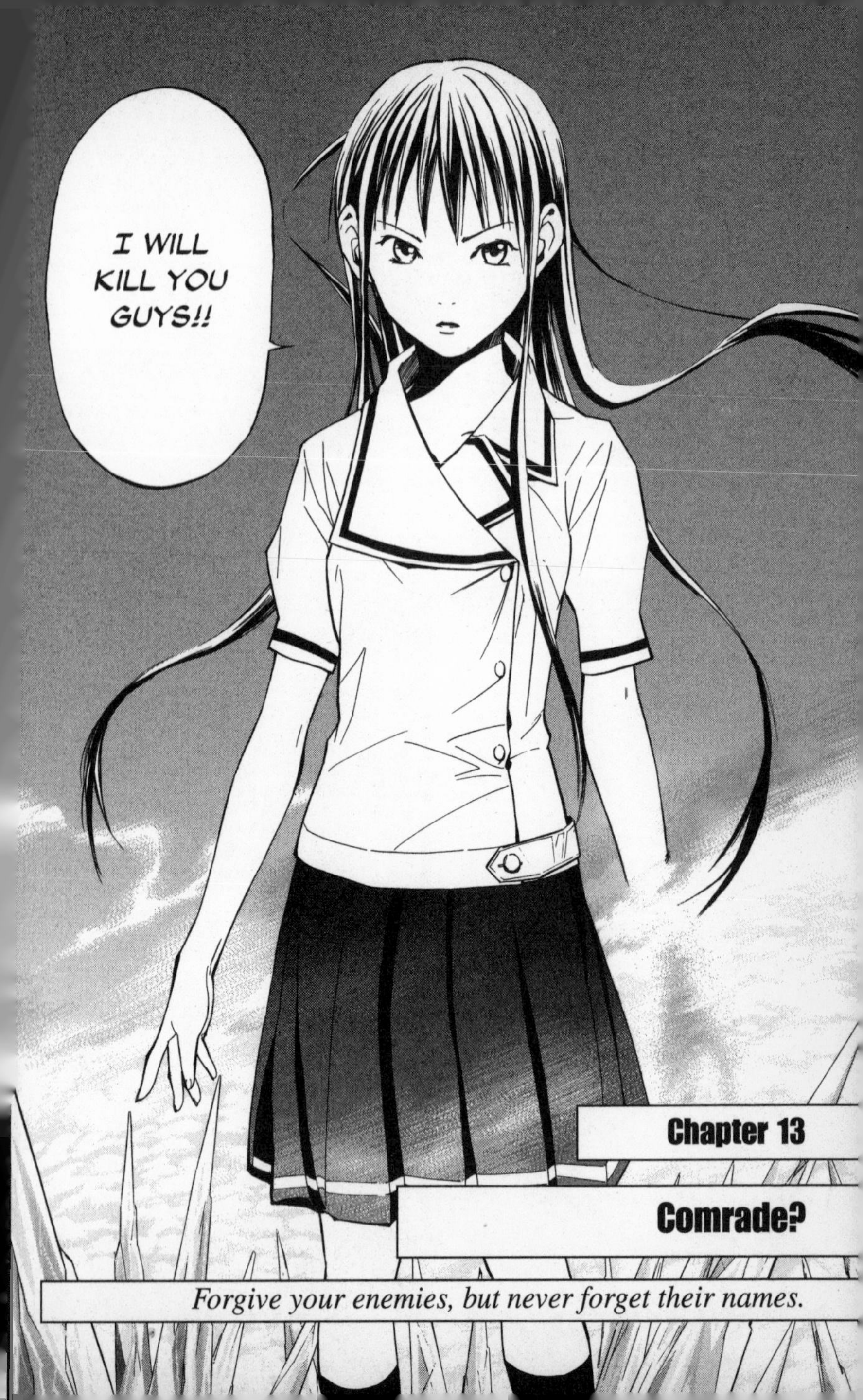
I WILL KILL YOU GUYS!!
Chapter 13
Comrade?
Forgive your enemies, but never forget their names.

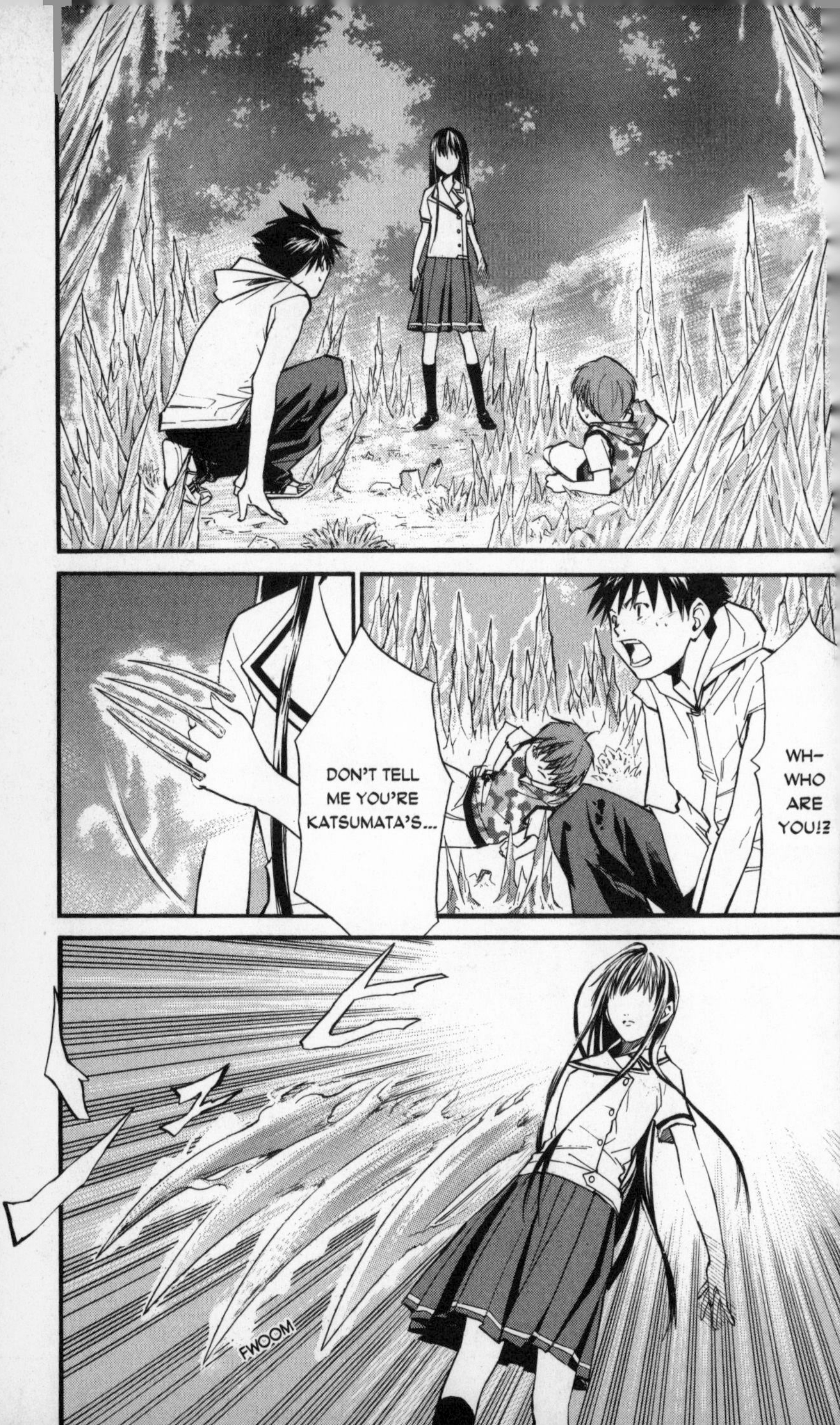
WH- WHO ARE YOU!?
DON'T TELL ME YOU'RE KATSUMATA'S...
FWOOM

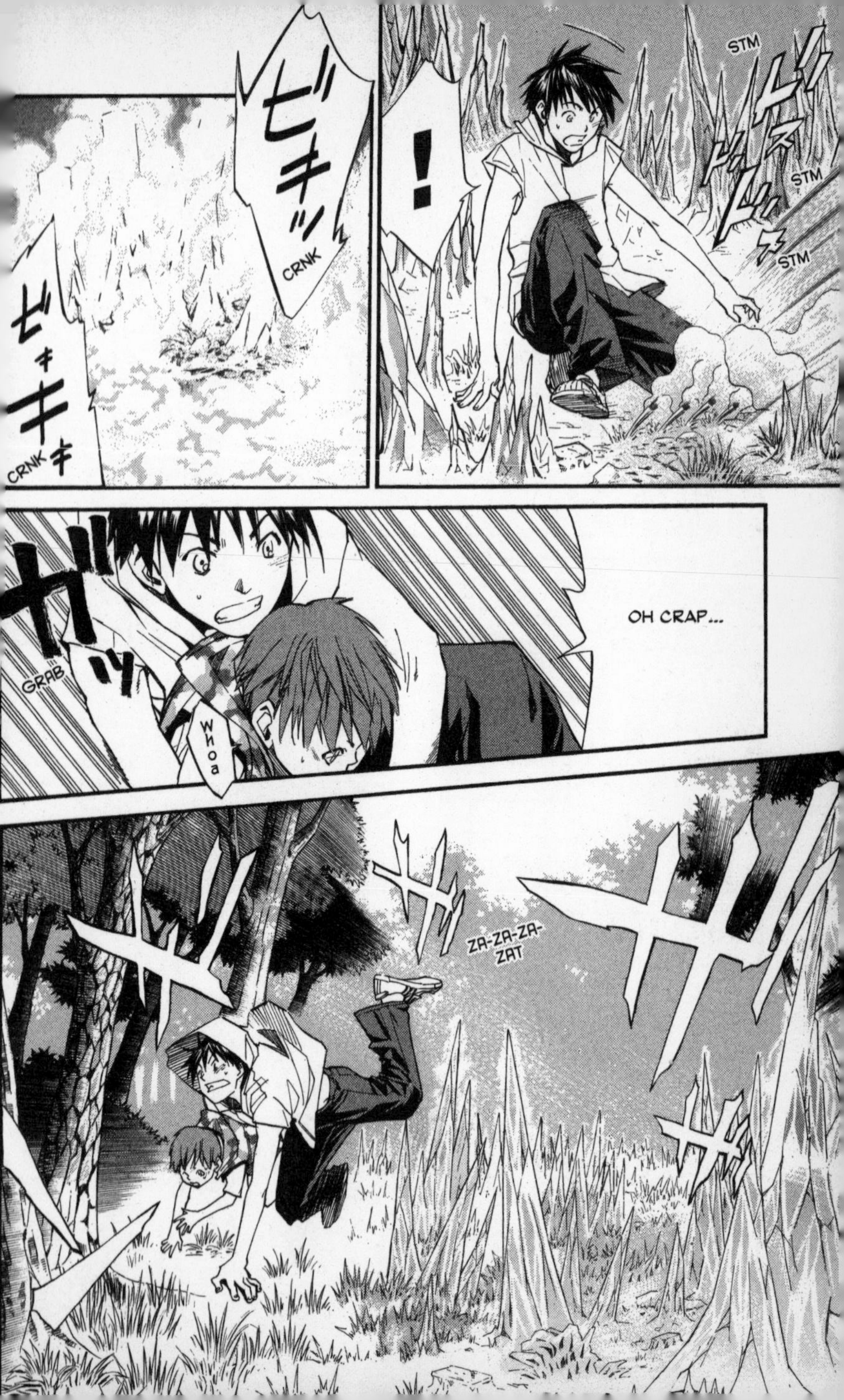
STM
STM
STM
!
ビキッ
CRNK
ビキキキ
CRNK
OH CRAP...
ガッ
GRAB
Whoa
ZA-ZA-ZA-ZAT

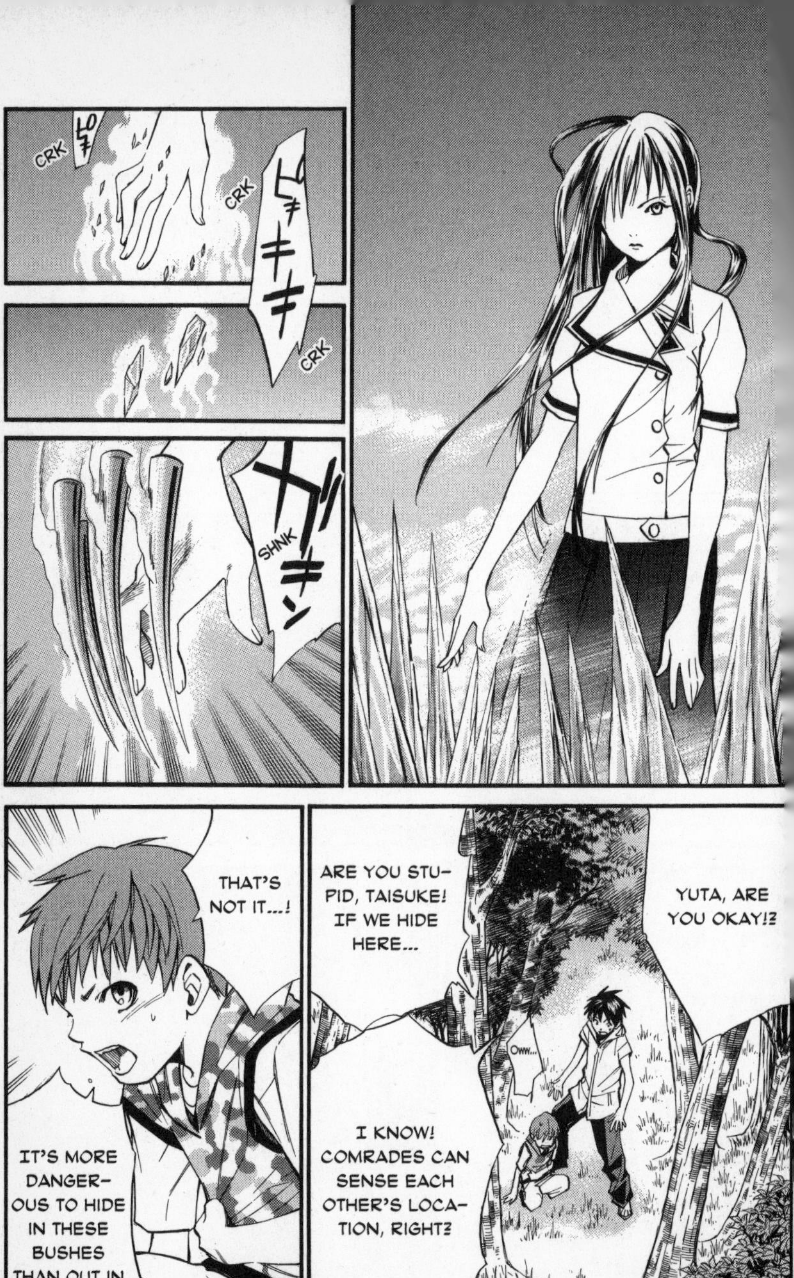
CRK
ピキ
CRK
ピキキキ
CRK
SHNK
ガキン
YUTA, ARE YOU OKAY!?
Oww...
ARE YOU STU-PID, TAISUKE! IF WE HIDE HERE...
I KNOW! COMRADES CAN SENSE EACH OTHER'S LOCA-TION, RIGHT?
THAT'S NOT IT...!
IT'S MORE DANGER-OUS TO HIDE IN THESE BUSHES THAN OUT IN THE OPEN!

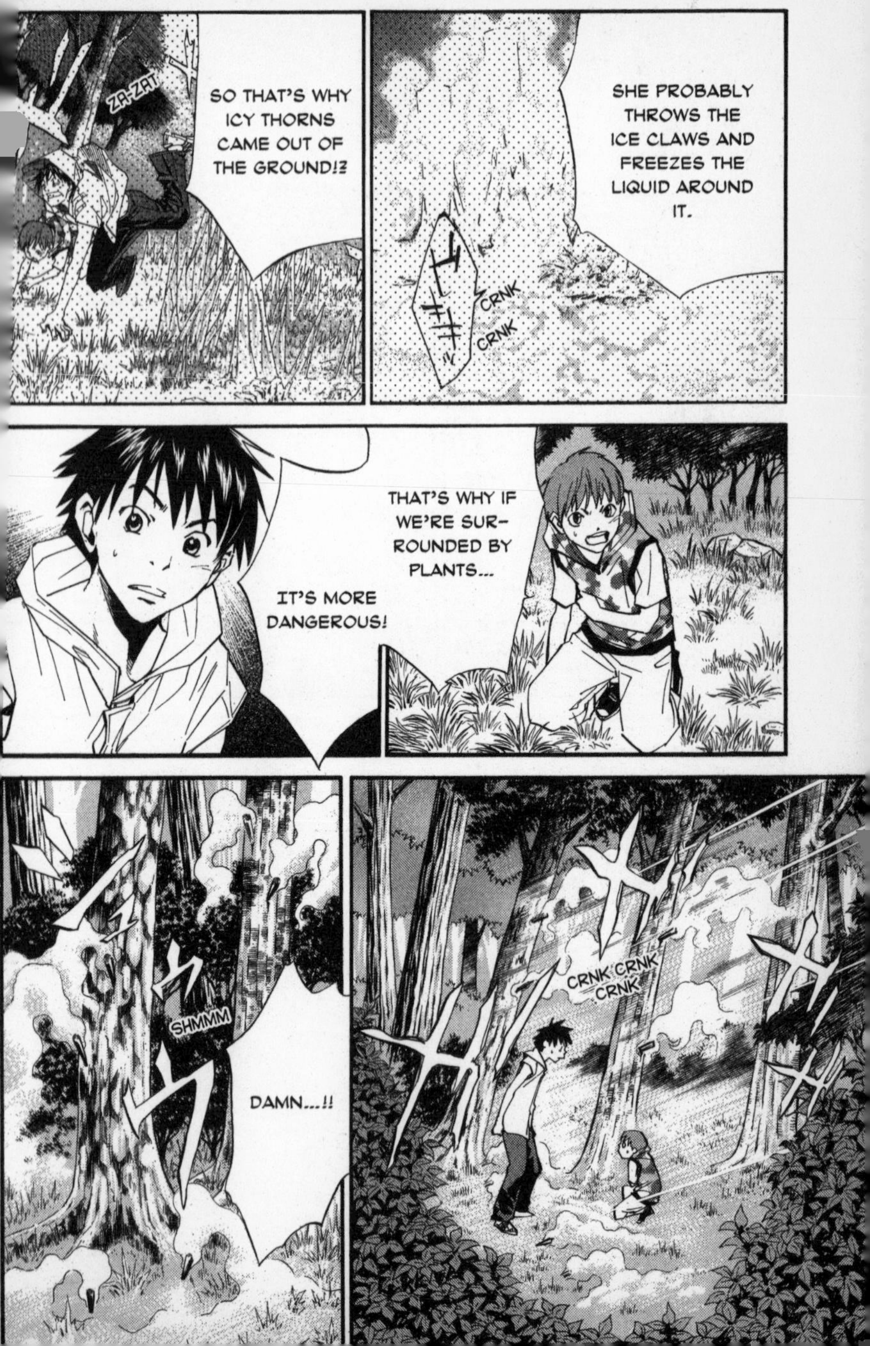
SHE PROBABLY THROWS THE ICE CLAWS AND FREEZES THE LIQUID AROUND IT.
CRNK
CRNK
ZA-ZAT
SO THAT'S WHY ICY THORNS CAME OUT OF THE GROUND!?
THAT'S WHY IF WE'RE SUR-ROUNDED BY PLANTS...
IT'S MORE DANGEROUS!
CRNK CRNK CRNK
SHMMM
DAMN...!!

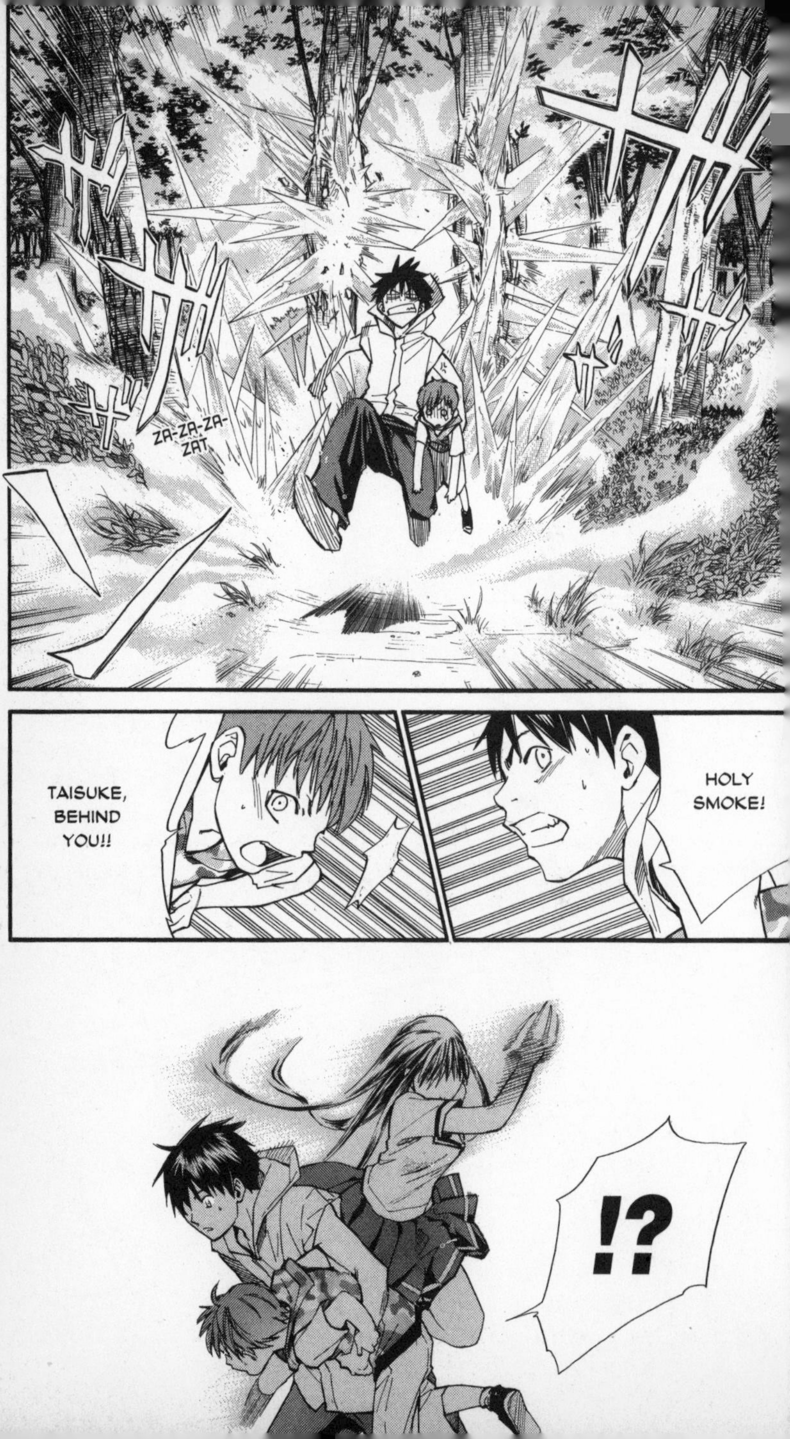
ZA-ZA-ZA-ZAT
HOLY SMOKE!
TAISUKE, BEHIND YOU!!
!?

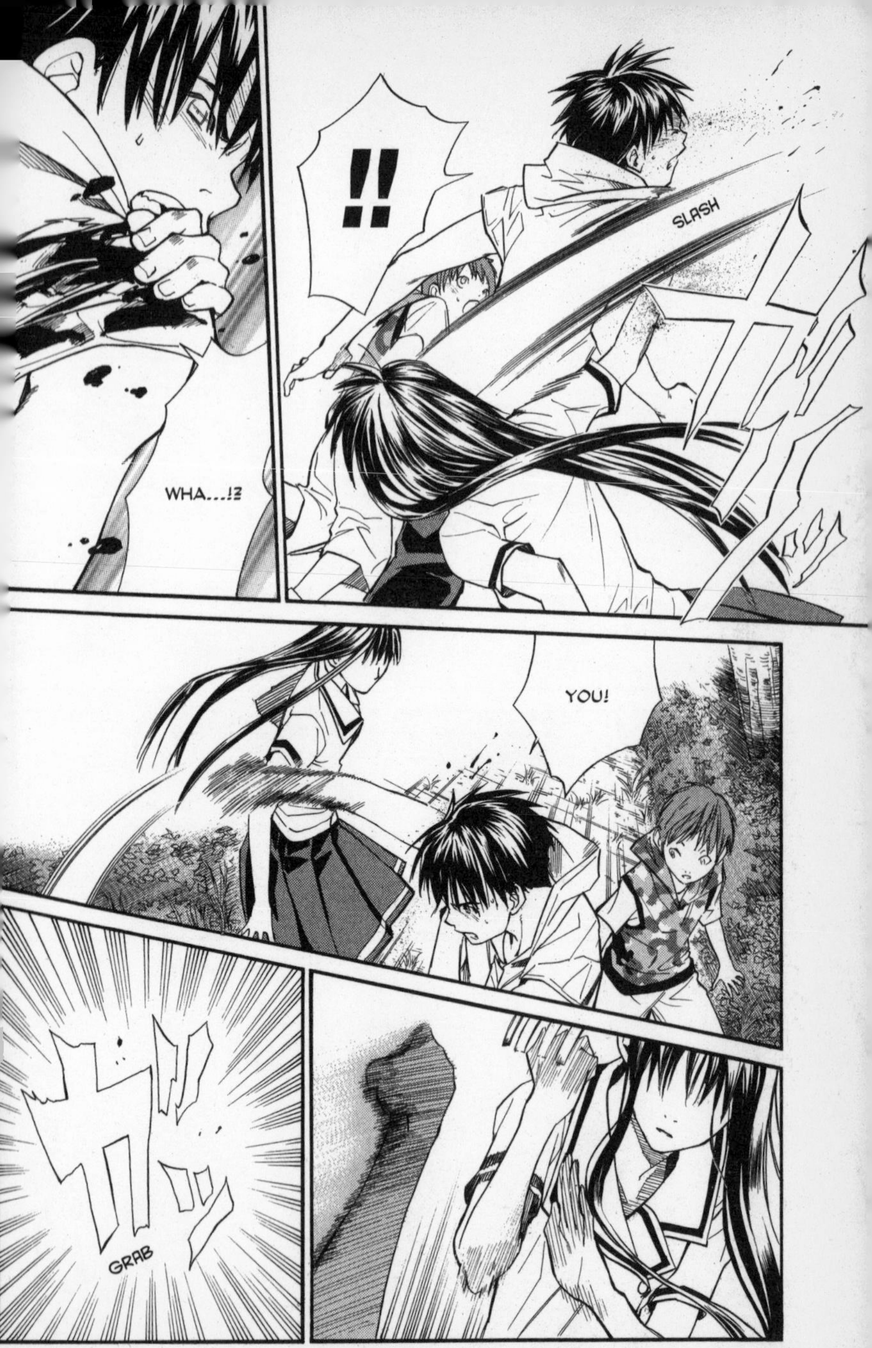

!!
SLASH
WHA...!?
YOU!
GRAB

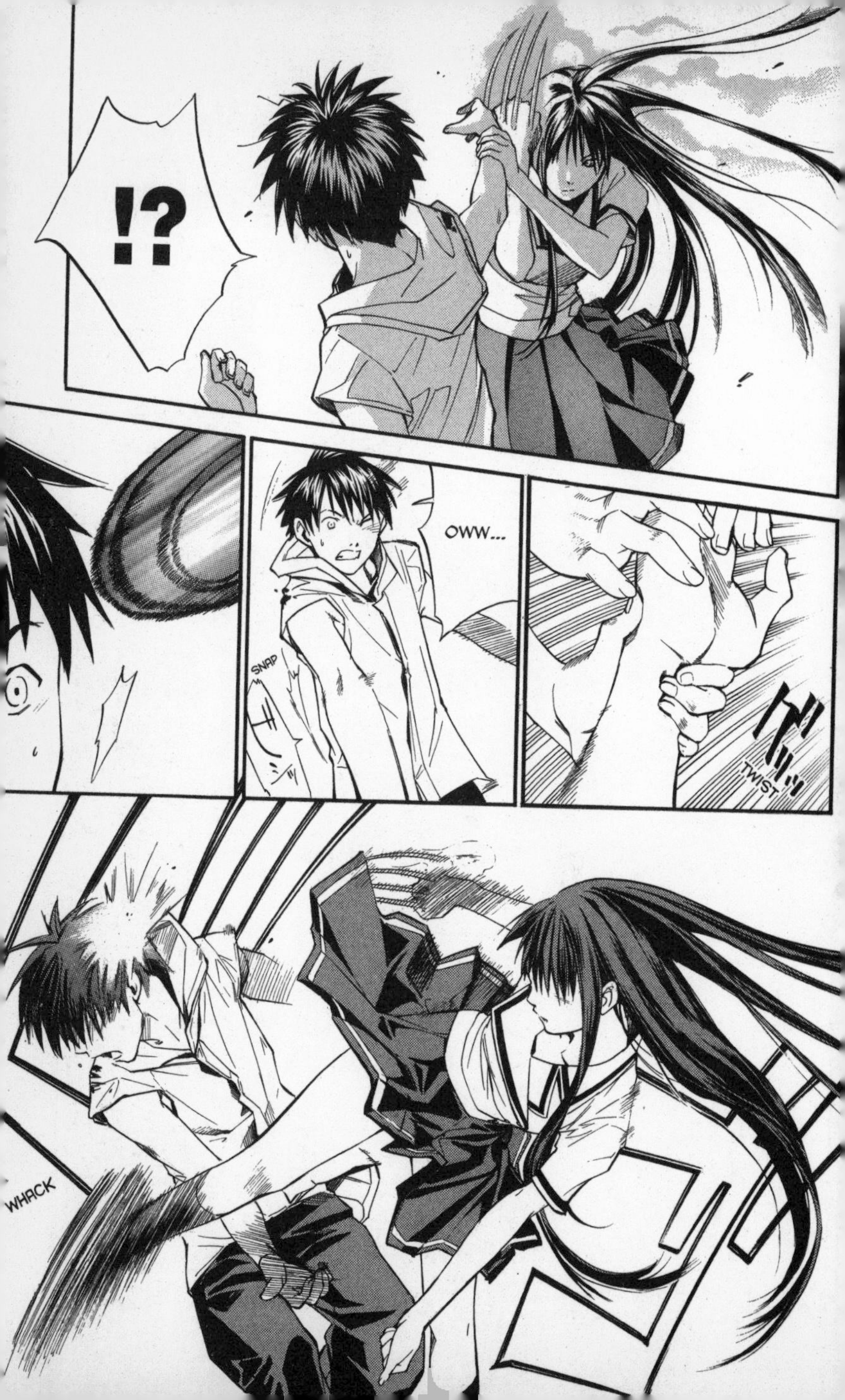
!?
TWIST
OWW...
SNAP
WHACK

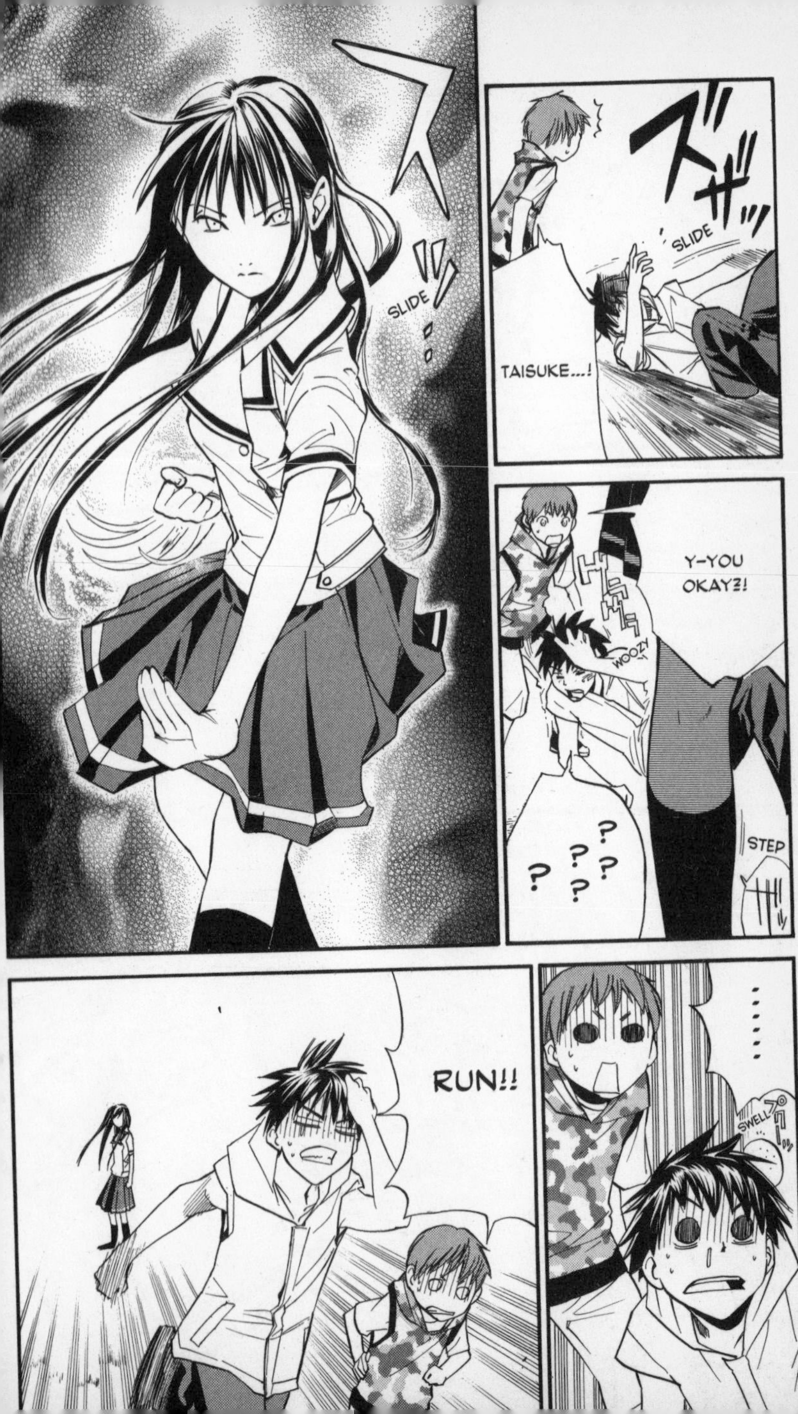

SLIDE
TAISUKE...!
Y-YOU OKAY?!
WOOZY
? ? ? ? ? ?
STEP
SLIDE
......
SWELL
RUN!!

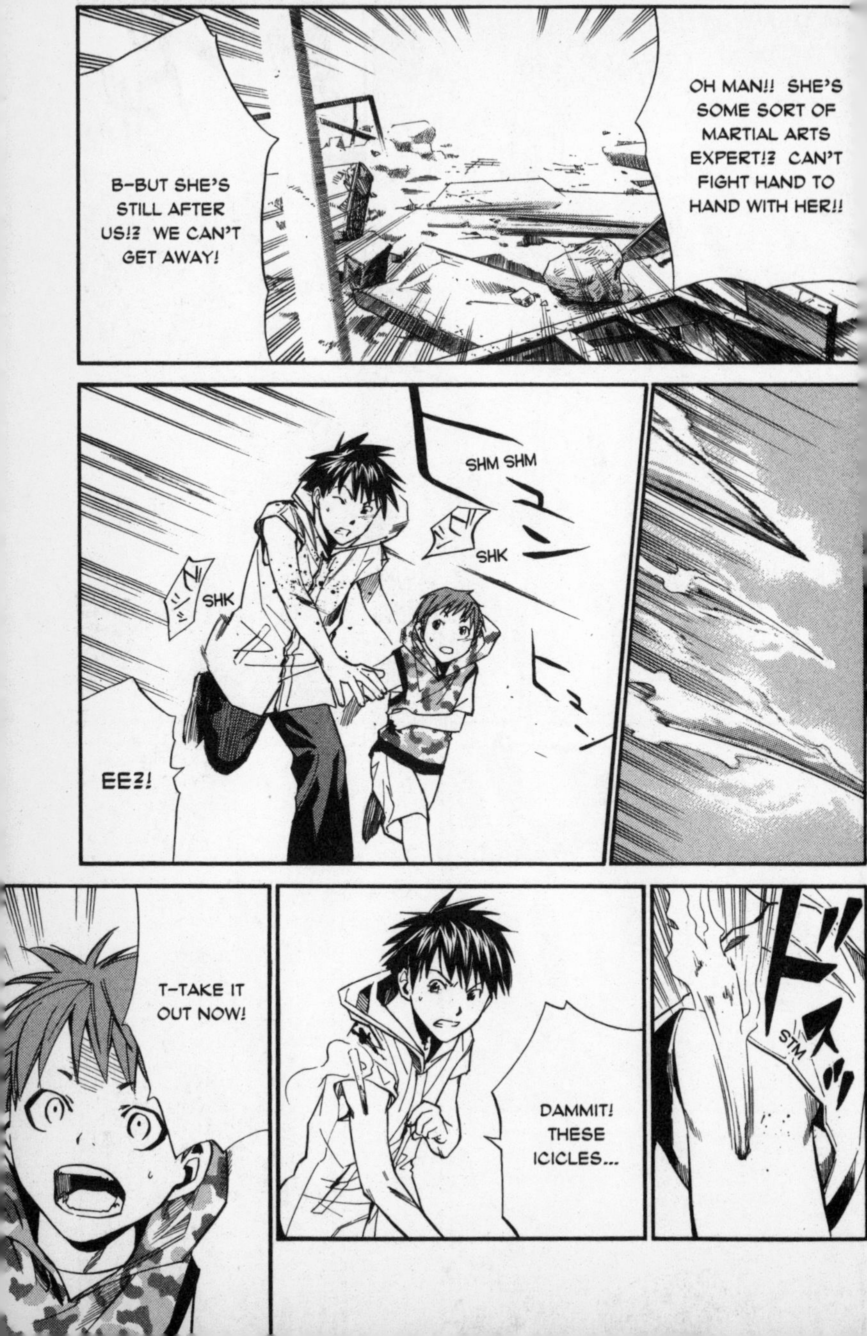
OH MAN!! SHE'S SOME SORT OF MARTIAL ARTS EXPERT!? CAN'T FIGHT HAND TO HAND WITH HER!!
B-BUT SHE'S STILL AFTER US!? WE CAN'T GET AWAY!
SHM SHM
SHK
SHK
EE?!
STM
DAMMIT! THESE ICICLES...
T-TAKE IT OUT NOW!

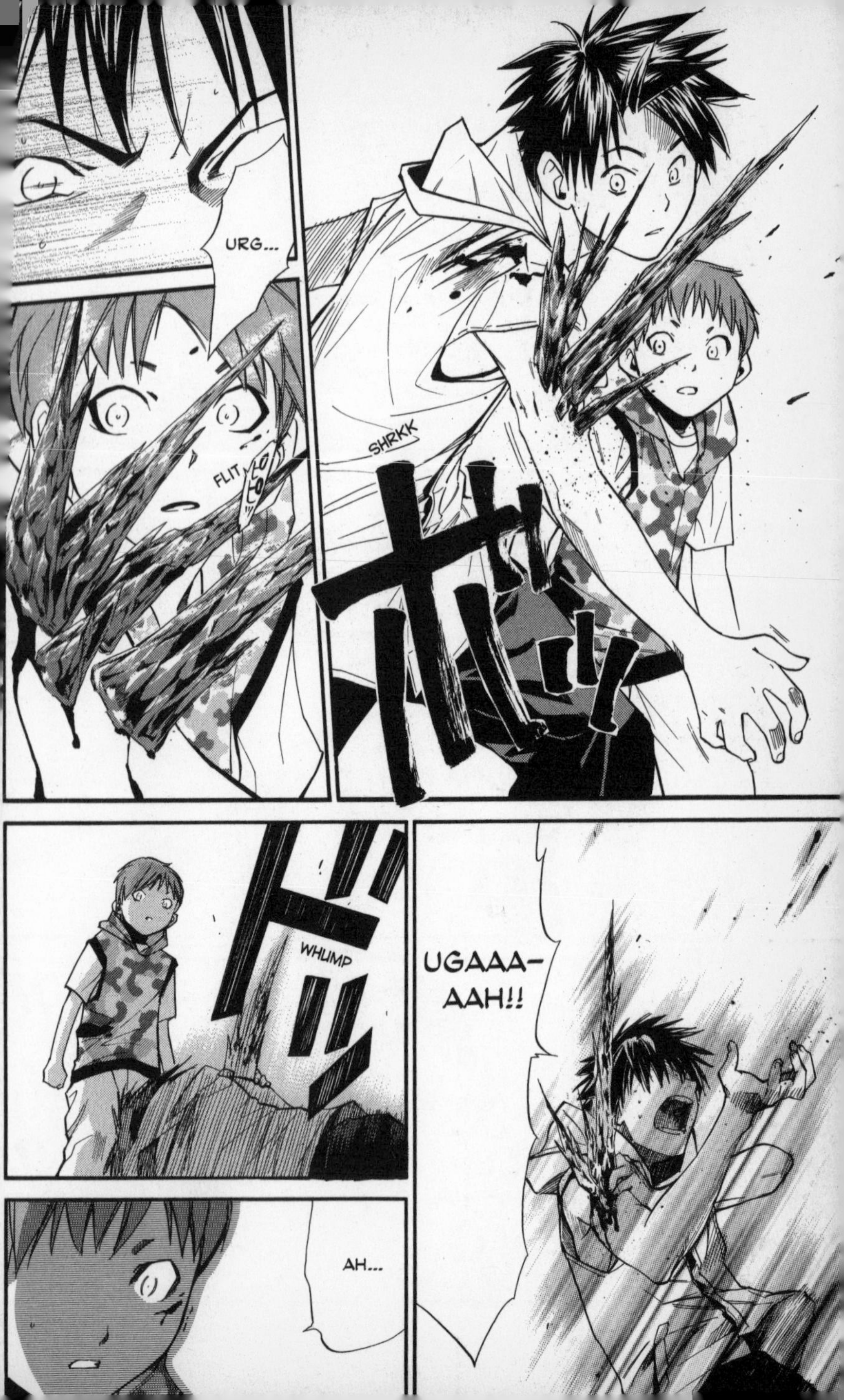
SHRKK
URG...
FLIT
UGAAA-
AAH!!
WHUMP
AH...

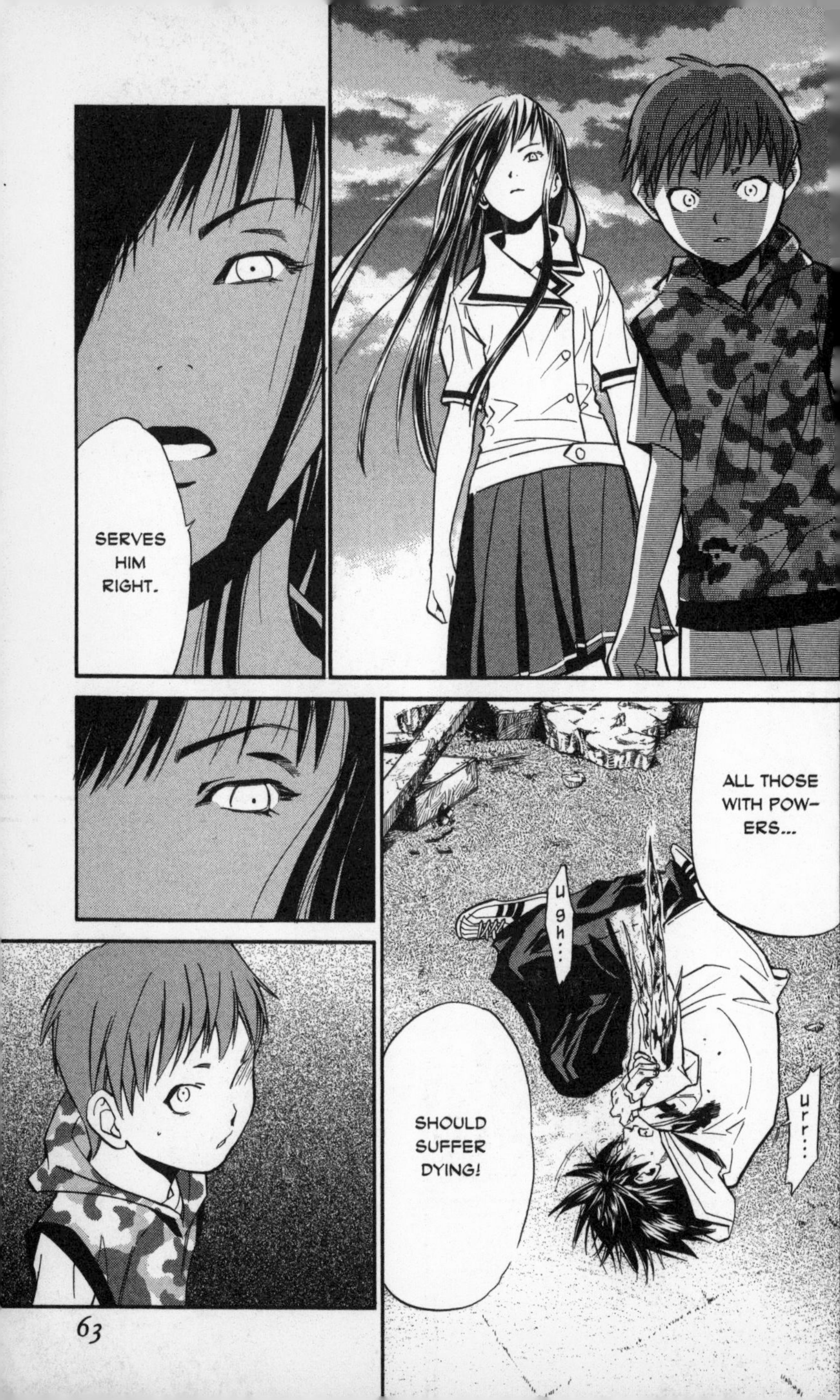
SERVES HIM RIGHT.
ALL THOSE WITH POW- ERS...
Ugh...
SHOULD SUFFER DYING!
Urr...

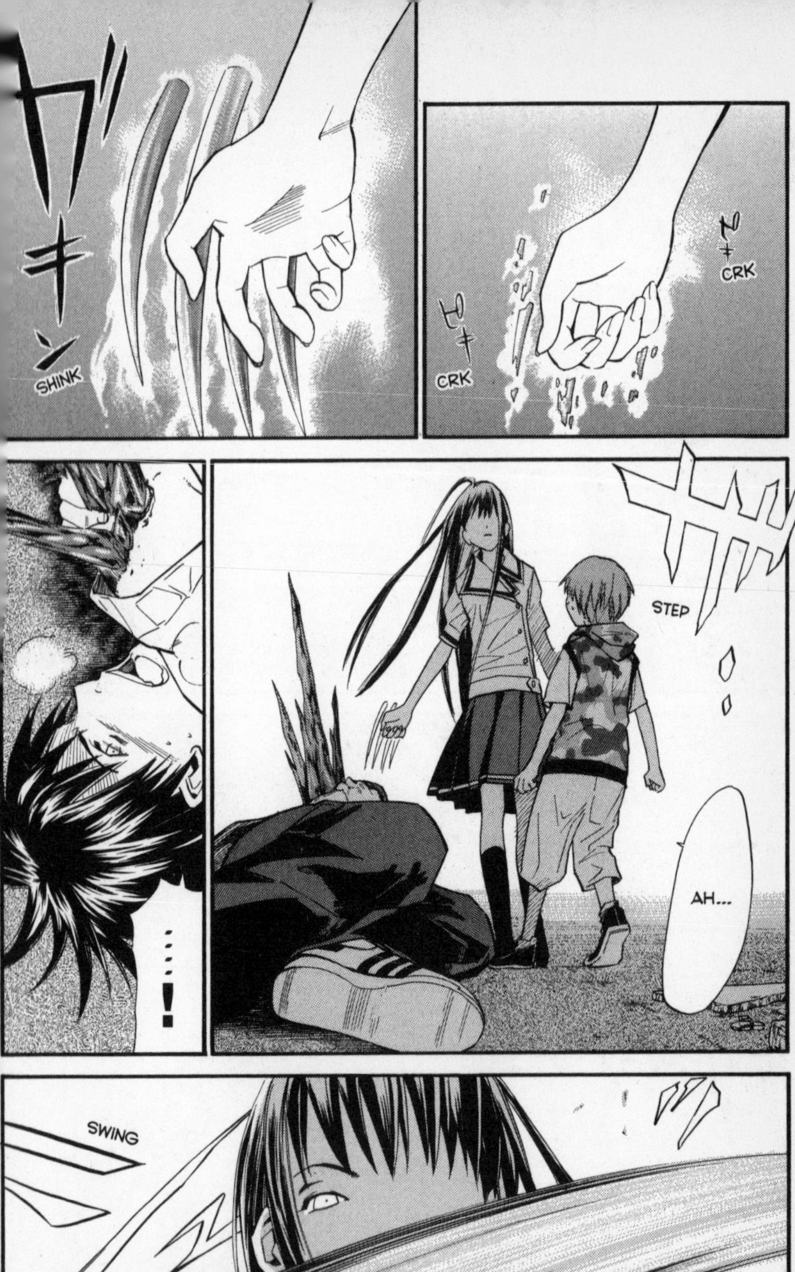
ピキ
CRK
ピキ
CRK
ヴキン
SHINK
ザッ
STEP
AH...
...!
SWING

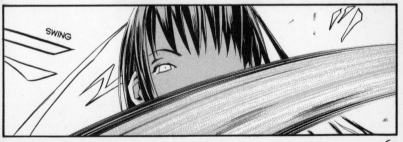

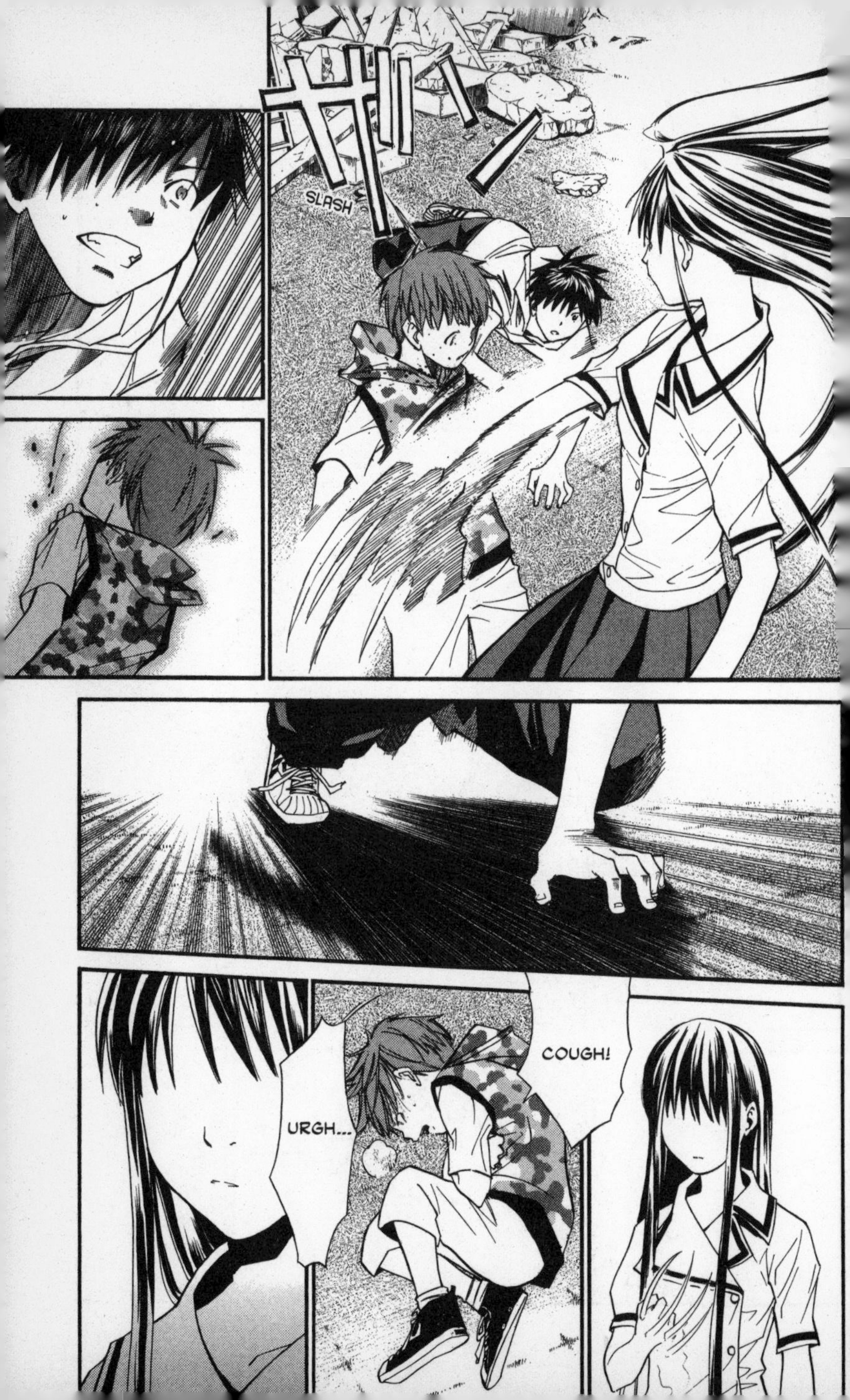
SLASH
COUGH!
URGH...

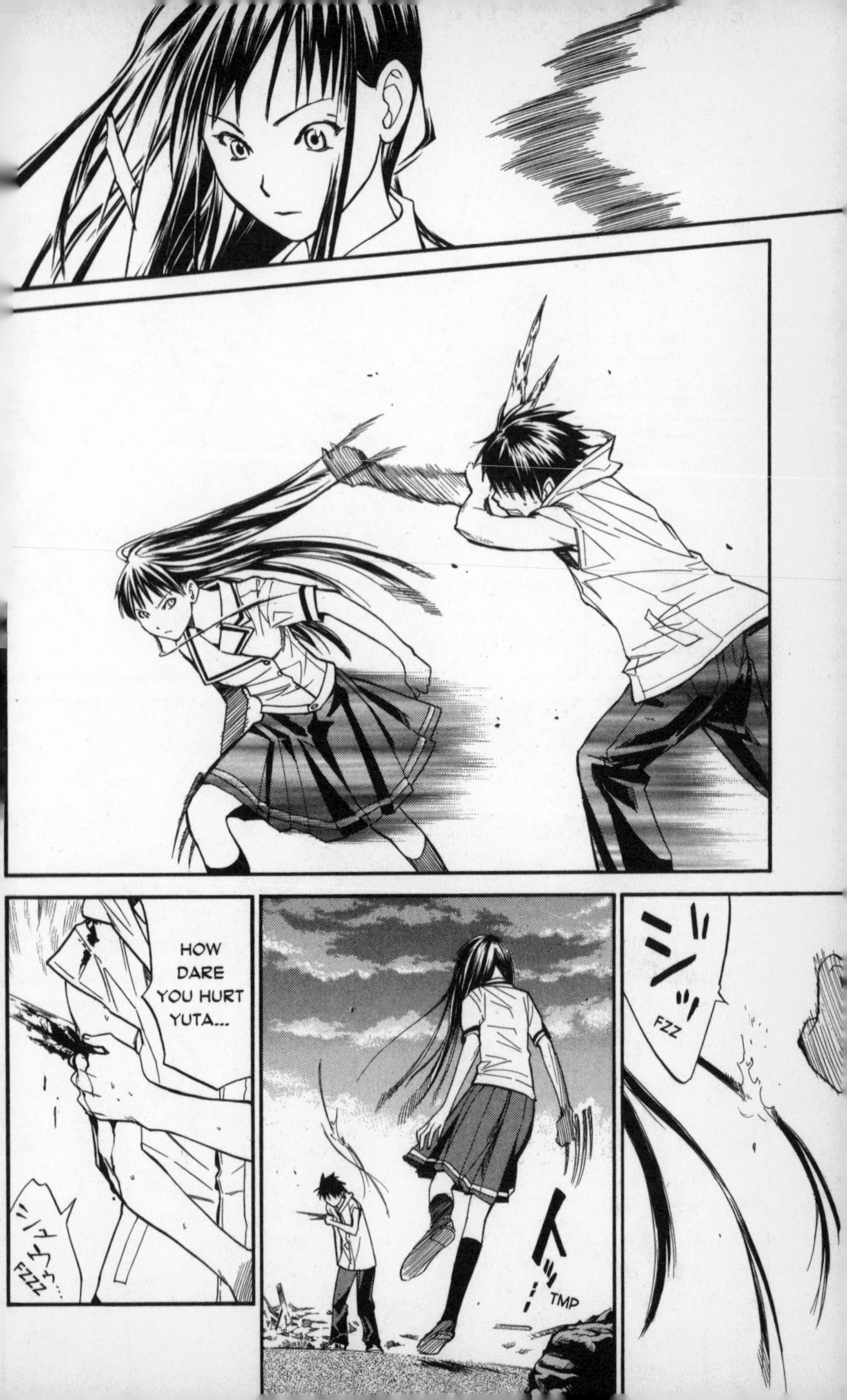
FZZ
TMP
HOW DARE YOU HURT YUTA...
FZZZZ...

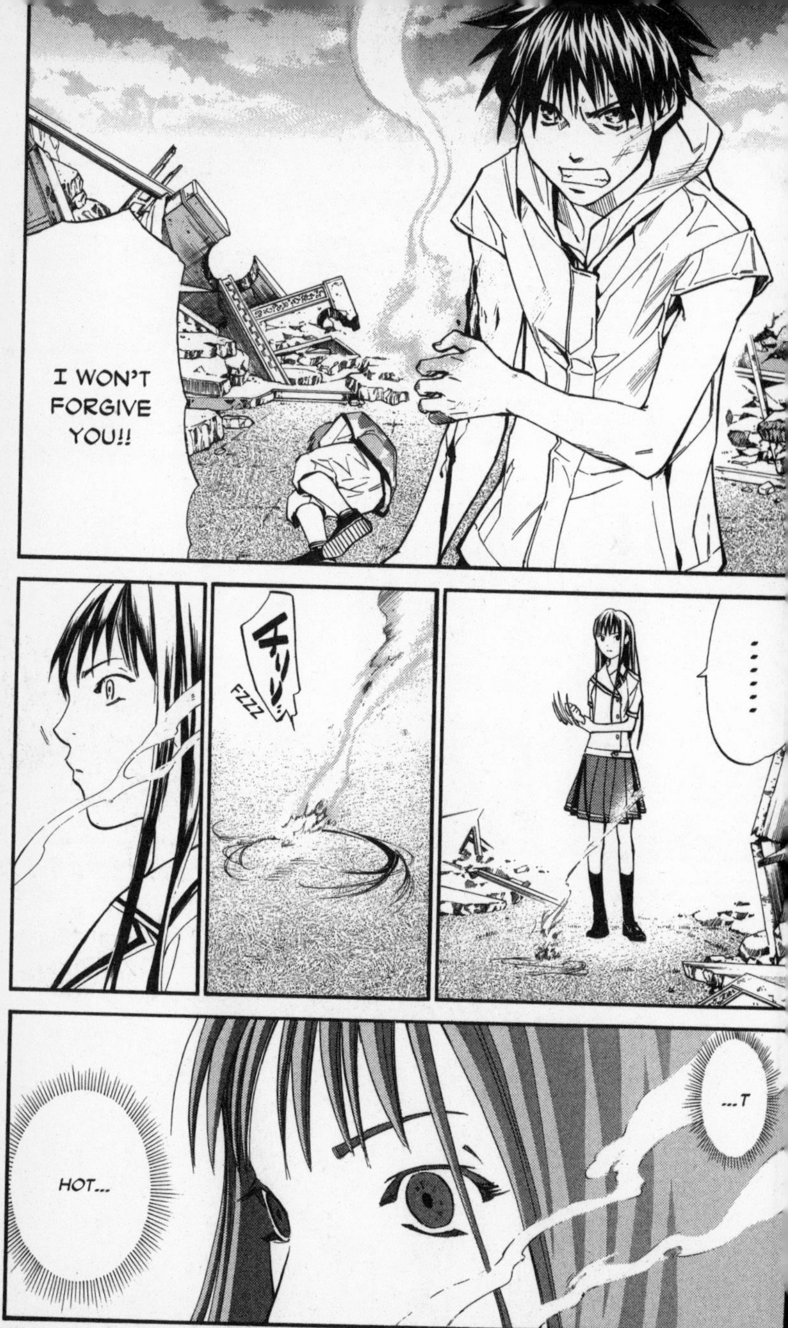
I WON'T FORGIVE YOU!!
......
FZZZ
...T
HOT...

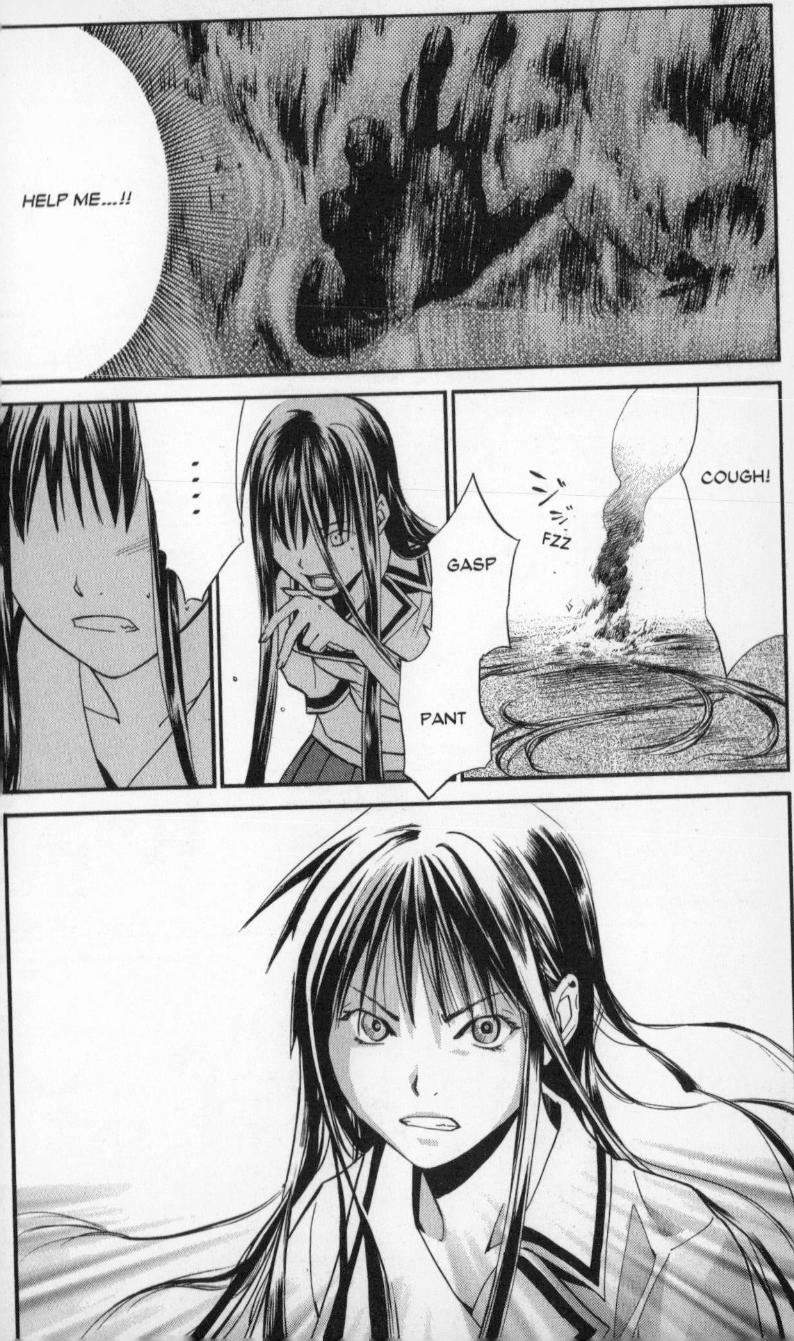
HELP ME...!!
COUGH!
FZZ
GASP
PANT
....

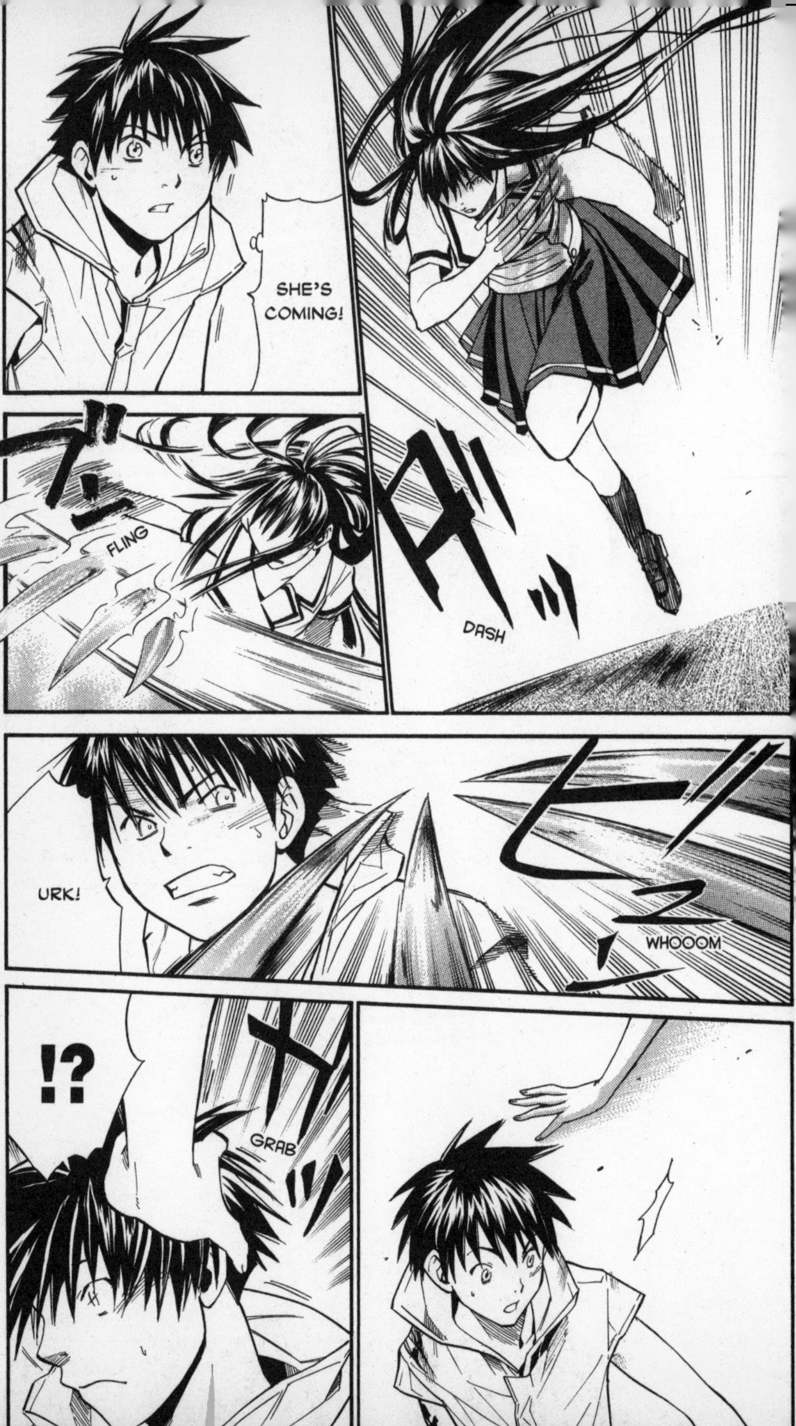
DASH
SHE'S COMING!
FLING
WHOOOM
URK!
GRAB
!?

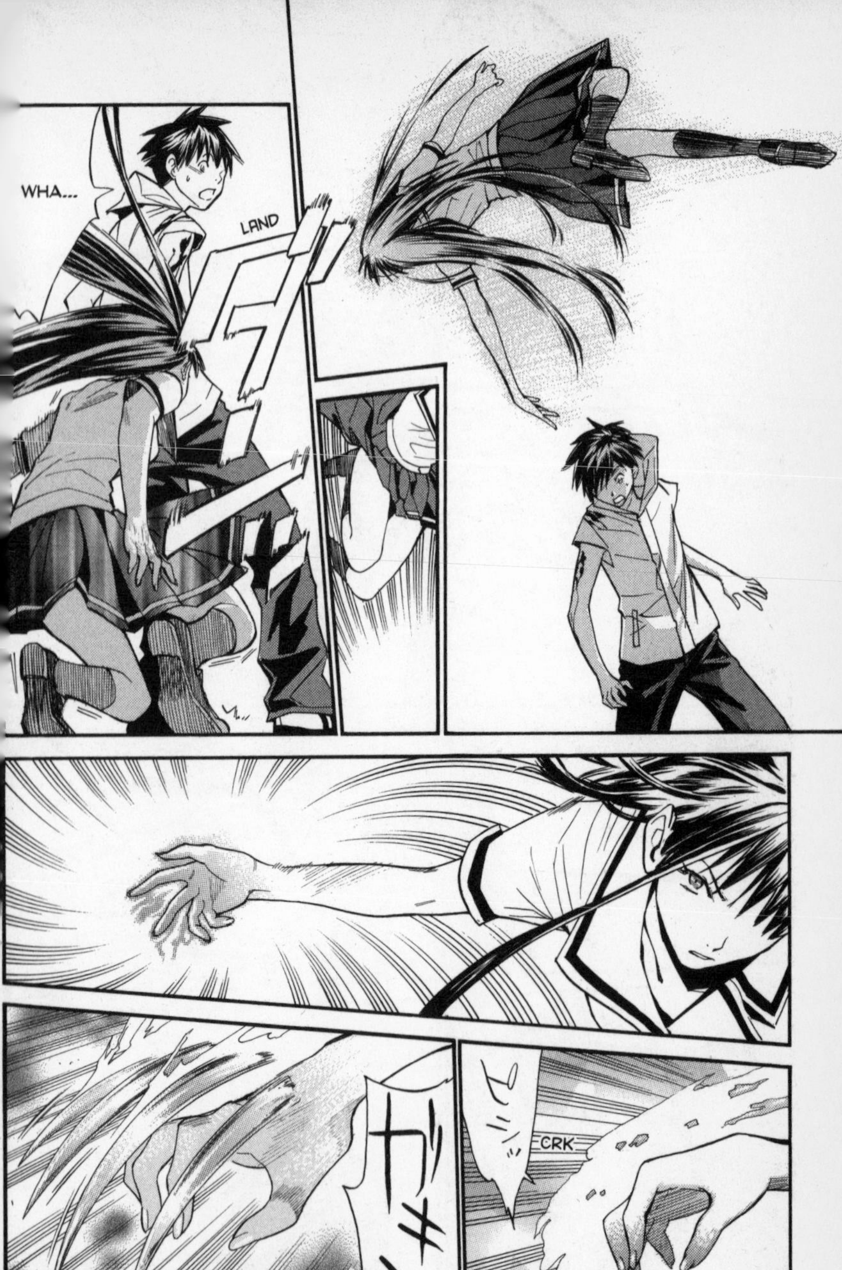
LAND
WHA...
CRK
SHNK

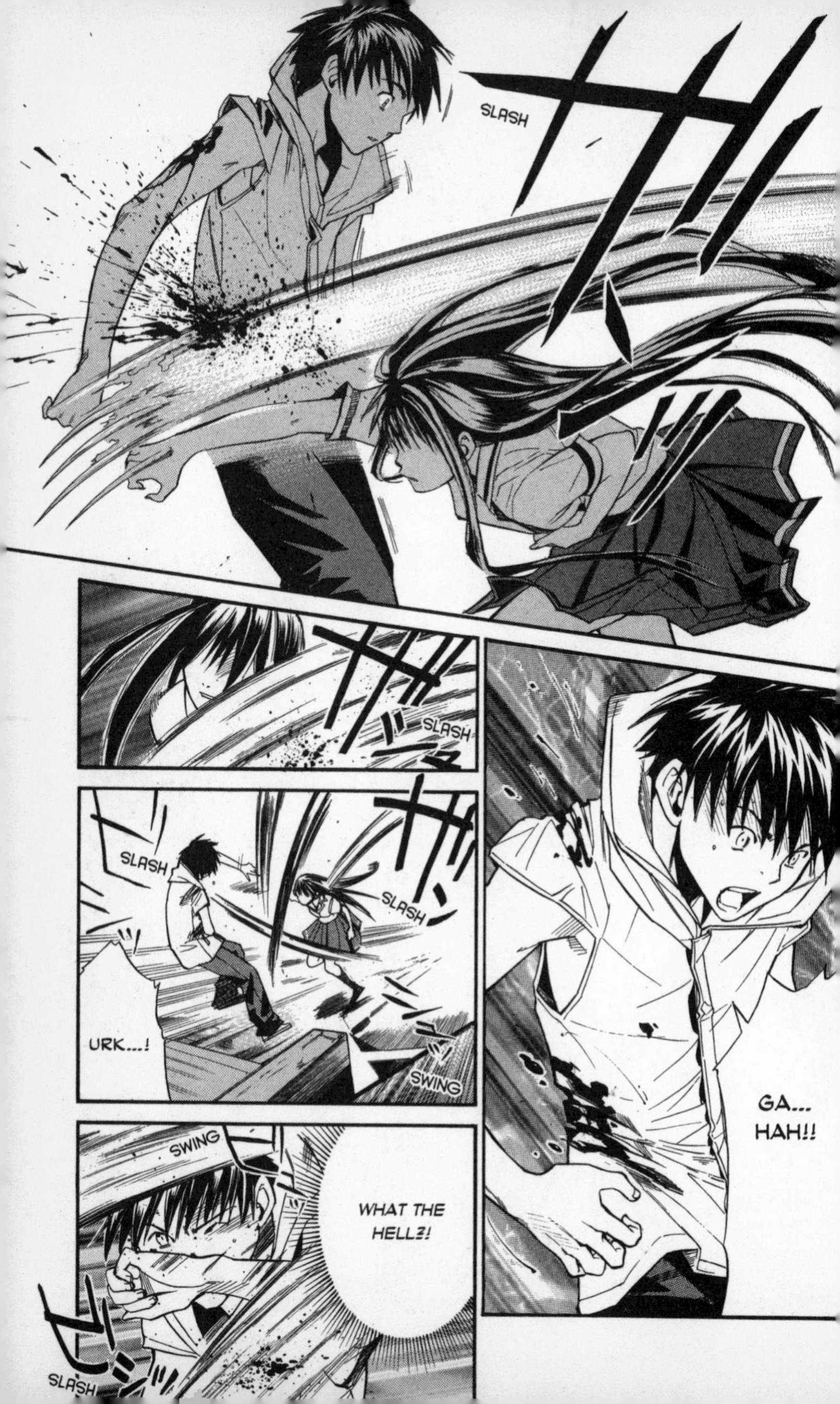
SLASH
GA... HAH!!
SLASH
SLASH
SLASH
SWING
URK...!
SWING
WHAT THE HELL?!
SLASH

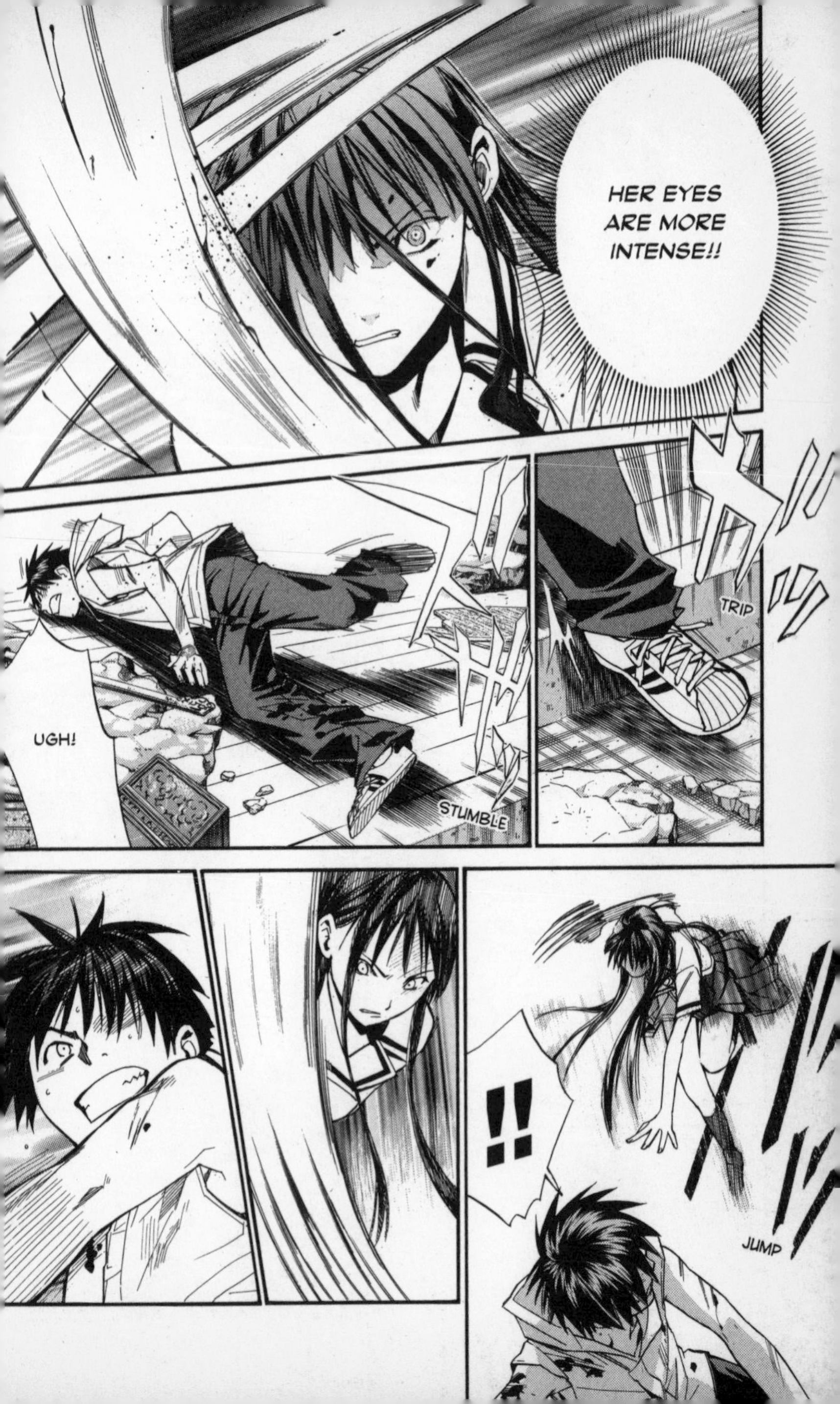
HER EYES ARE MORE INTENSE!!
TRIP
STUMBLE
UGH!
!!
JUMP

K-SHING

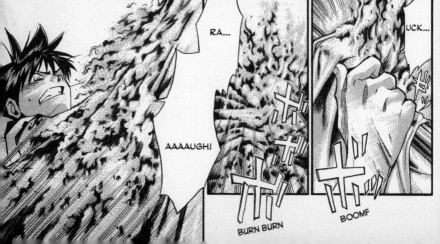

RA...

AAAAUGH!

BURN BURN

UCK...

BOOMF

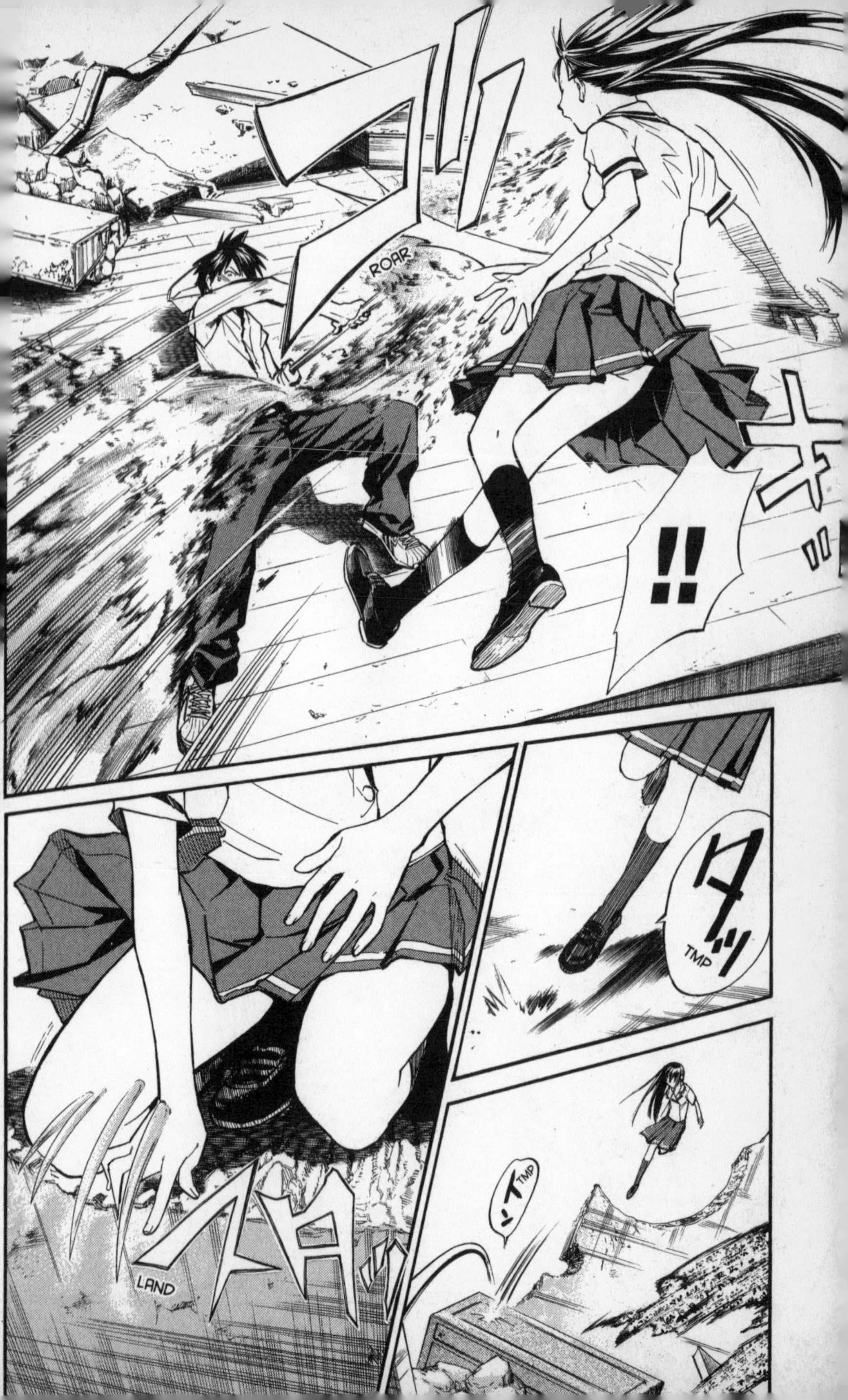
ROAR
!!
TMP
TMP
LAND

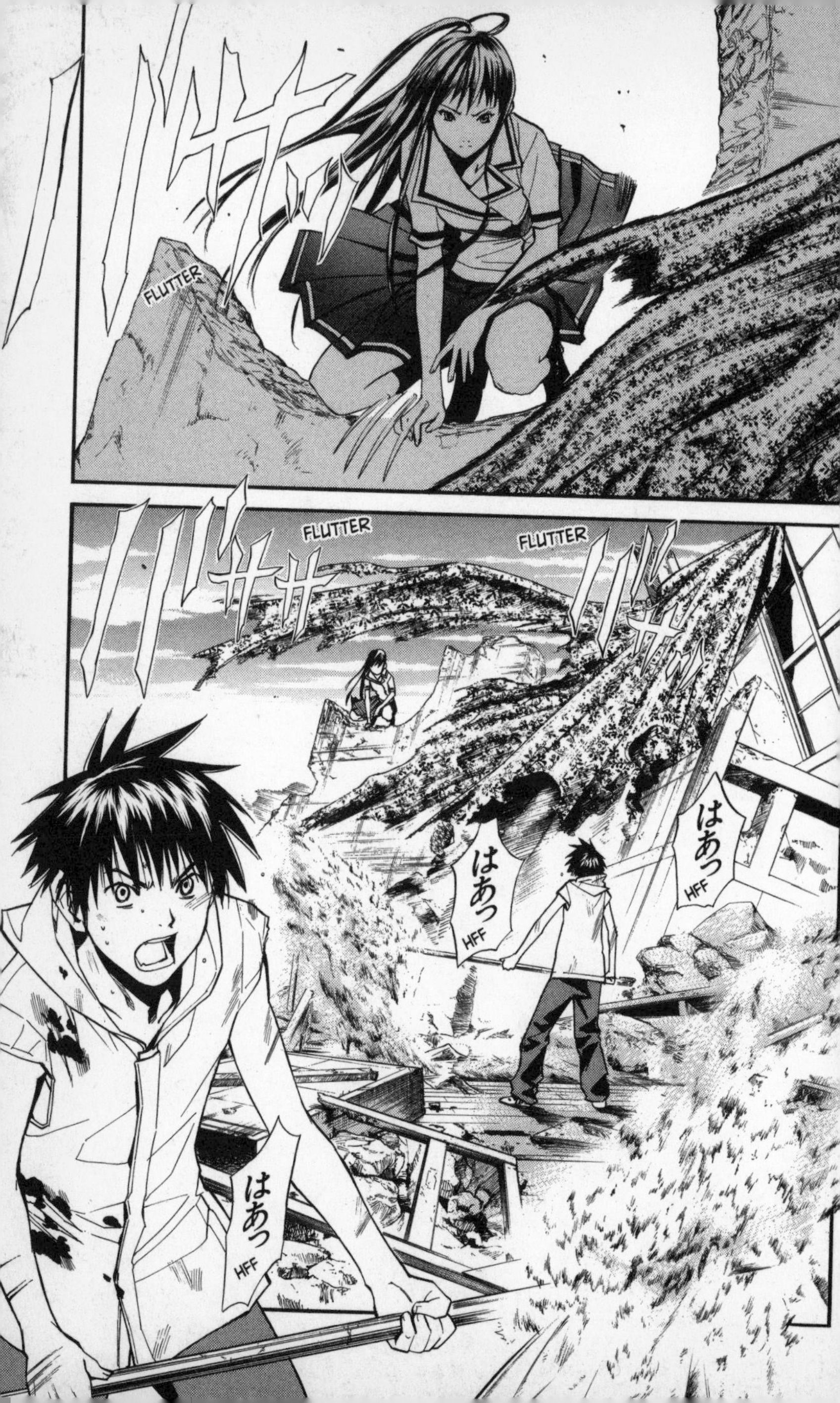
FLUTTER
FLUTTER
FLUTTER
はあっ
HFF
はあっ
HFF
はあっ
HFF

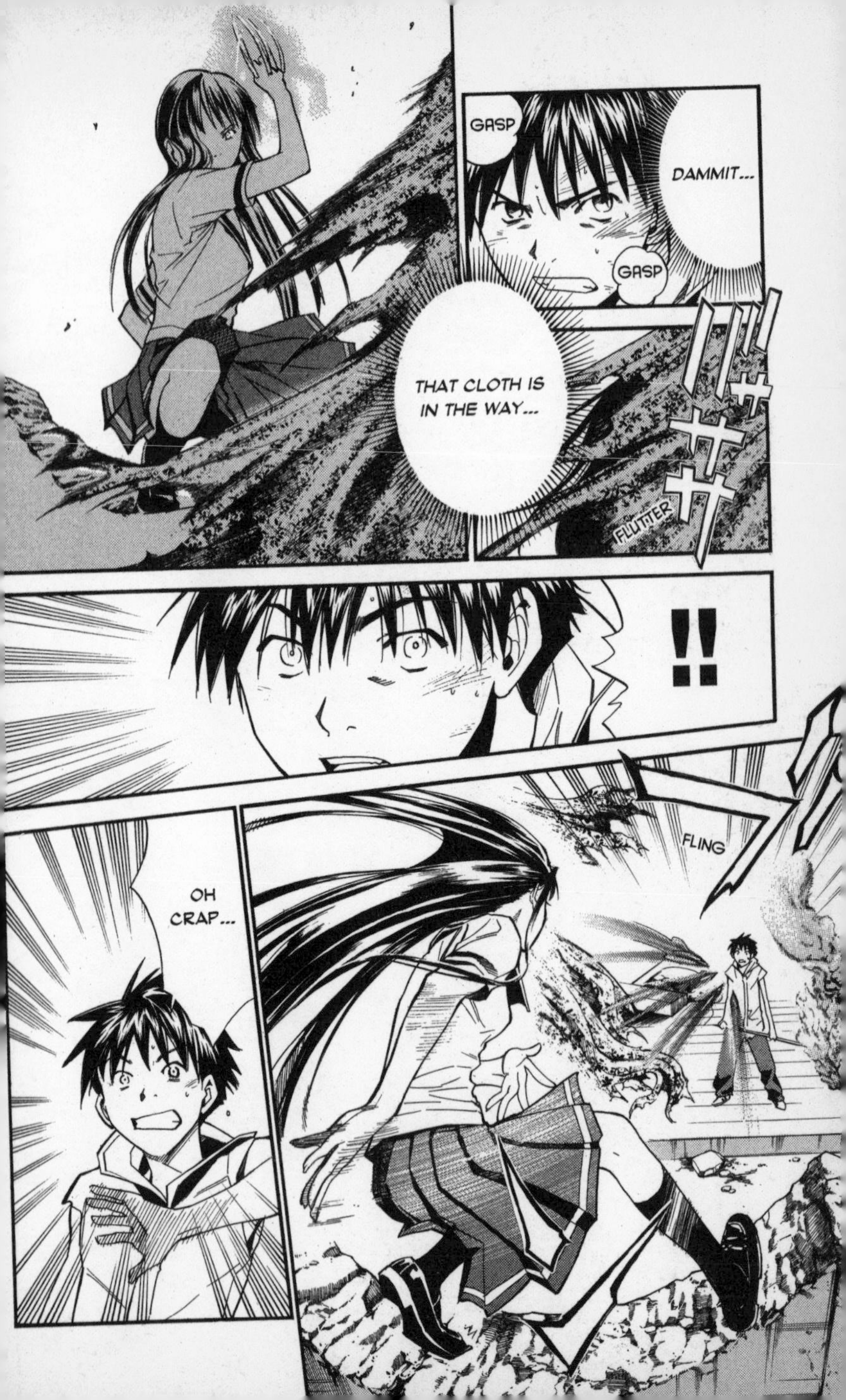
GASP
DAMMIT...
GASP
THAT CLOTH IS IN THE WAY...
FLUTTER
!!
FLING
OH CRAP...

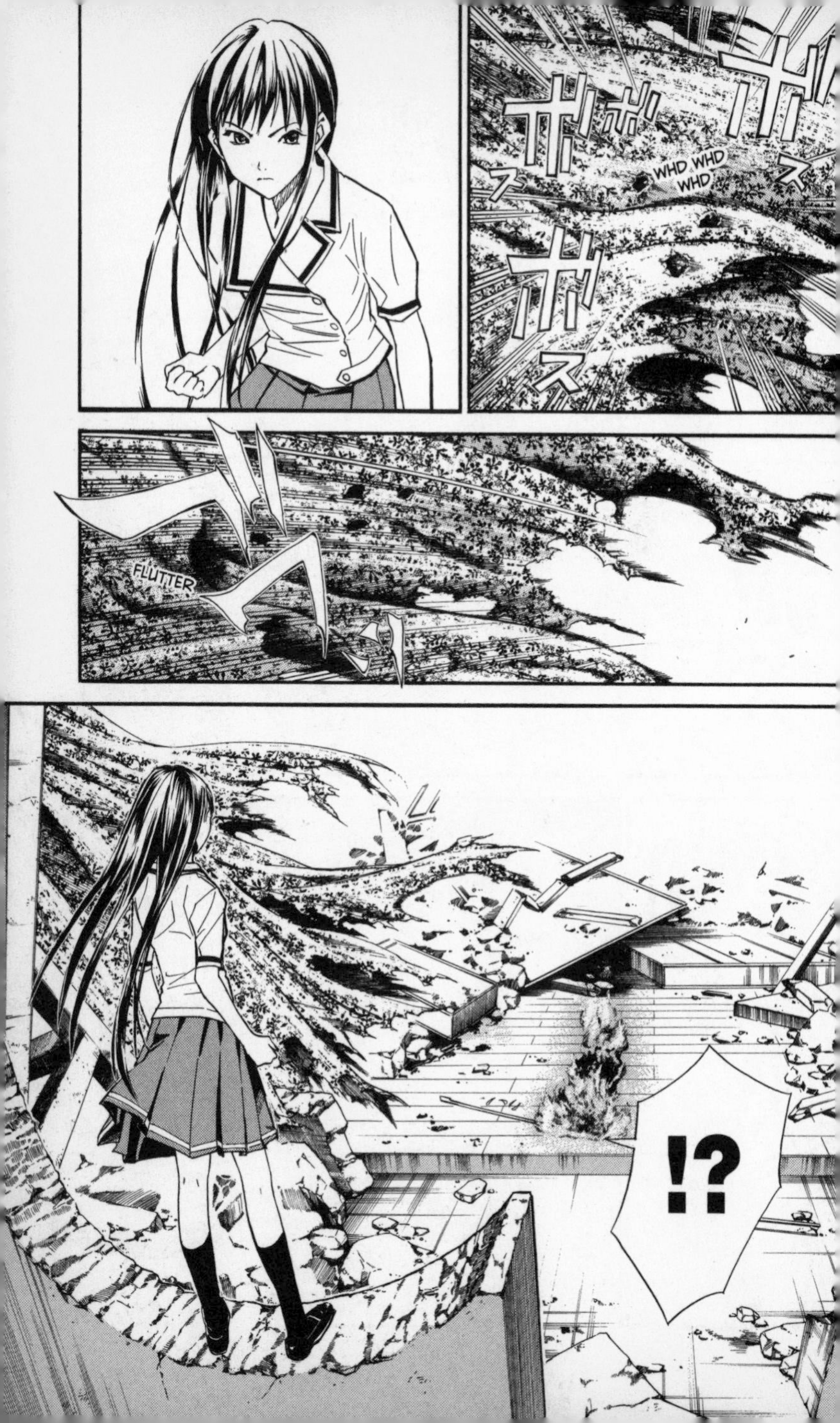
WHD WHD WHD
FLUTTER
!?

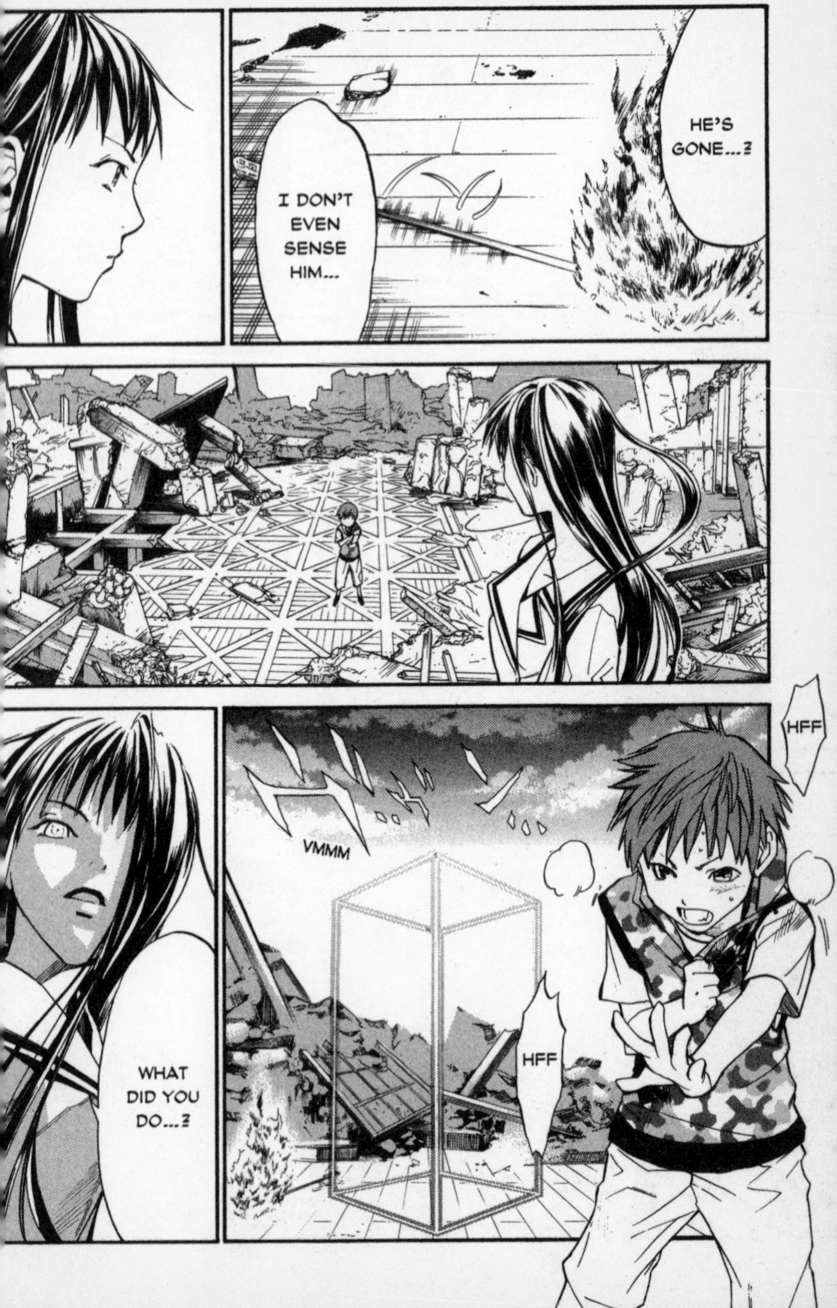

HE'S GONE...?
I DON'T EVEN SENSE HIM...
HFF
VMMM
HFF
WHAT DID YOU DO...?

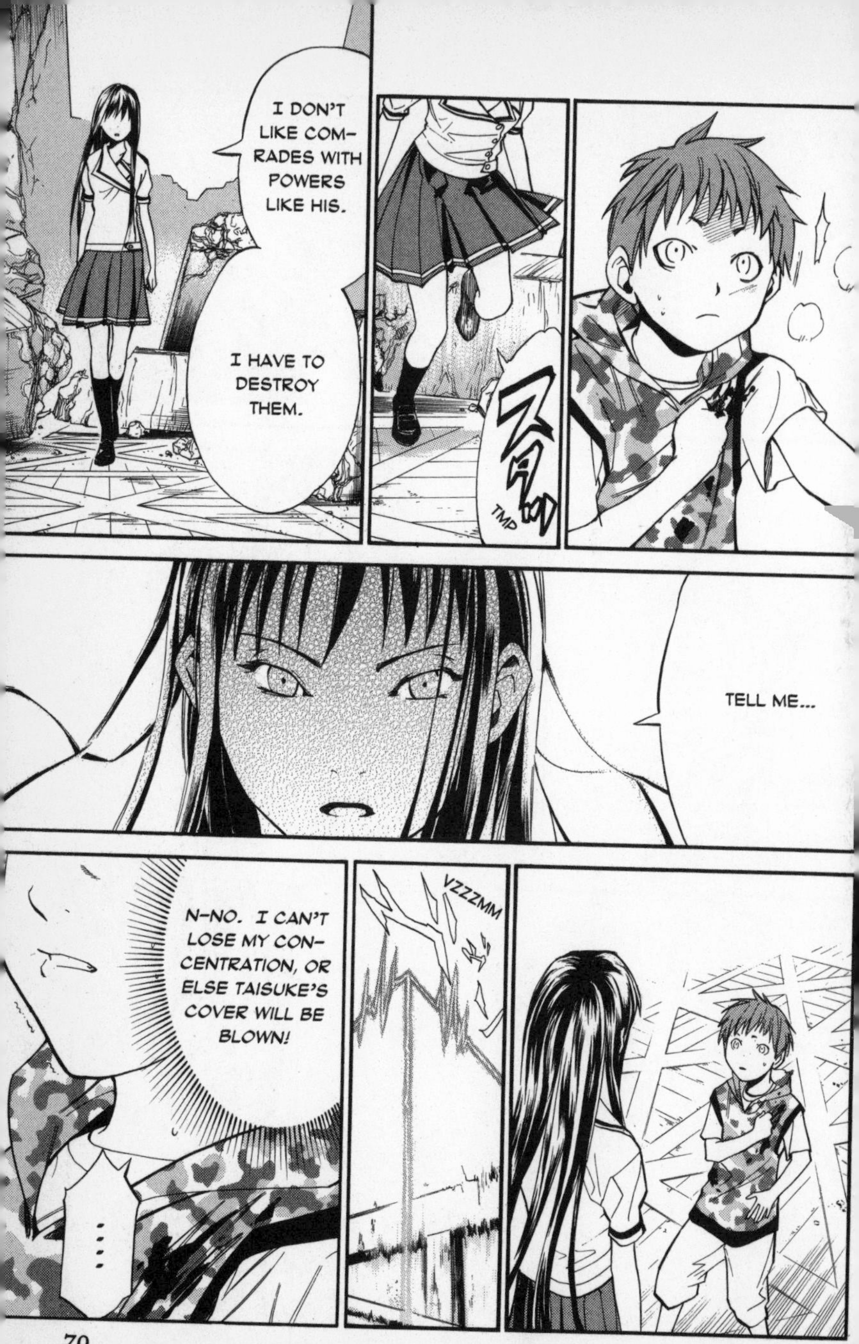
TMP
I DON'T LIKE COM-RADES WITH POWERS LIKE HIS.
I HAVE TO DESTROY THEM.
TELL ME...
VZZZMM
N-NO. I CAN'T LOSE MY CON-CENTRATION, OR ELSE TAISUKE'S COVER WILL BE BLOWN!
....

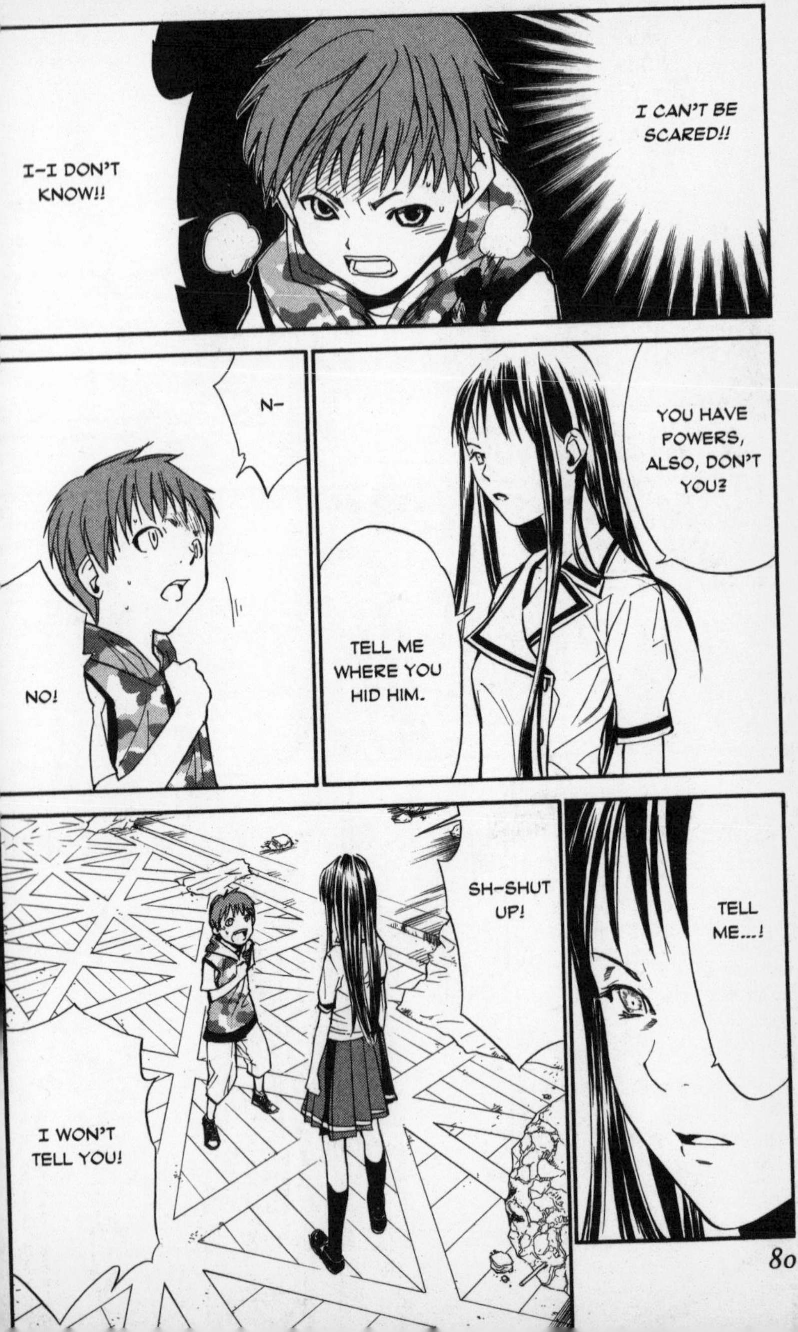

I CAN'T BE SCARED!!
I-I DON'T KNOW!!
YOU HAVE POWERS, ALSO, DON'T YOU?
TELL ME WHERE YOU HID HIM.
N-
NO!
TELL ME...!
SH-SHUT UP!
I WON'T TELL YOU!

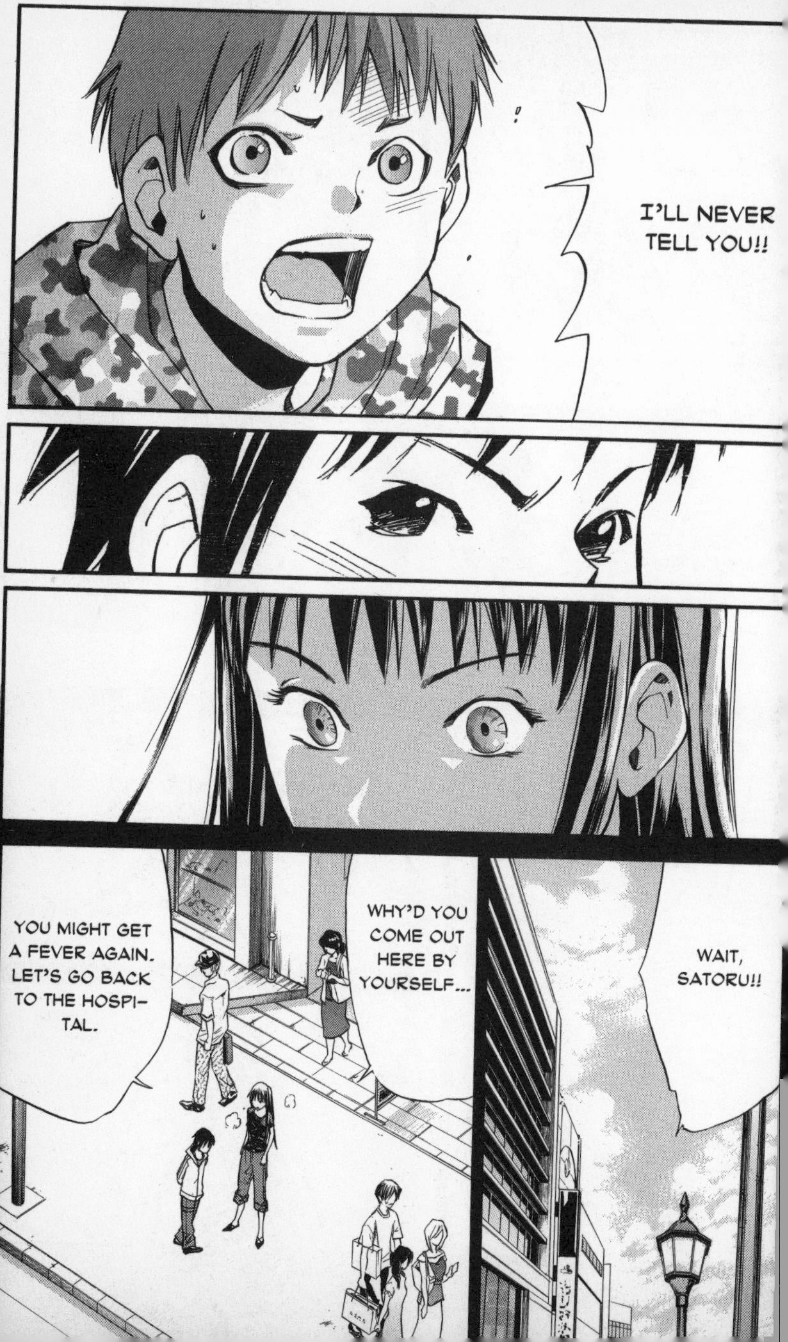
I'LL NEVER TELL YOU!!
WAIT, SATORU!!
WHY'D YOU COME OUT HERE BY YOURSELF...
YOU MIGHT GET A FEVER AGAIN. LET'S GO BACK TO THE HOSPI-TAL.

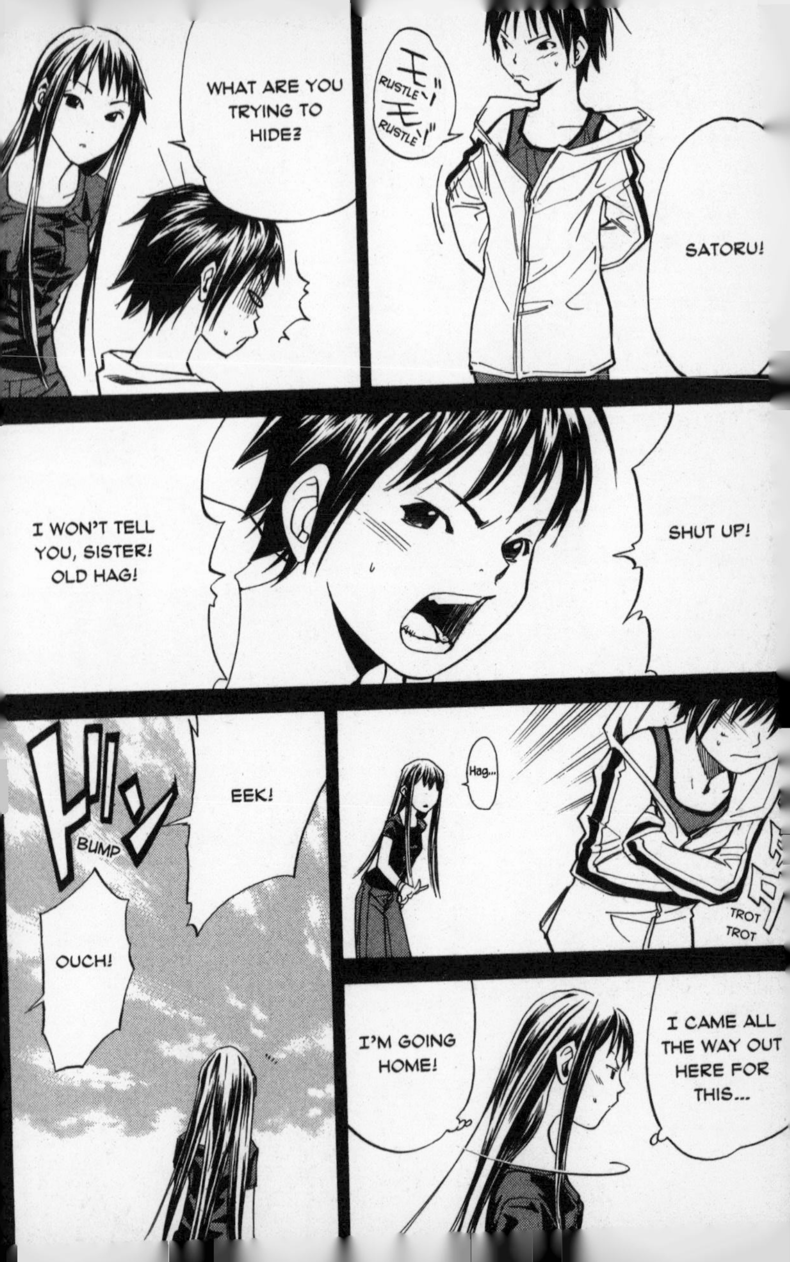
SATORU!
RUSTLE
RUSTLE
WHAT ARE YOU TRYING TO HIDE?
SHUT UP!
I WON'T TELL YOU, SISTER! OLD HAG!
Hag...
TROT
TROT
I CAME ALL THE WAY OUT HERE FOR THIS...
I'M GOING HOME!
BUMP
EEK!
OUCH!

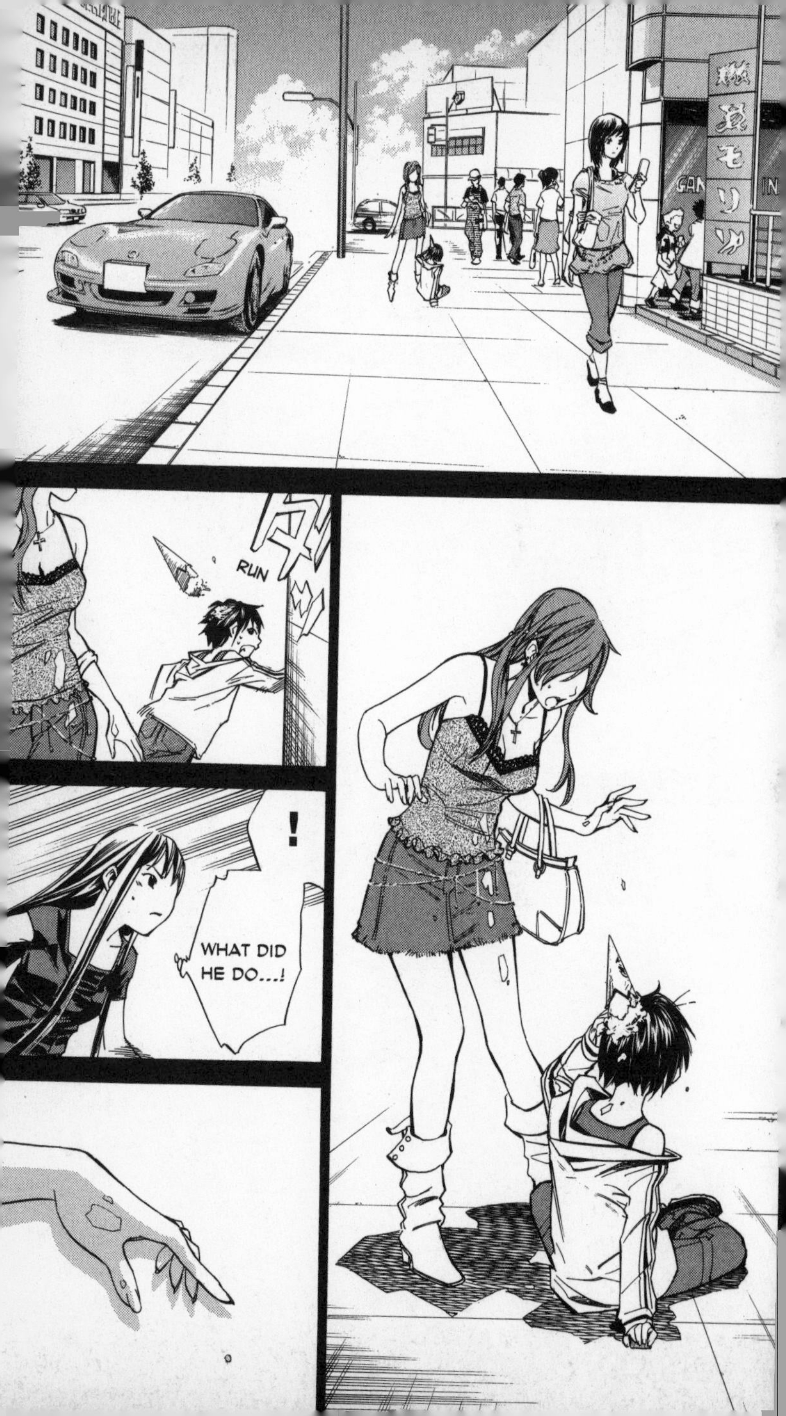
RUN
!
WHAT DID HE DO...!

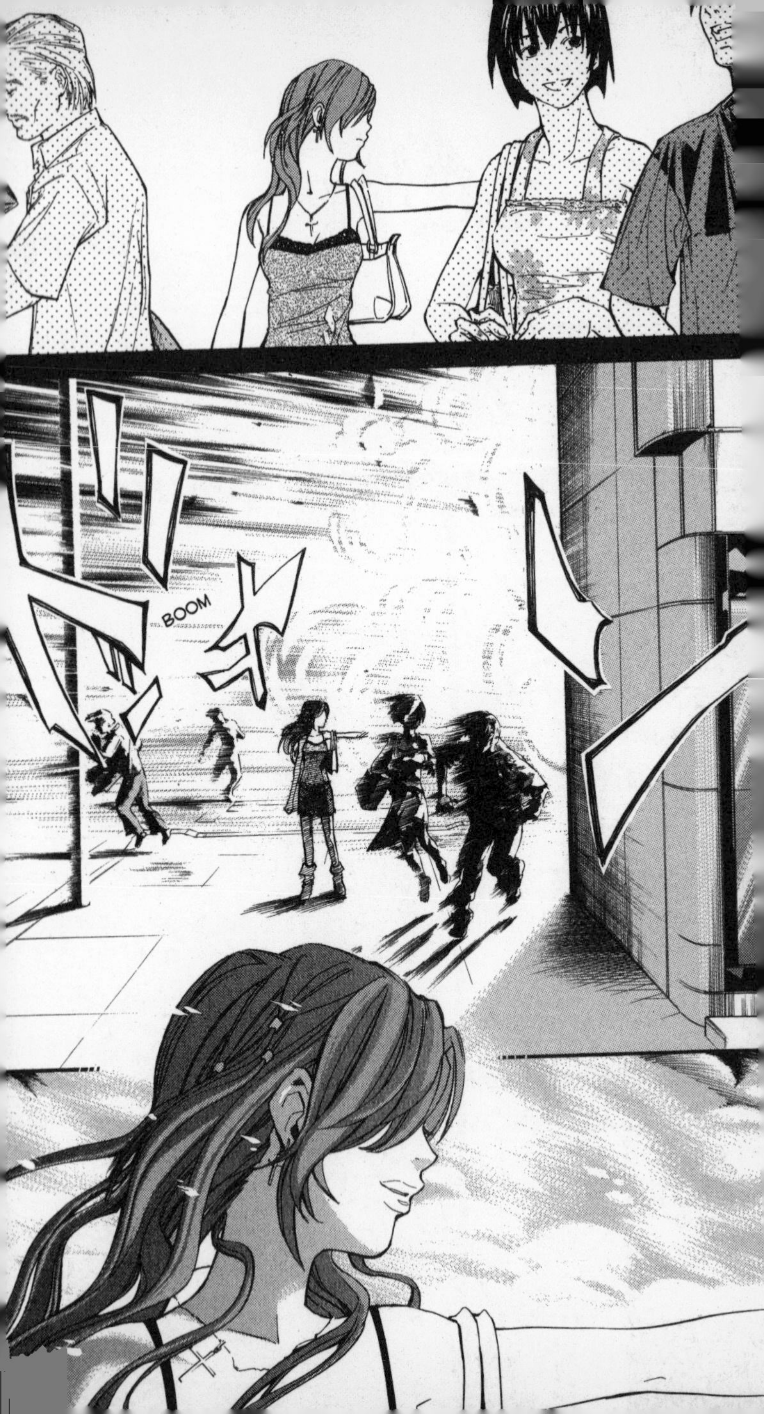
BOOM

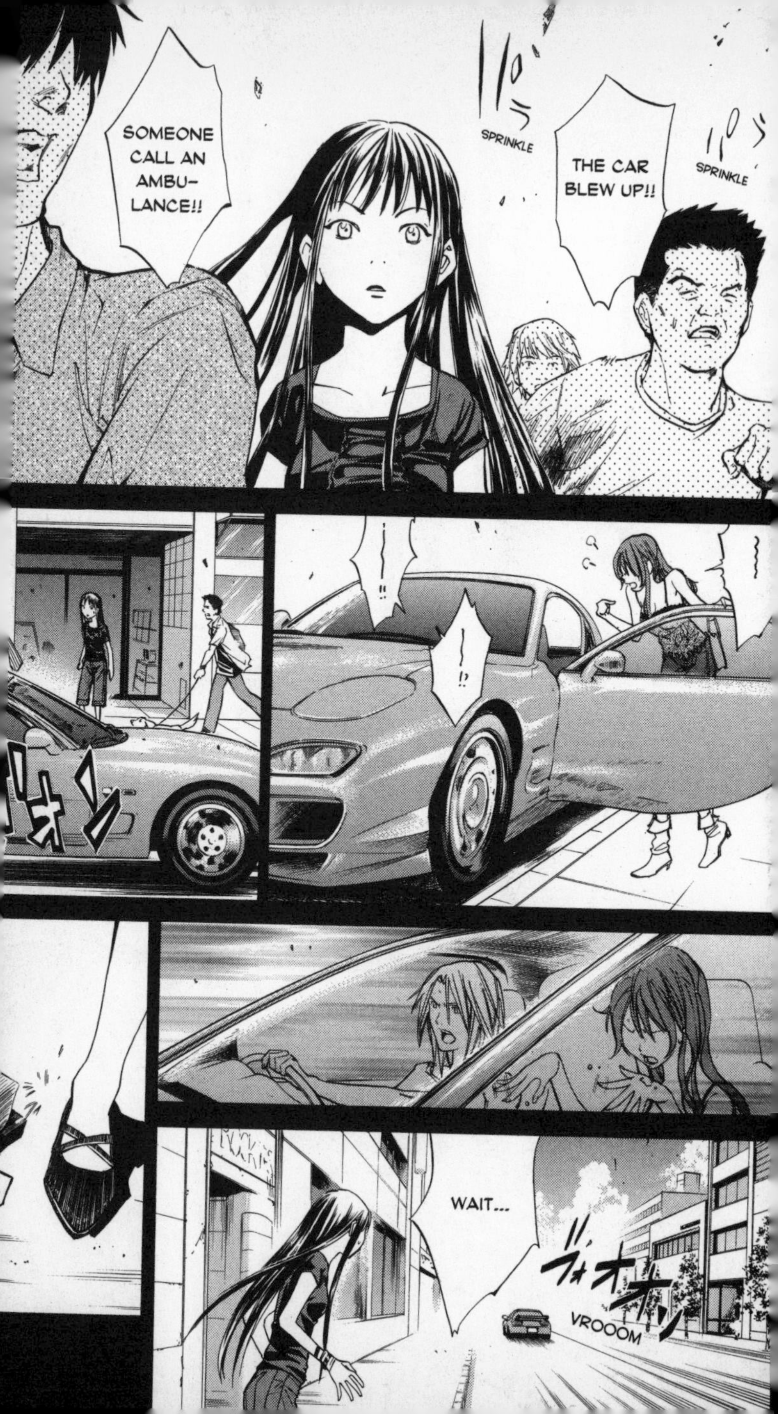
SPRINKLE
THE CAR BLEW UP!!
SPRINKLE
SOMEONE CALL AN AMBULANCE!!
—!!
—!?
WAIT...
VROOOM

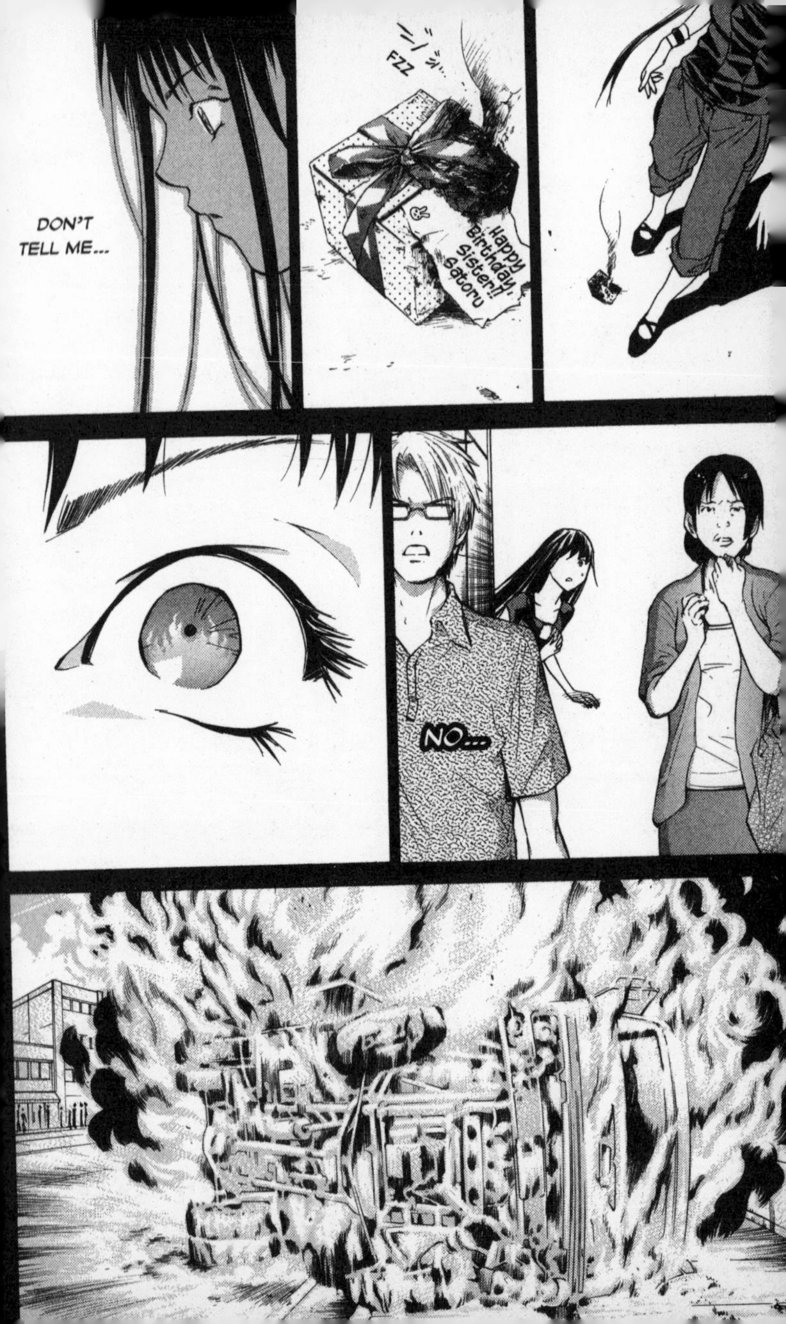
FZZ
Happy Birthday, sister!! Satoru
DON'T TELL ME...
NO...

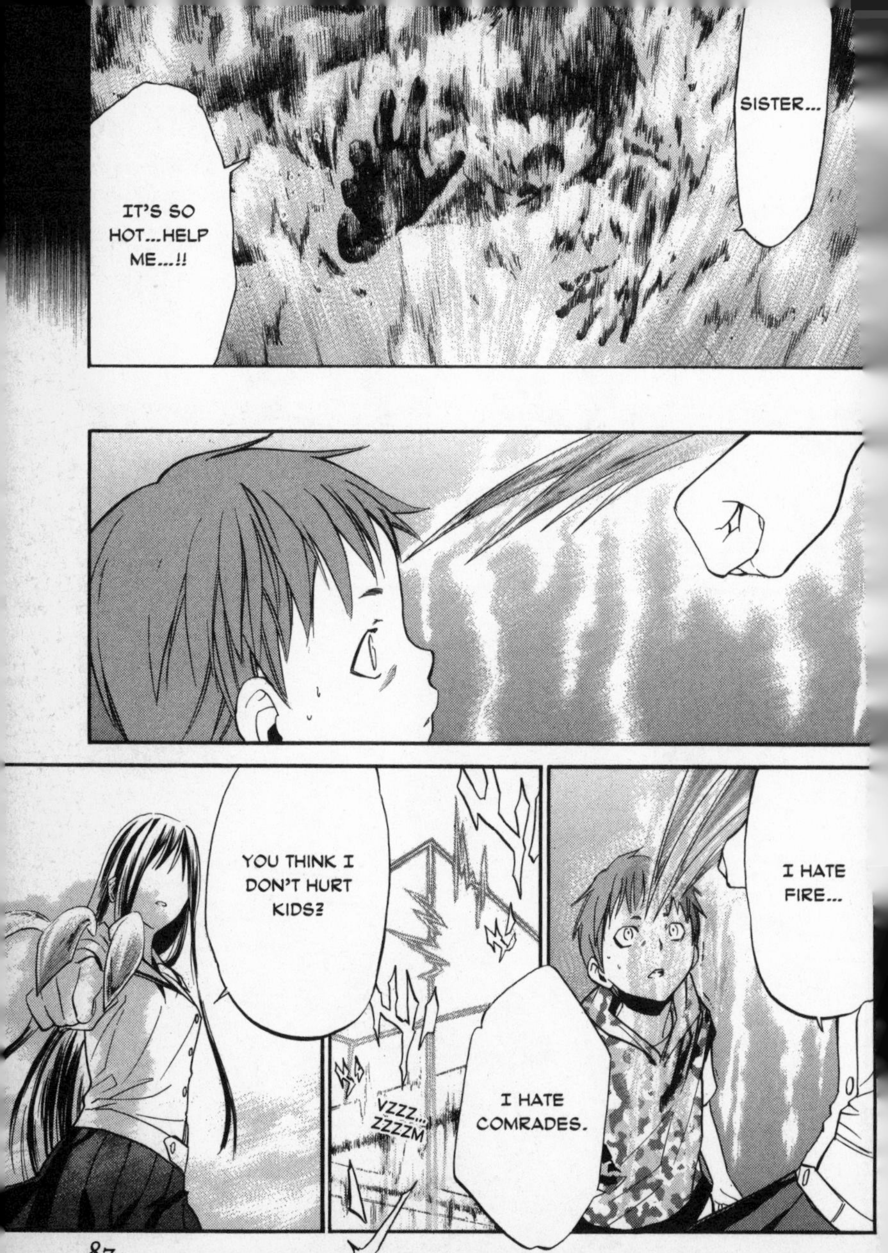
SISTER...
IT'S SO HOT...HELP ME...!!
I HATE FIRE...
I HATE COMRADES.
VZZZ... ZZZZM
YOU THINK I DON'T HURT KIDS?

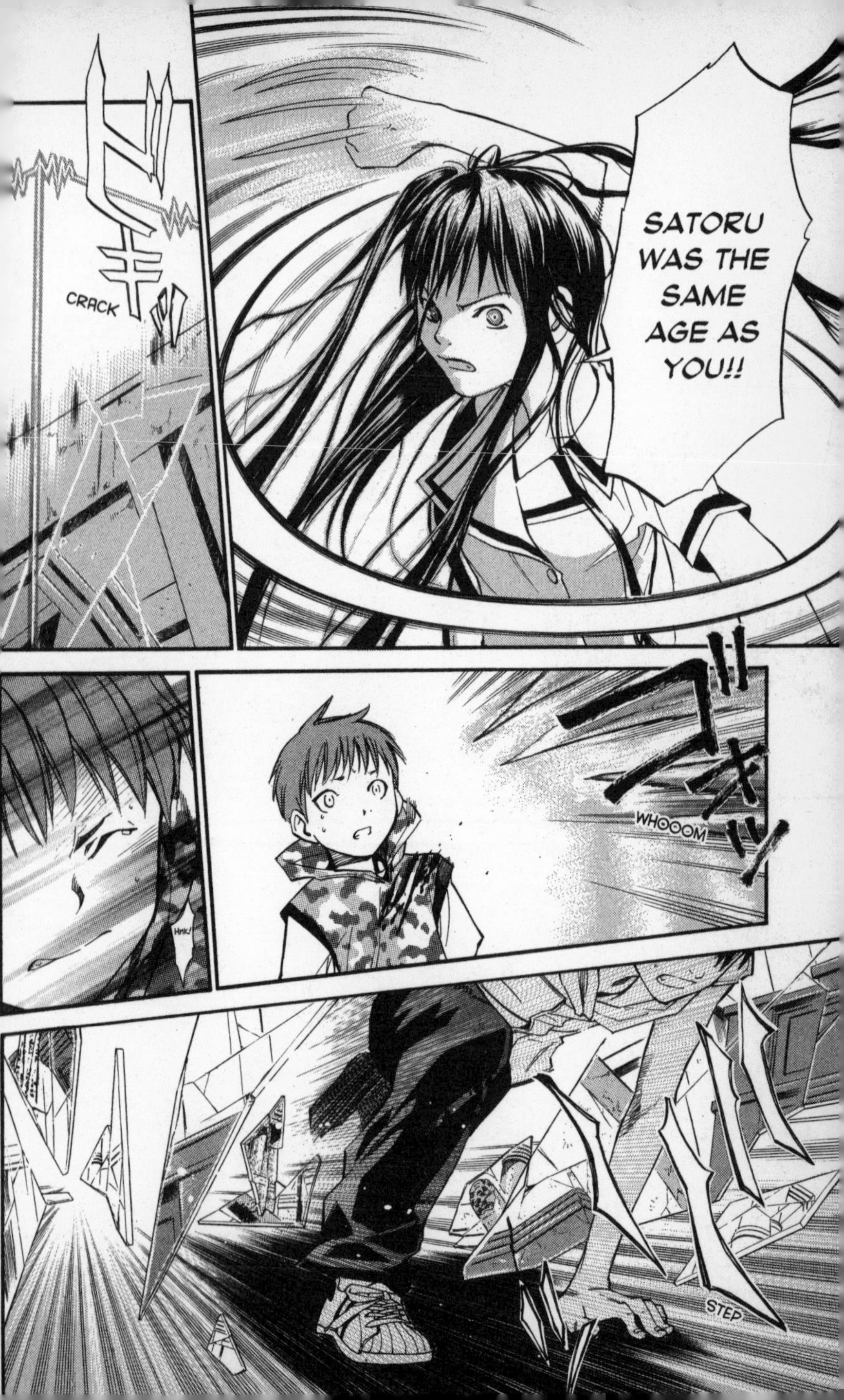
SATORU WAS THE SAME AGE AS YOU!!
CRACK
WHOOOM
HNK!
STEP

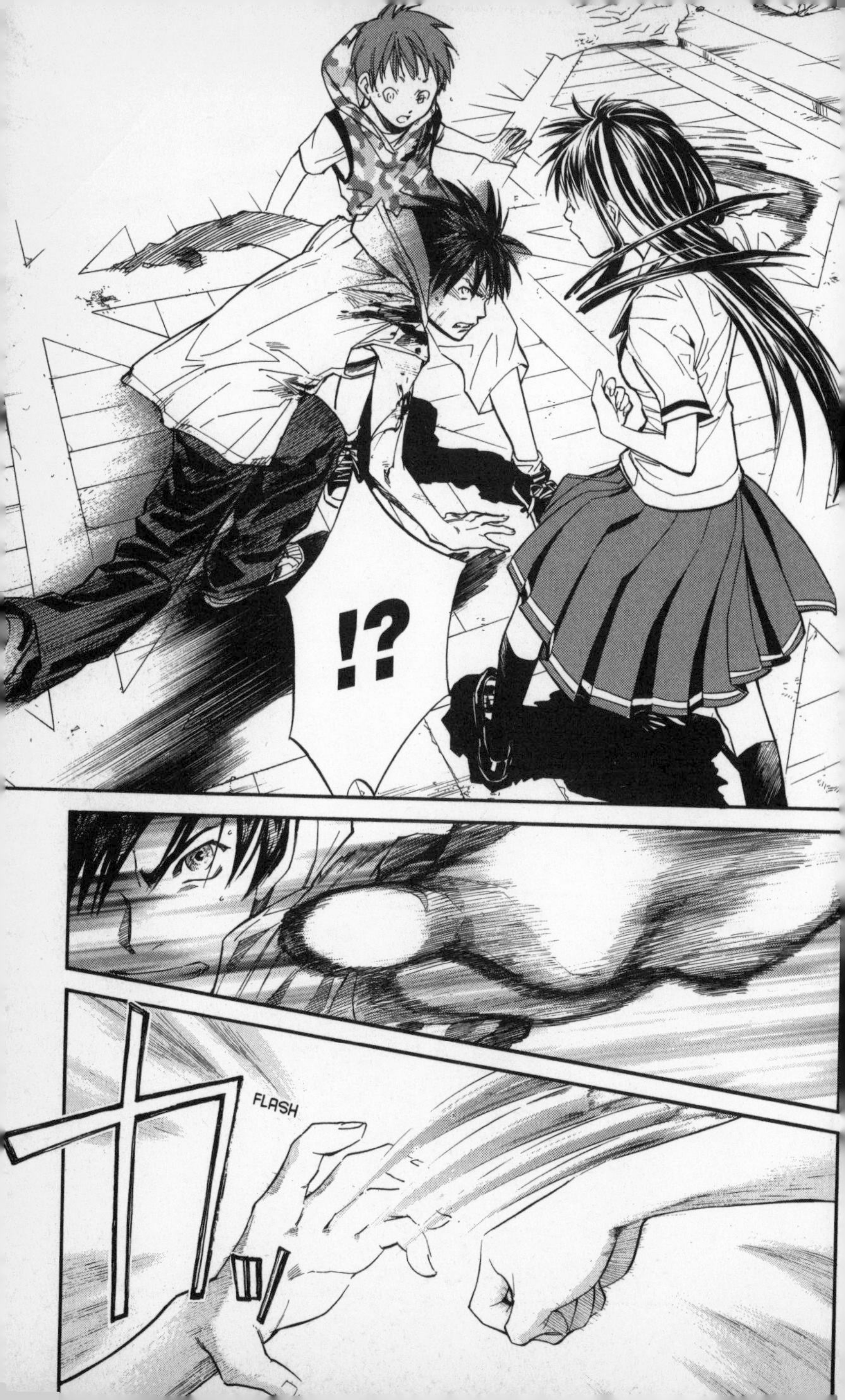
!?
FLASH

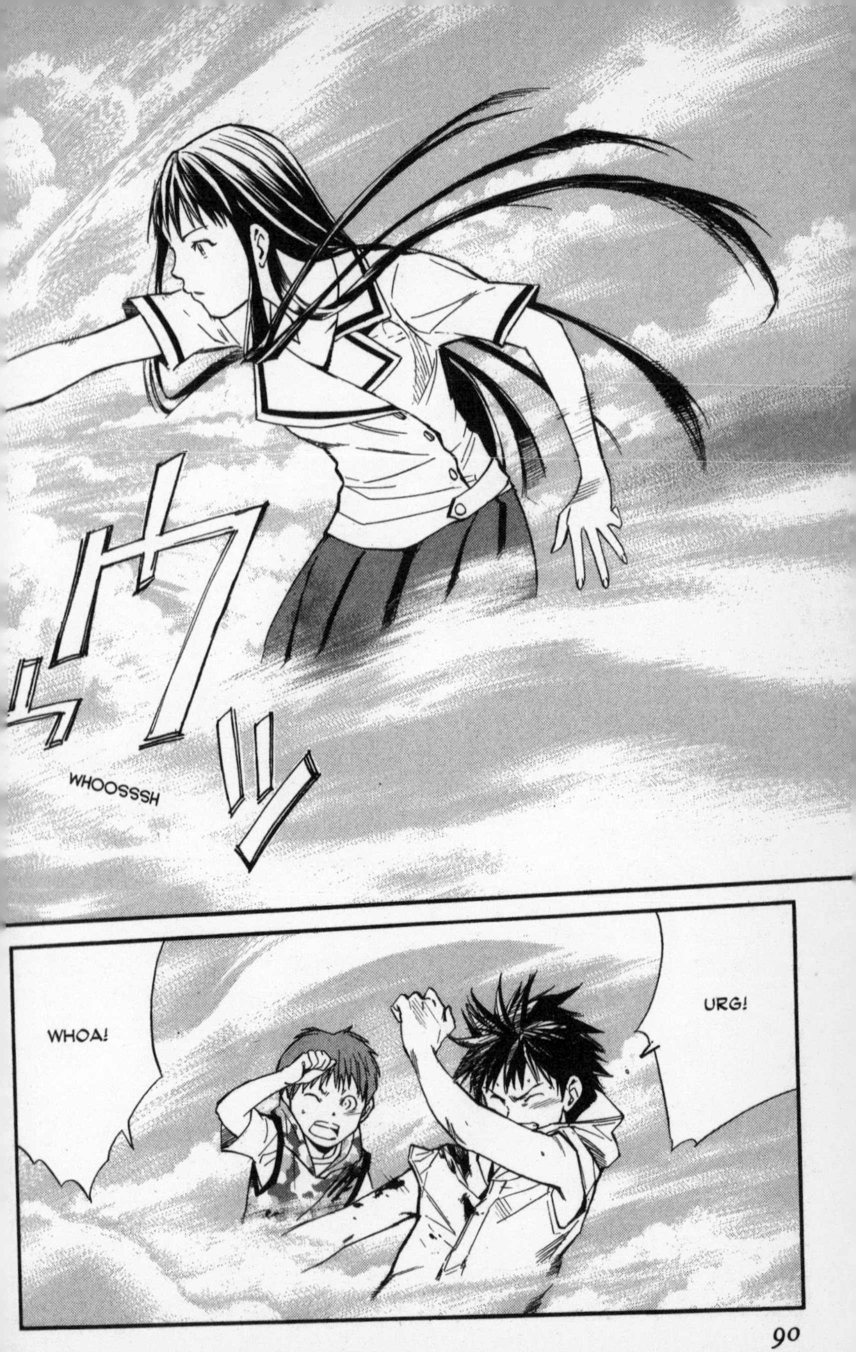
WHOOSSSH
URG!
WHOA!

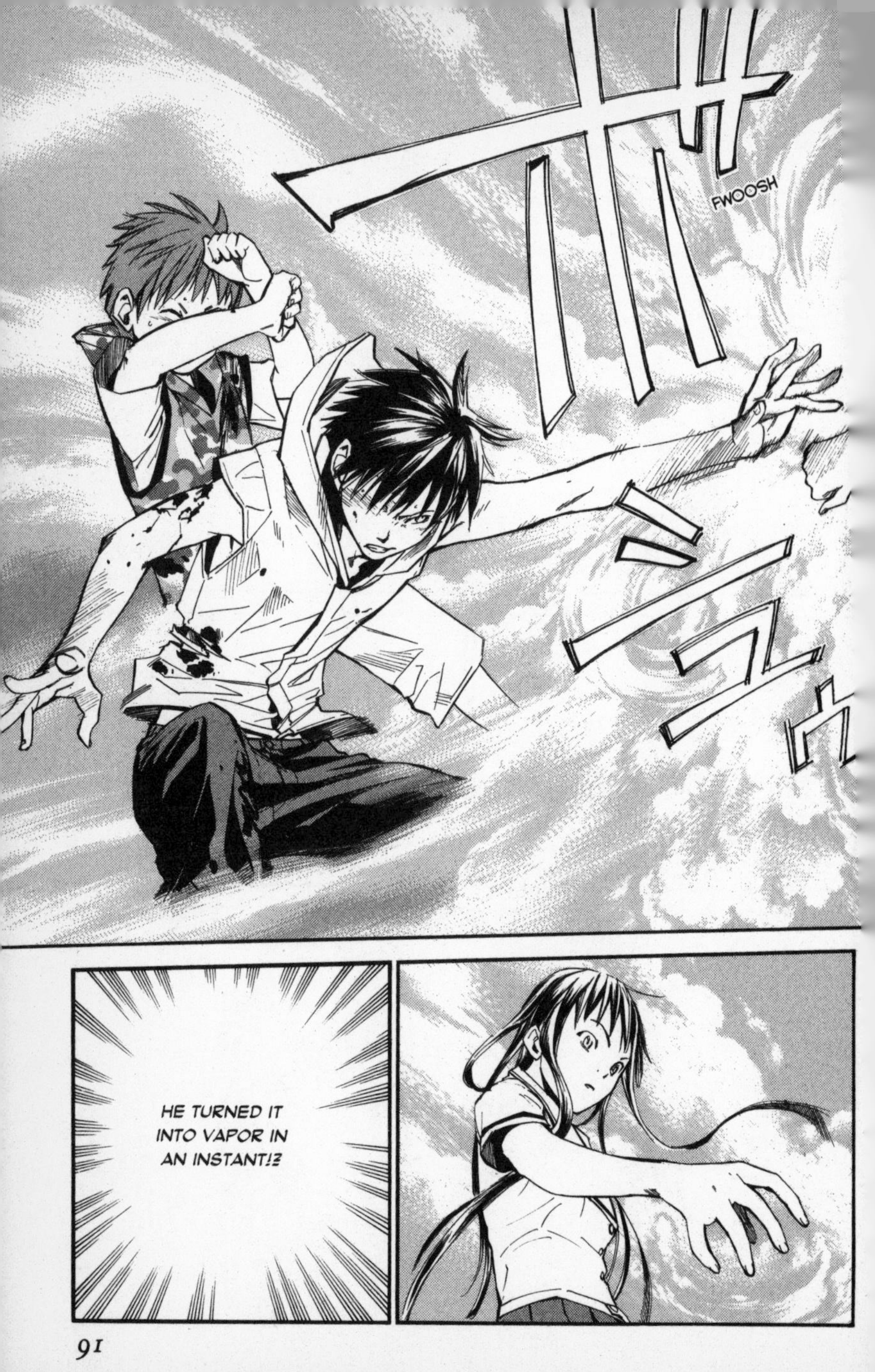
FWOOSH
HE TURNED IT INTO VAPOR IN AN INSTANT!?

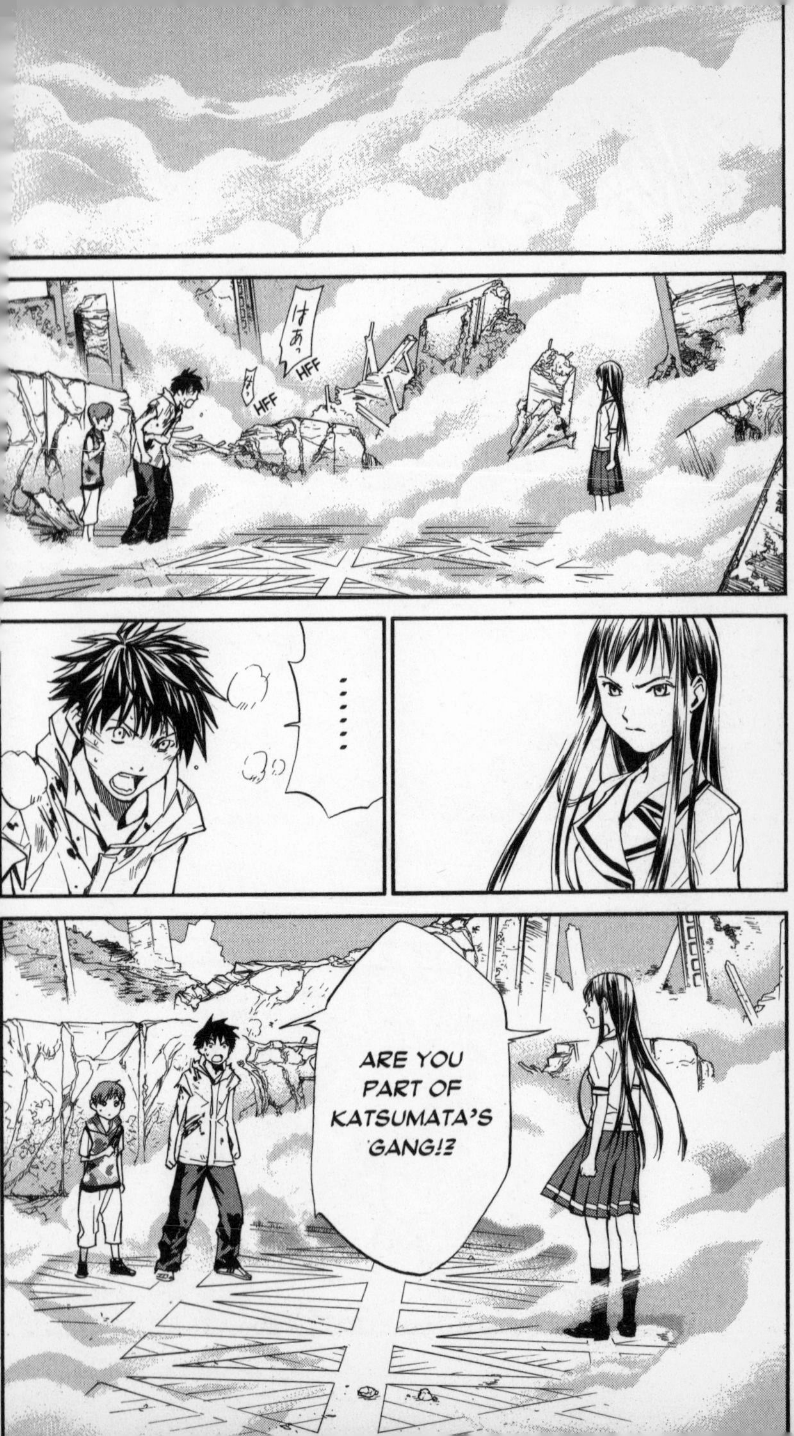
はあっ HFF
はっ HFF
......
ARE YOU PART OF KATSUMATA'S GANG!?

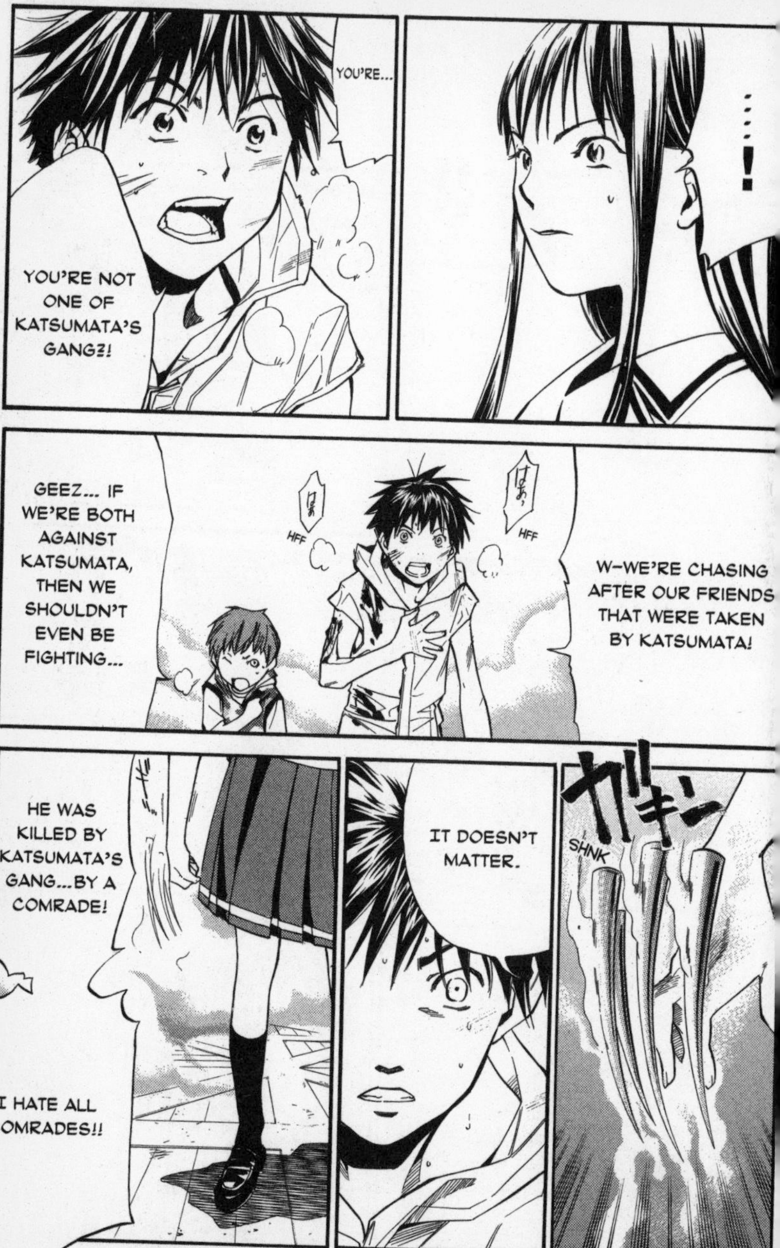
...!
YOU'RE...
YOU'RE NOT ONE OF KATSUMATA'S GANG?!
W-WE'RE CHASING AFTER OUR FRIENDS THAT WERE TAKEN BY KATSUMATA!
HFF
HFF
GEEZ... IF WE'RE BOTH AGAINST KATSUMATA, THEN WE SHOULDN'T EVEN BE FIGHTING...
SHNK
IT DOESN'T MATTER.
HE WAS KILLED BY KATSUMATA'S GANG...BY A COMRADE!
I HATE ALL COMRADES!!

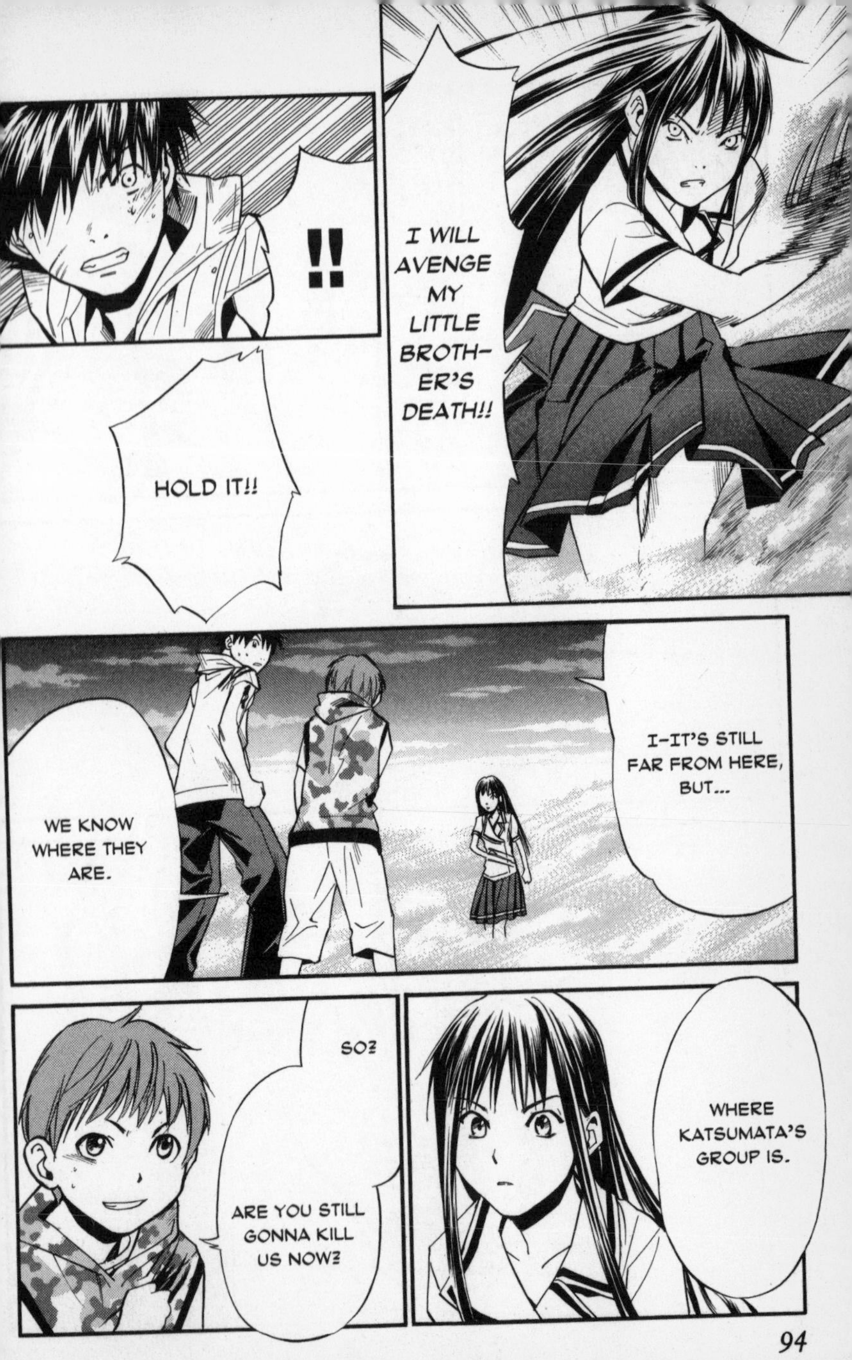
I WILL AVENGE MY LITTLE BROTH-ER'S DEATH!!
!!
HOLD IT!!
I-IT'S STILL FAR FROM HERE, BUT...
WE KNOW WHERE THEY ARE.
WHERE KATSUMATA'S GROUP IS.
SO?
ARE YOU STILL GONNA KILL US NOW?

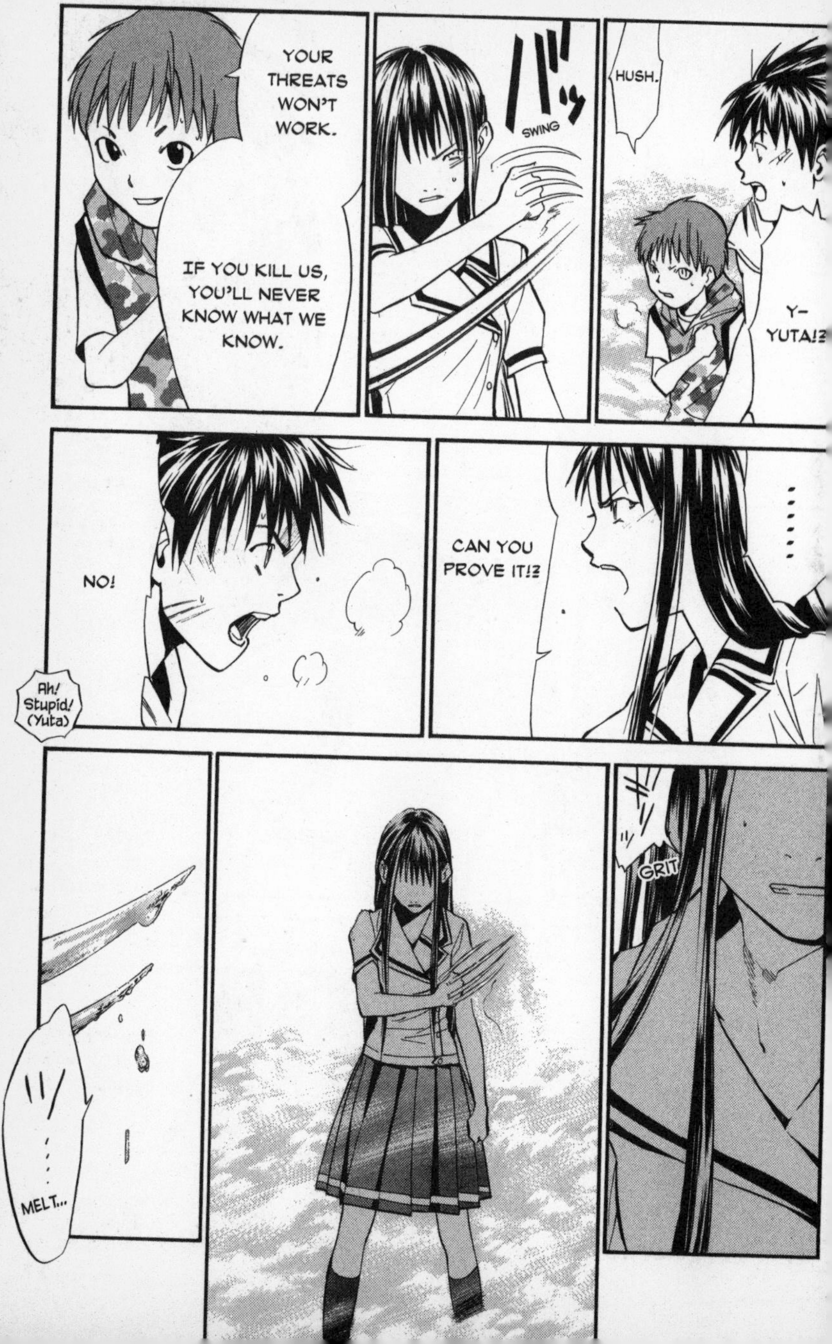
HUSH.
Y–
YUTA!?
SWING
YOUR THREATS WON'T WORK.
IF YOU KILL US, YOU'LL NEVER KNOW WHAT WE KNOW.
......
CAN YOU PROVE IT!?
NO!
Ah! Stupid! (Yuta)
GRIT
MELT...

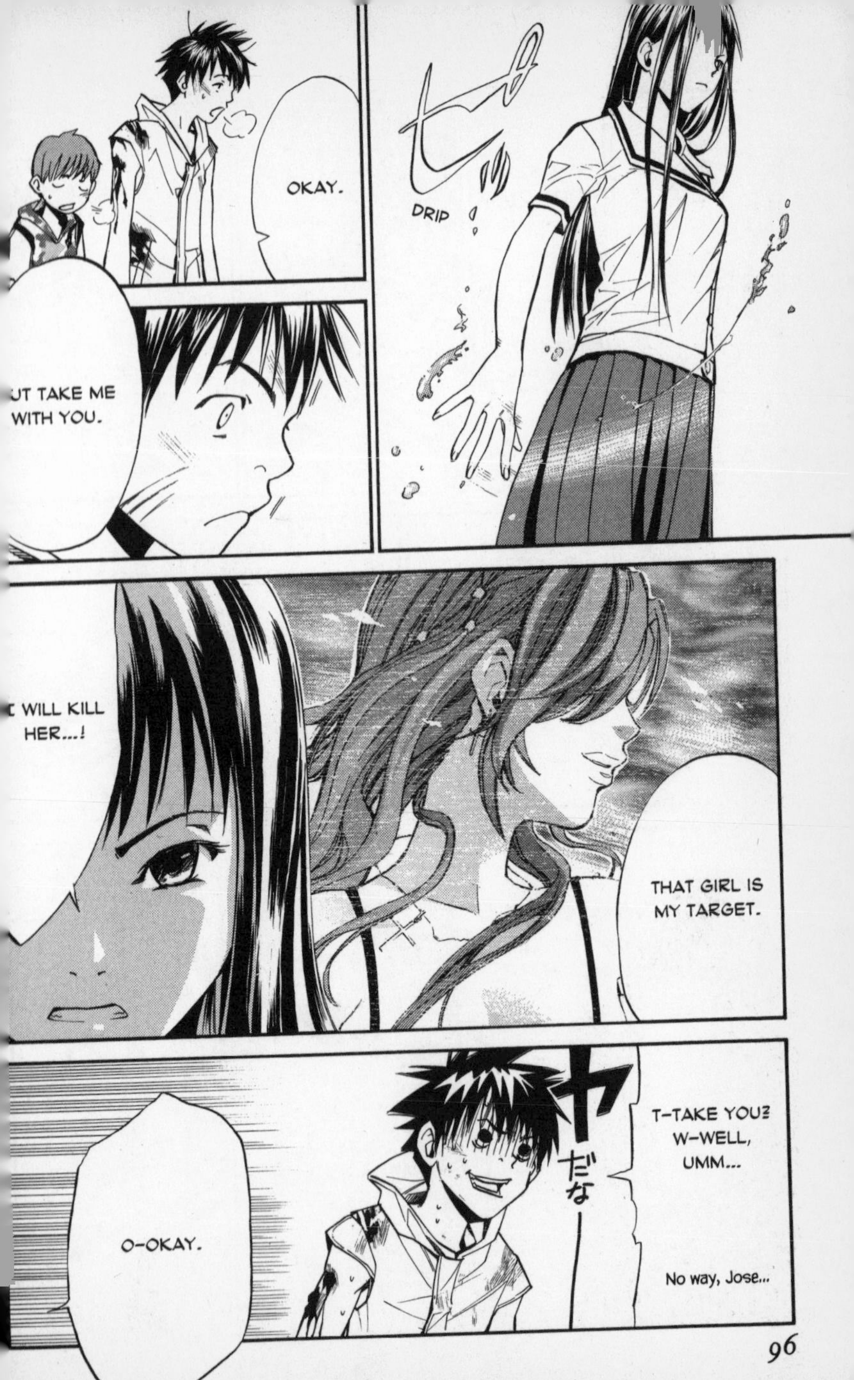
DRIP
OKAY.
UT TAKE ME WITH YOU.
THAT GIRL IS MY TARGET.
I WILL KILL HER...!
ヤだな
T-TAKE YOU? W-WELL, UMM...
No way, Jose...
O-OKAY.

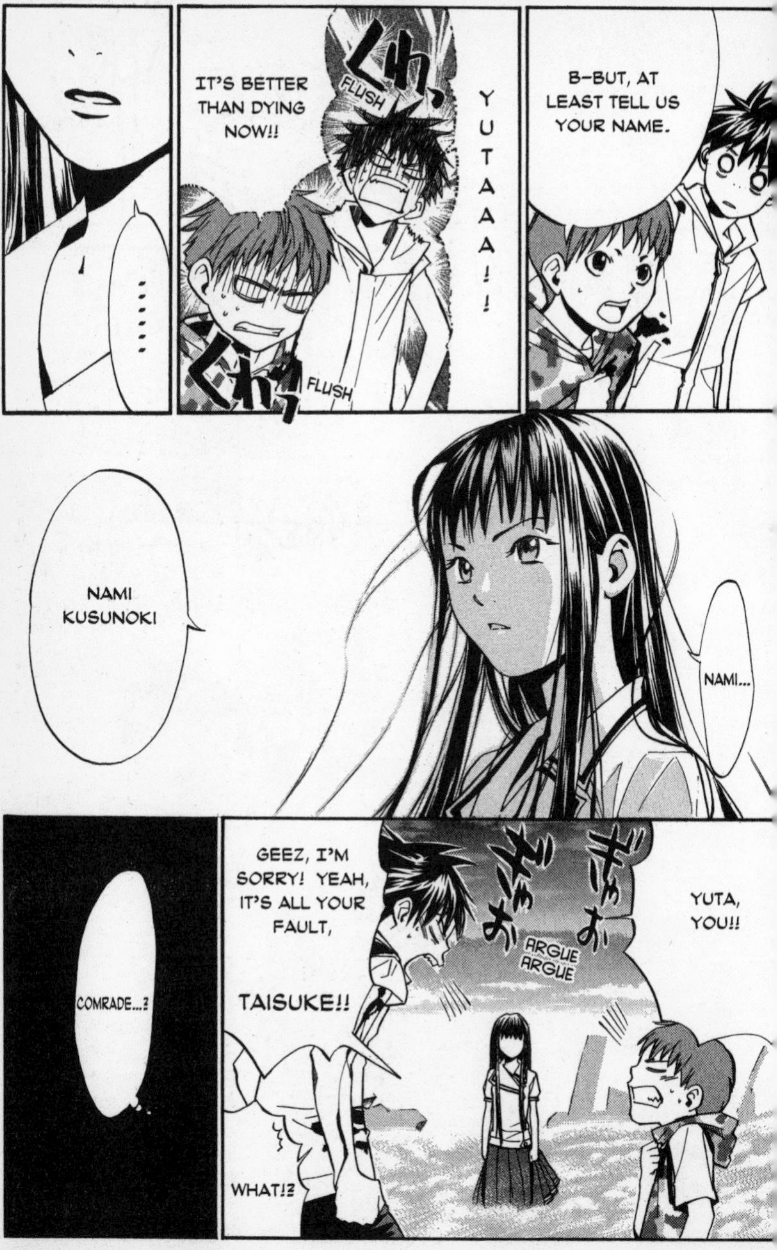
B-BUT, AT LEAST TELL US YOUR NAME.
YUTAAAA!!
くわっ
FLUSH
IT'S BETTER THAN DYING NOW!!
くわっ
FLUSH
......
NAMI...
NAMI KUSUNOKI
YUTA, YOU!!
ぎゃお ぎゃお
ARGUE ARGUE
GEEZ, I'M SORRY! YEAH, IT'S ALL YOUR FAULT,
TAISUKE!!
WHAT!?
COMRADE...?

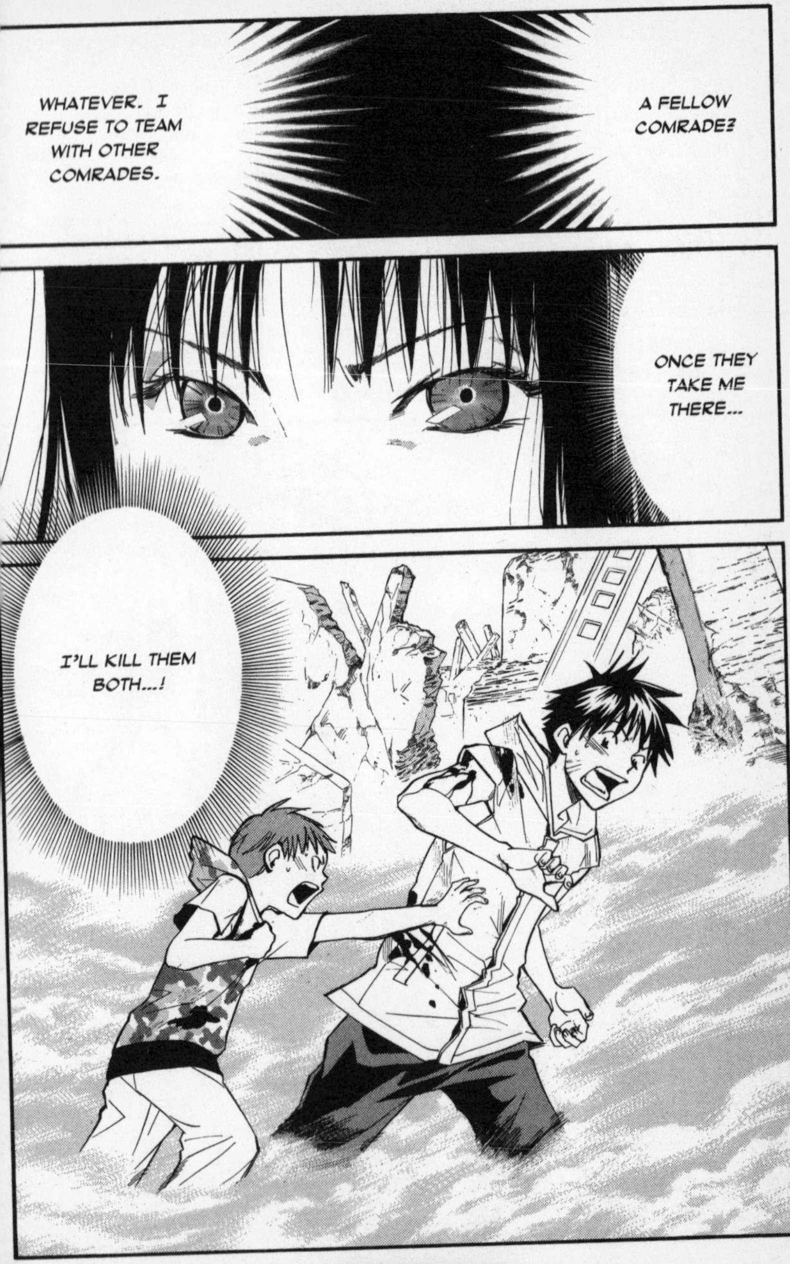
A FELLOW COMRADE?
WHATEVER. I REFUSE TO TEAM WITH OTHER COMRADES.
ONCE THEY TAKE ME THERE...
I'LL KILL THEM BOTH...!

**Chapter 13/ End**

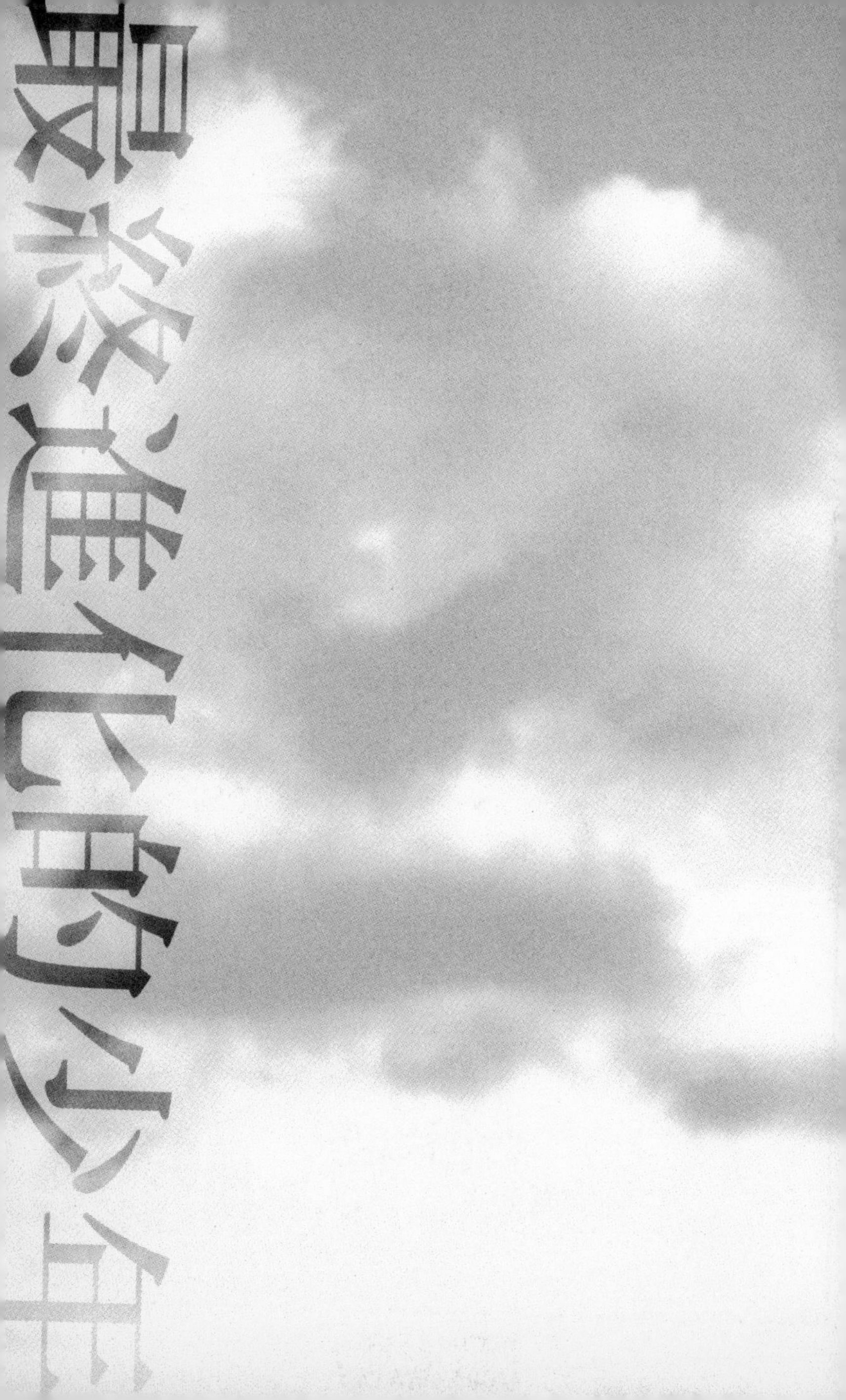
最後進化的少年

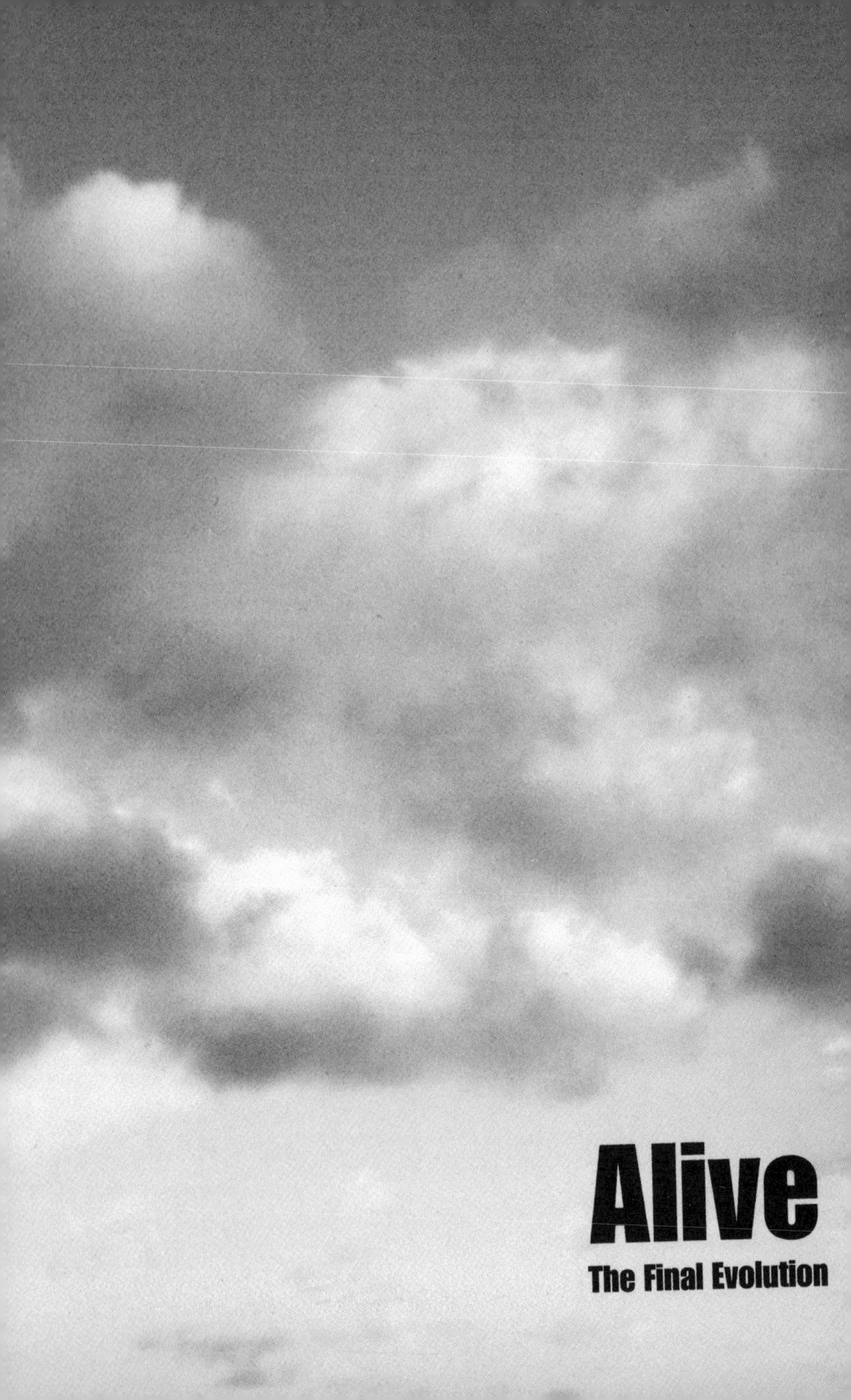

# Alive

## The Final Evolution

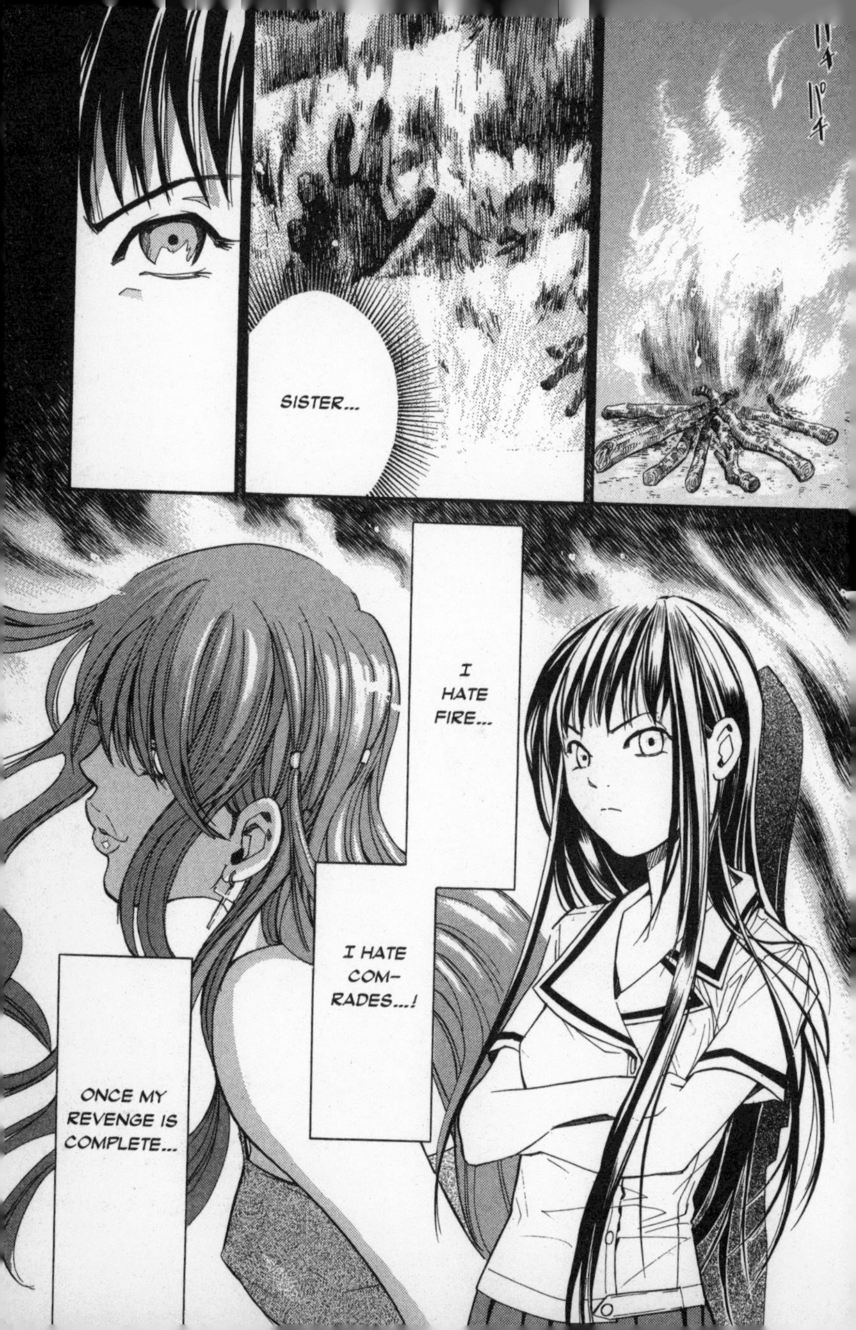
パチパチ
SISTER...
I HATE FIRE...
I HATE COM-RADES...!
ONCE MY REVENGE IS COMPLETE...

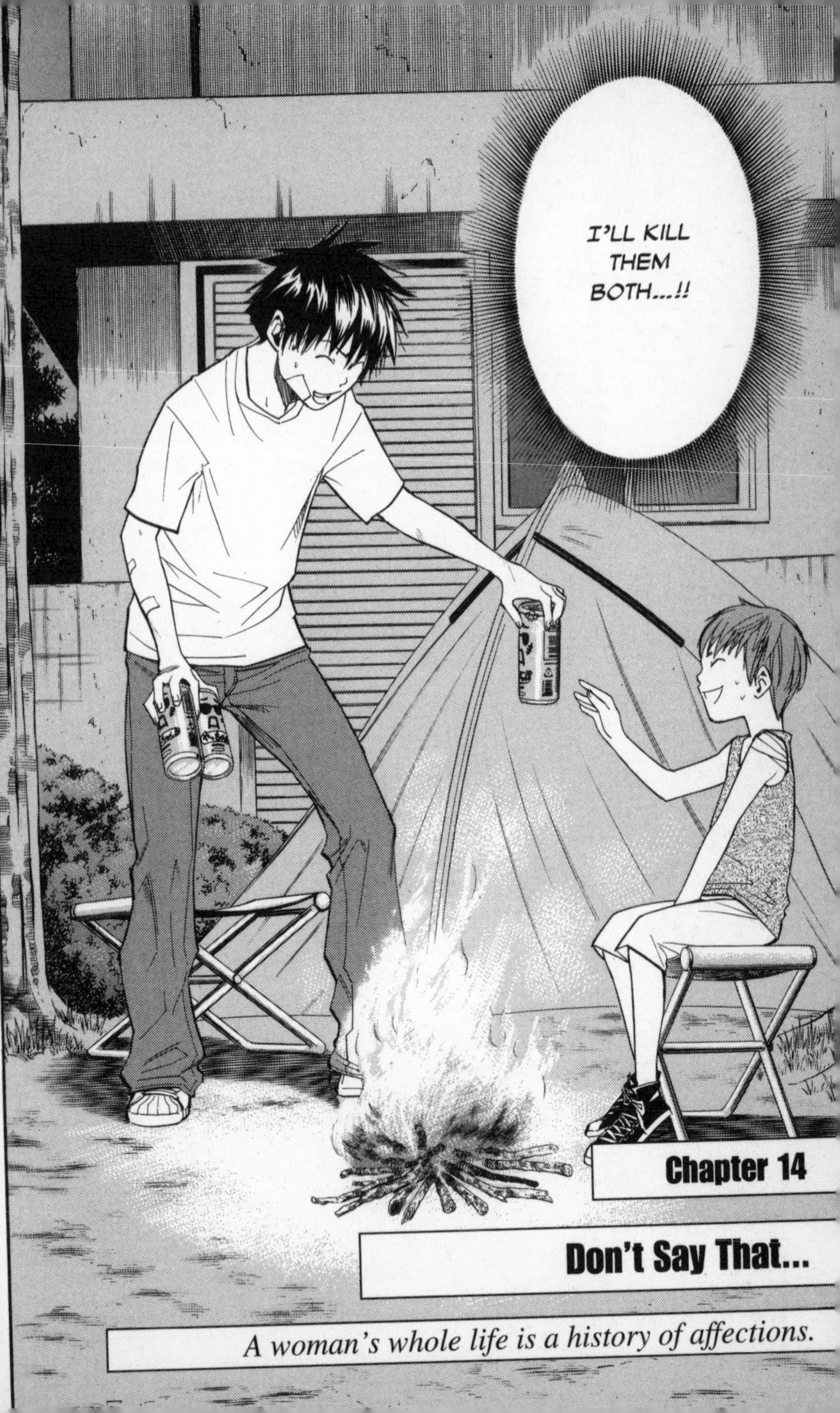
I'LL KILL THEM BOTH...!!
Chapter 14
Don't Say That...
A woman's whole life is a history of affections.

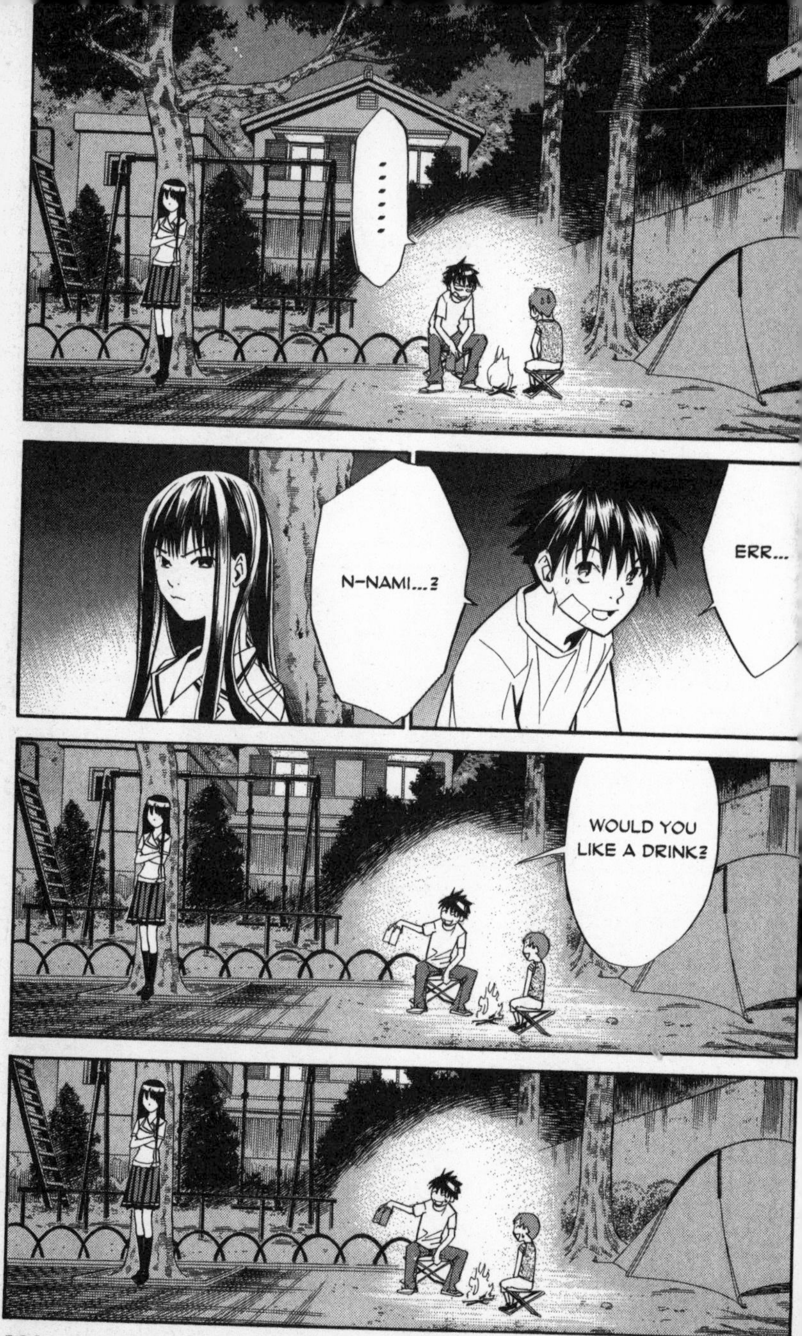
......
ERR...
N-NAMI...?
WOULD YOU LIKE A DRINK?

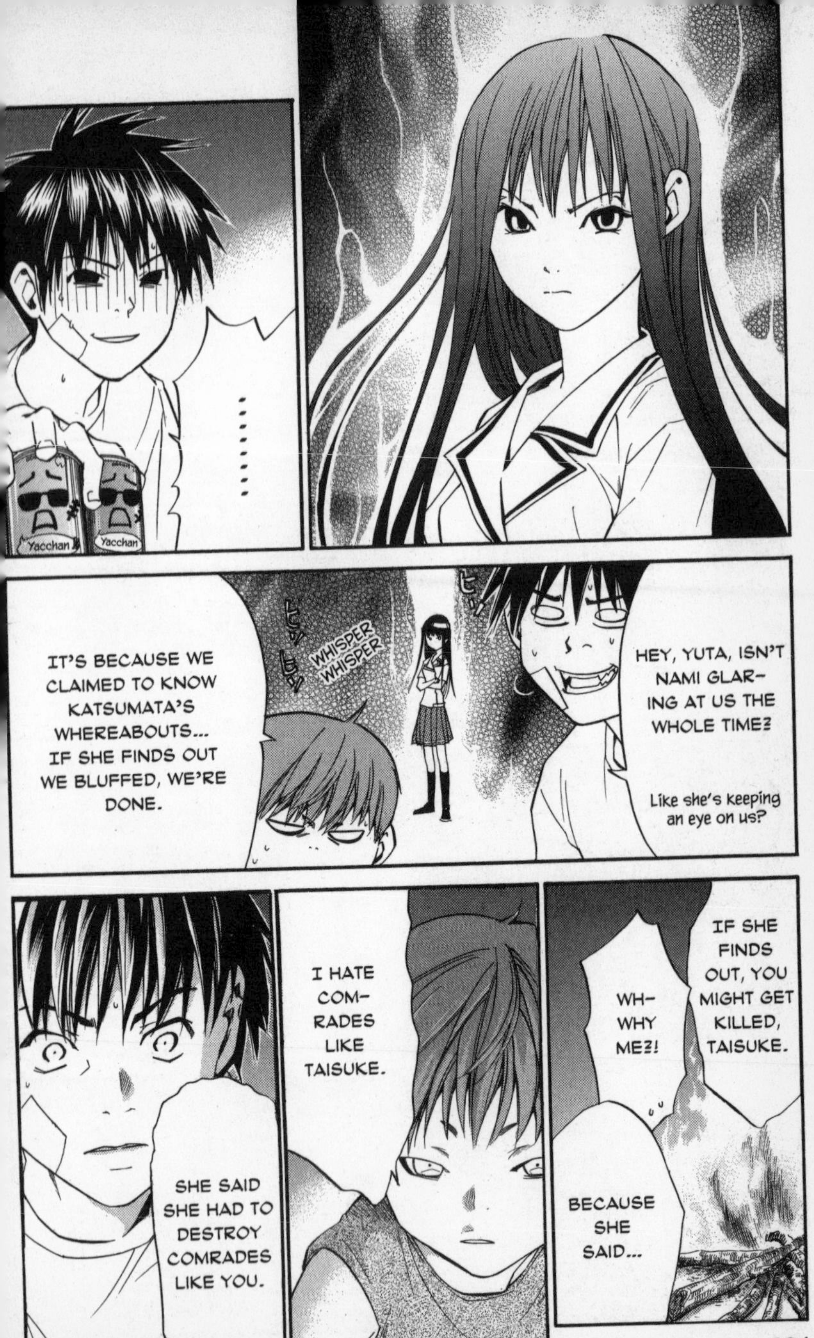

......
Yacchan
Yacchan
HEY, YUTA, ISN'T NAMI GLARING AT US THE WHOLE TIME?
Like she's keeping an eye on us?
WHISPER WHISPER
IT'S BECAUSE WE CLAIMED TO KNOW KATSUMATA'S WHEREABOUTS... IF SHE FINDS OUT WE BLUFFED, WE'RE DONE.
IF SHE FINDS OUT, YOU MIGHT GET KILLED, TAISUKE.
WH-WHY ME?!
BECAUSE SHE SAID...
I HATE COMRADES LIKE TAISUKE.
SHE SAID SHE HAD TO DESTROY COMRADES LIKE YOU.

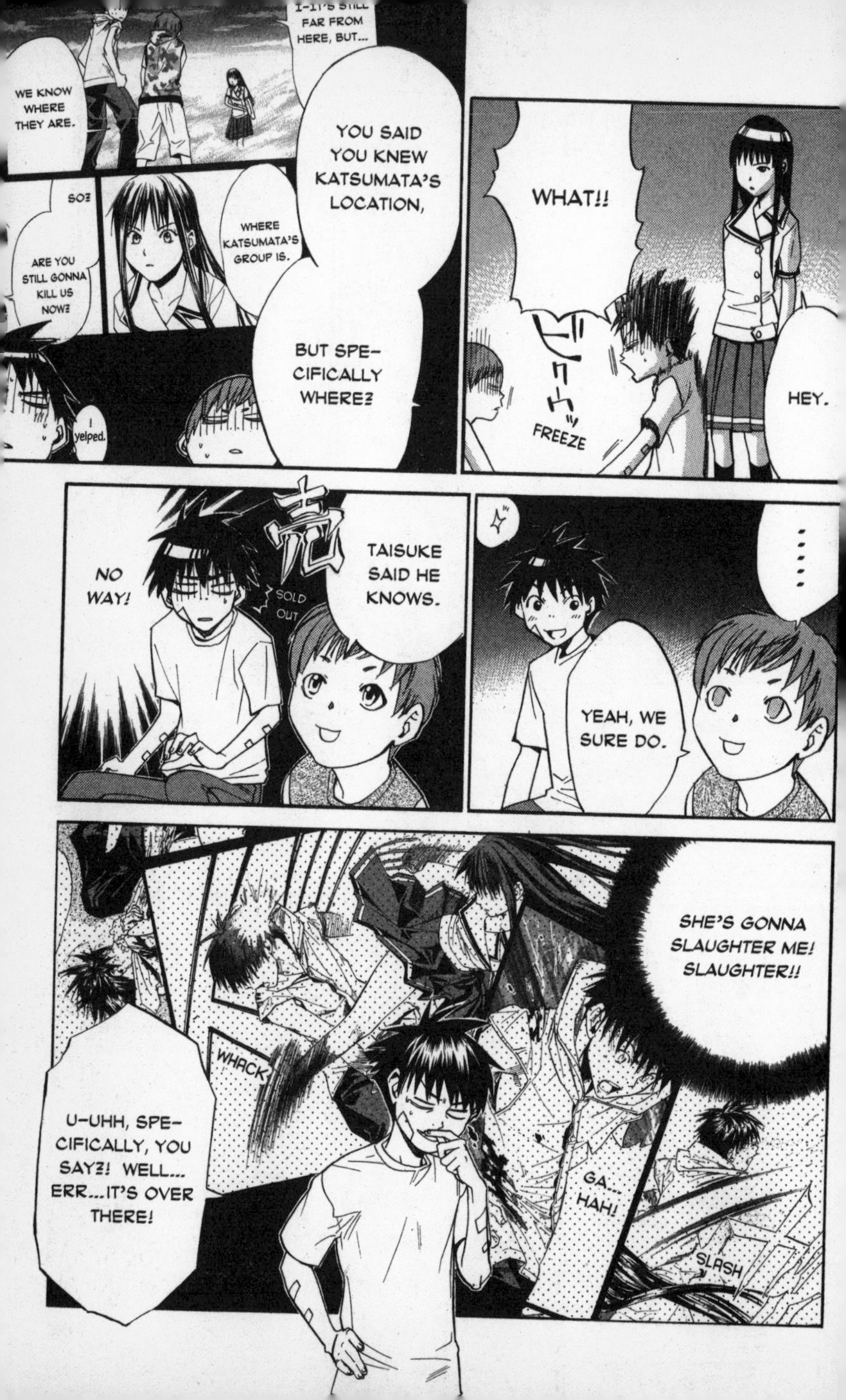

HEY.
WHAT!!
FREEZE
I-IT'S STILL FAR FROM HERE, BUT...
WE KNOW WHERE THEY ARE.
WHERE KATSUMATA'S GROUP IS.
SO?
ARE YOU STILL GONNA KILL US NOW?
YOU SAID YOU KNEW KATSUMATA'S LOCATION,
BUT SPE-CIFICALLY WHERE?
I yelped.
......
YEAH, WE SURE DO.
TAISUKE SAID HE KNOWS.
SOLD OUT
NO WAY!
SHE'S GONNA SLAUGHTER ME! SLAUGHTER!!
GA... HAH!
SLASH
WHACK
U-UHH, SPE-CIFICALLY, YOU SAY?! WELL... ERR...IT'S OVER THERE!

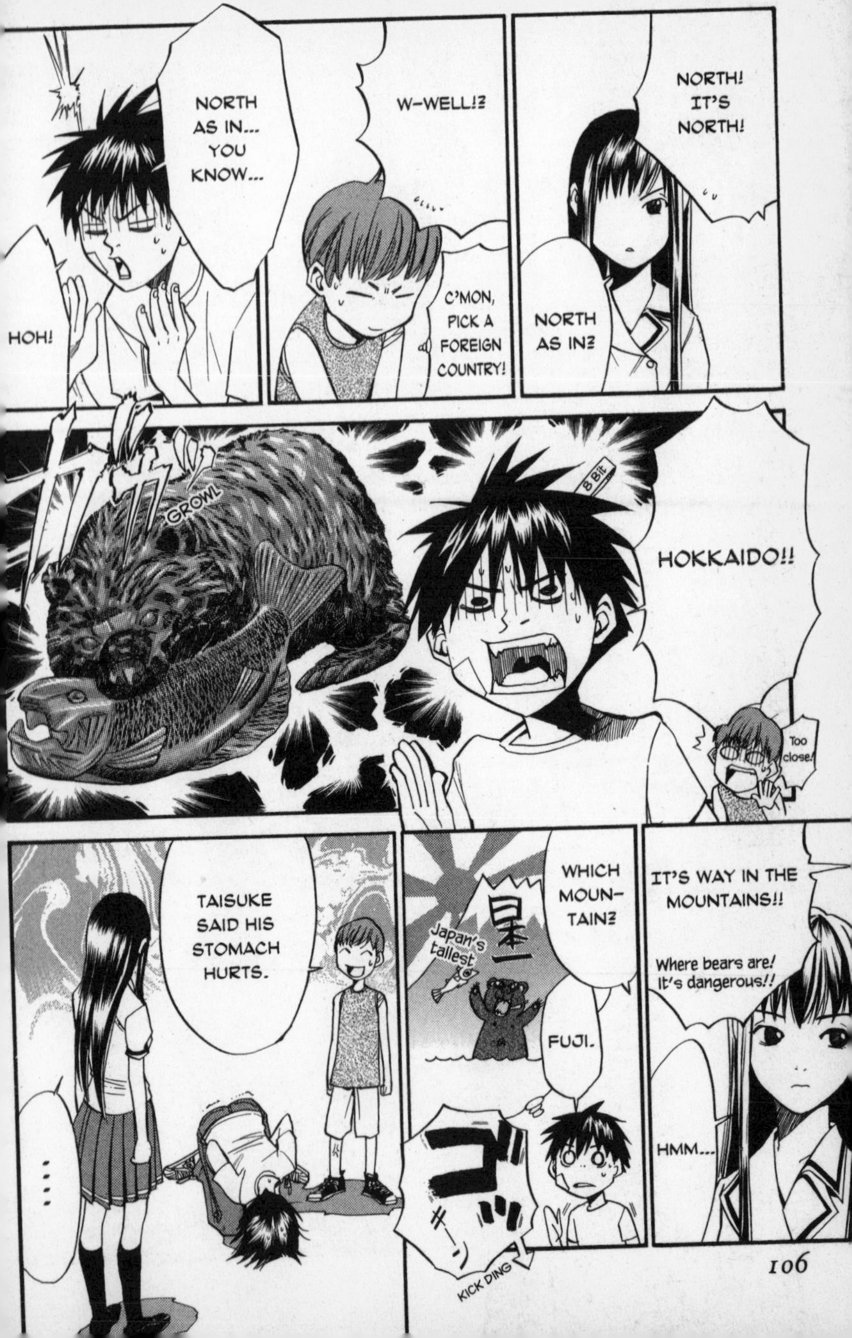
NORTH! IT'S NORTH!
NORTH AS IN?
W-WELL!?
C'MON, PICK A FOREIGN COUNTRY!
NORTH AS IN... YOU KNOW...
HOH!
HOKKAIDO!!
8 Bit
GROWL
Too close!
IT'S WAY IN THE MOUNTAINS!!
Where bears are! It's dangerous!!
HMM...
WHICH MOUNTAIN?
Japan's tallest
FUJI.
KICK DING
TAISUKE SAID HIS STOMACH HURTS.
....

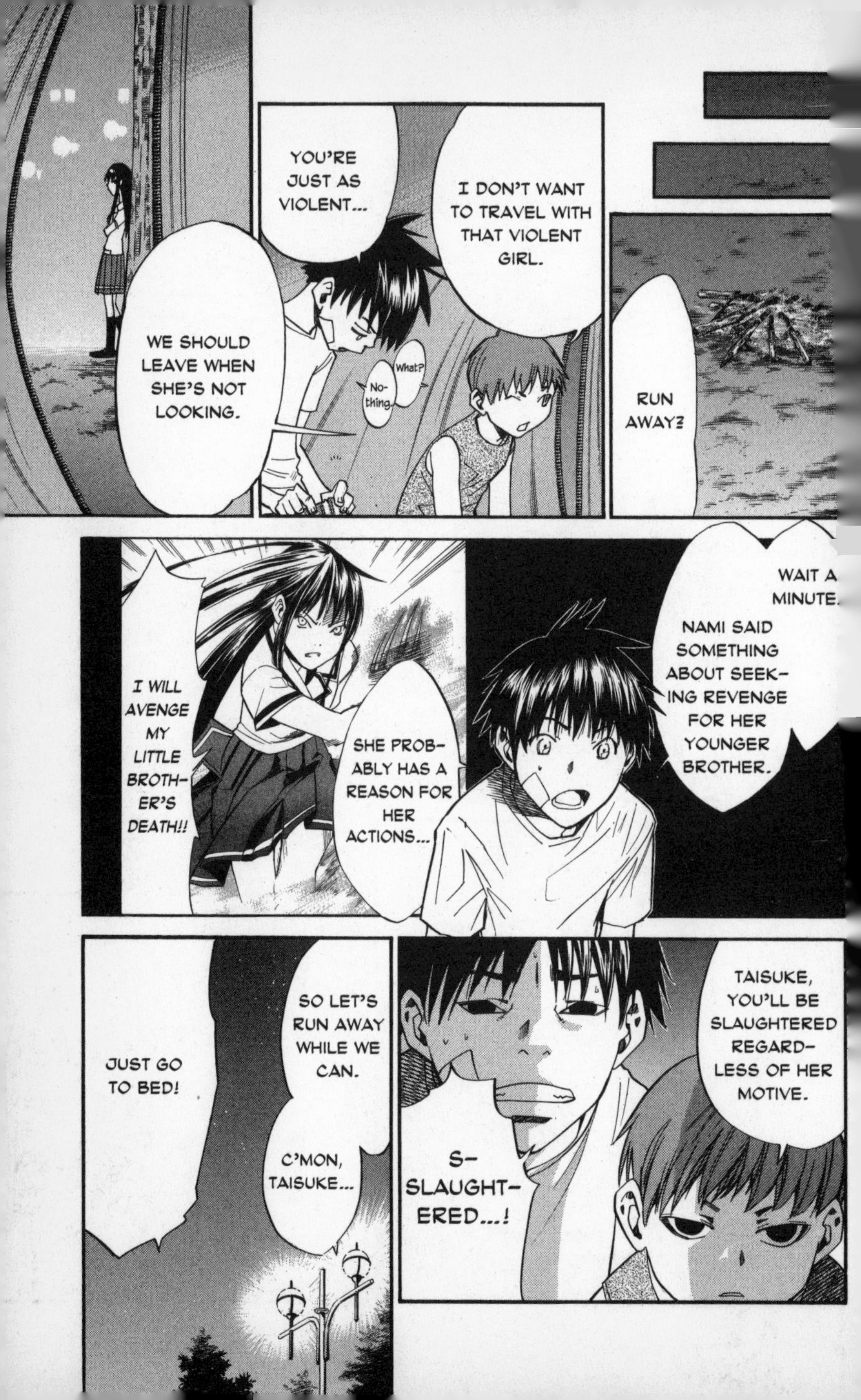
RUN AWAY?
I DON'T WANT TO TRAVEL WITH THAT VIOLENT GIRL.
What?
YOU'RE JUST AS VIOLENT...
No-thing.
WE SHOULD LEAVE WHEN SHE'S NOT LOOKING.
WAIT A MINUTE.
NAMI SAID SOMETHING ABOUT SEEK-ING REVENGE FOR HER YOUNGER BROTHER.
SHE PROB-ABLY HAS A REASON FOR HER ACTIONS...
I WILL AVENGE MY LITTLE BROTH-ER'S DEATH!!
TAISUKE, YOU'LL BE SLAUGHTERED REGARD-LESS OF HER MOTIVE.
S-SLAUGHT-ERED...!
SO LET'S RUN AWAY WHILE WE CAN.
C'MON, TAISUKE...
JUST GO TO BED!

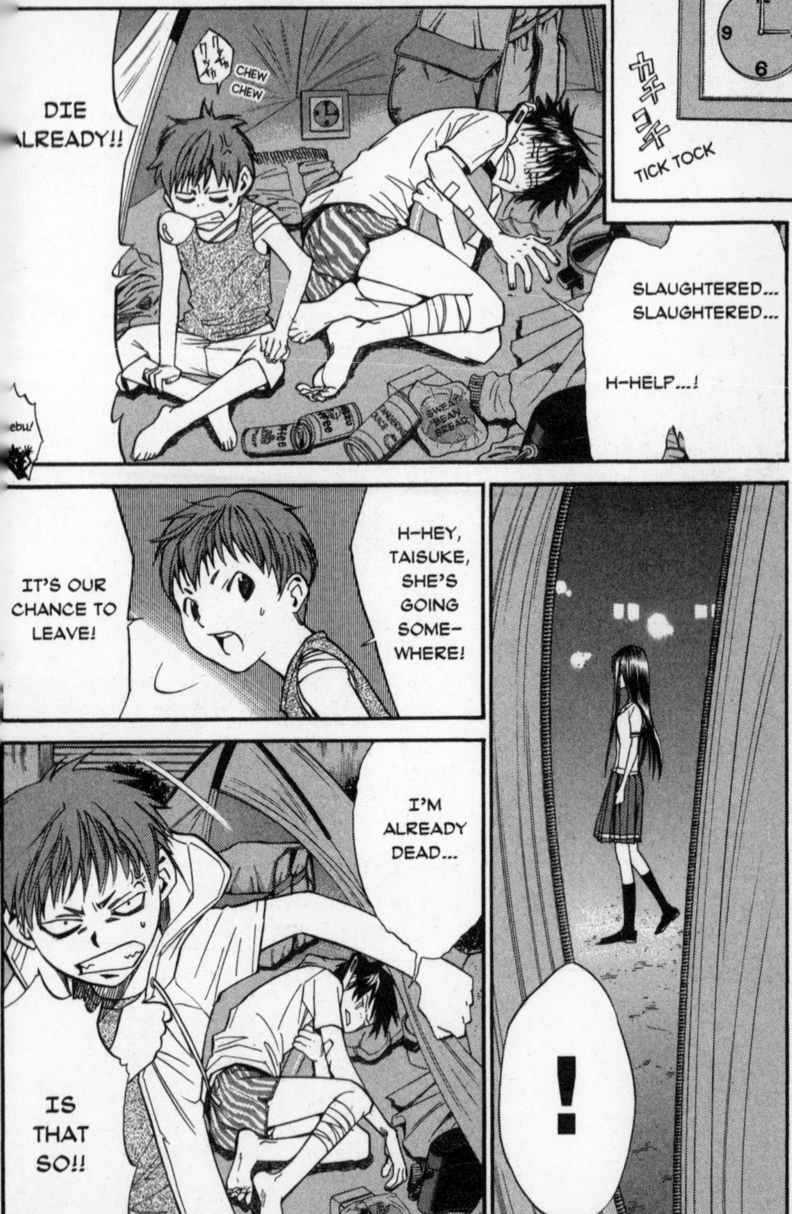
TICK TOCK
SLAUGHTERED... SLAUGHTERED...
H-HELP...!
DIE ALREADY!!
CHEW CHEW
SWEET BEAN BREAD
!
H-HEY, TAISUKE, SHE'S GOING SOME-WHERE!
IT'S OUR CHANCE TO LEAVE!
I'M ALREADY DEAD...
IS THAT SO!!

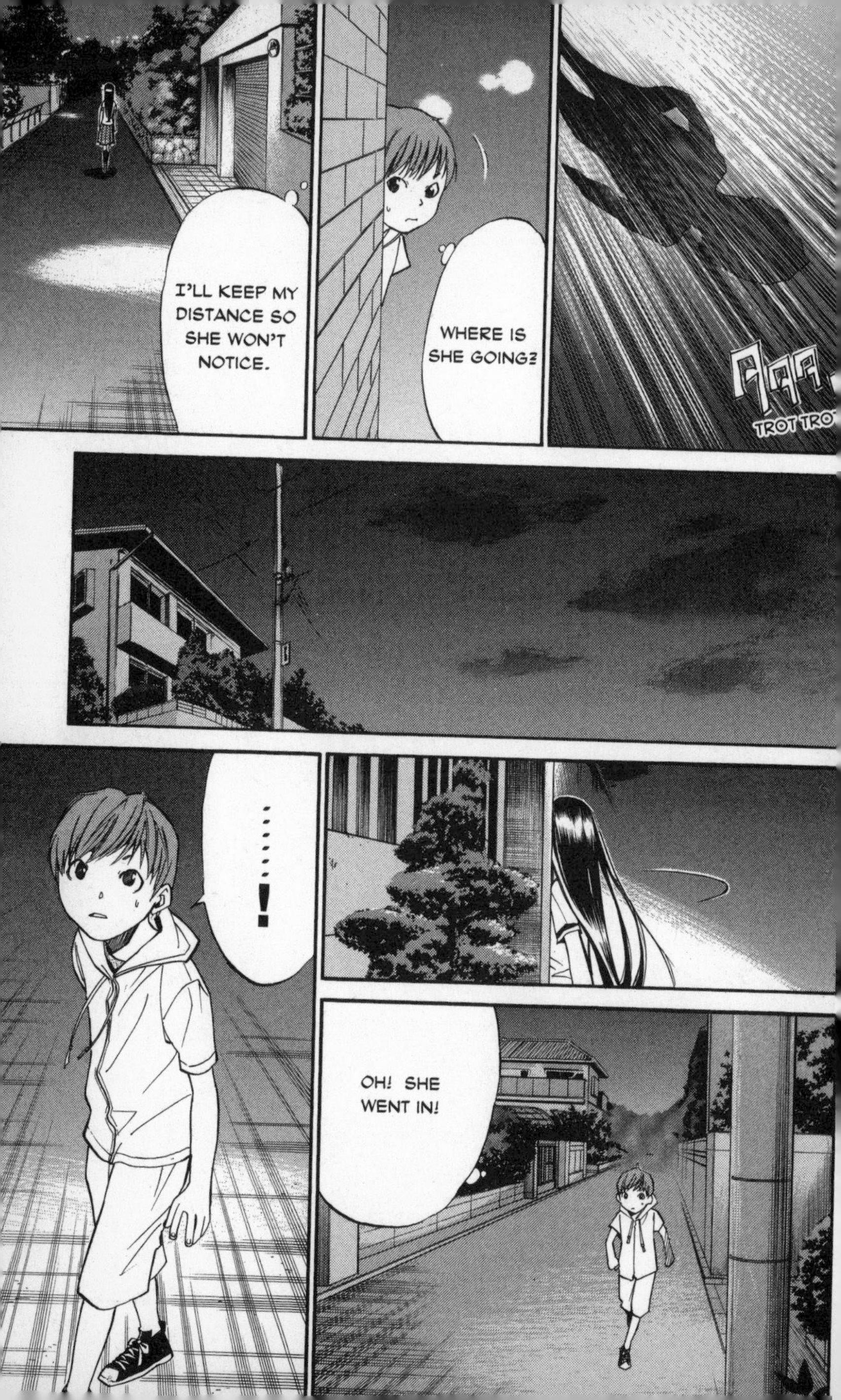
TROT TROT
WHERE IS SHE GOING?
I'LL KEEP MY DISTANCE SO SHE WON'T NOTICE.
OH! SHE WENT IN!
......!

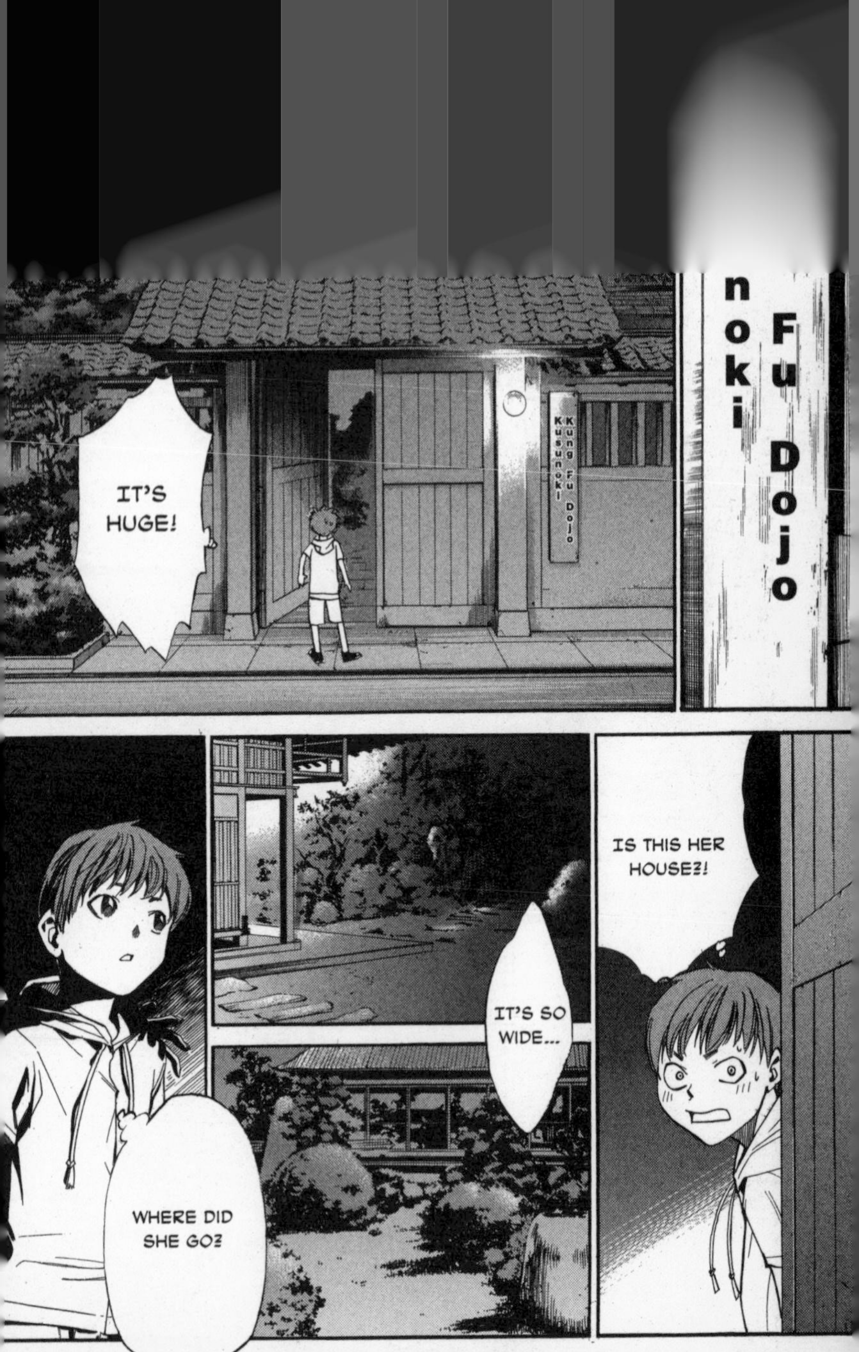
noki Fu Dojo
Kusunoki Kung Fu Dojo
IT'S HUGE!
IS THIS HER HOUSE?!
IT'S SO WIDE...
WHERE DID SHE GO?

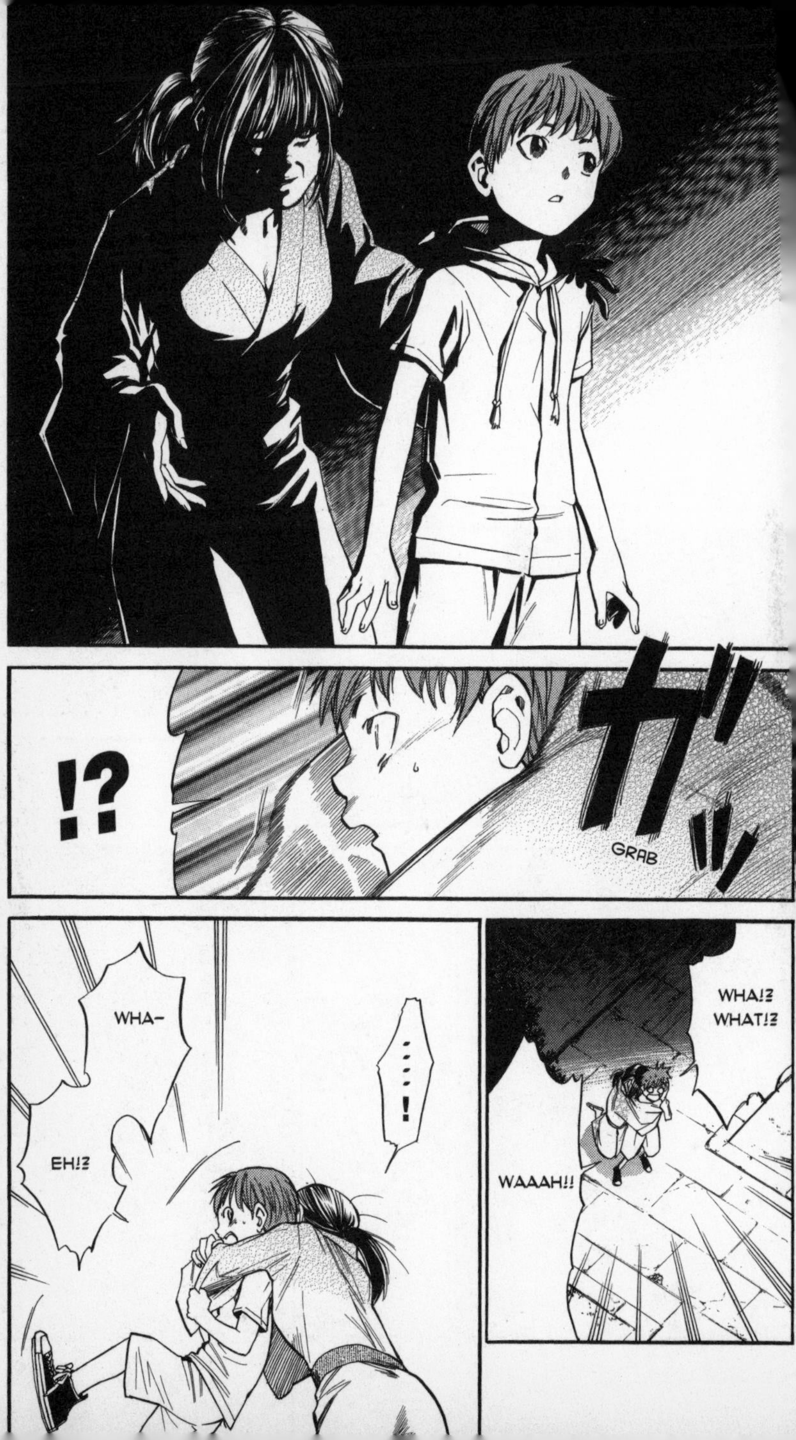

ガッ
GRAB
!?
WHA!? WHAT!?
WAAAH!!
……!
WHA-
EH!?

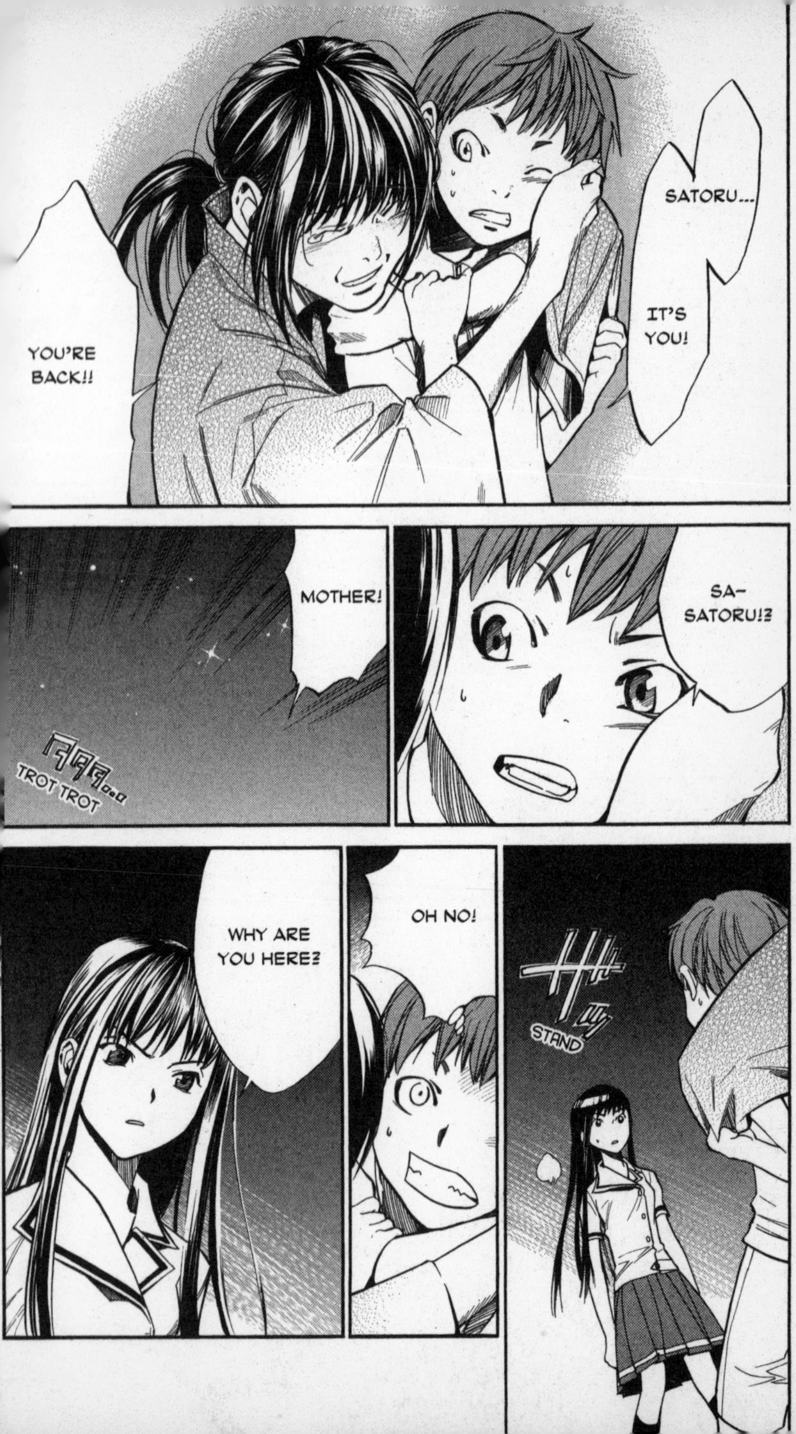
SATORU...
IT'S YOU!
YOU'RE BACK!!
SA-SATORU!?
MOTHER!
TROT TROT
STAND
OH NO!
WHY ARE YOU HERE?

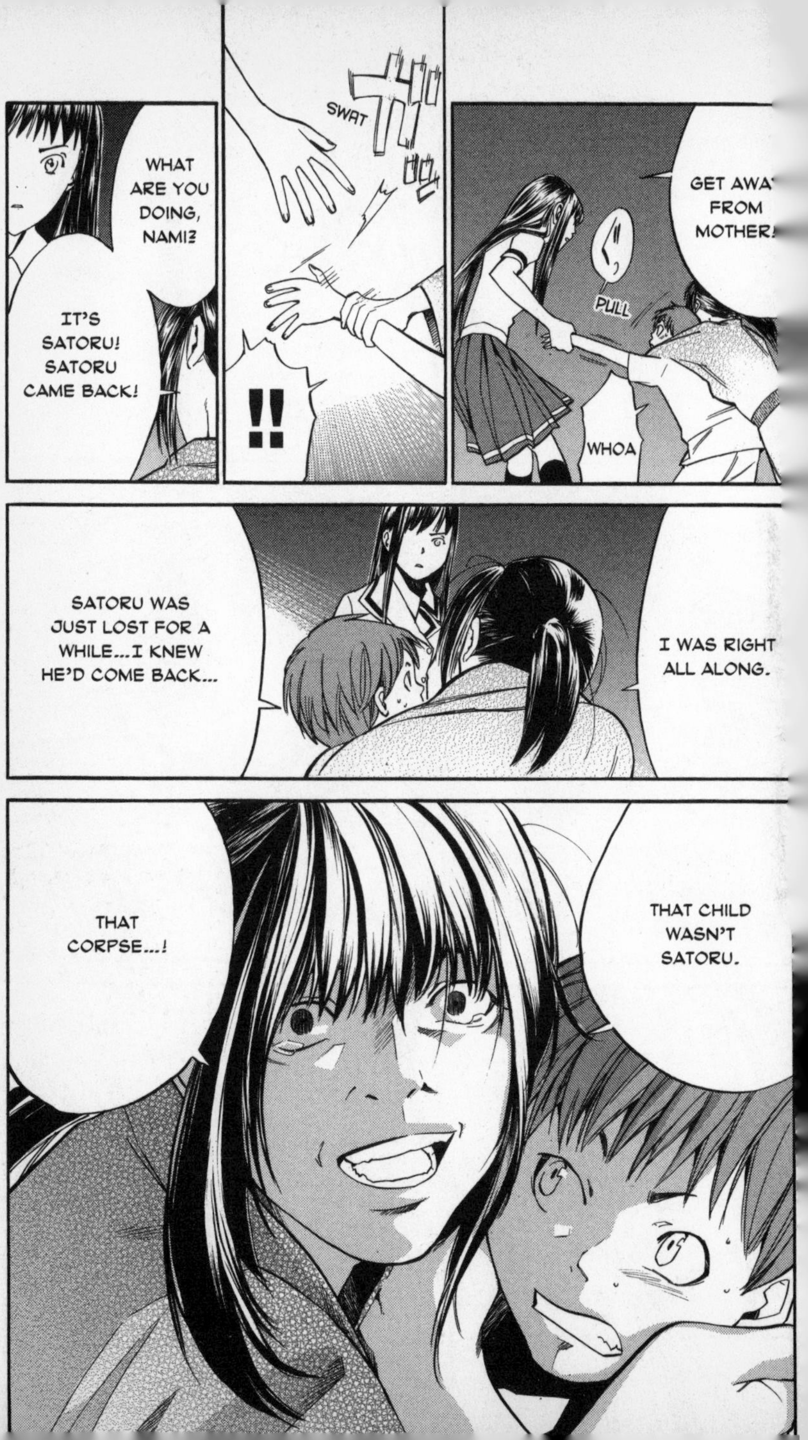
GET AWA
FROM MOTHER!
PULL
WHOA
SWAT
!!
WHAT ARE YOU DOING, NAMI?
IT'S SATORU! SATORU CAME BACK!
I WAS RIGHT ALL ALONG.
SATORU WAS JUST LOST FOR A WHILE...I KNEW HE'D COME BACK...
THAT CHILD WASN'T SATORU.
THAT CORPSE...!

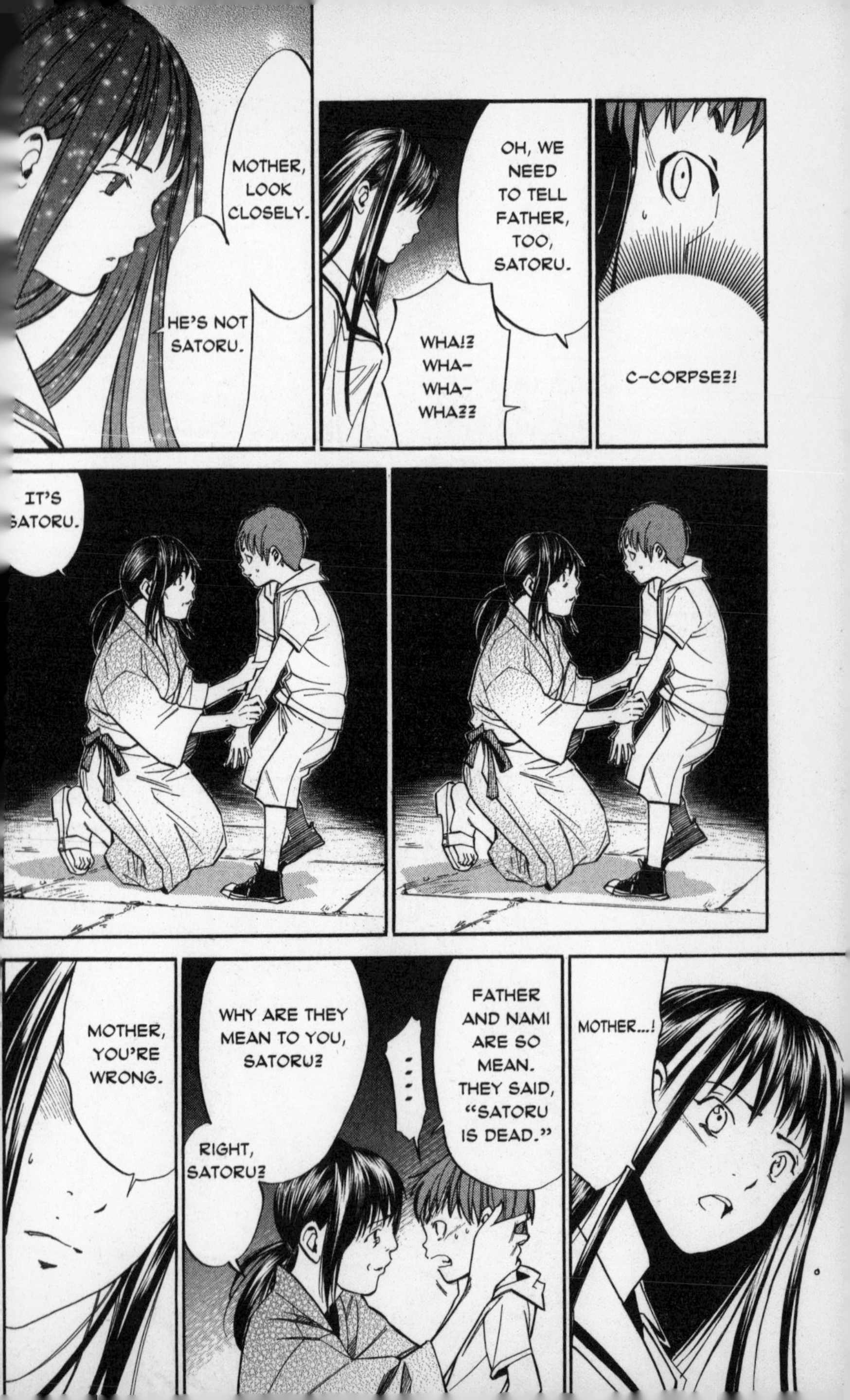

C-CORPSE?!
OH, WE NEED TO TELL FATHER, TOO, SATORU.
WHA!? WHA- WHA- WHA??
MOTHER, LOOK CLOSELY.
HE'S NOT SATORU.
IT'S SATORU.
MOTHER...!
FATHER AND NAMI ARE SO MEAN. THEY SAID, "SATORU IS DEAD."
....
WHY ARE THEY MEAN TO YOU, SATORU?
RIGHT, SATORU?
MOTHER, YOU'RE WRONG.

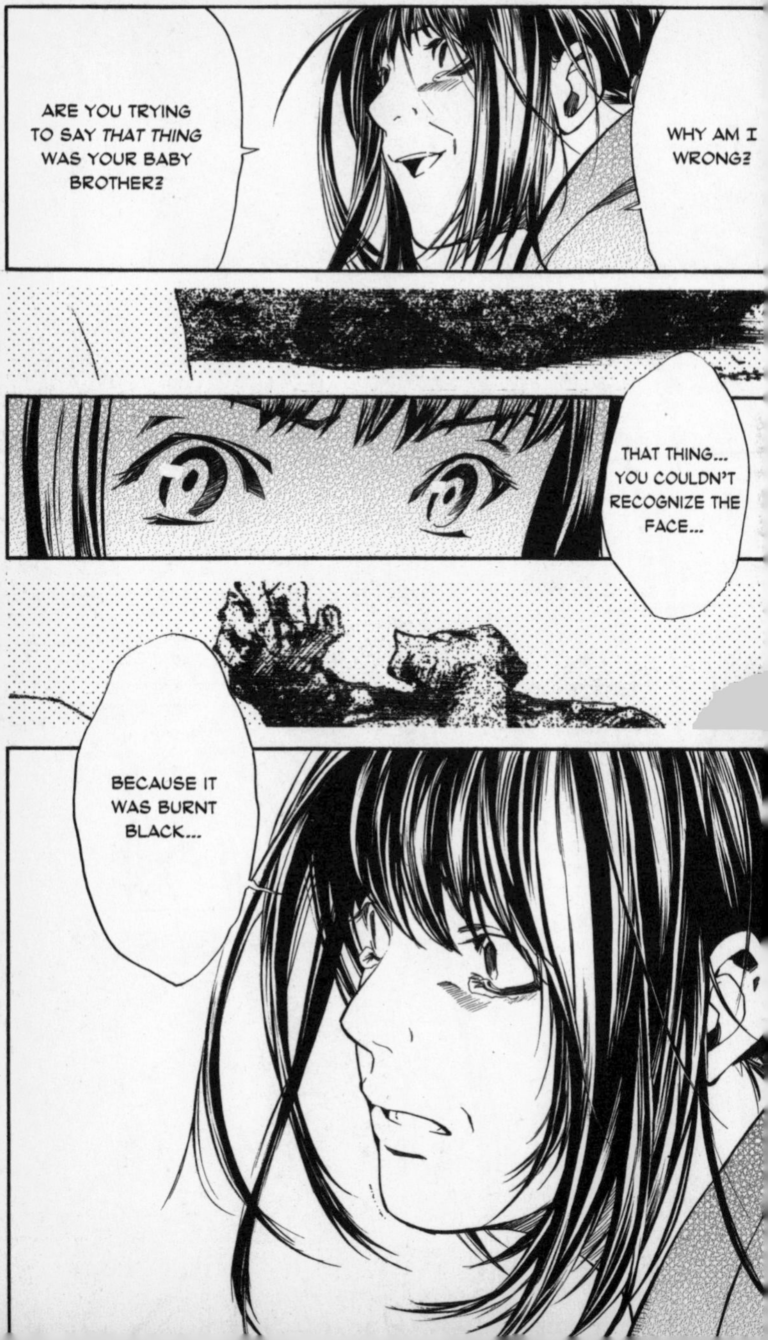
WHY AM I WRONG?
ARE YOU TRYING TO SAY *THAT THING* WAS YOUR BABY BROTHER?
THAT THING... YOU COULDN'T RECOGNIZE THE FACE...
BECAUSE IT WAS BURNT BLACK...

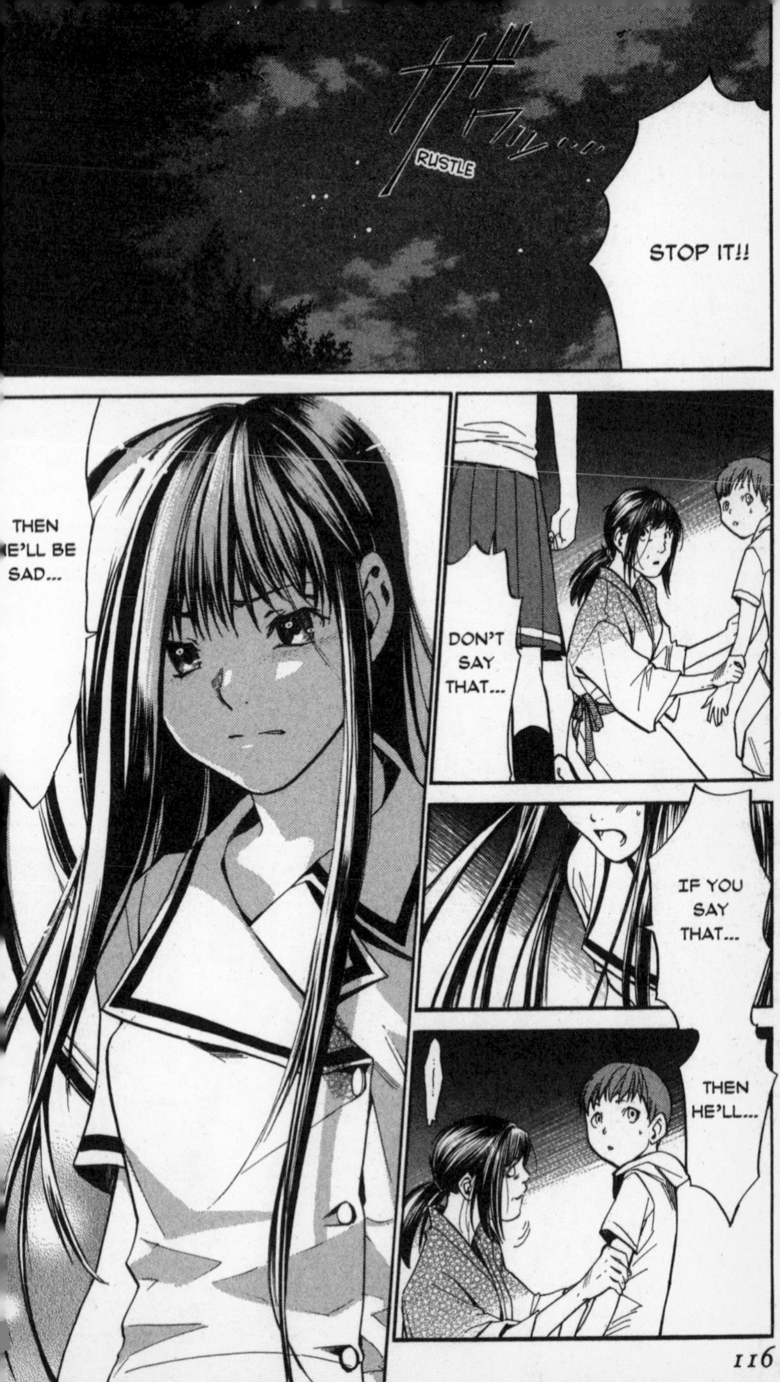
RUSTLE
STOP IT!!
DON'T SAY THAT...
IF YOU SAY THAT...
!
THEN HE'LL...
THEN
E'LL BE
SAD...

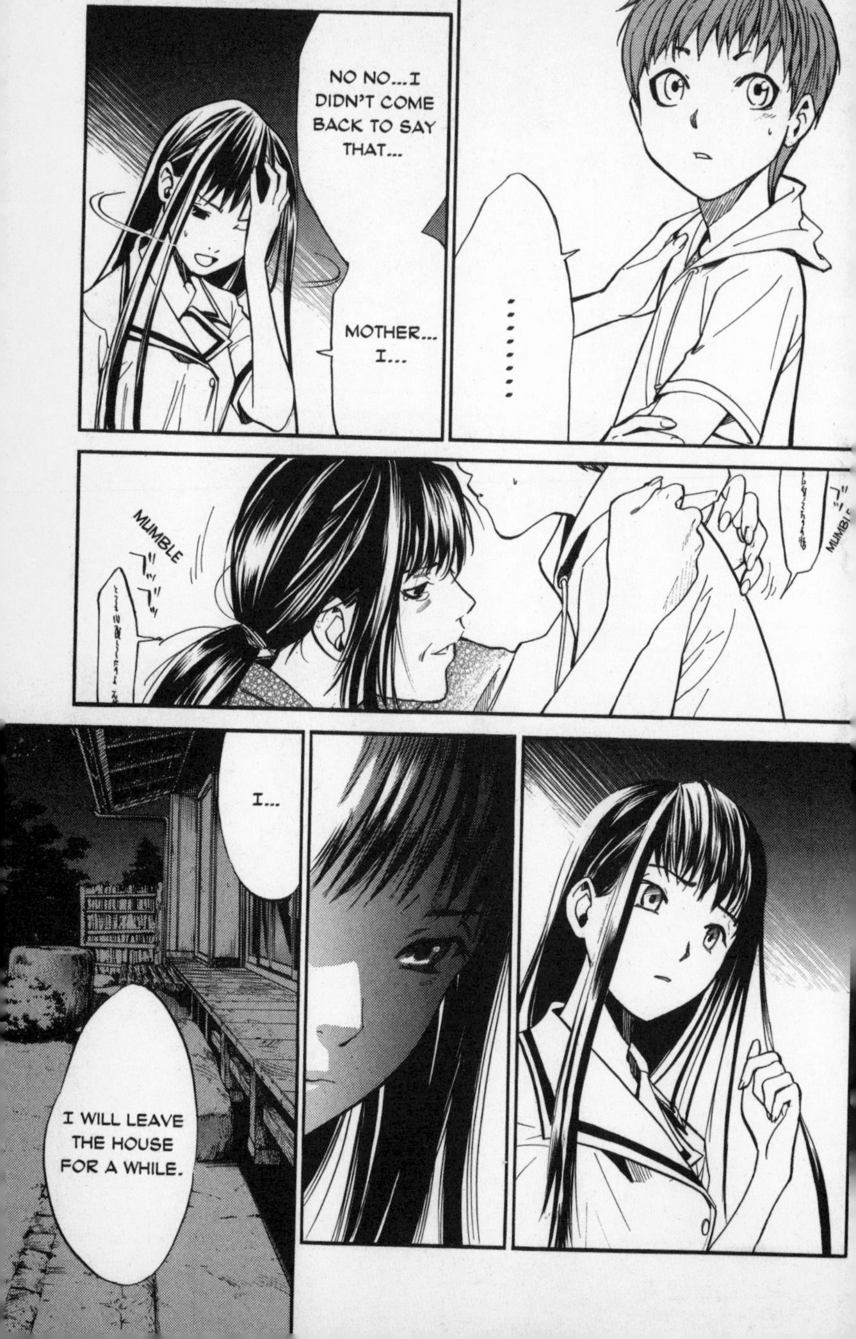
......
NO NO...I DIDN'T COME BACK TO SAY THAT...
MOTHER... I...
MUMBLE
MUMBLE
I...
I WILL LEAVE THE HOUSE FOR A WHILE.

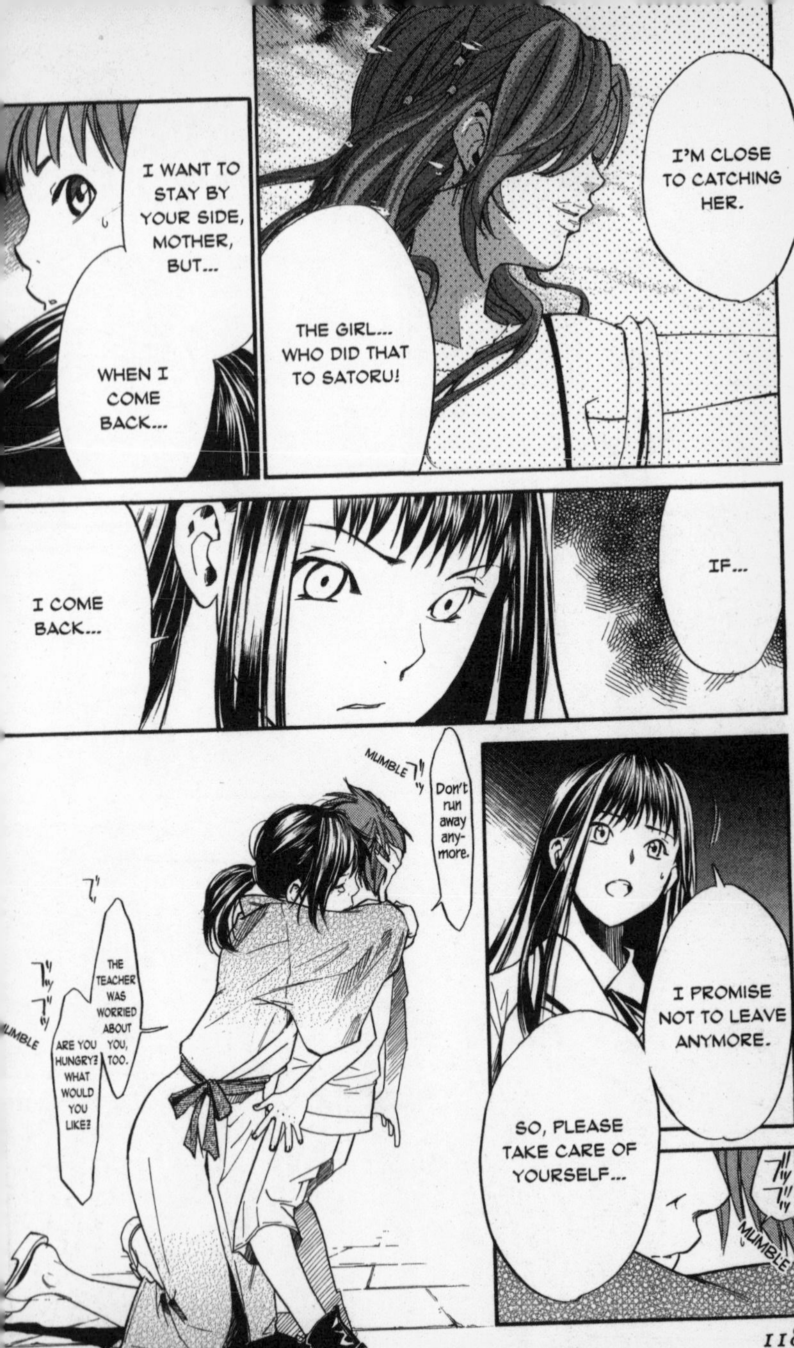
I'M CLOSE TO CATCHING HER.
THE GIRL... WHO DID THAT TO SATORU!
I WANT TO STAY BY YOUR SIDE, MOTHER, BUT...
WHEN I COME BACK...
IF...
I COME BACK...
I PROMISE NOT TO LEAVE ANYMORE.
SO, PLEASE TAKE CARE OF YOURSELF...
MUMBLE
MUMBLE
Don't run away anymore.
THE TEACHER WAS WORRIED ABOUT YOU, TOO.
ARE YOU HUNGRY? WHAT WOULD YOU LIKE?

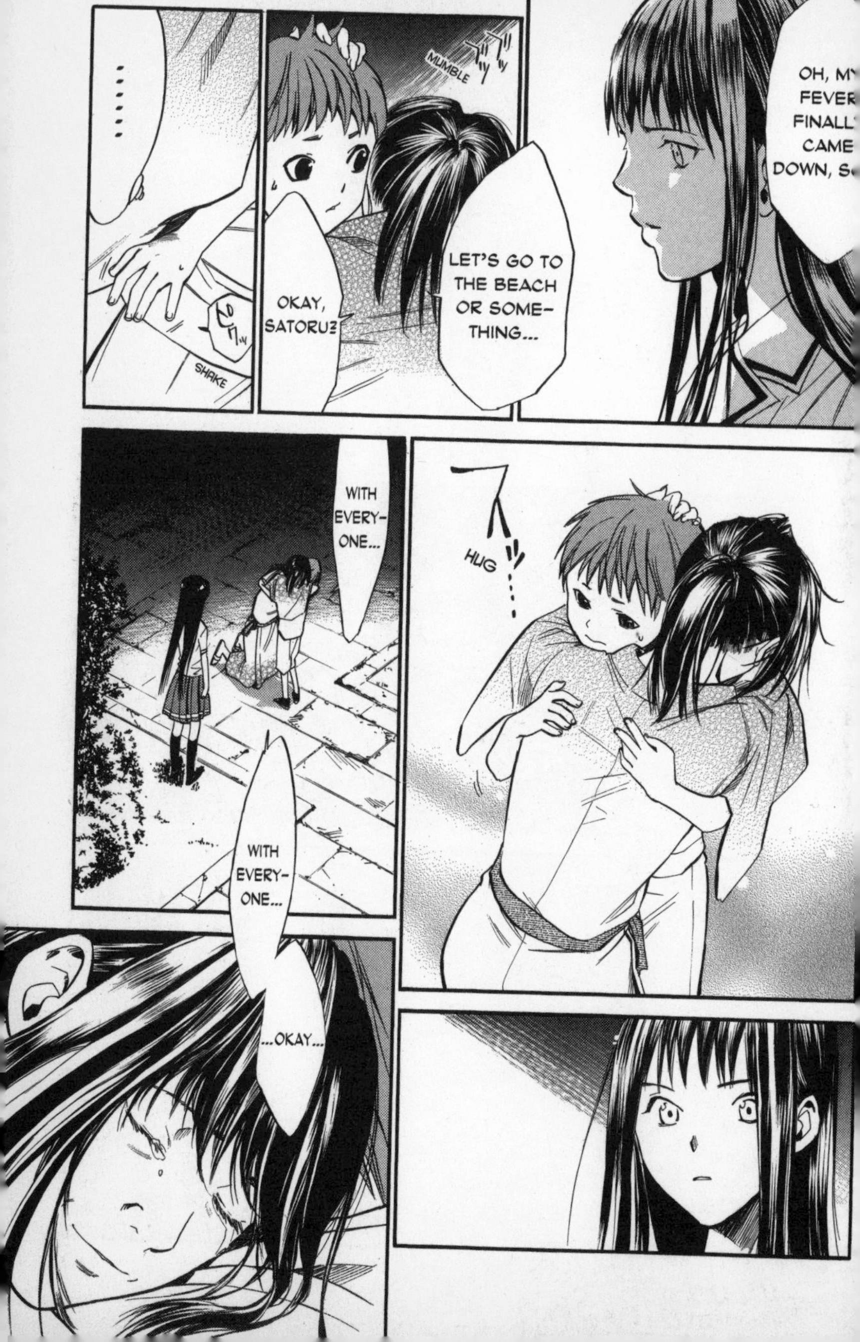
OH, M
FEVER
FINALL
CAME
DOWN, S
MUMBLE
LET'S GO TO THE BEACH OR SOME-THING...
OKAY, SATORU?
......
SHAKE
HUG
WITH EVERY-ONE...
WITH EVERY-ONE...
...OKAY...

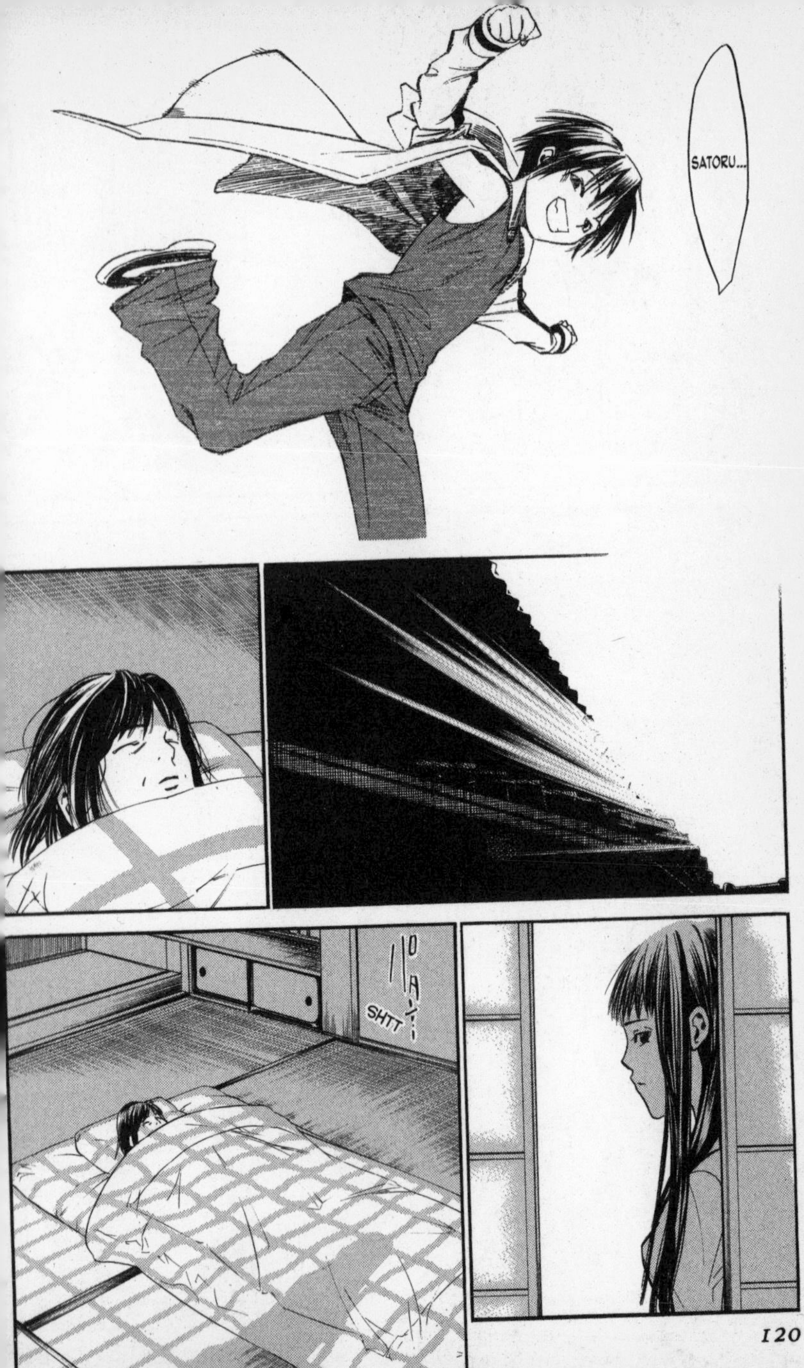
SATORU...
SHTT

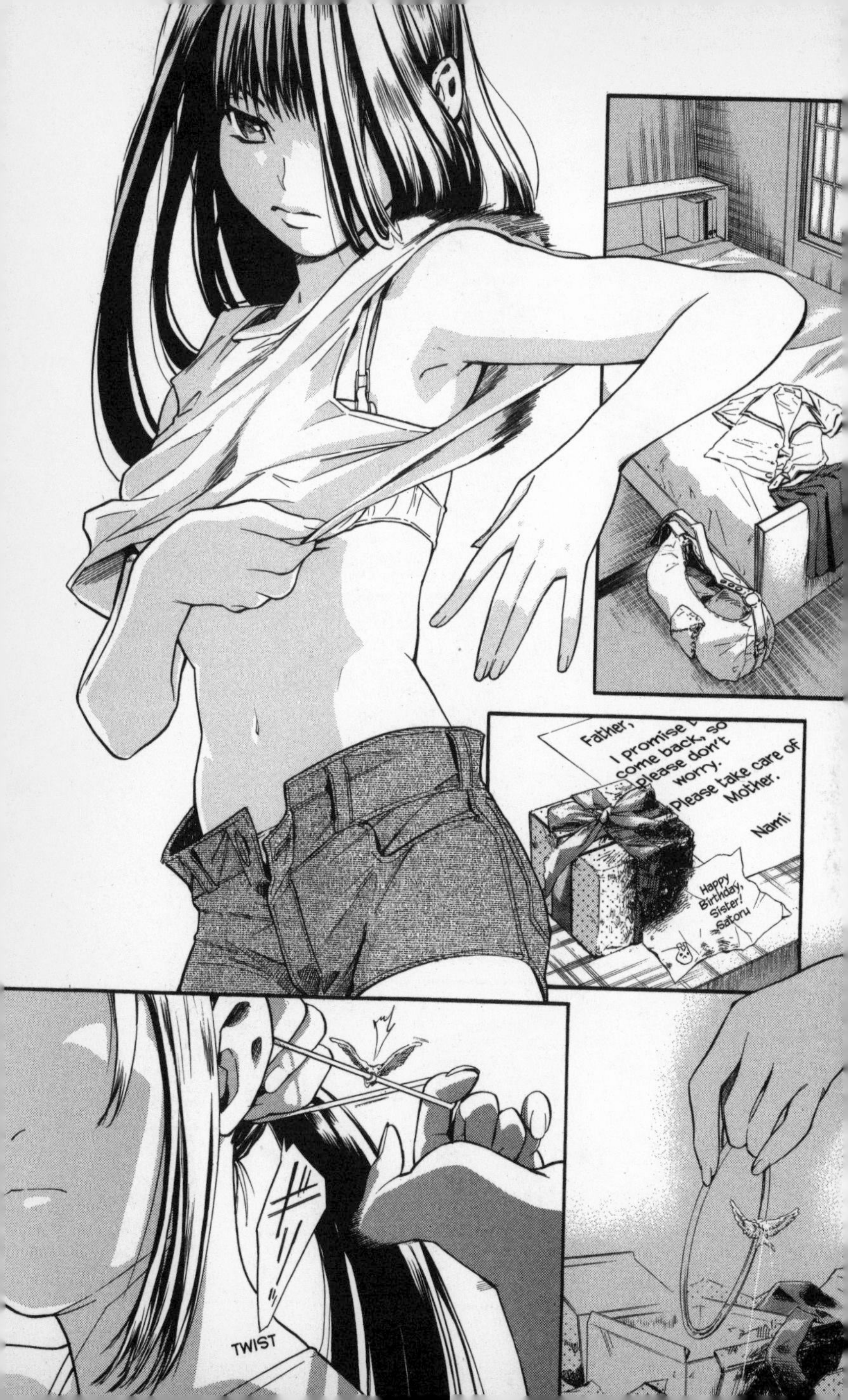
Father,
I promise
come back, so
please don't
worry.
Please take care of
Mother.
Nami
Happy
Birthday,
Sister!
Satoru
TWIST

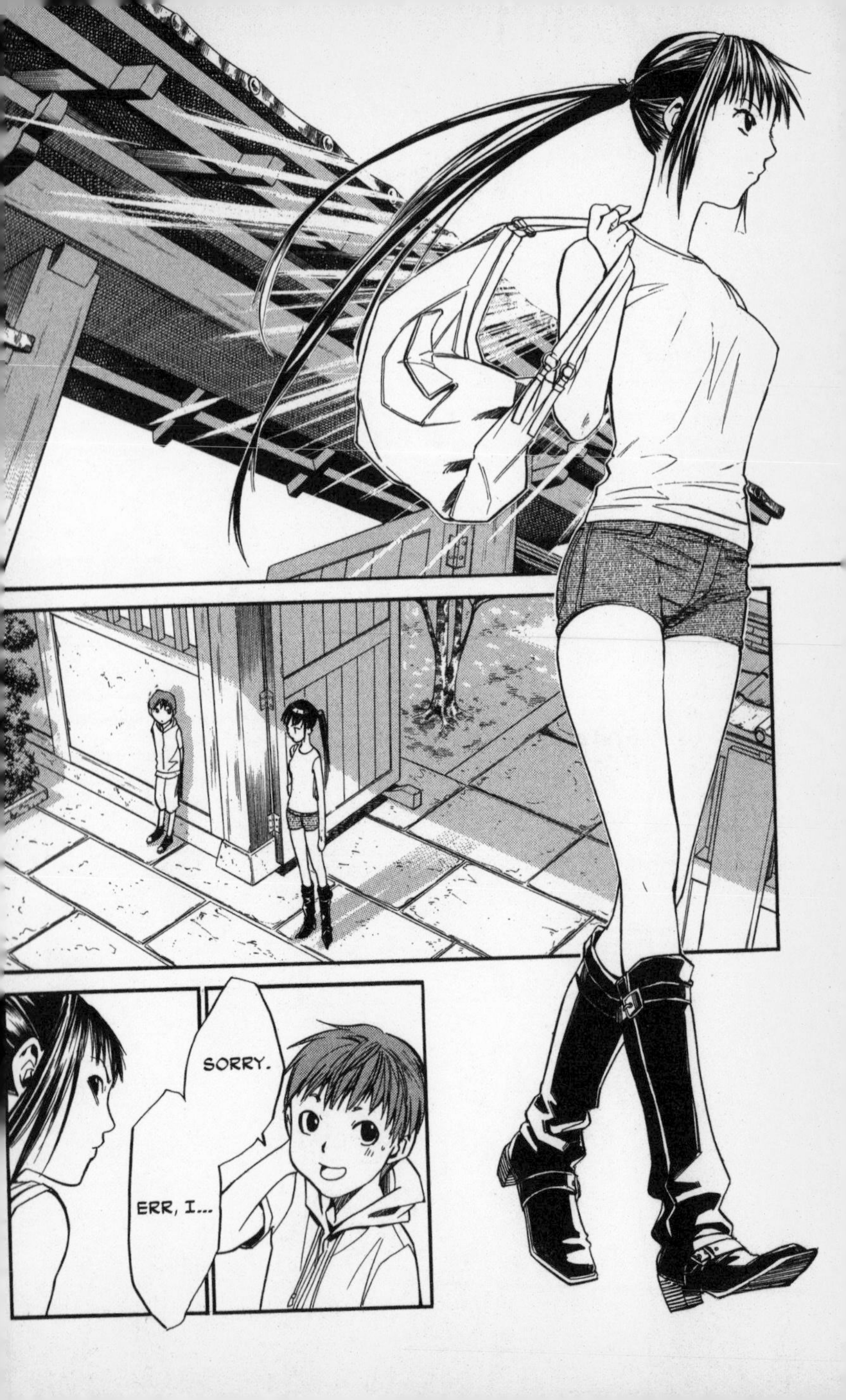
SORRY.
ERR, I...

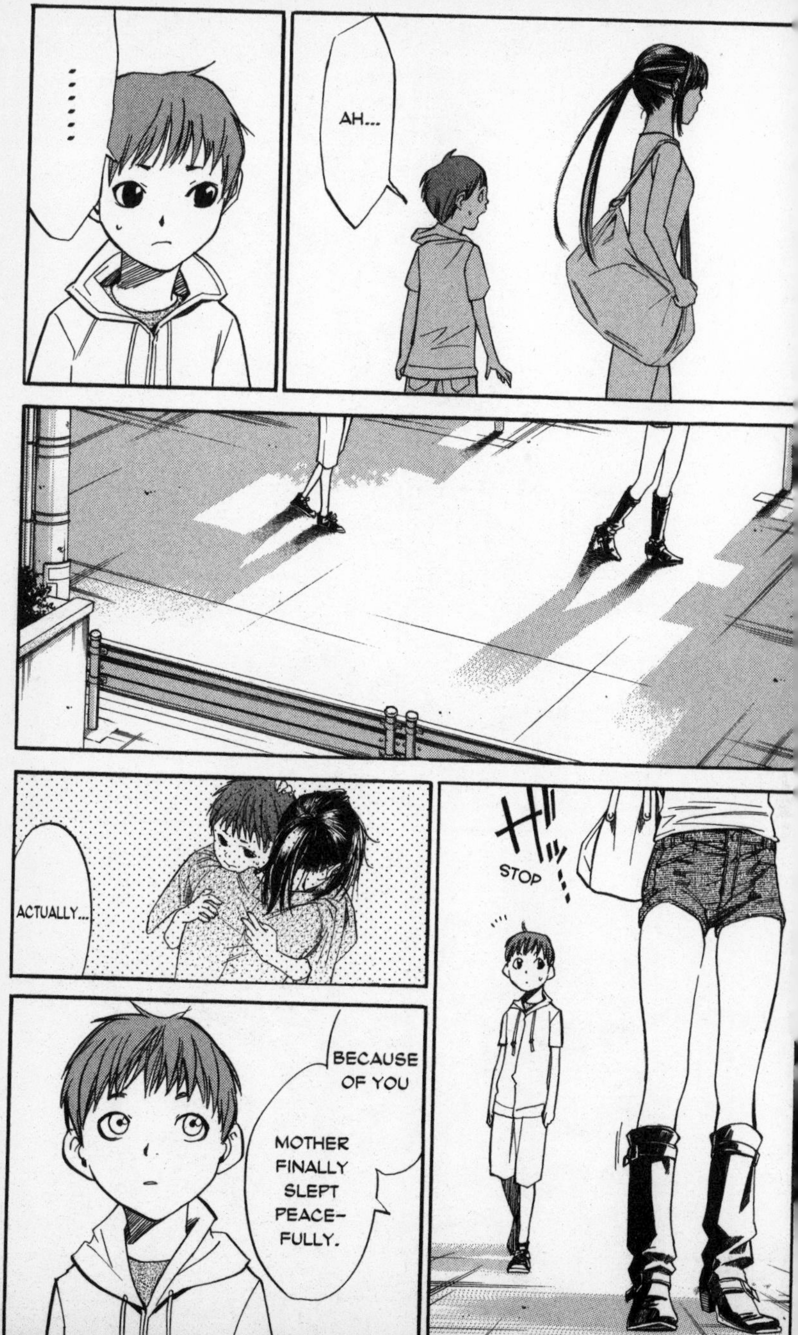
AH...
......
STOP
ACTUALLY...
BECAUSE OF YOU
MOTHER FINALLY SLEPT PEACE-FULLY.

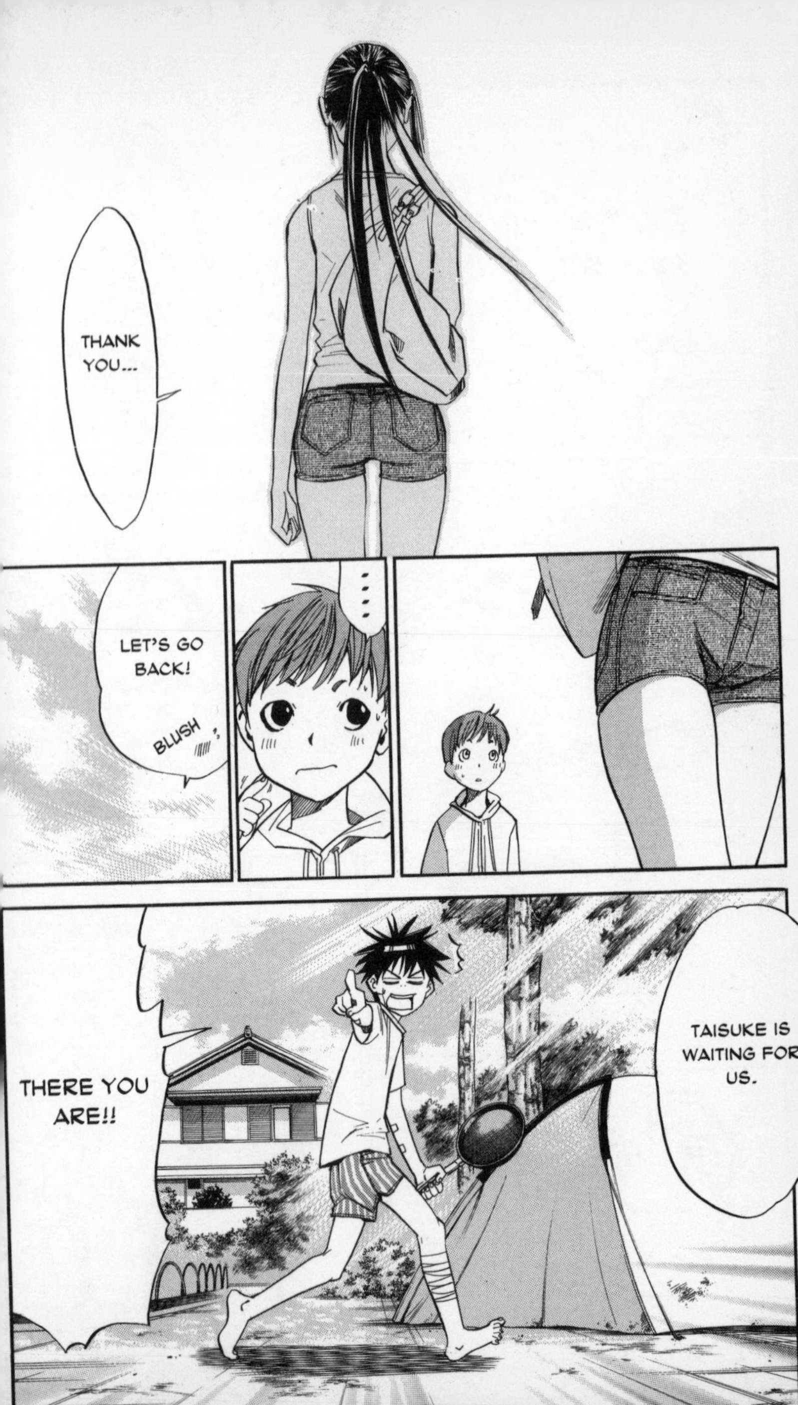
THANK YOU...
....
LET'S GO BACK!
BLUSH
TAISUKE IS WAITING FOR US.
THERE YOU ARE!!

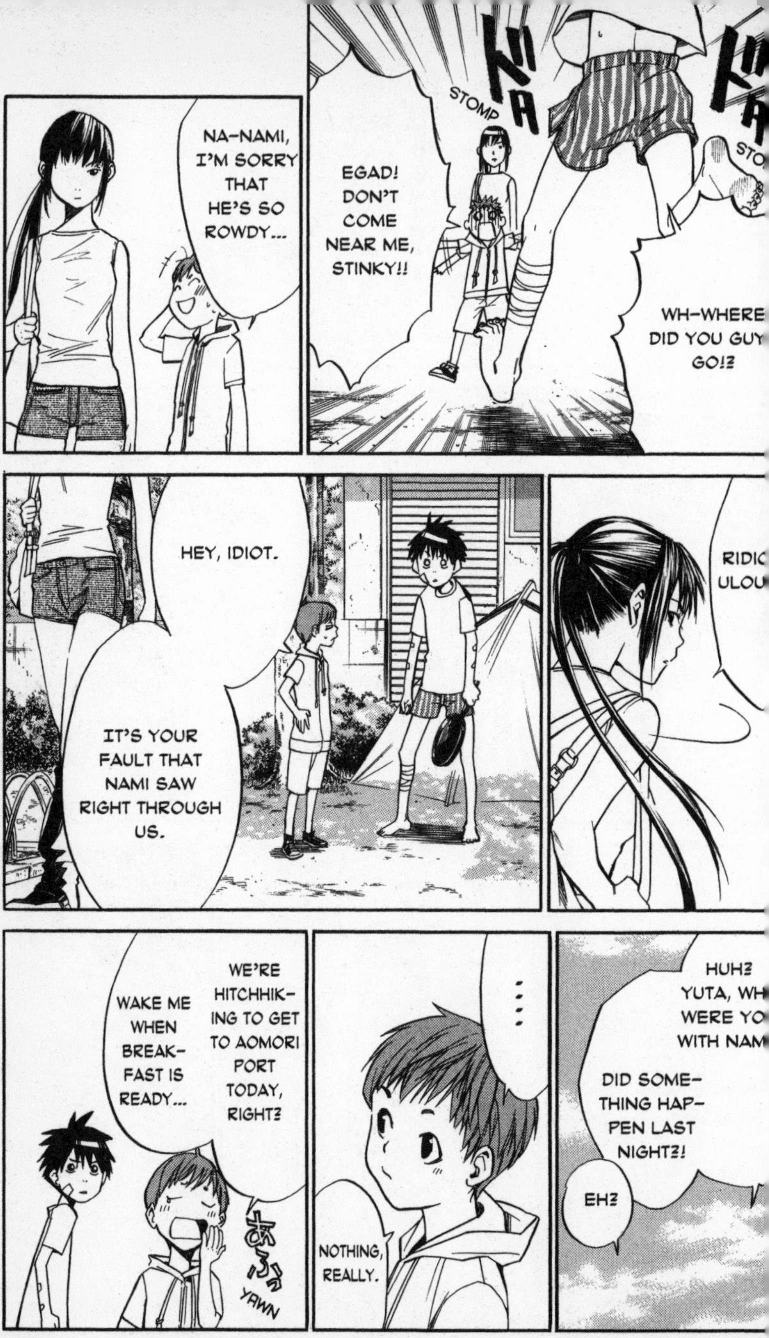
STOMP
WH-WHERE DID YOU GUY GO!?
EGAD! DON'T COME NEAR ME, STINKY!!
STOMP
NA-NAMI, I'M SORRY THAT HE'S SO ROWDY...
RIDIC ULOU
HEY, IDIOT.
IT'S YOUR FAULT THAT NAMI SAW RIGHT THROUGH US.
HUH? YUTA, WH WERE YO WITH NAM
DID SOME-THING HAP-PEN LAST NIGHT?!
EH?
....
NOTHING, REALLY.
WE'RE HITCHHIK-ING TO GET TO AOMORI PORT TODAY, RIGHT?
WAKE ME WHEN BREAK-FAST IS READY...
YAWN

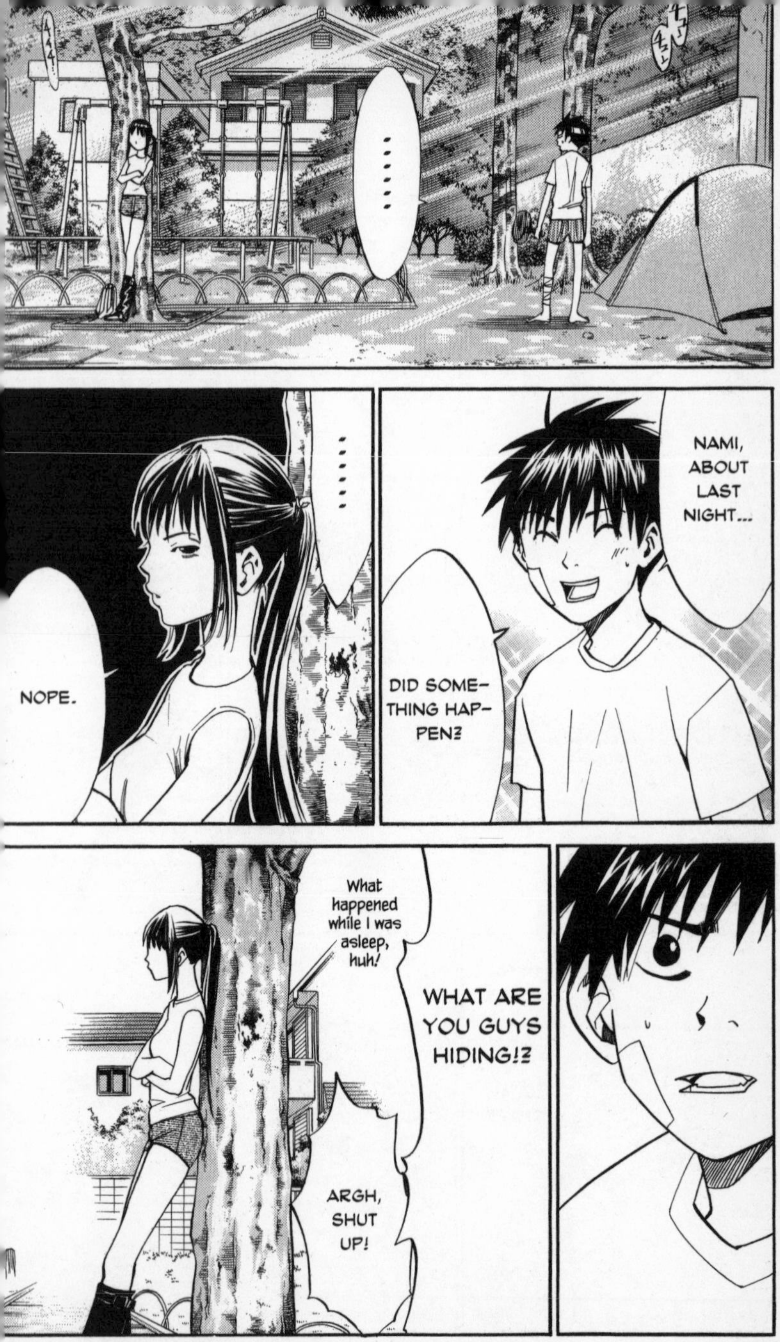

......
NAMI, ABOUT LAST NIGHT...
DID SOME-THING HAP-PEN?
......
NOPE.
What happened while I was asleep, huh!
WHAT ARE YOU GUYS HIDING!?
ARGH, SHUT UP!

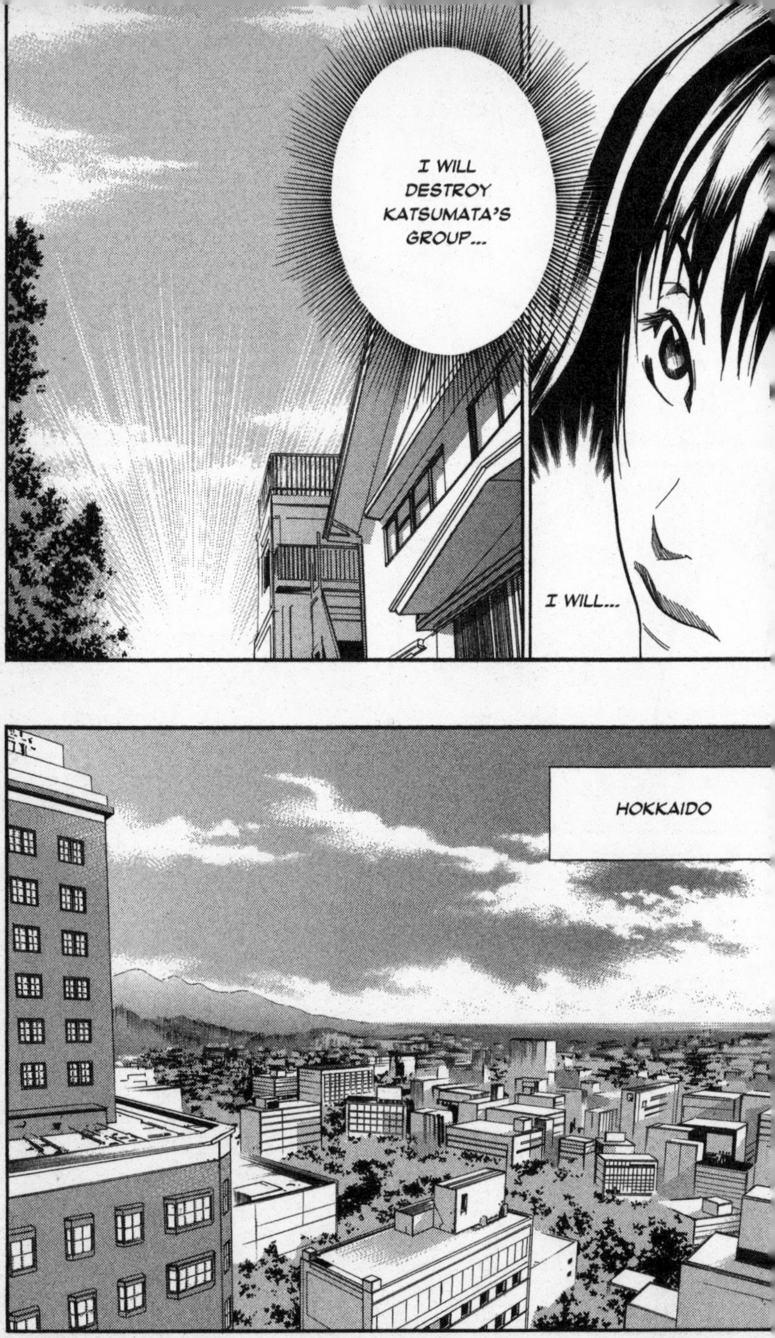
I WILL DESTROY KATSUMATA'S GROUP...
I WILL...
HOKKAIDO

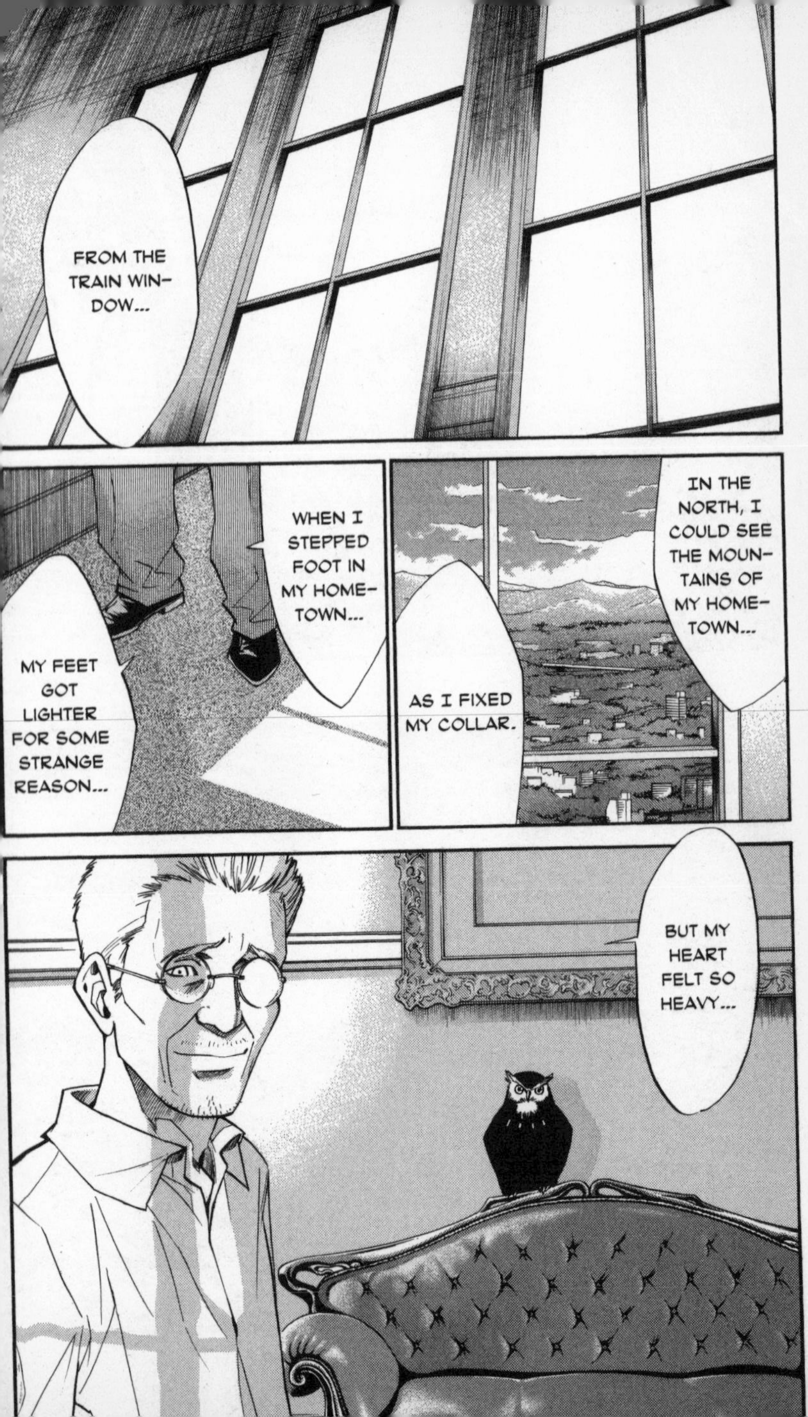
FROM THE TRAIN WIN-DOW...
IN THE NORTH, I COULD SEE THE MOUN-TAINS OF MY HOME-TOWN...
AS I FIXED MY COLLAR.
WHEN I STEPPED FOOT IN MY HOME-TOWN...
MY FEET GOT LIGHTER FOR SOME STRANGE REASON...
BUT MY HEART FELT SO HEAVY...

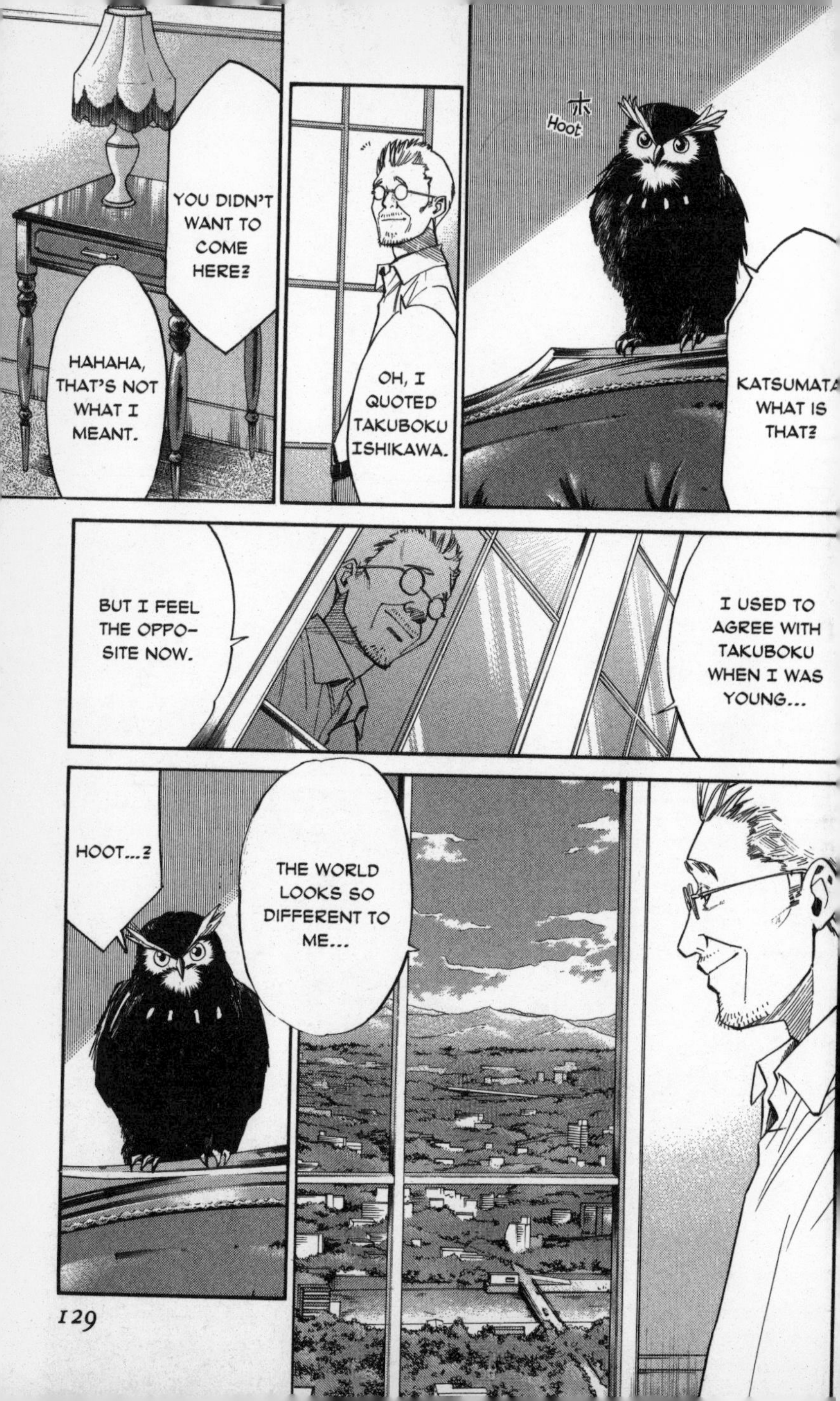
ホ
Hoot
KATSUMATA WHAT IS THAT?
OH, I QUOTED TAKUBOKU ISHIKAWA.
YOU DIDN'T WANT TO COME HERE?
HAHAHA, THAT'S NOT WHAT I MEANT.
I USED TO AGREE WITH TAKUBOKU WHEN I WAS YOUNG...
BUT I FEEL THE OPPOSITE NOW.
THE WORLD LOOKS SO DIFFERENT TO ME...
HOOT...?

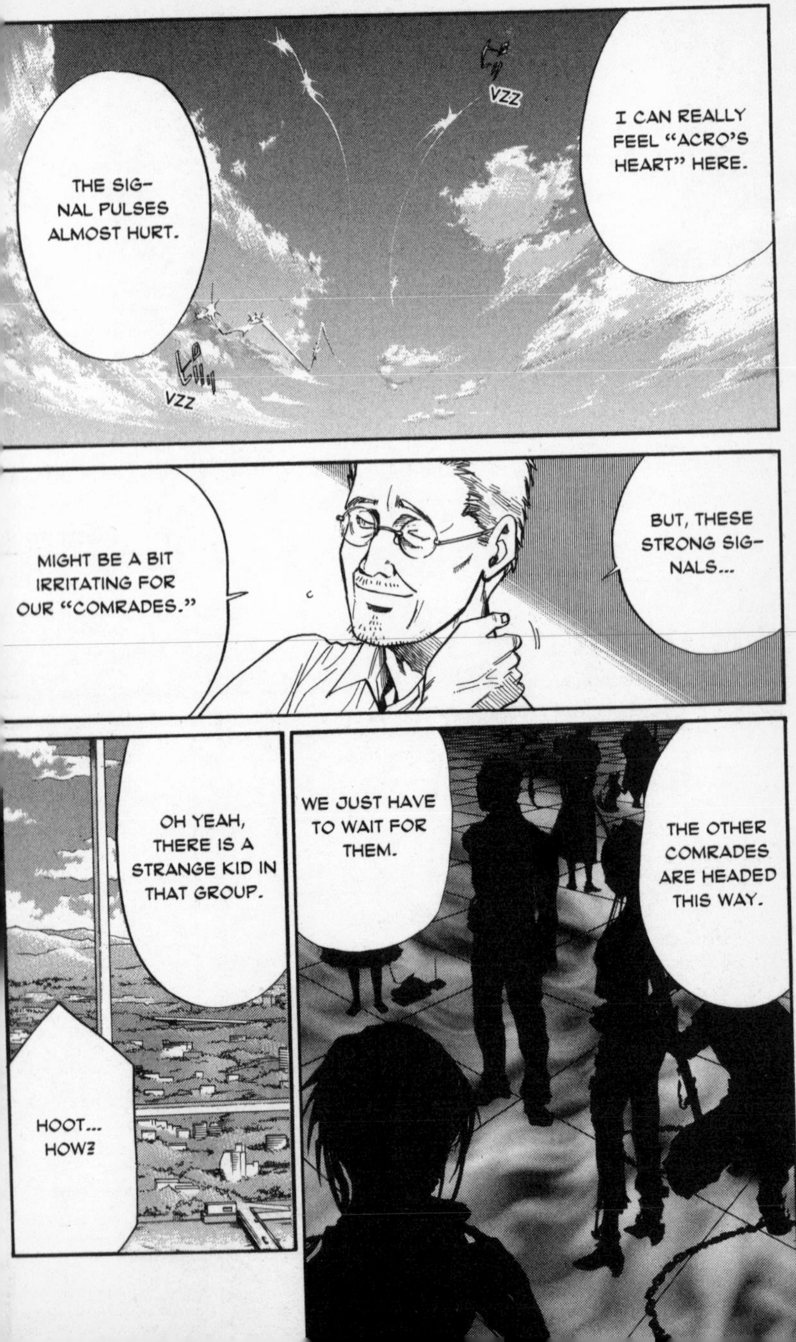
I CAN REALLY FEEL "ACRO'S HEART" HERE.
VZZ
THE SIG-NAL PULSES ALMOST HURT.
VZZ
BUT, THESE STRONG SIG-NALS...
MIGHT BE A BIT IRRITATING FOR OUR "COMRADES."
THE OTHER COMRADES ARE HEADED THIS WAY.
WE JUST HAVE TO WAIT FOR THEM.
OH YEAH, THERE IS A STRANGE KID IN THAT GROUP.
HOOT... HOW?

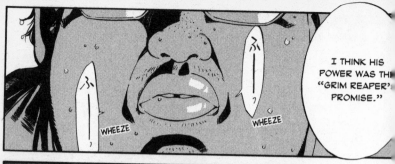

I THINK HIS POWER WAS THE "GRIM REAPER'S PROMISE."
ふーっ
WHEEZE
ふーっ
WHEEZE
THE KID IS GOING TO RIDE THE FERRY TODAY TO COME HERE.
FERRY
ふーっ
WHEEZE
ふーっ
WHEEZE
PASSENGER LIST (MANIFEST)
Please enter your name. (Children under six require supervision.)
NAME
Gou Okada
SCRIT SCRIT
THE "GRIM REAPER'S PROMISE," EH...?

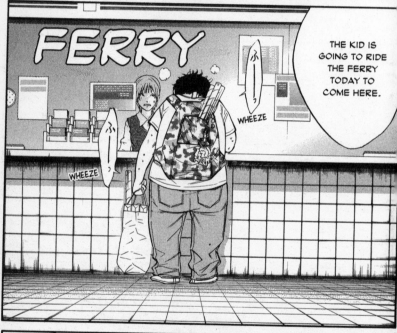

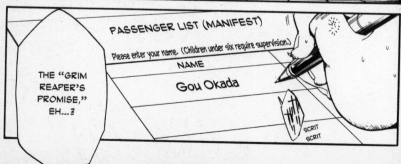

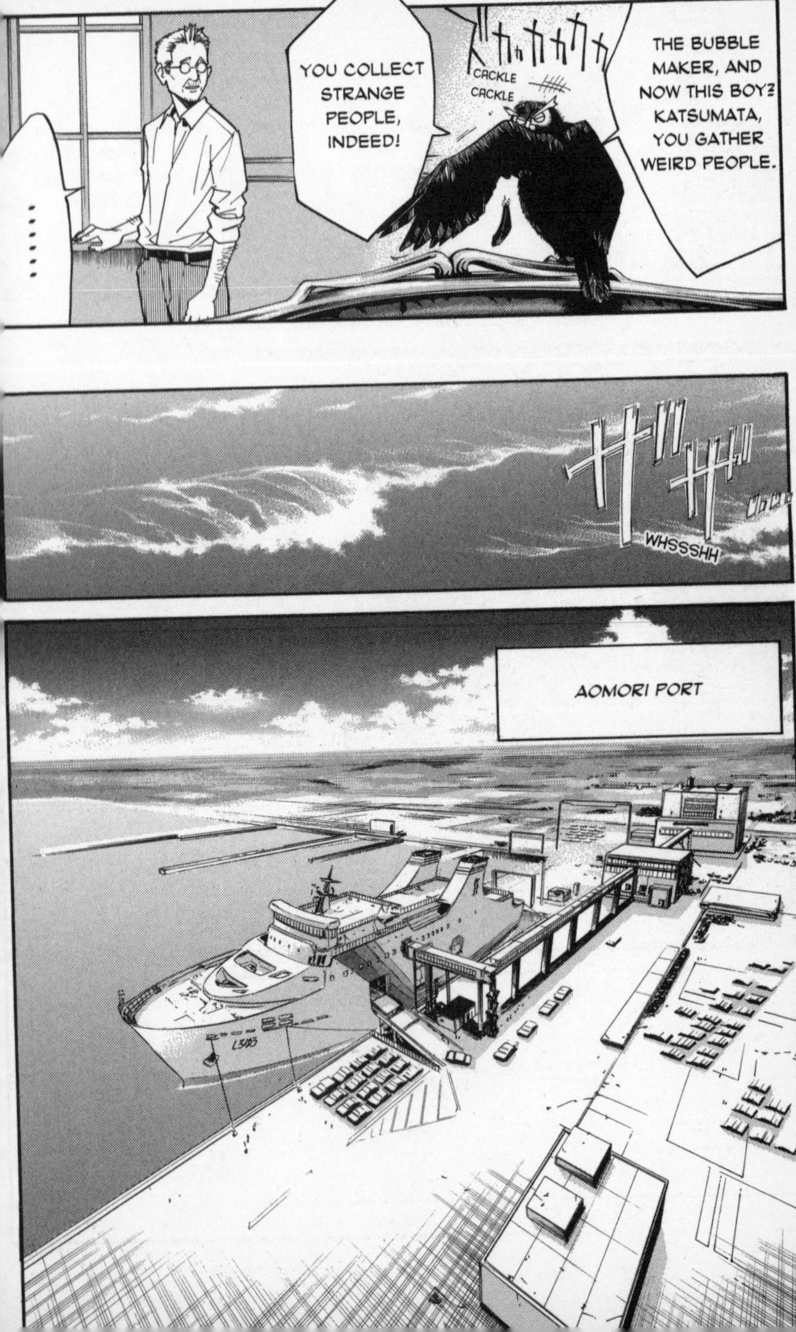
THE BUBBLE MAKER, AND NOW THIS BOY? KATSUMATA, YOU GATHER WEIRD PEOPLE.
CACKLE CACKLE
YOU COLLECT STRANGE PEOPLE, INDEED!
......
WHSSSHH
AOMORI PORT

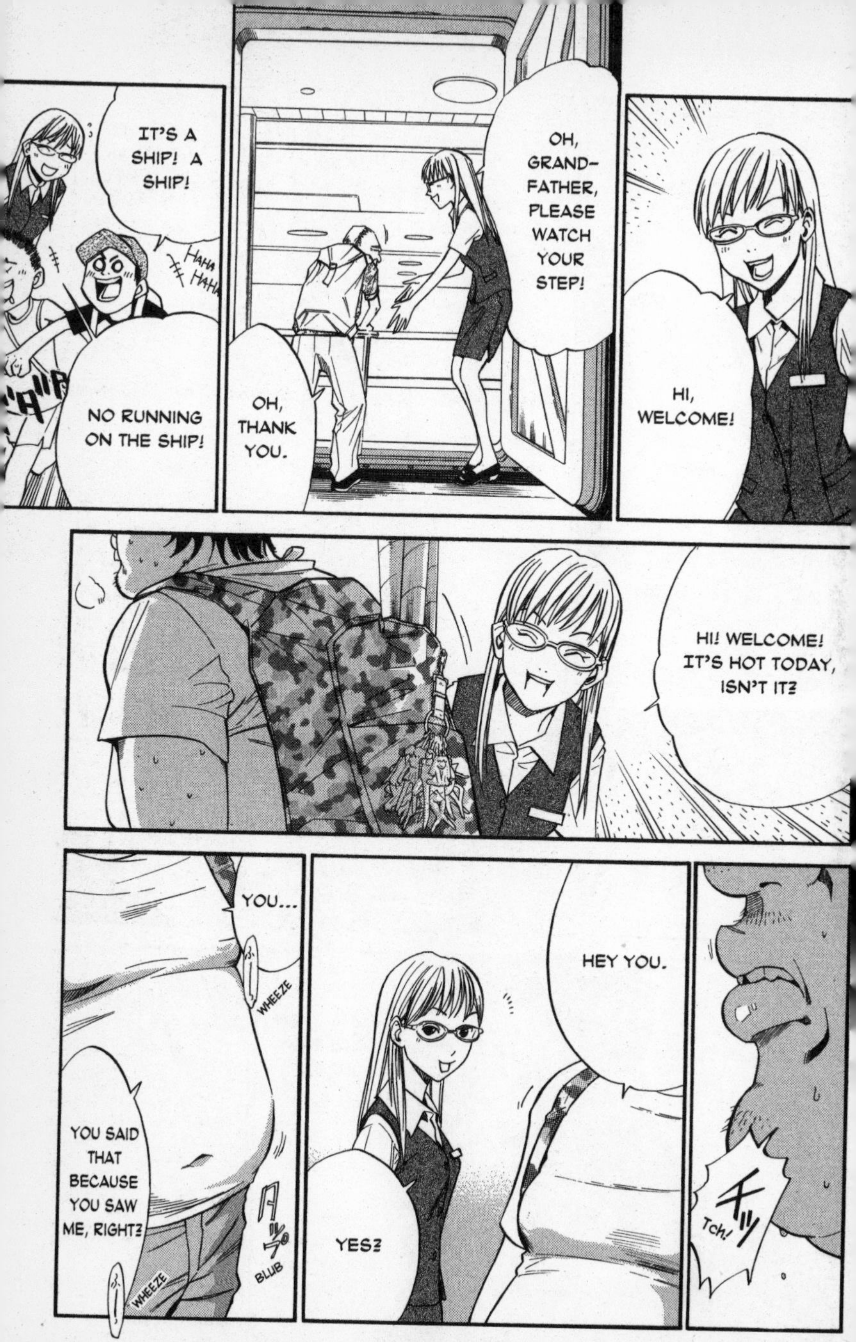
HI, WELCOME!
OH, GRAND-FATHER, PLEASE WATCH YOUR STEP!
OH, THANK YOU.
IT'S A SHIP! A SHIP!
HAHA HAHA
NO RUNNING ON THE SHIP!
HI! WELCOME! IT'S HOT TODAY, ISN'T IT?
Tch!
HEY YOU.
YES?
YOU...
WHEEZE
YOU SAID THAT BECAUSE YOU SAW ME, RIGHT?
BLUB
WHEEZE

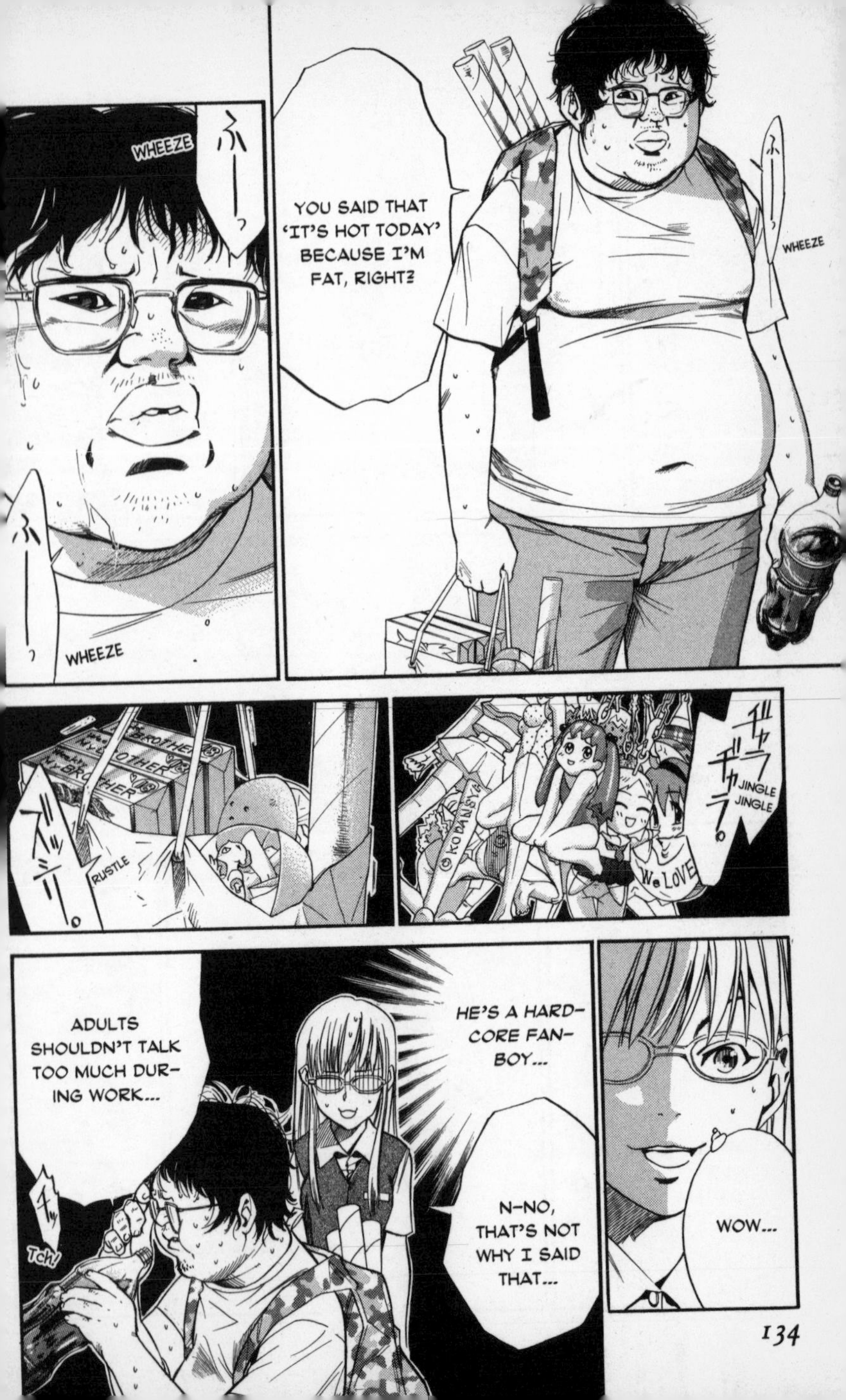
YOU SAID THAT 'IT'S HOT TODAY' BECAUSE I'M FAT, RIGHT?
ふーっ
WHEEZE
ふーっ
WHEEZE
ふーっ
WHEEZE
ジャラジャラ。
JINGLE JINGLE
KODANSYA
W LOVE
ズッシリ。
RUSTLE
MY BROTHER
WOW...
HE'S A HARD-CORE FAN-BOY...
N-NO, THAT'S NOT WHY I SAID THAT...
ADULTS SHOULDN'T TALK TOO MUCH DUR-ING WORK...
チッ
Tch!

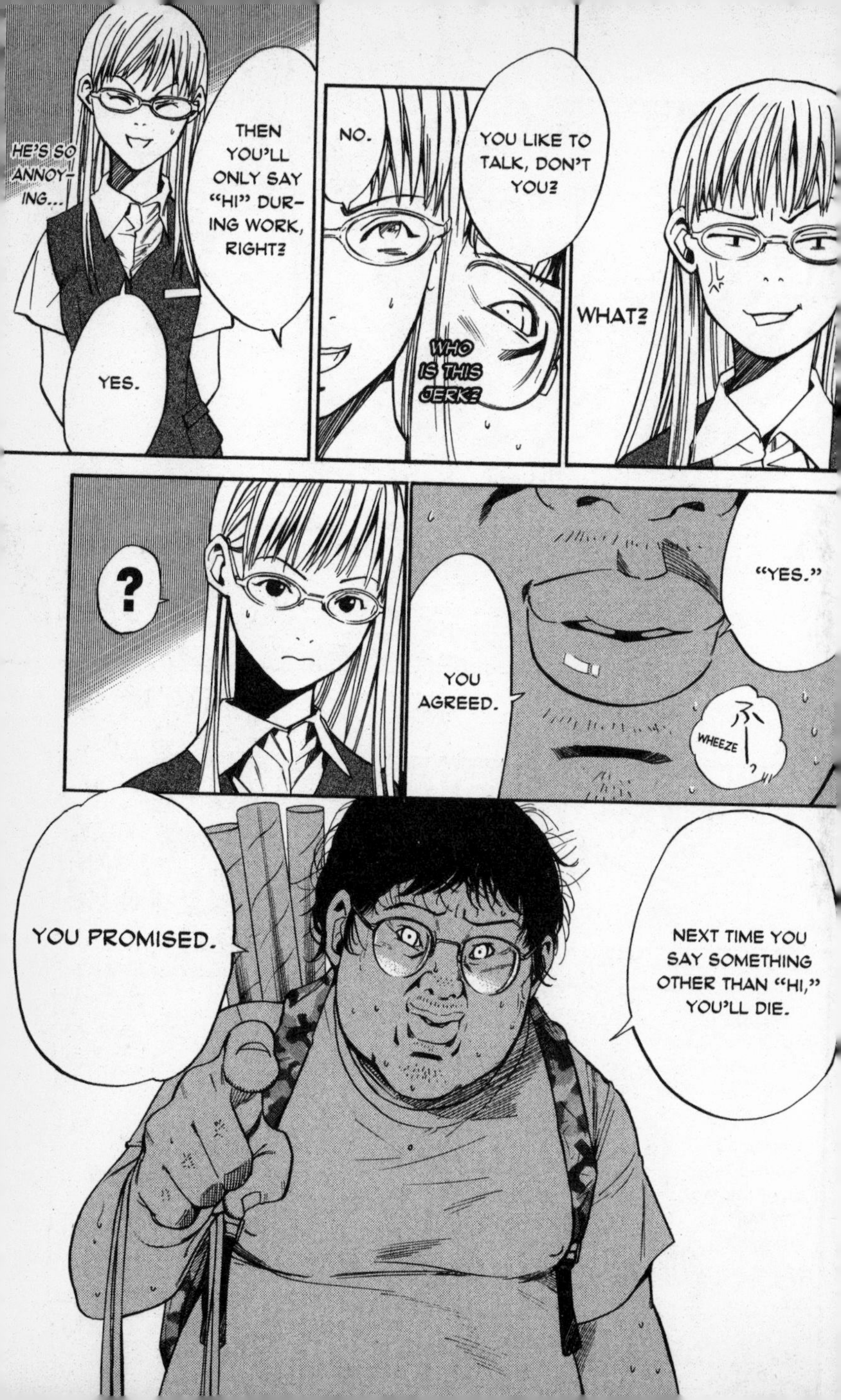
WHAT?
YOU LIKE TO TALK, DON'T YOU?
NO.
WHO IS THIS JERK?
THEN YOU'LL ONLY SAY "HI" DURING WORK, RIGHT?
HE'S SO ANNOYING...
YES.
"YES."
YOU AGREED.
ふー
WHEEZE
?
NEXT TIME YOU SAY SOMETHING OTHER THAN "HI," YOU'LL DIE.
YOU PROMISED.

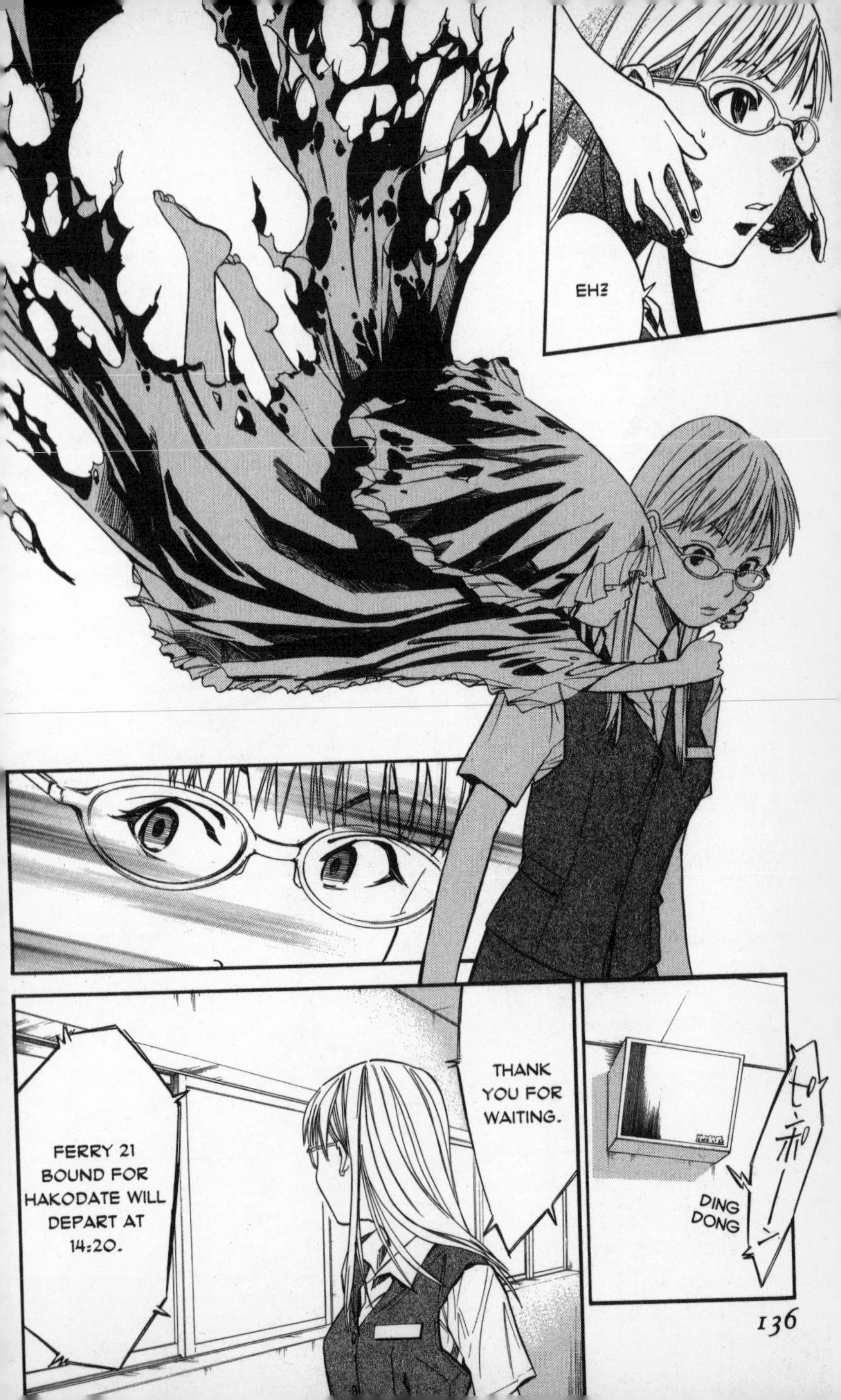
EH?
DING DONG
THANK YOU FOR WAITING.
FERRY 21 BOUND FOR HAKODATE WILL DEPART AT 14:20.

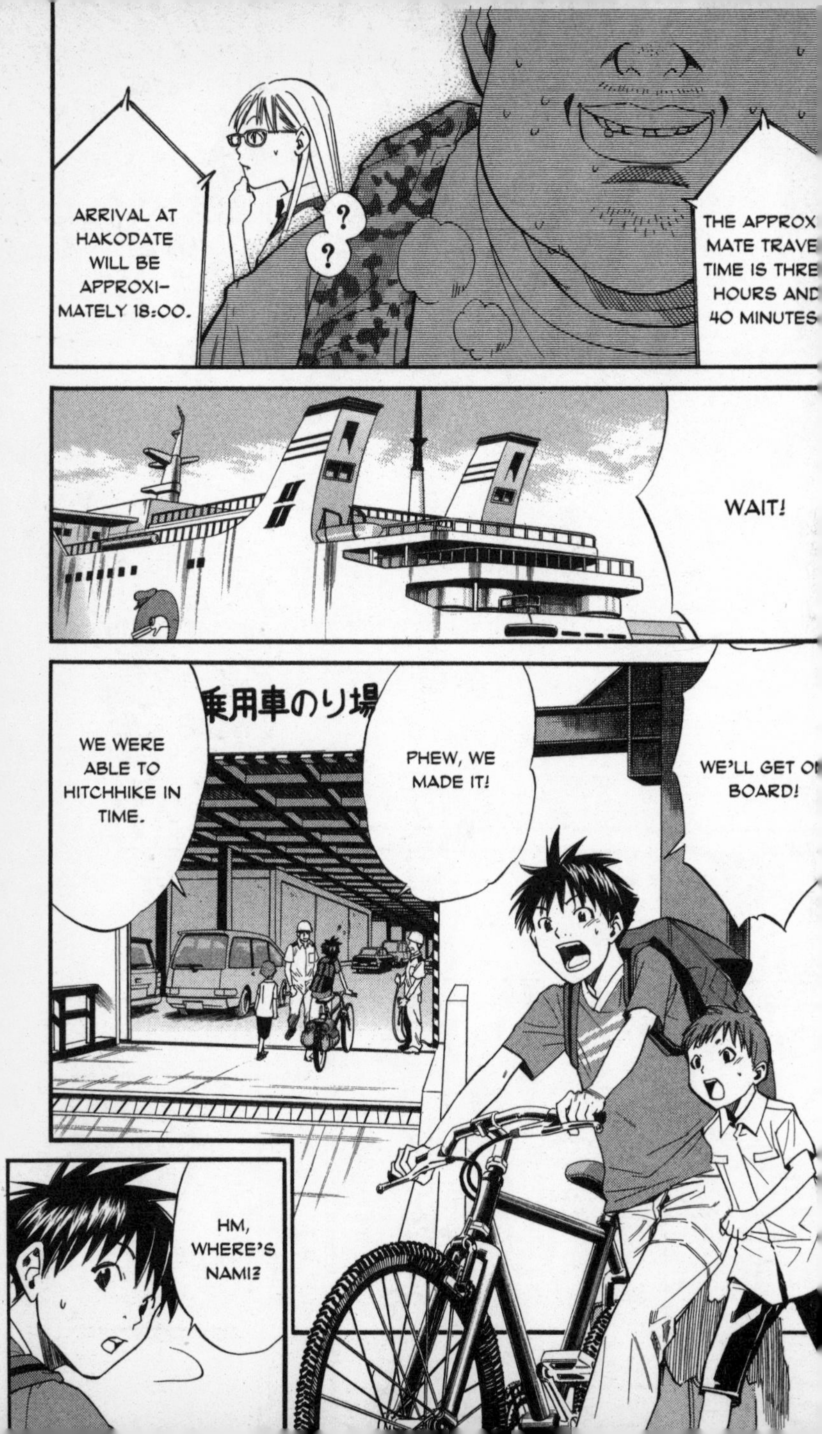
THE APPROX MATE TRAVE TIME IS THRE HOURS AND 40 MINUTES
?
?
ARRIVAL AT HAKODATE WILL BE APPROXI-MATELY 18:00.
WAIT!
WE'LL GET O BOARD!
PHEW, WE MADE IT!
乗用車のり場
WE WERE ABLE TO HITCHHIKE IN TIME.
HM, WHERE'S NAMI!?

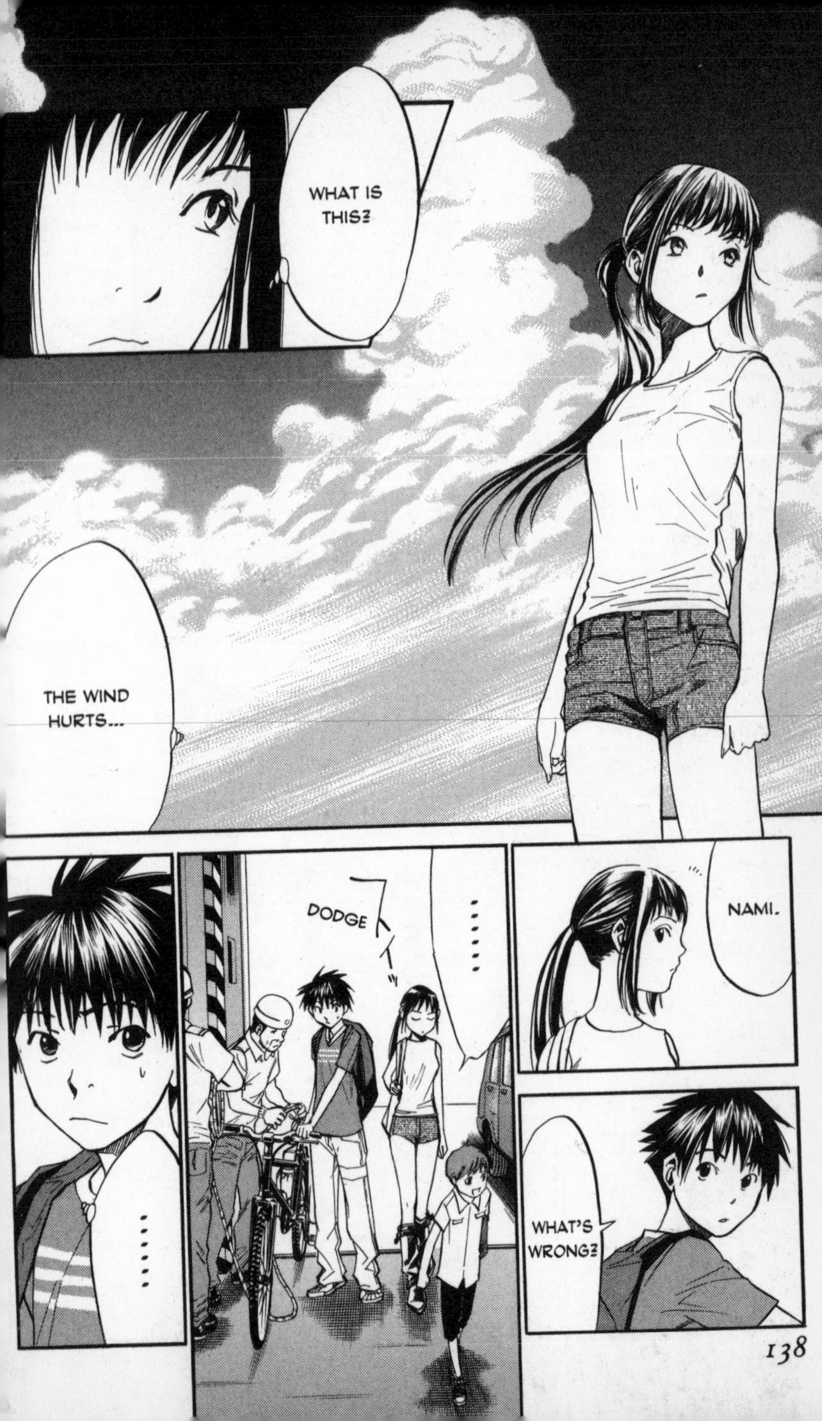
WHAT IS THIS?
THE WIND HURTS...
NAMI.
WHAT'S WRONG?
......
DODGE
......

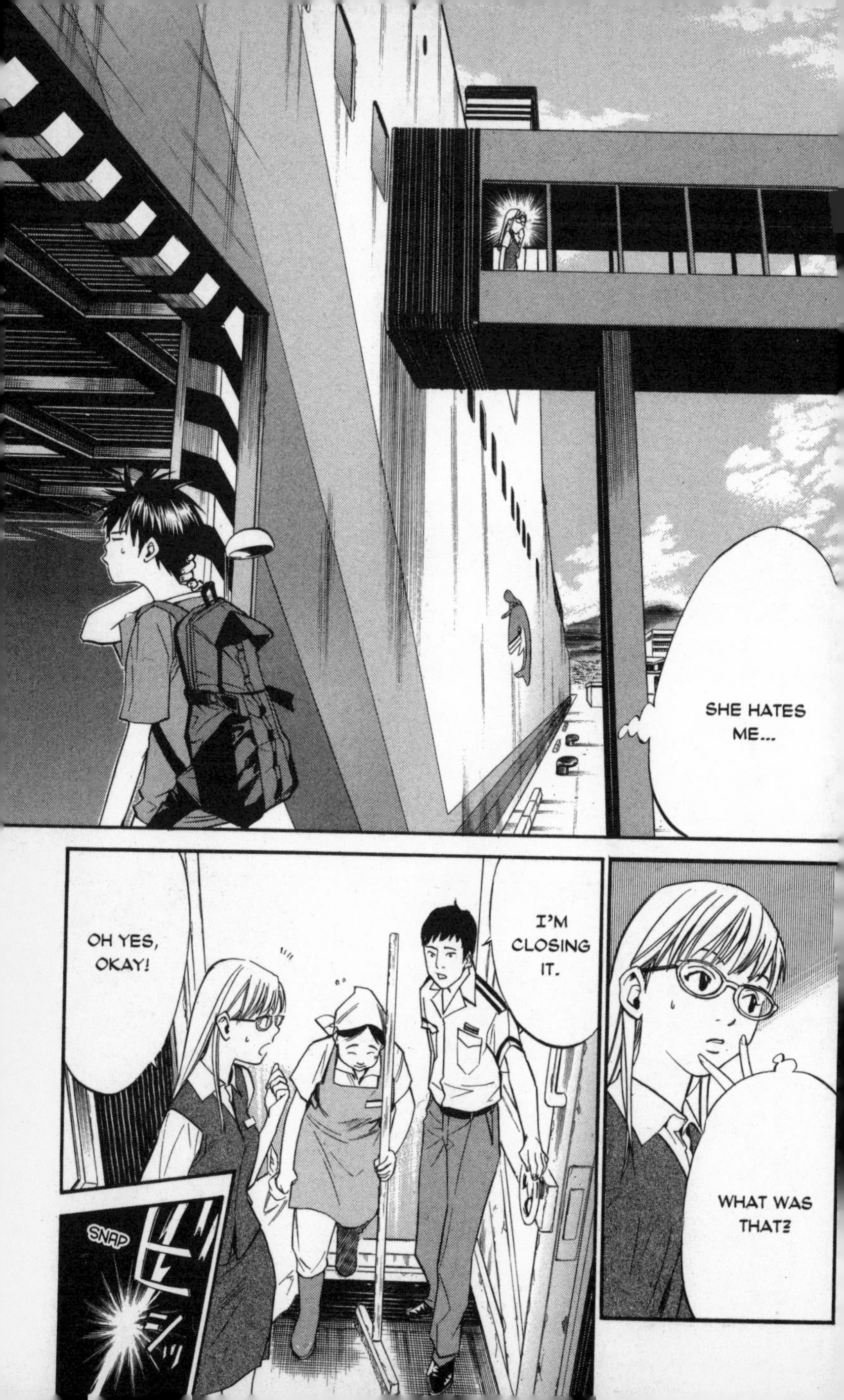
SHE HATES ME...
WHAT WAS THAT?
I'M CLOSING IT.
OH YES, OKAY!
SNAP

OUCH!
B-TAM

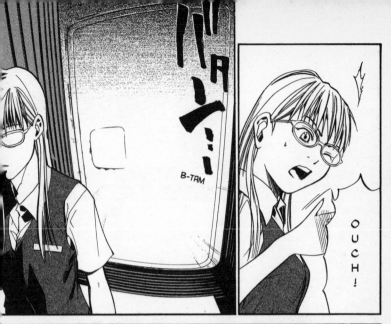

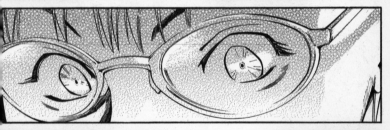

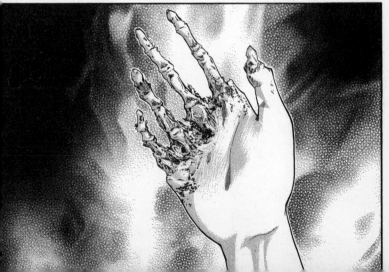

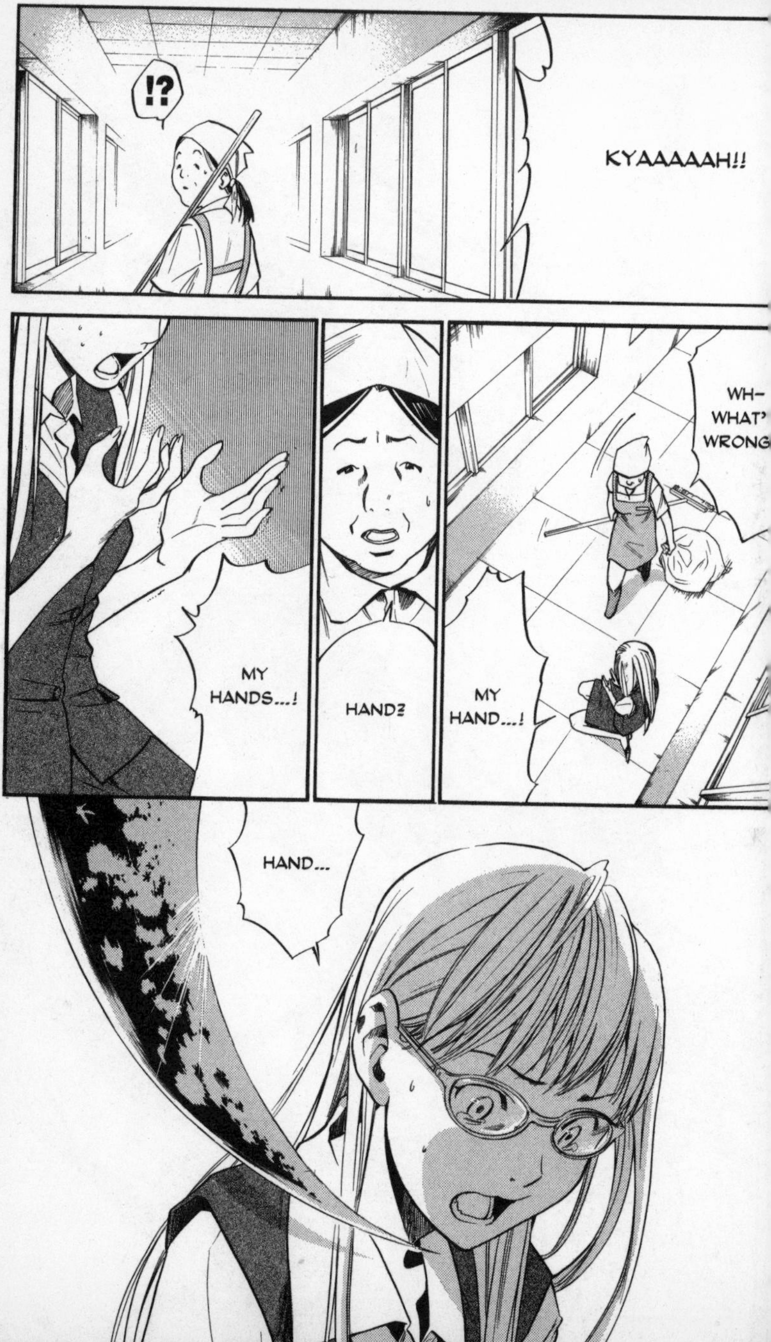
KYAAAAAH!!
!?
WH- WHAT' WRONG
MY HAND...!
HAND?
MY HANDS...!
HAND...

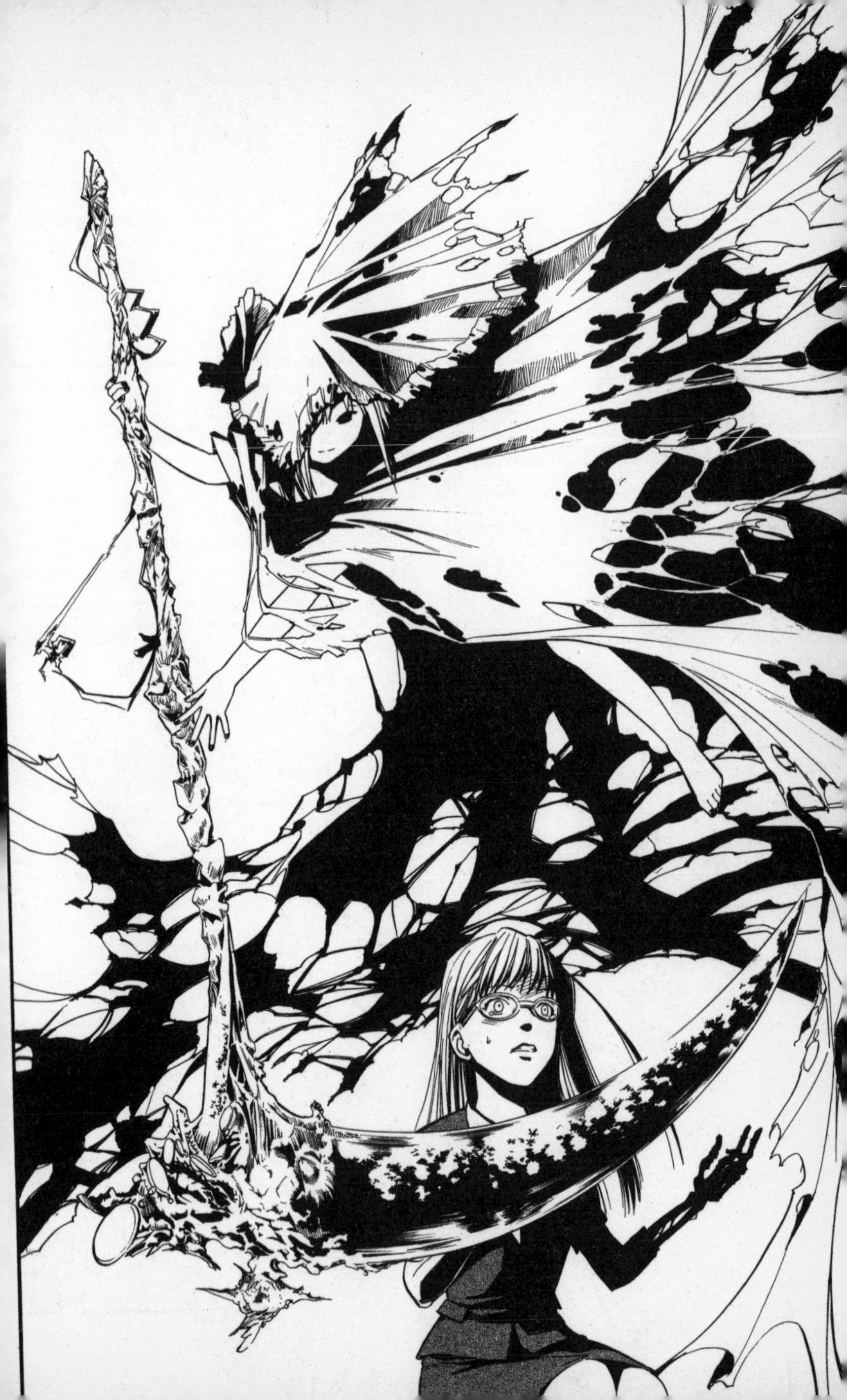

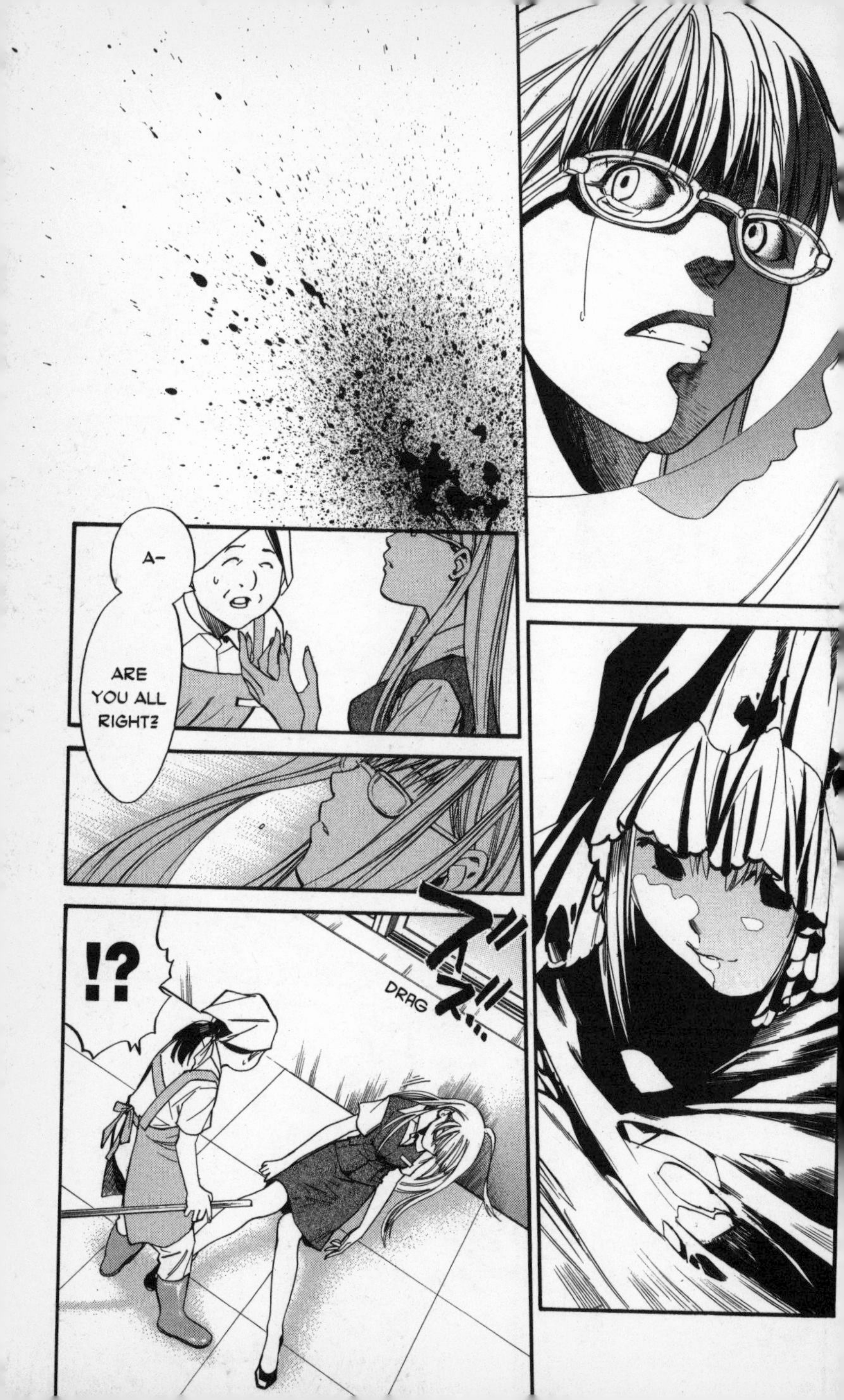
A-
ARE YOU ALL RIGHT?
DRAG
!?

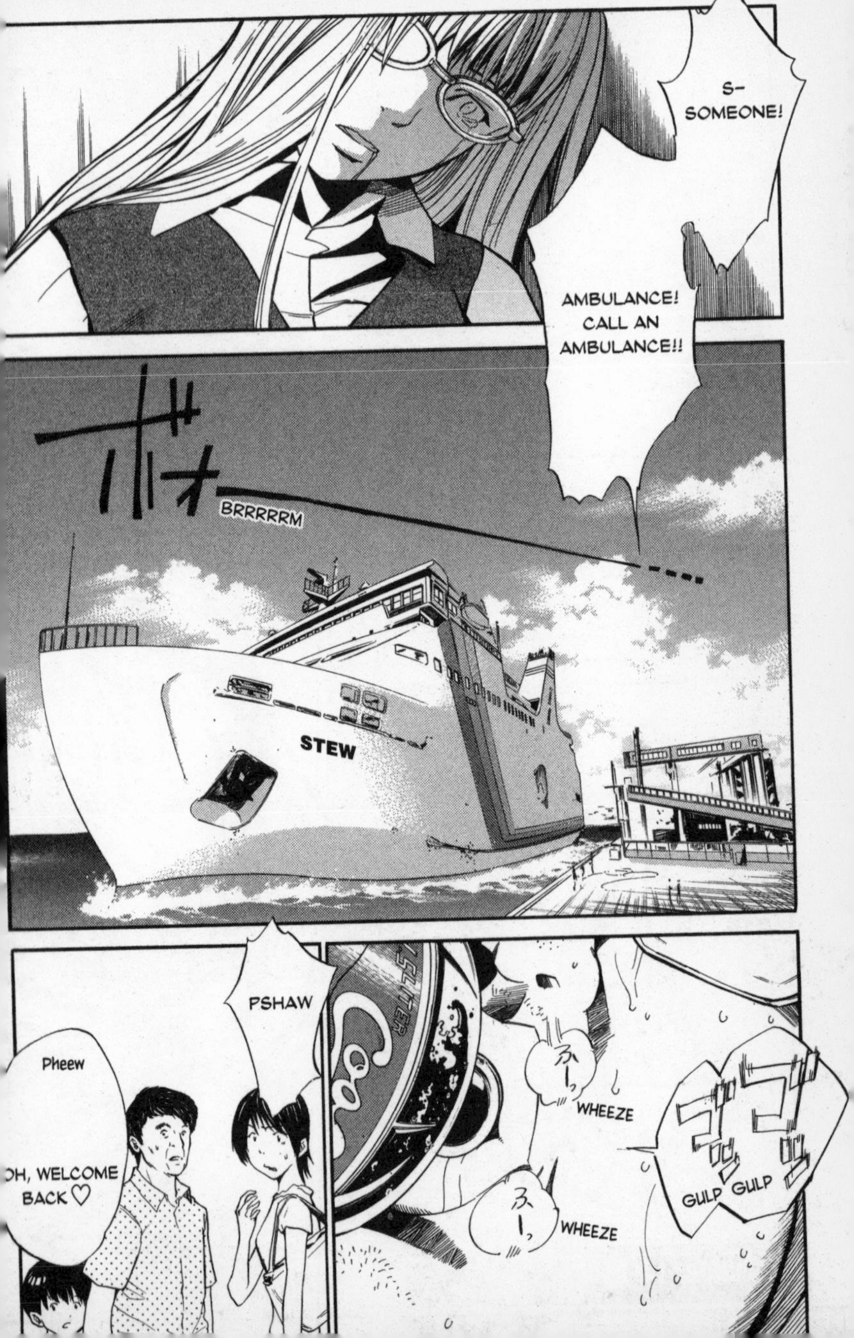
S-SOMEONE!
AMBULANCE! CALL AN AMBULANCE!!
ボォー
BRRRRRM
STEW
GULP GULP
WHEEZE
WHEEZE
PSHAW
Pheew
OH, WELCOME BACK ♡

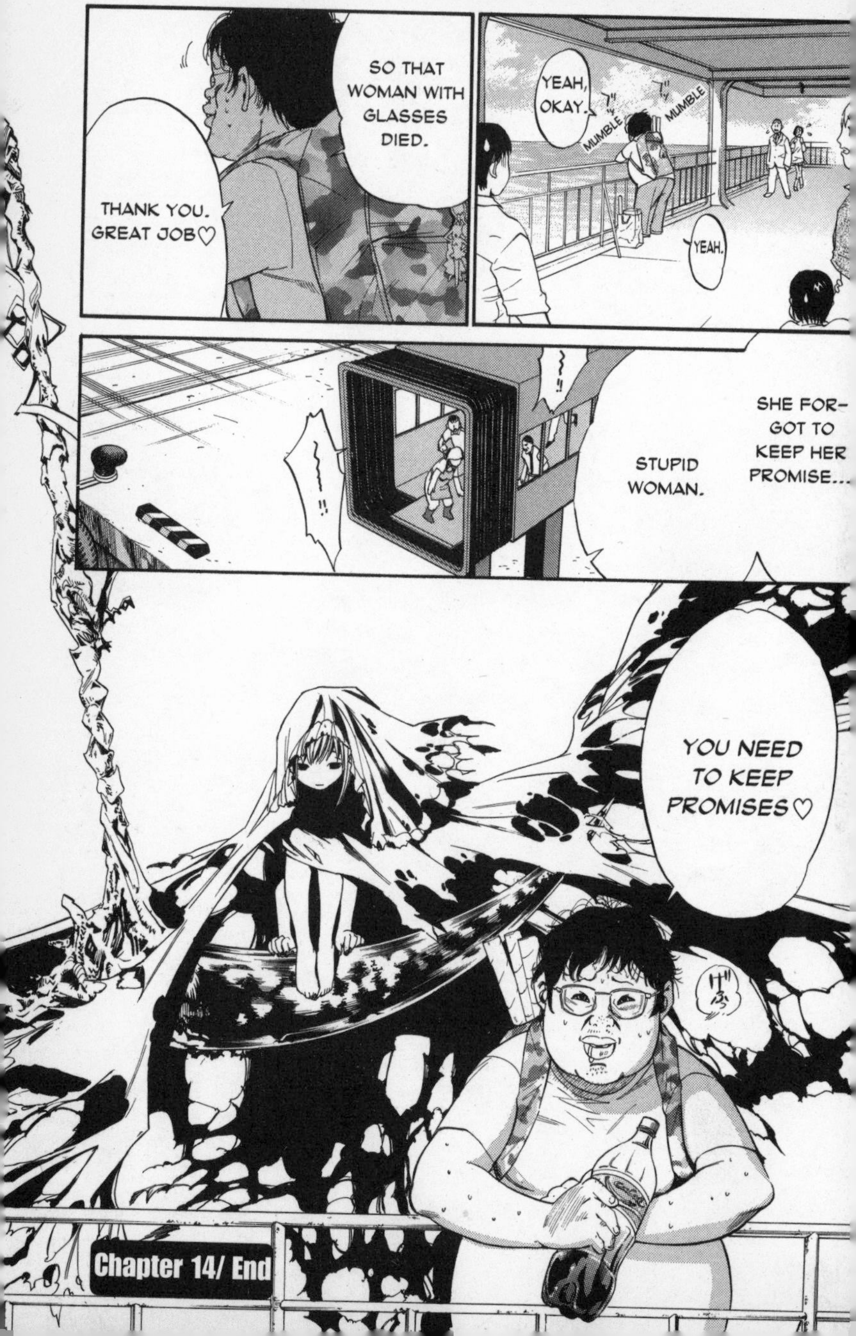
YEAH, OKAY.
MUMBLE
MUMBLE
YEAH.
SO THAT WOMAN WITH GLASSES DIED.
THANK YOU. GREAT JOB♡
SHE FOR-GOT TO KEEP HER PROMISE...
STUPID WOMAN.
YOU NEED TO KEEP PROMISES♡
Chapter 14/ End

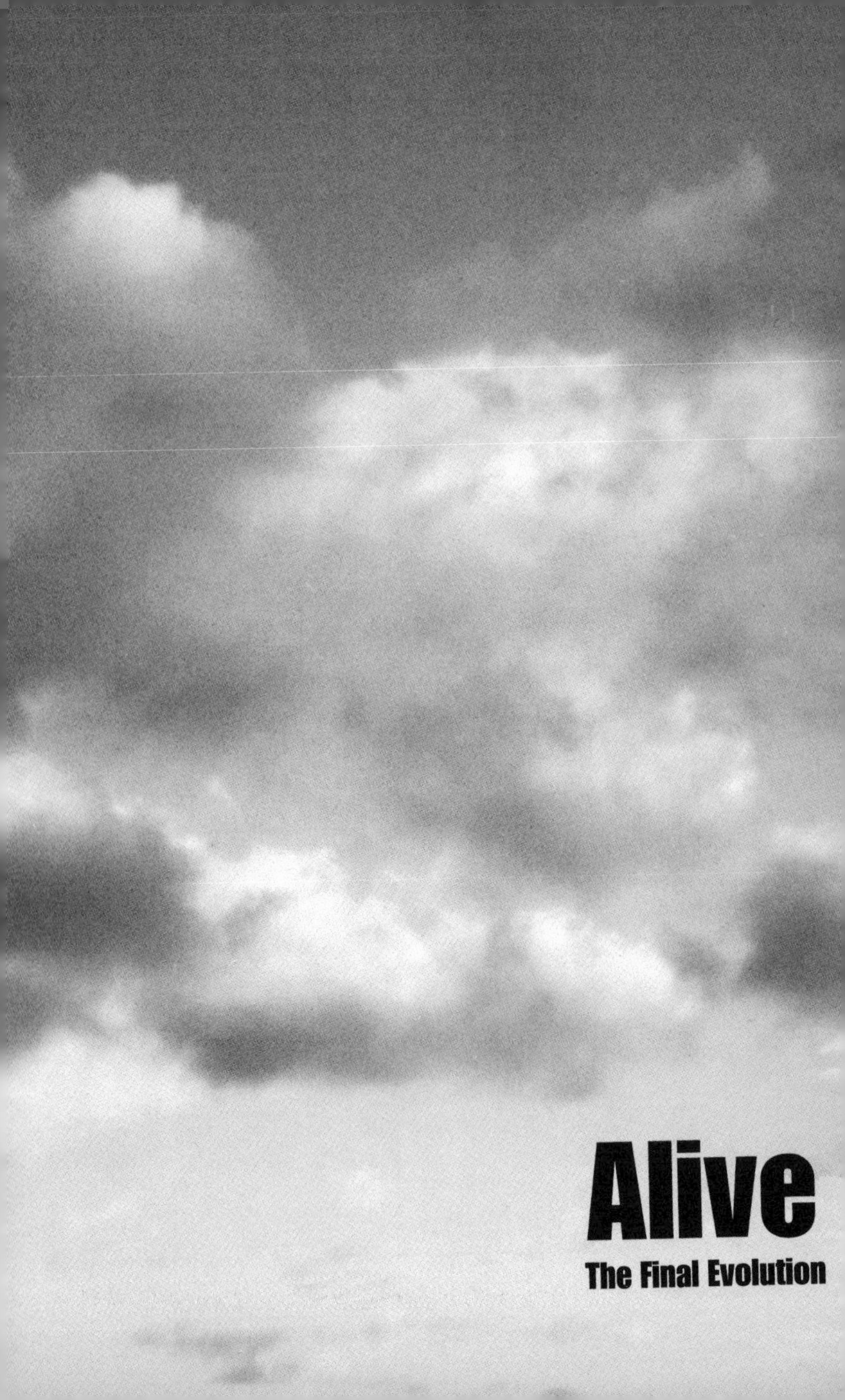

# Alive

## The Final Evolution

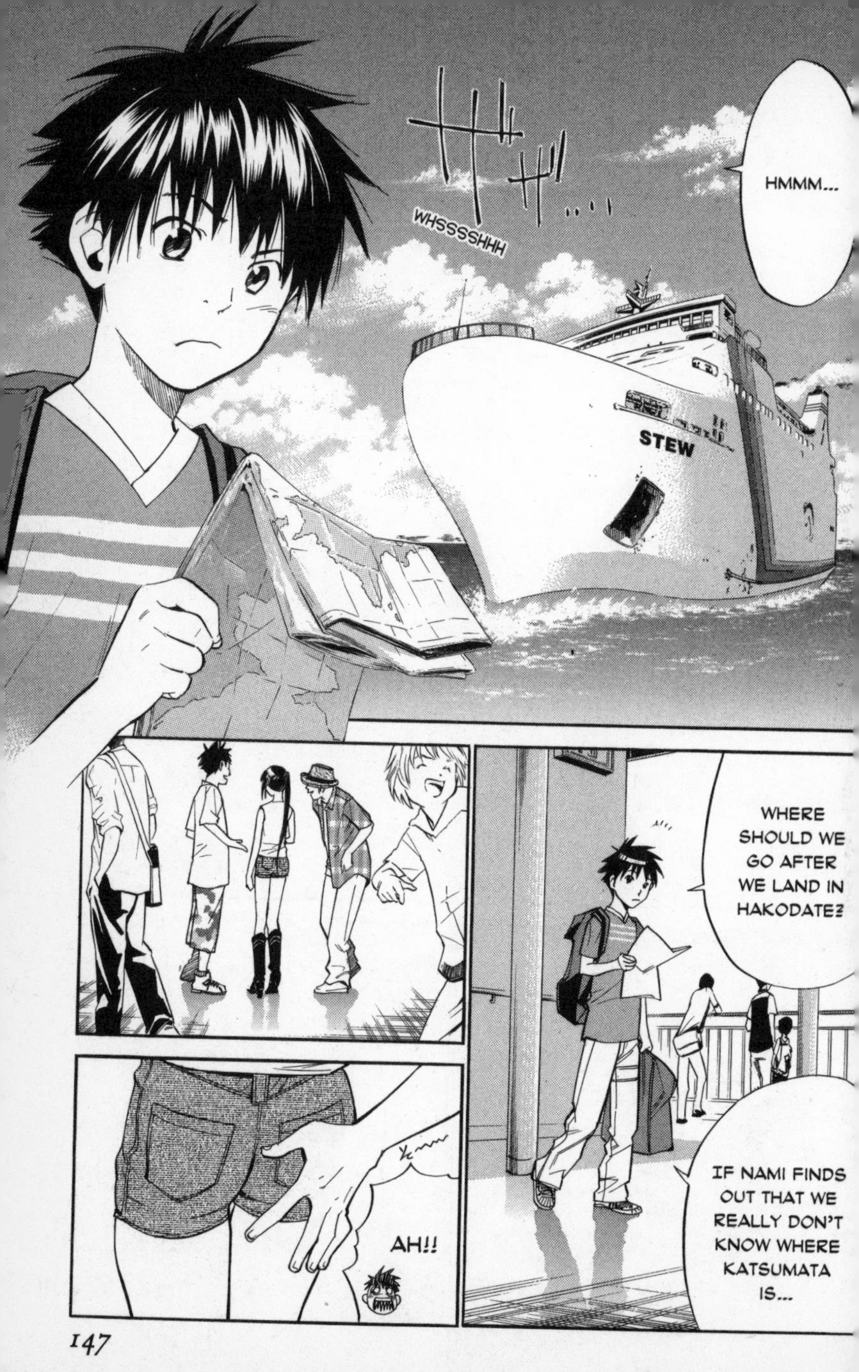
HMMM...
WHSSSSHHH
STEW
WHERE SHOULD WE GO AFTER WE LAND IN HAKODATE?
IF NAMI FINDS OUT THAT WE REALLY DON'T KNOW WHERE KATSUMATA IS...
AH!!

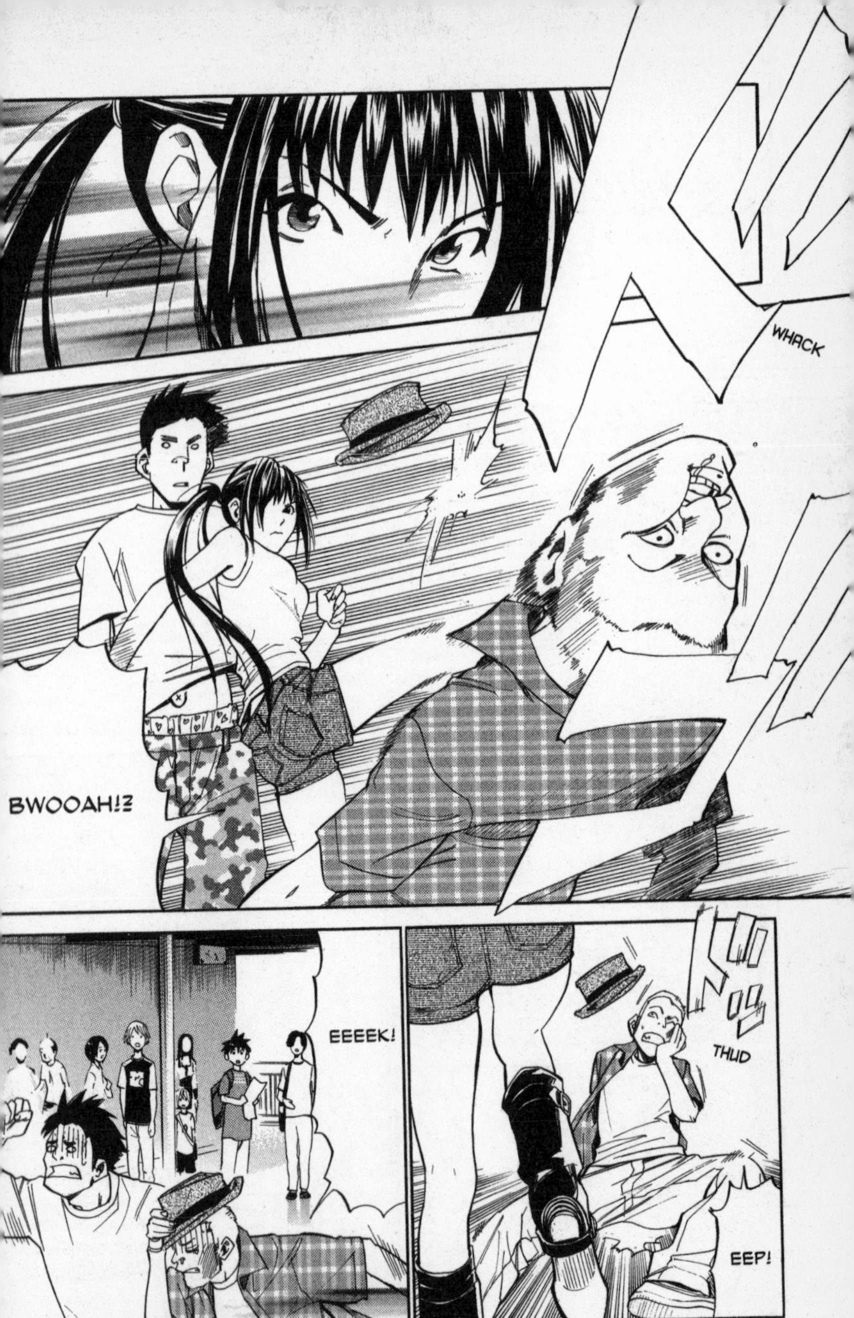
WHACK
BWOOAH!?
THUD
EEP!
EEEEK!

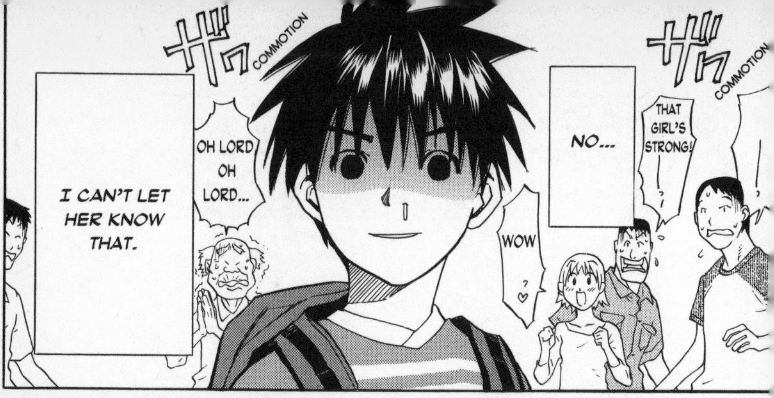
COMMOTION
THAT GIRL'S STRONG!
NO...
WOW
COMMOTION
OH LORD OH LORD...
I CAN'T LET HER KNOW THAT.

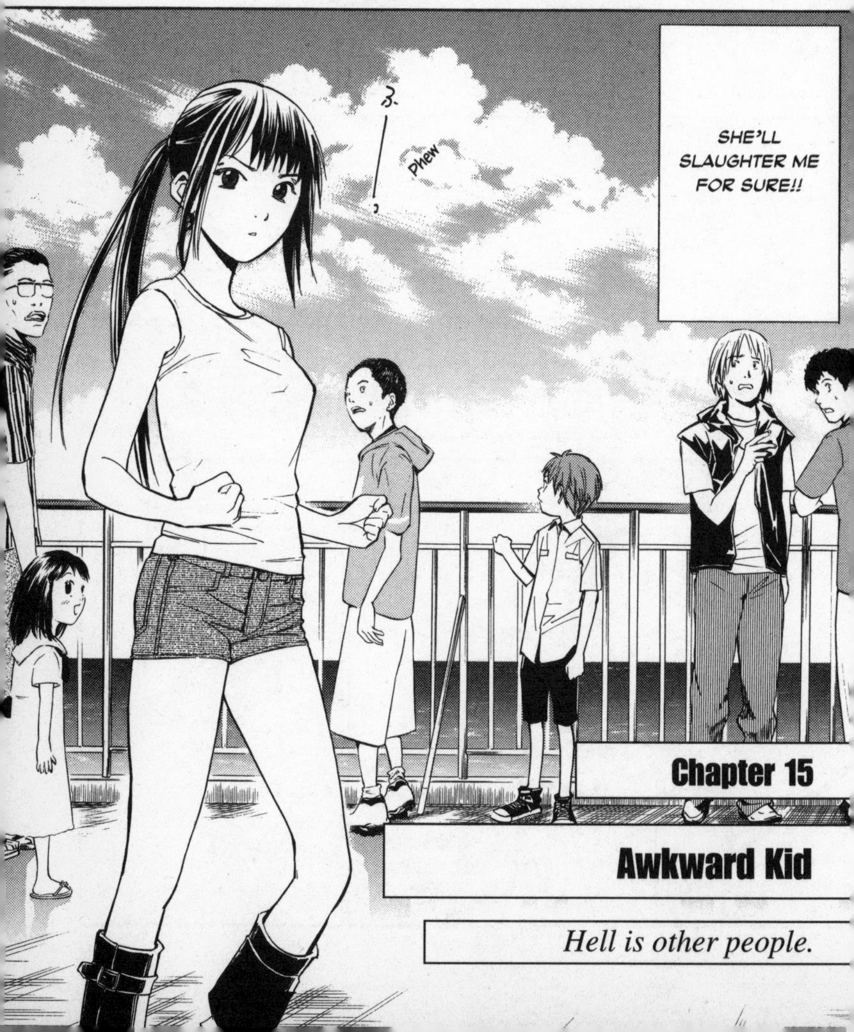
SHE'LL SLAUGHTER ME FOR SURE!!
Phew

# Chapter 15

## Awkward Kid

*Hell is other people.*

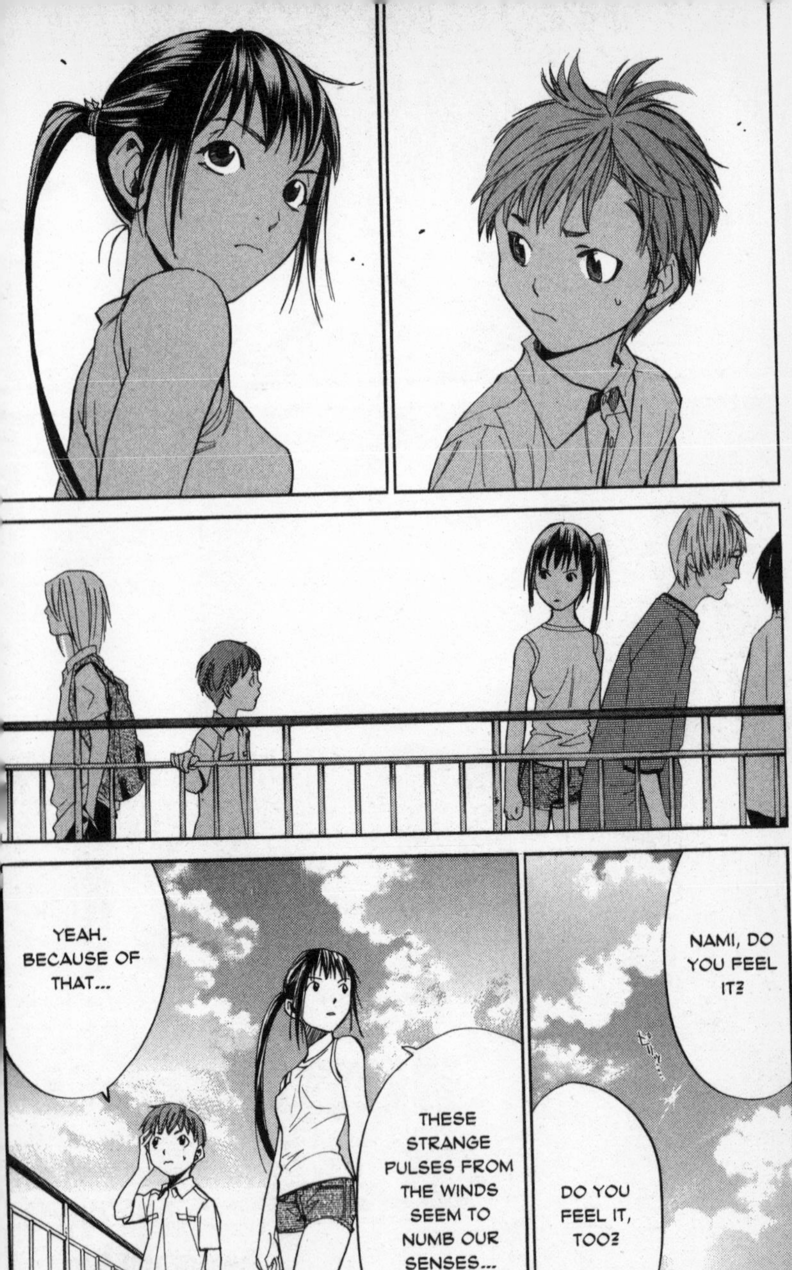
NAMI, DO YOU FEEL IT?
DO YOU FEEL IT, TOO?
YEAH. BECAUSE OF THAT...
THESE STRANGE PULSES FROM THE WINDS SEEM TO NUMB OUR SENSES...

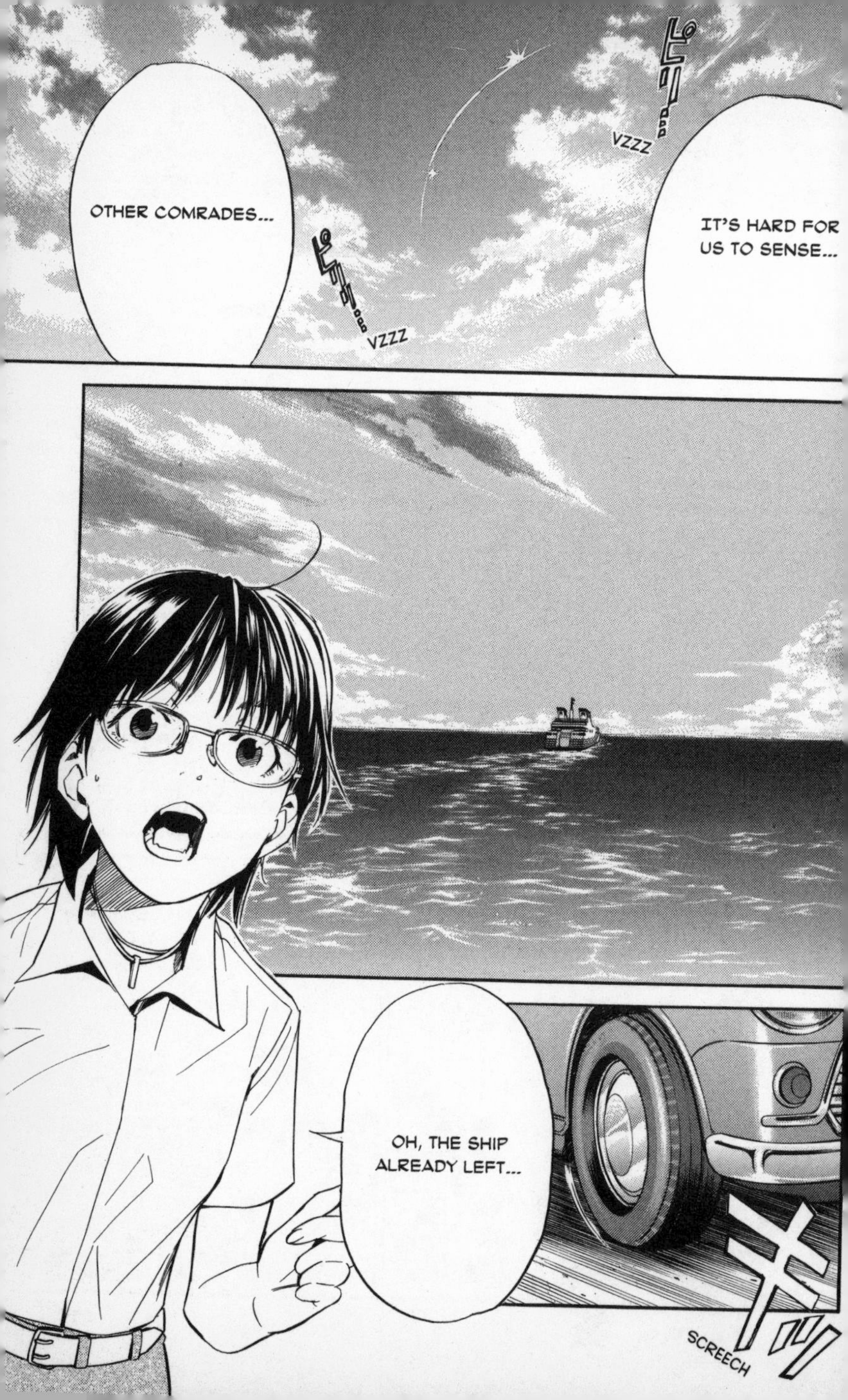
IT'S HARD FOR US TO SENSE...
VZZZ
OTHER COMRADES...
VZZZ
SCREECH
OH, THE SHIP ALREADY LEFT...

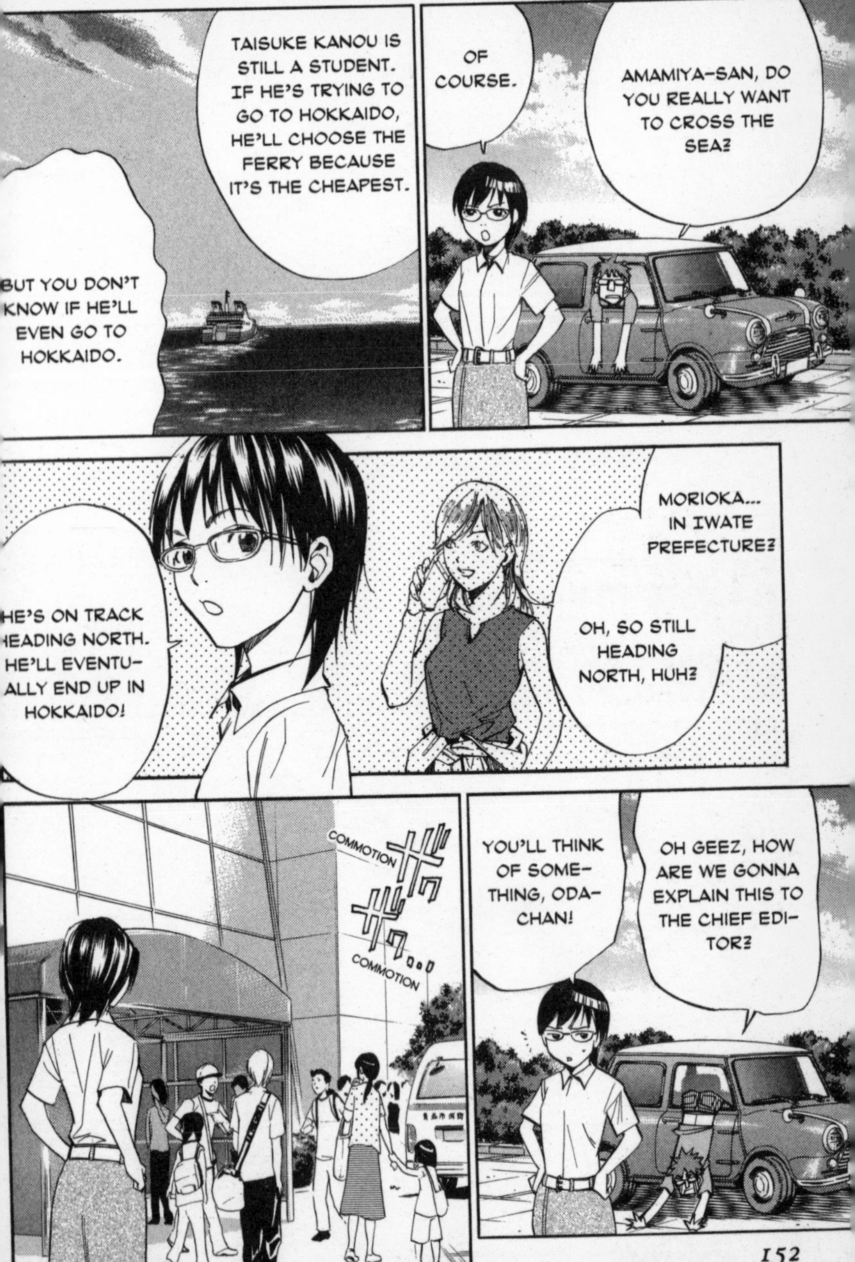
AMAMIYA-SAN, DO YOU REALLY WANT TO CROSS THE SEA?
OF COURSE.
TAISUKE KANOU IS STILL A STUDENT. IF HE'S TRYING TO GO TO HOKKAIDO, HE'LL CHOOSE THE FERRY BECAUSE IT'S THE CHEAPEST.
BUT YOU DON'T KNOW IF HE'LL EVEN GO TO HOKKAIDO.
MORIOKA... IN IWATE PREFECTURE?
OH, SO STILL HEADING NORTH, HUH?
HE'S ON TRACK HEADING NORTH. HE'LL EVENTUALLY END UP IN HOKKAIDO!
OH GEEZ, HOW ARE WE GONNA EXPLAIN THIS TO THE CHIEF EDITOR?
YOU'LL THINK OF SOMETHING, ODA-CHAN!
COMMOTION
COMMOTION

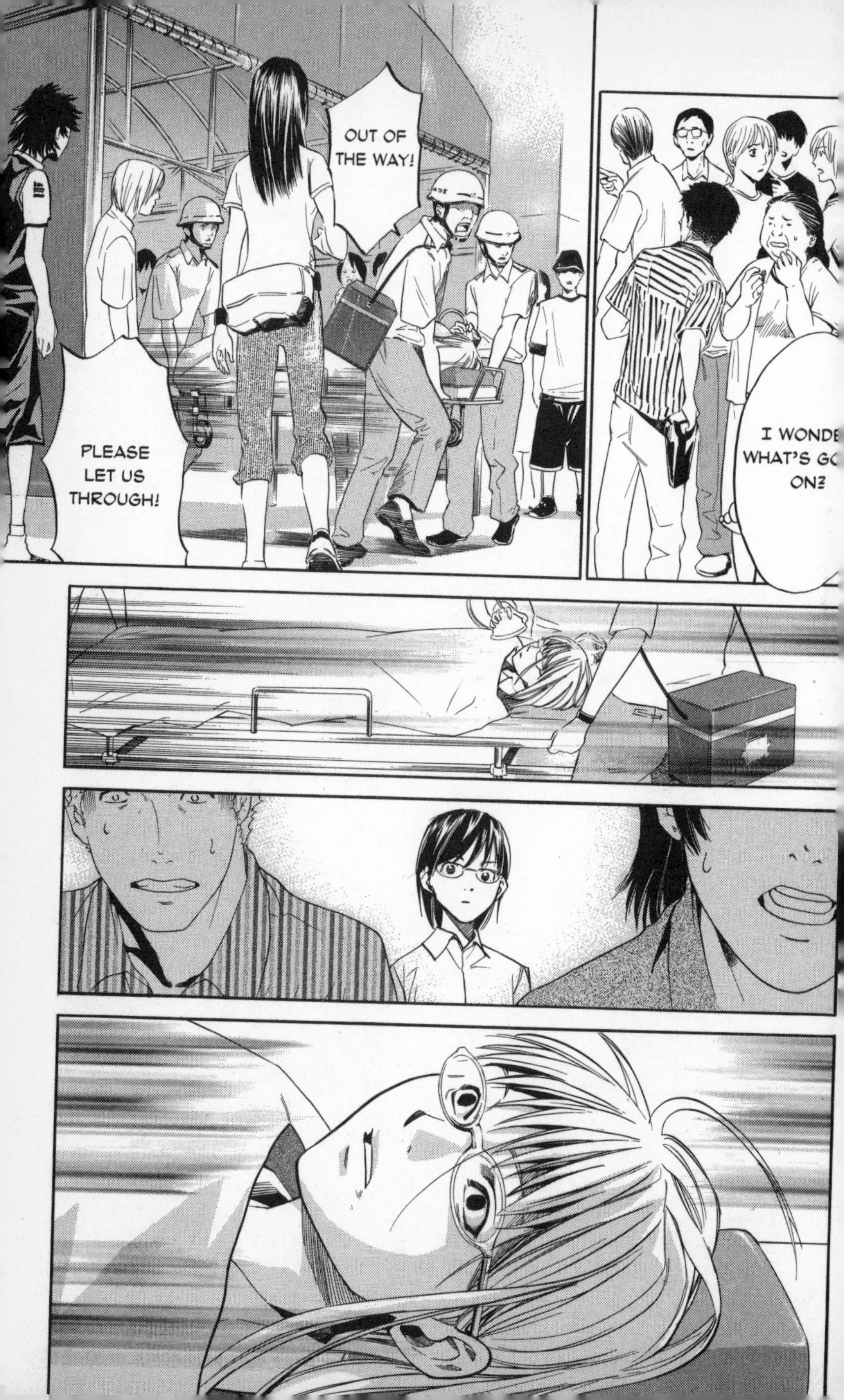
I WONDE WHAT'S GO ON?
OUT OF THE WAY!
PLEASE LET US THROUGH!

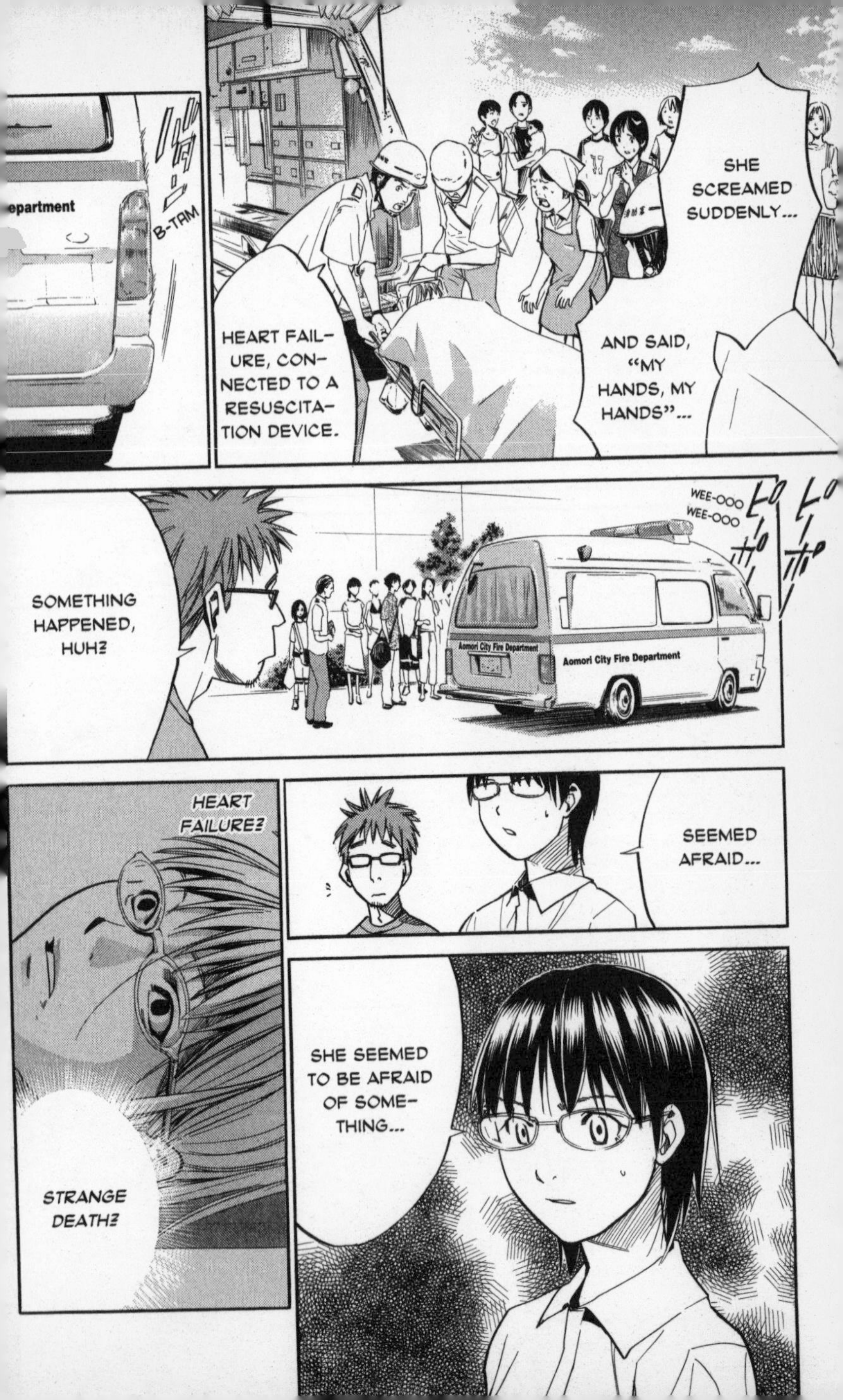
SHE SCREAMED SUDDENLY...
AND SAID, "MY HANDS, MY HANDS"...
HEART FAIL-URE, CON-NECTED TO A RESUSCITA-TION DEVICE.
B-TAM
epartment
WEE-OOO
WEE-OOO
Aomori City Fire Department
Aomori City Fire Department
SOMETHING HAPPENED, HUH?
SEEMED AFRAID...
SHE SEEMED TO BE AFRAID OF SOME-THING...
HEART FAILURE?
STRANGE DEATH?

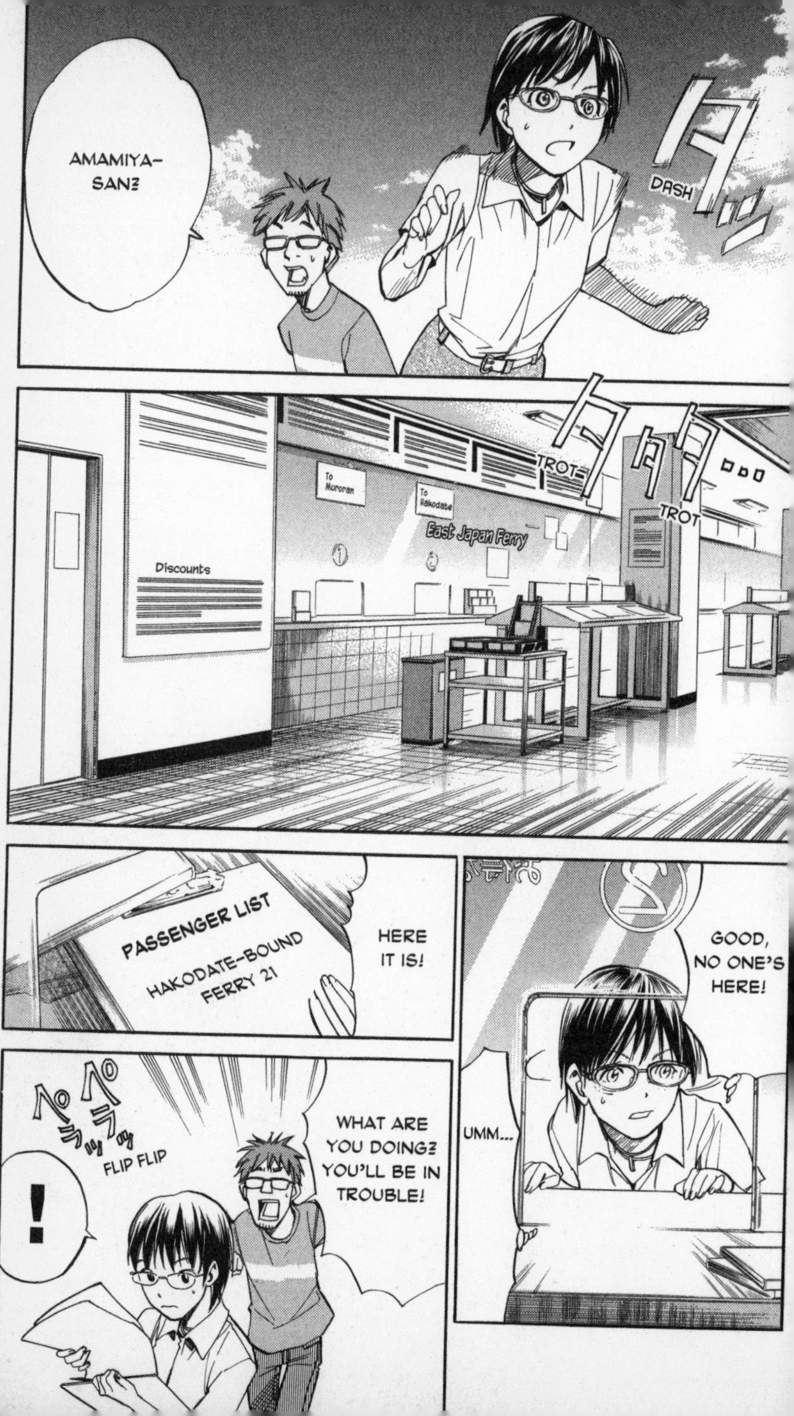
DASH
AMAMIYA-SAN?
TROT
TROT
To Muroran
To Hakodate
East Japan Ferry
Discounts
GOOD, NO ONE'S HERE!
UMM...
HERE IT IS!
PASSENGER LIST
HAKODATE-BOUND FERRY 21
WHAT ARE YOU DOING? YOU'LL BE IN TROUBLE!
FLIP FLIP
!

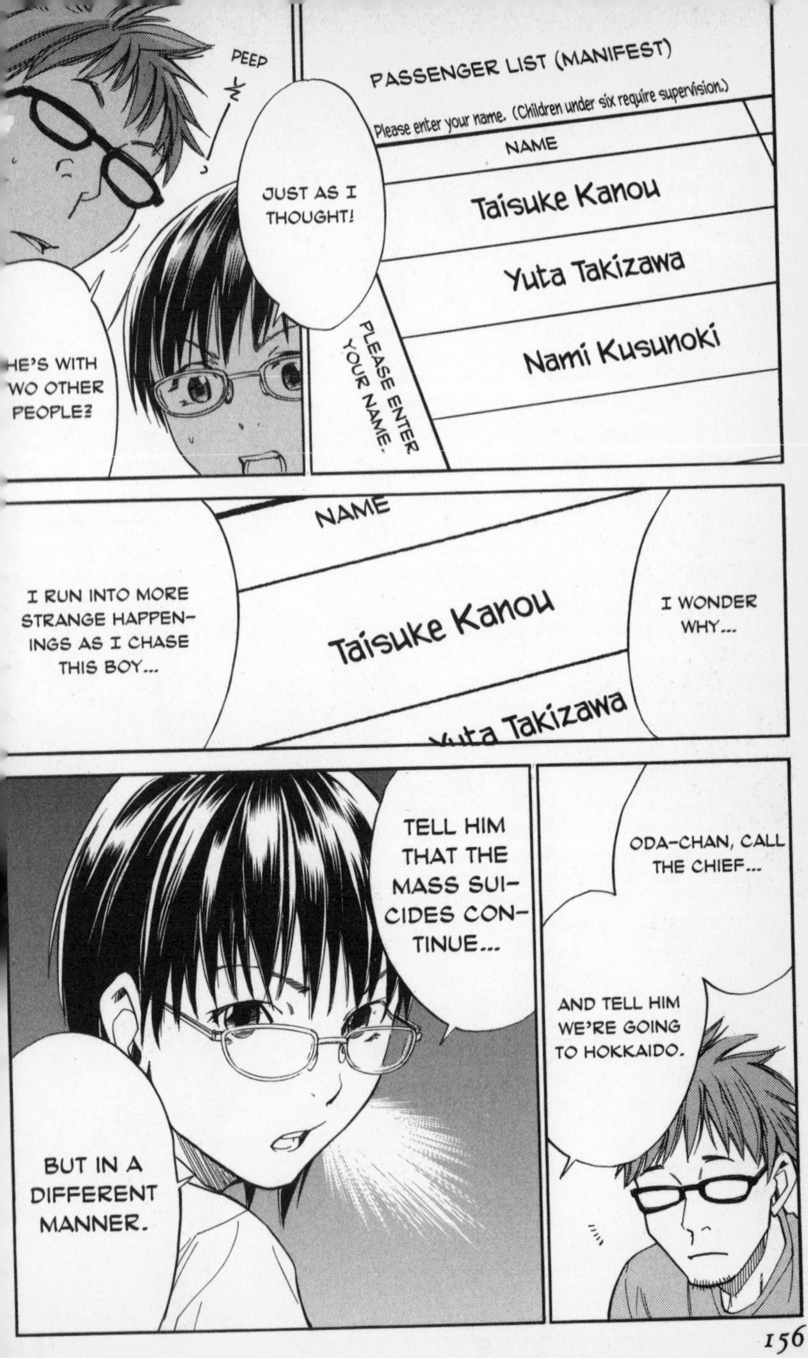
PASSENGER LIST (MANIFEST)
Please enter your name. (Children under six require supervision.)
NAME
Taisuke Kanou
Yuta Takizawa
Nami Kusunoki
JUST AS I THOUGHT!
PLEASE ENTER YOUR NAME.
PEEP
HE'S WITH TWO OTHER PEOPLE?
I WONDER WHY...
NAME
Taisuke Kanou
Yuta Takizawa
I RUN INTO MORE STRANGE HAPPEN-INGS AS I CHASE THIS BOY...
ODA-CHAN, CALL THE CHIEF...
AND TELL HIM WE'RE GOING TO HOKKAIDO.
TELL HIM THAT THE MASS SUI-CIDES CON-TINUE...
BUT IN A DIFFERENT MANNER.

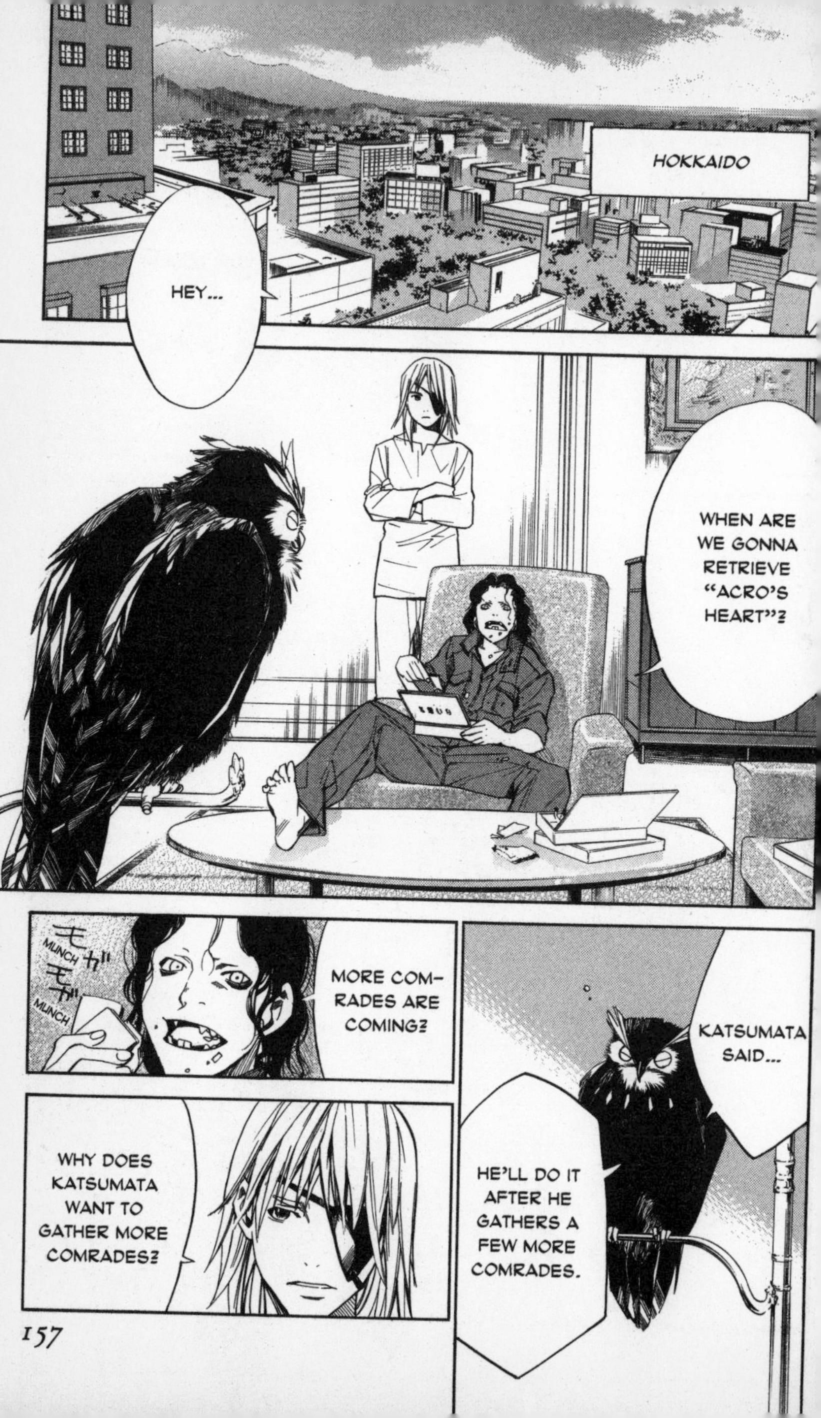
HOKKAIDO
HEY...
WHEN ARE WE GONNA RETRIEVE "ACRO'S HEART"?
KATSUMATA SAID...
HE'LL DO IT AFTER HE GATHERS A FEW MORE COMRADES.
MUNCH
MUNCH
MORE COM-RADES ARE COMING?
WHY DOES KATSUMATA WANT TO GATHER MORE COMRADES?

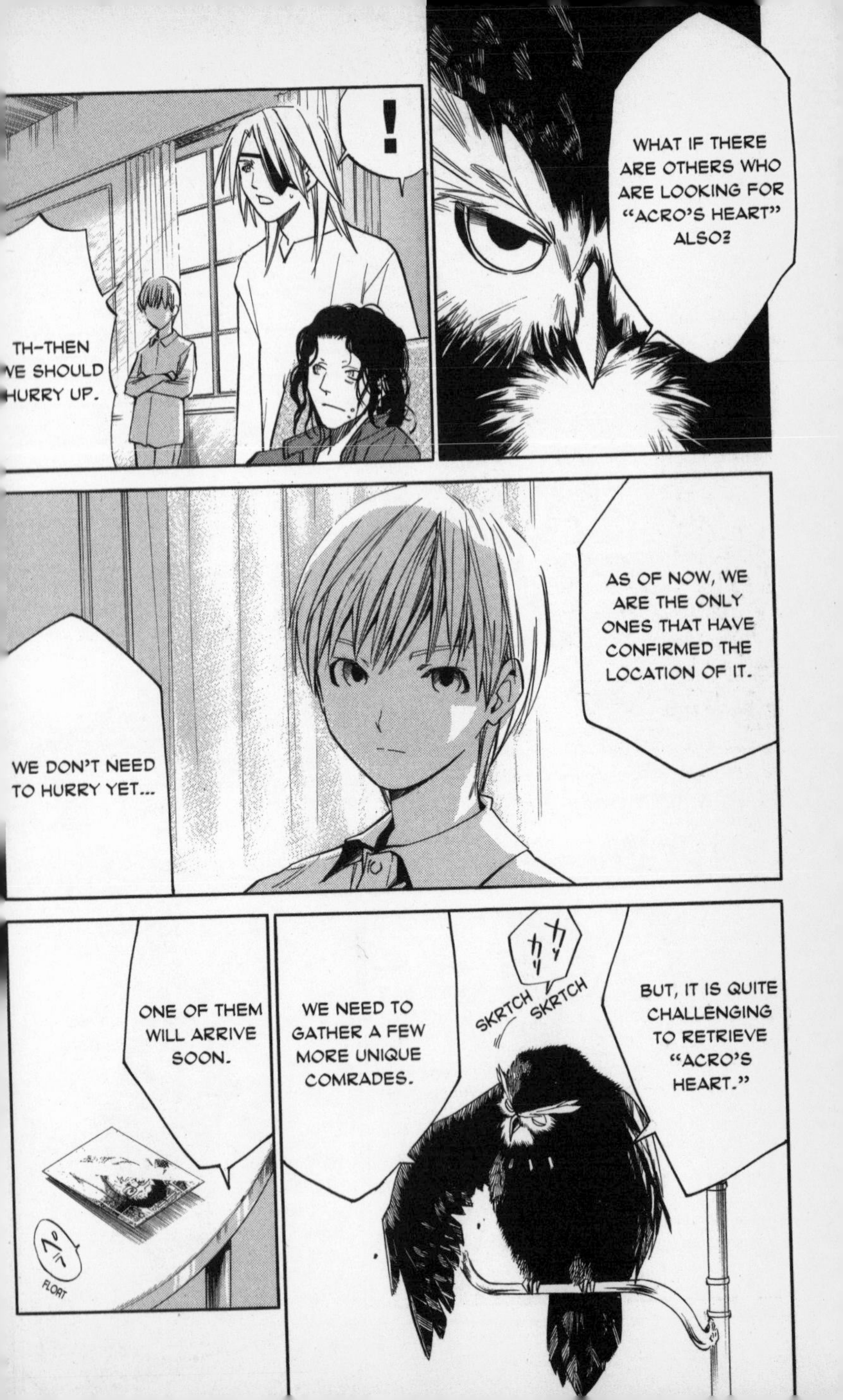
WHAT IF THERE ARE OTHERS WHO ARE LOOKING FOR "ACRO'S HEART" ALSO?
!
TH-THEN VE SHOULD HURRY UP.
AS OF NOW, WE ARE THE ONLY ONES THAT HAVE CONFIRMED THE LOCATION OF IT.
WE DON'T NEED TO HURRY YET...
BUT, IT IS QUITE CHALLENGING TO RETRIEVE "ACRO'S HEART."
SKRTCH SKRTCH
WE NEED TO GATHER A FEW MORE UNIQUE COMRADES.
ONE OF THEM WILL ARRIVE SOON.
FLOAT

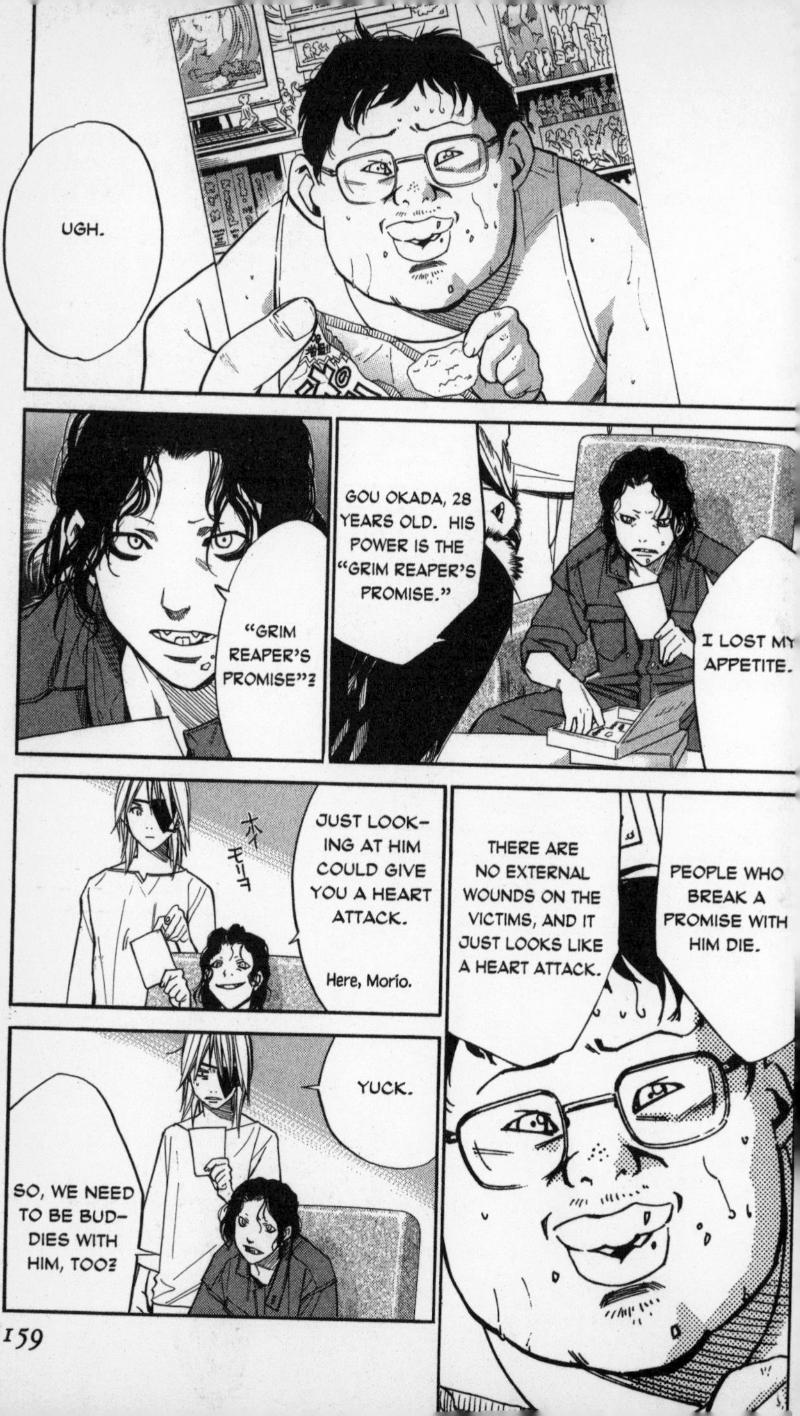

UGH.
I LOST MY APPETITE.
GOU OKADA, 28 YEARS OLD. HIS POWER IS THE "GRIM REAPER'S PROMISE."
"GRIM REAPER'S PROMISE"?
PEOPLE WHO BREAK A PROMISE WITH HIM DIE.
THERE ARE NO EXTERNAL WOUNDS ON THE VICTIMS, AND IT JUST LOOKS LIKE A HEART ATTACK.
JUST LOOK-ING AT HIM COULD GIVE YOU A HEART ATTACK.
Here, Morio.
YUCK.
SO, WE NEED TO BE BUD-DIES WITH HIM, TOO?

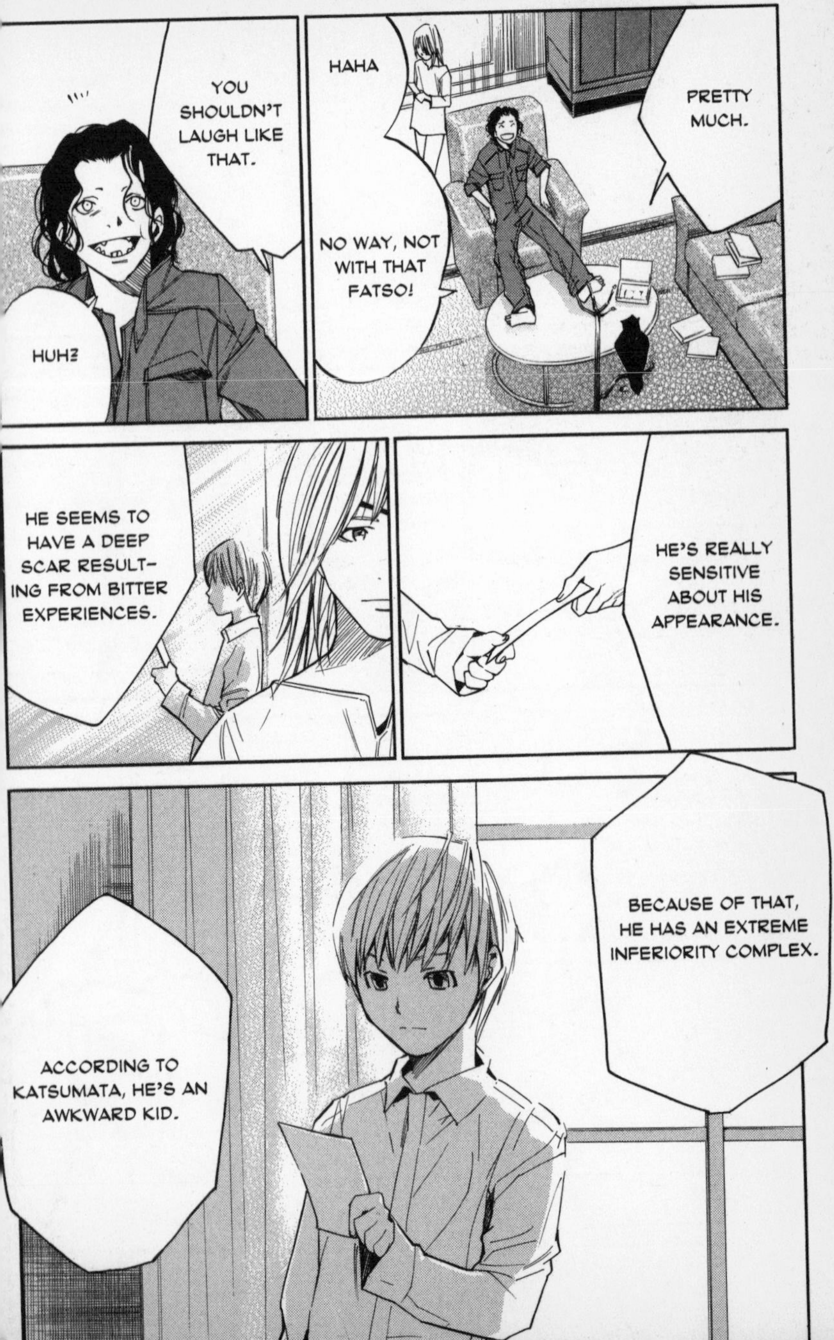
PRETTY MUCH.
HAHA
NO WAY, NOT WITH THAT FATSO!
YOU SHOULDN'T LAUGH LIKE THAT.
HUH?
HE'S REALLY SENSITIVE ABOUT HIS APPEARANCE.
HE SEEMS TO HAVE A DEEP SCAR RESULT-ING FROM BITTER EXPERIENCES.
BECAUSE OF THAT, HE HAS AN EXTREME INFERIORITY COMPLEX.
ACCORDING TO KATSUMATA, HE'S AN AWKWARD KID.

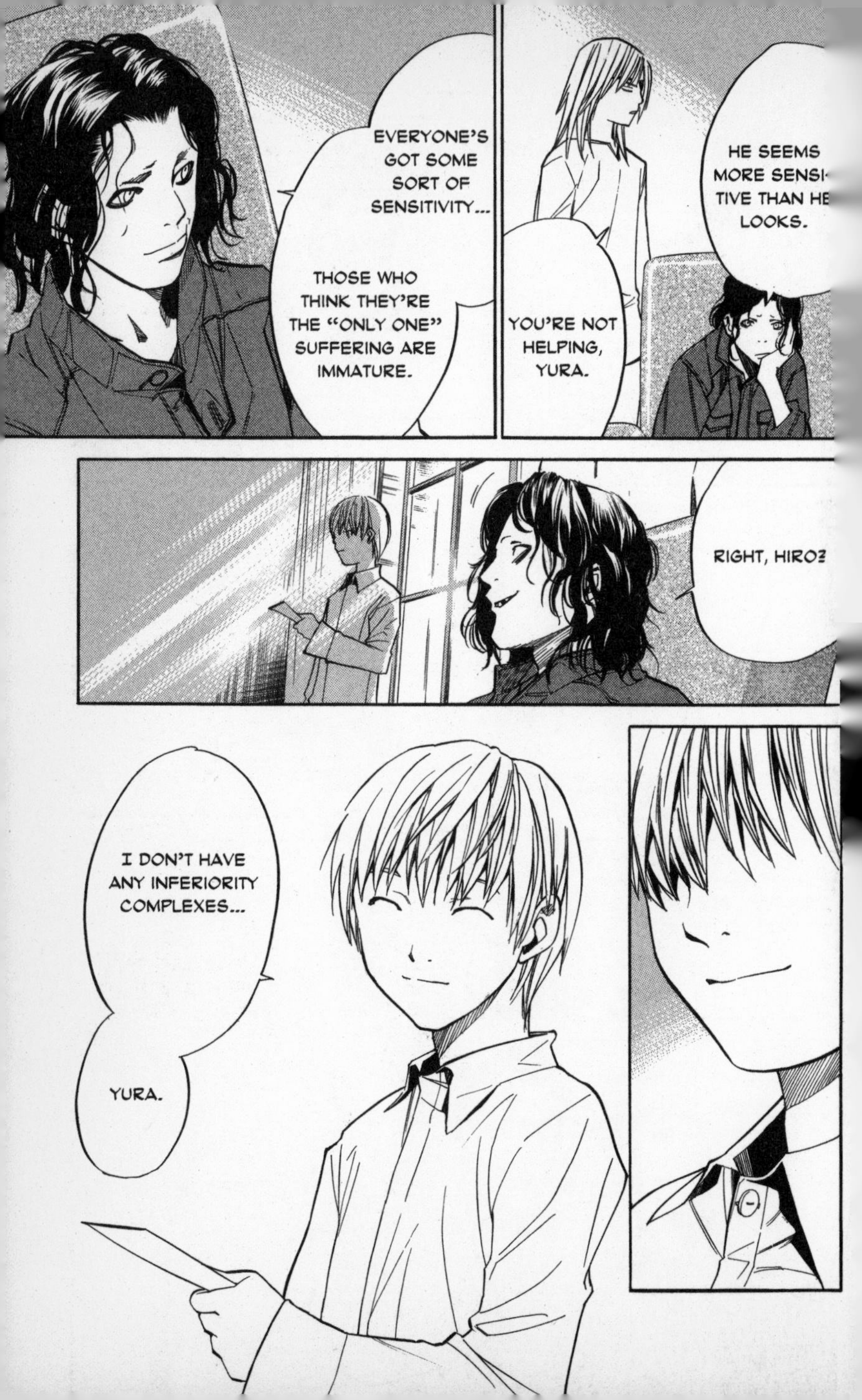
HE SEEMS MORE SENSI- TIVE THAN HE LOOKS.
YOU'RE NOT HELPING, YURA.
EVERYONE'S GOT SOME SORT OF SENSITIVITY...
THOSE WHO THINK THEY'RE THE "ONLY ONE" SUFFERING ARE IMMATURE.
RIGHT, HIRO?
I DON'T HAVE ANY INFERIORITY COMPLEXES...
YURA.

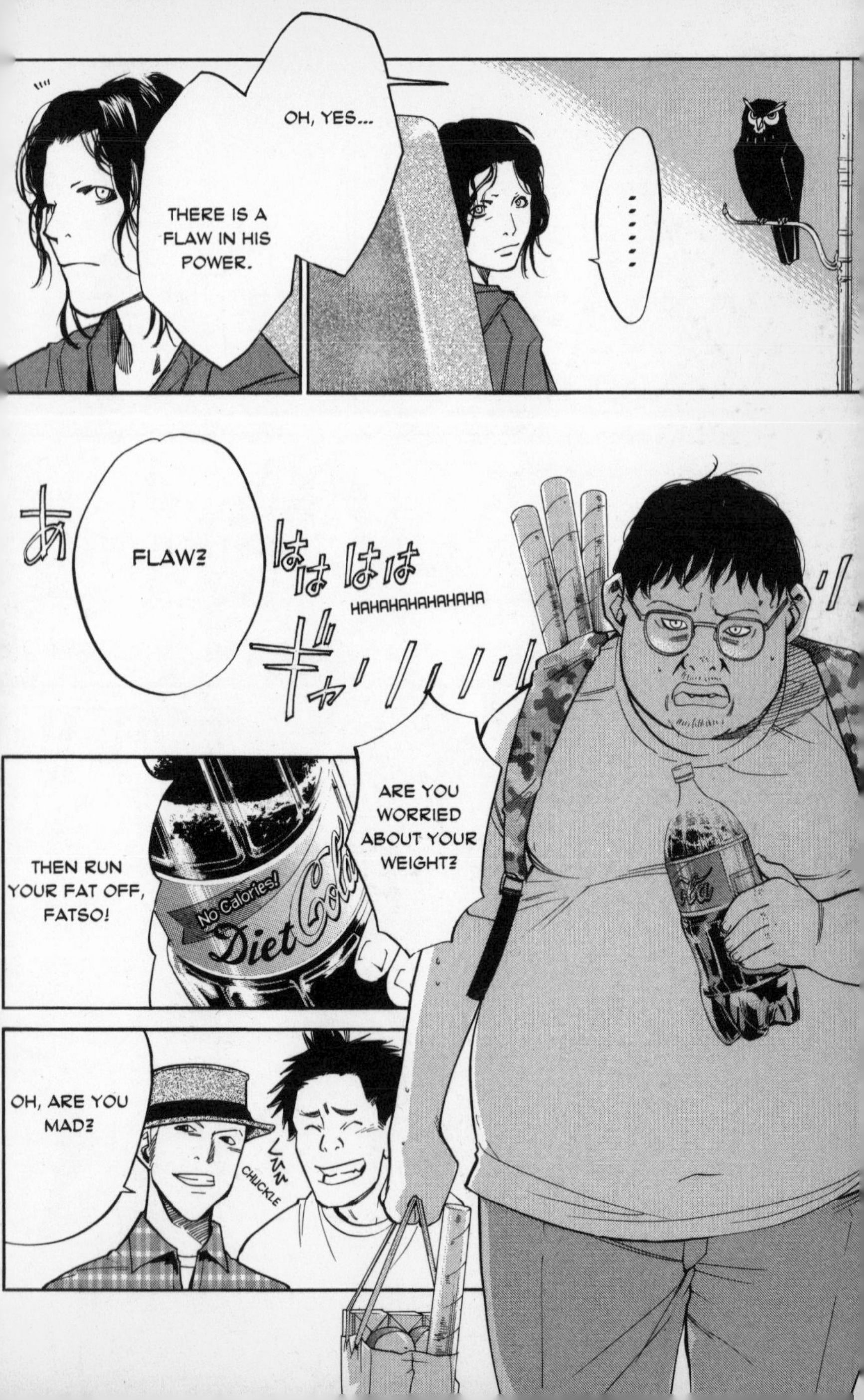
......
OH, YES...
THERE IS A FLAW IN HIS POWER.
FLAW?
あはははは
HAHAHAHAHAHAHA
ギャハハハ
ARE YOU WORRIED ABOUT YOUR WEIGHT?
THEN RUN YOUR FAT OFF, FATSO!
No Calories!
Diet Cola
OH, ARE YOU MAD?
CHUCKLE

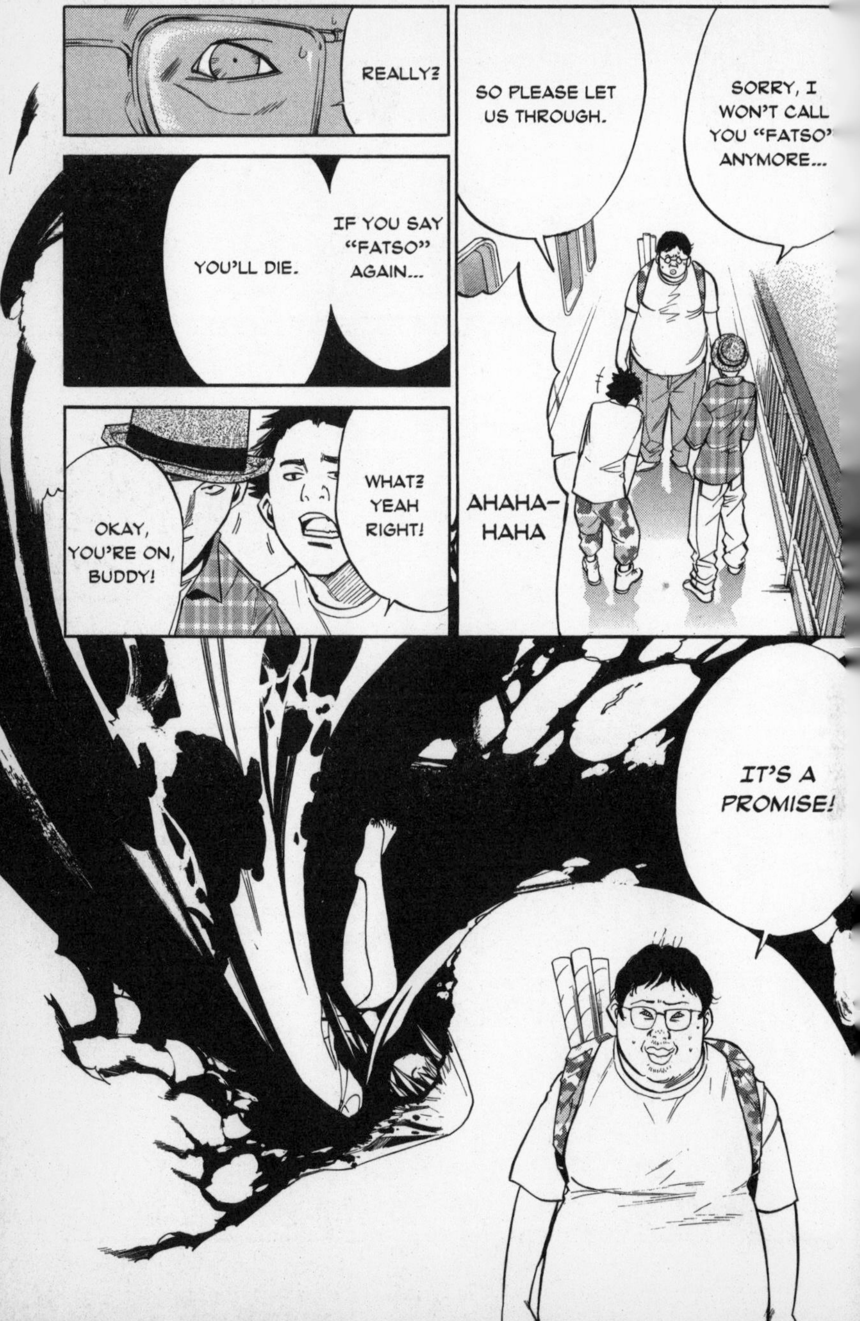
SORRY, I WON'T CALL YOU "FATSO" ANYMORE...
SO PLEASE LET US THROUGH.
AHAHA-HAHA
REALLY?
IF YOU SAY "FATSO" AGAIN...
YOU'LL DIE.
WHAT? YEAH RIGHT!
OKAY, YOU'RE ON, BUDDY!
IT'S A PROMISE!

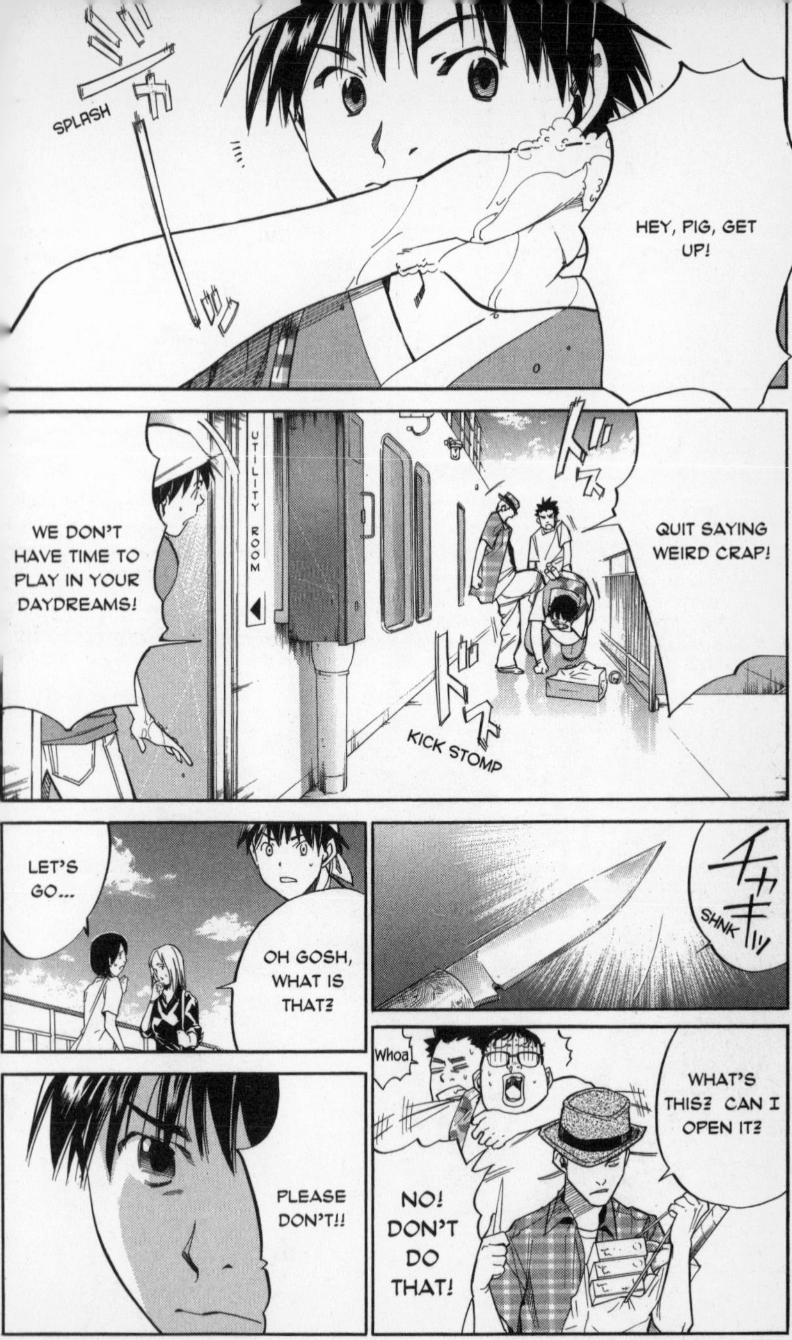
HEY, PIG, GET UP!
SPLASH
QUIT SAYING WEIRD CRAP!
KICK STOMP
UTILITY ROOM
WE DON'T HAVE TIME TO PLAY IN YOUR DAYDREAMS!
SHNK
LET'S GO...
OH GOSH, WHAT IS THAT?
WHAT'S THIS? CAN I OPEN IT?
Whoa
NO! DON'T DO THAT!
PLEASE DON'T!!

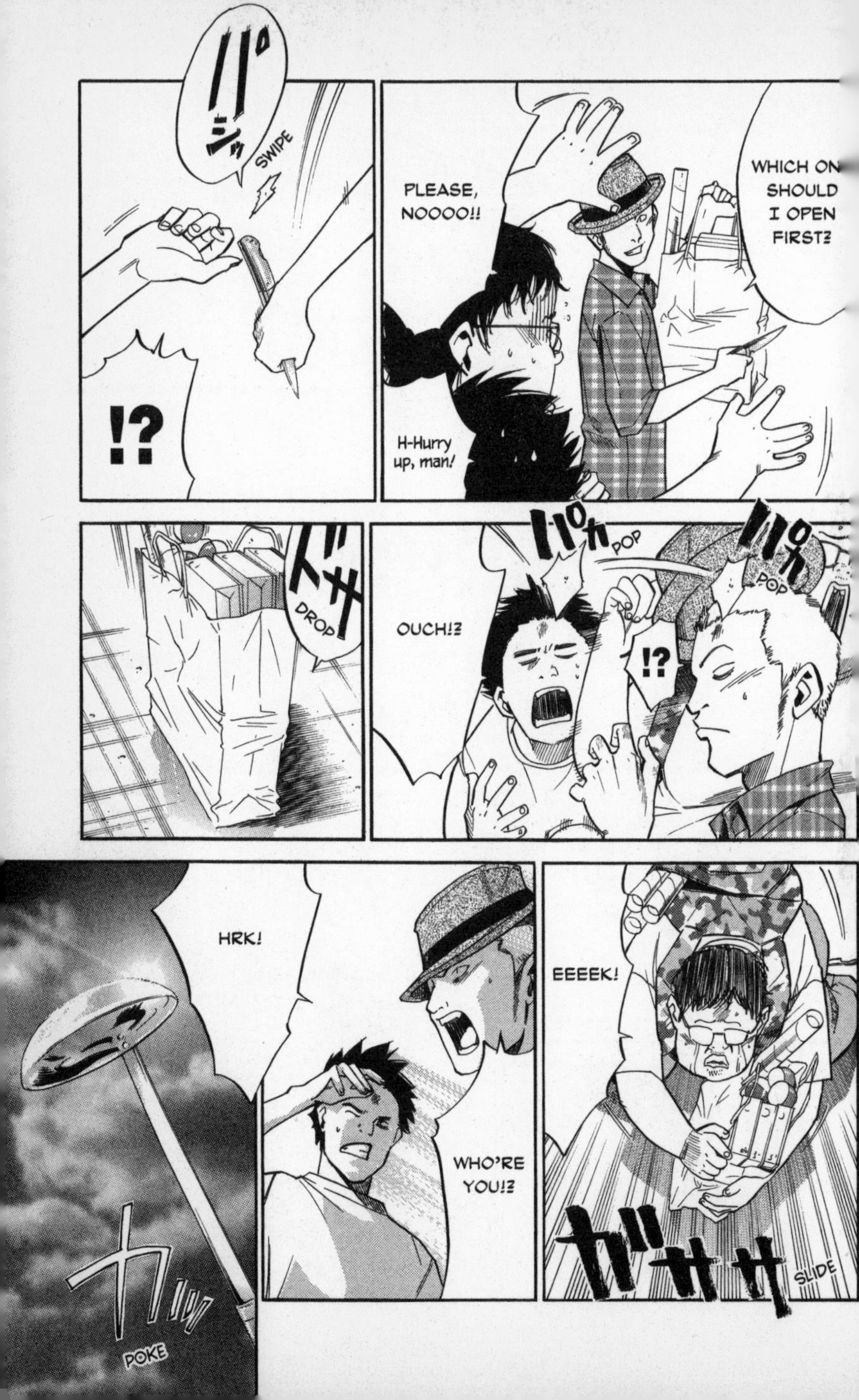
WHICH ON
SHOULD
I OPEN
FIRST?
PLEASE,
NOOOO!!
H-Hurry
up, man!
SWIPE
!?
POP
POP
OUCH!?
!?
DROP
EEEEK!
SLIDE
HRK!
WHO'RE
YOU!?
POKE

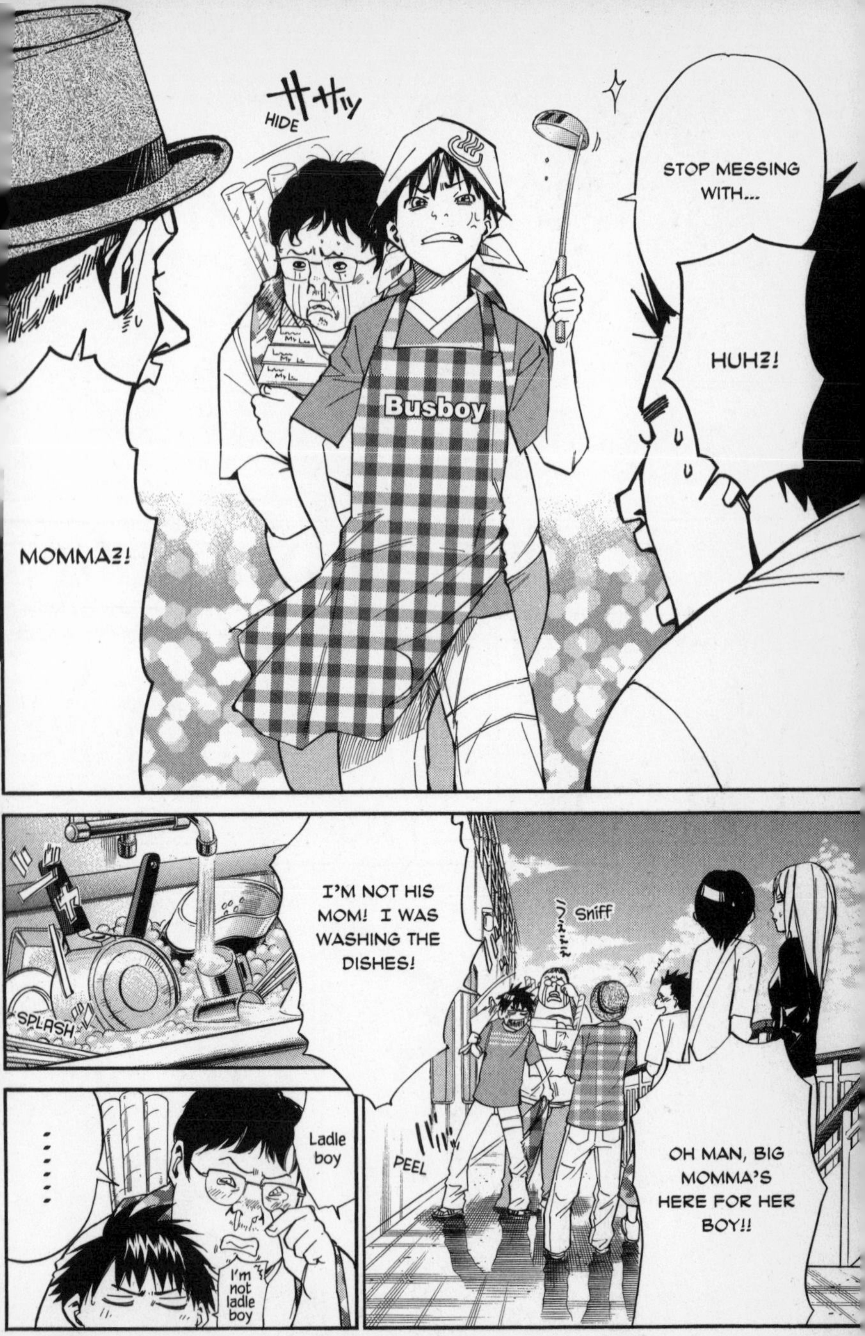
STOP MESSING WITH...
HUH?!
HIDE
MOMMA?!
I'M NOT HIS MOM! I WAS WASHING THE DISHES!
Sniff
OH MAN, BIG MOMMA'S HERE FOR HER BOY!!
PEEL
SPLASH
Ladle boy
......
I'm not ladle boy

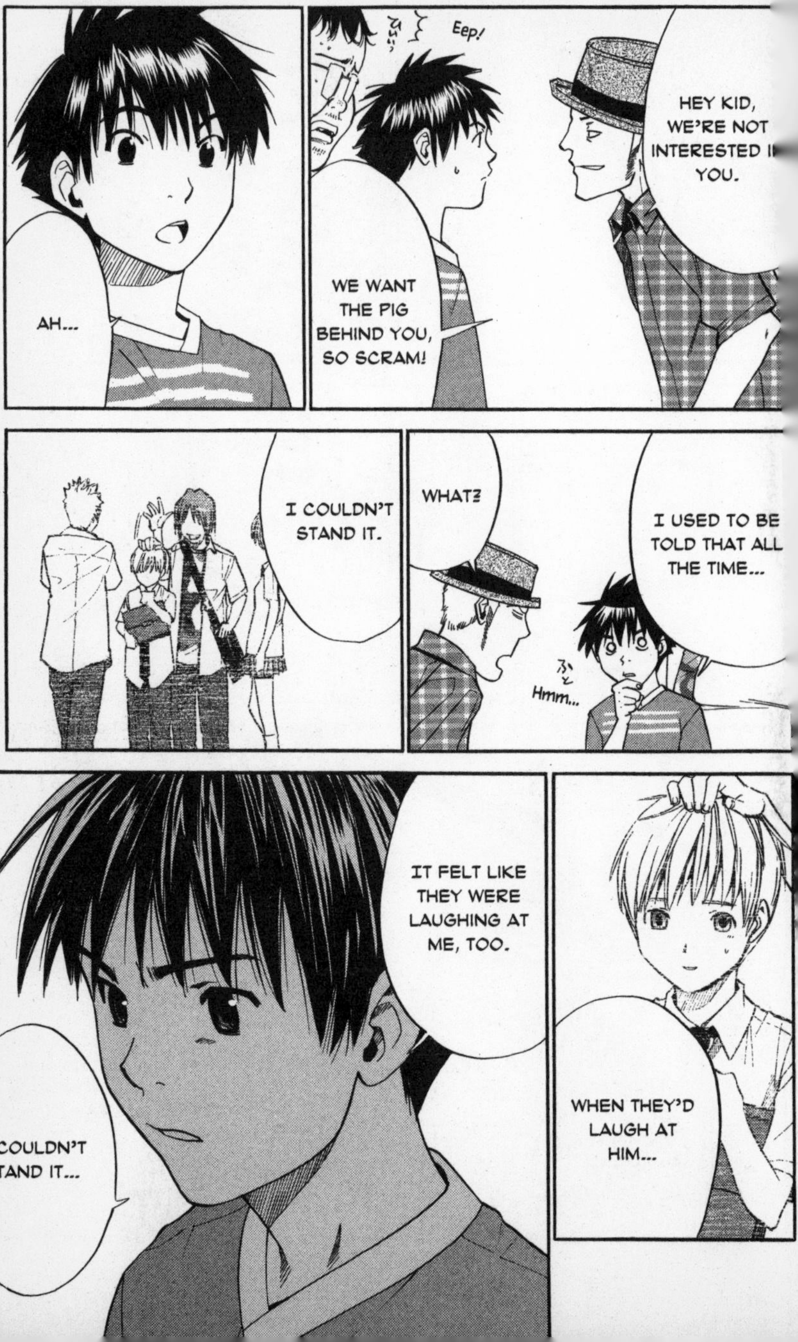

HEY KID, WE'RE NOT INTERESTED I YOU.
Eep!
WE WANT THE PIG BEHIND YOU, SO SCRAM!
AH...
I USED TO BE TOLD THAT ALL THE TIME...
WHAT?
Hmm...
I COULDN'T STAND IT.
WHEN THEY'D LAUGH AT HIM...
IT FELT LIKE THEY WERE LAUGHING AT ME, TOO.
I COULDN'T STAND IT...

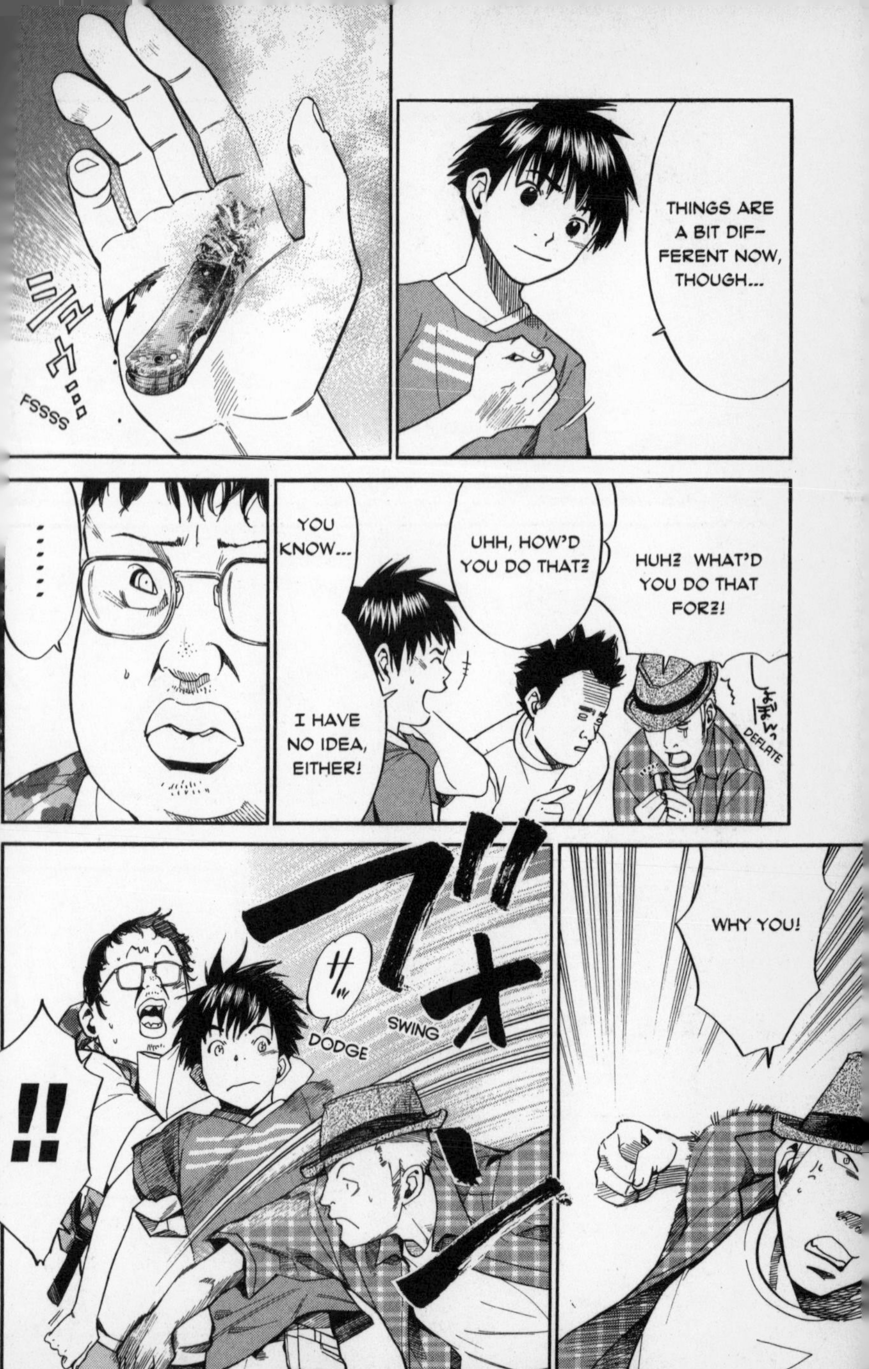

THINGS ARE A BIT DIF-FERENT NOW, THOUGH...
FSSSS
HUH? WHAT'D YOU DO THAT FOR?!
DEFLATE
UHH, HOW'D YOU DO THAT?
YOU KNOW...
I HAVE NO IDEA, EITHER!
......
WHY YOU!
SWING
DODGE
!!

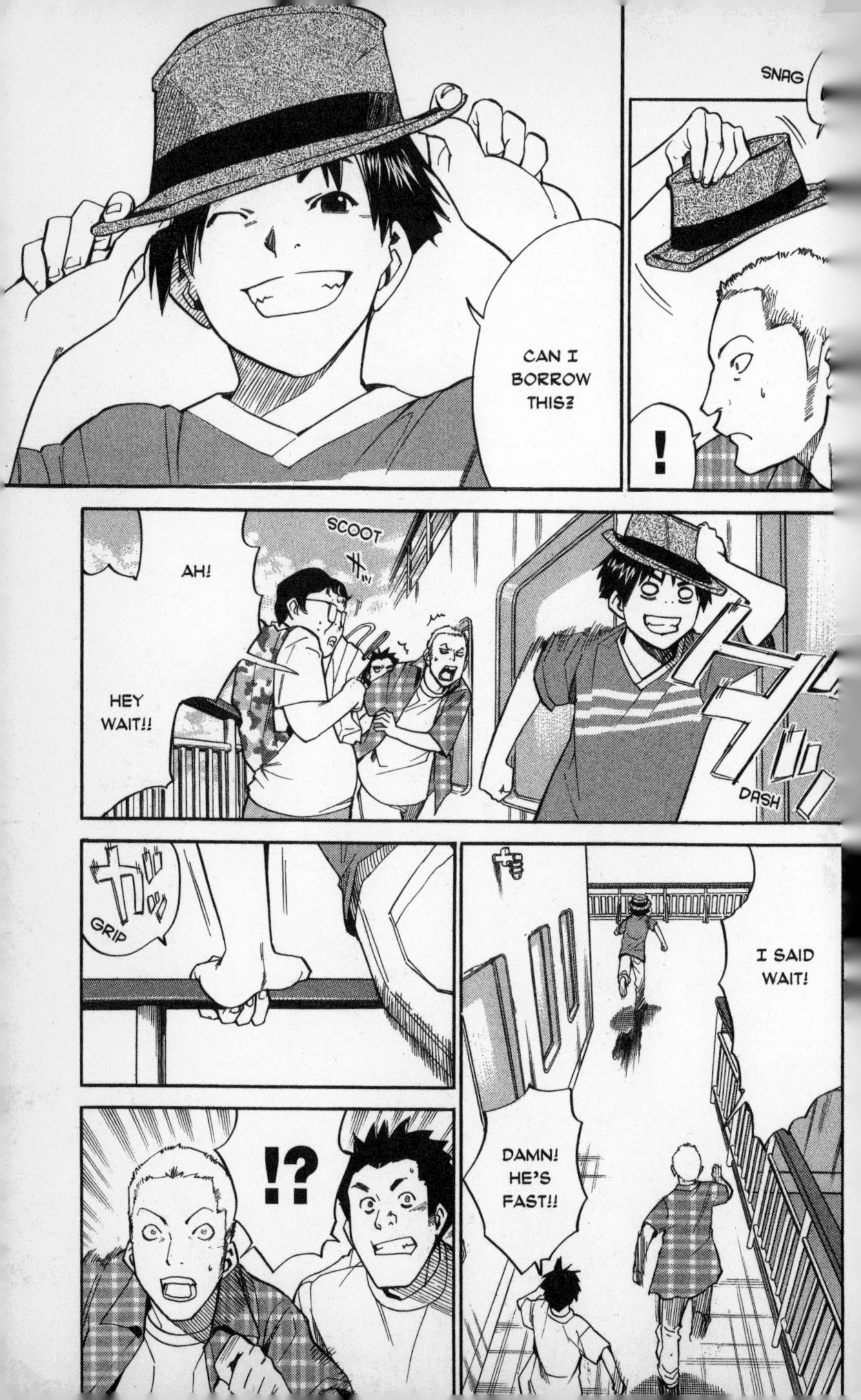
SNAG
!
CAN I BORROW THIS?
SCOOT
DASH
AH!
HEY WAIT!!
I SAID WAIT!
DAMN! HE'S FAST!!
GRIP
!?

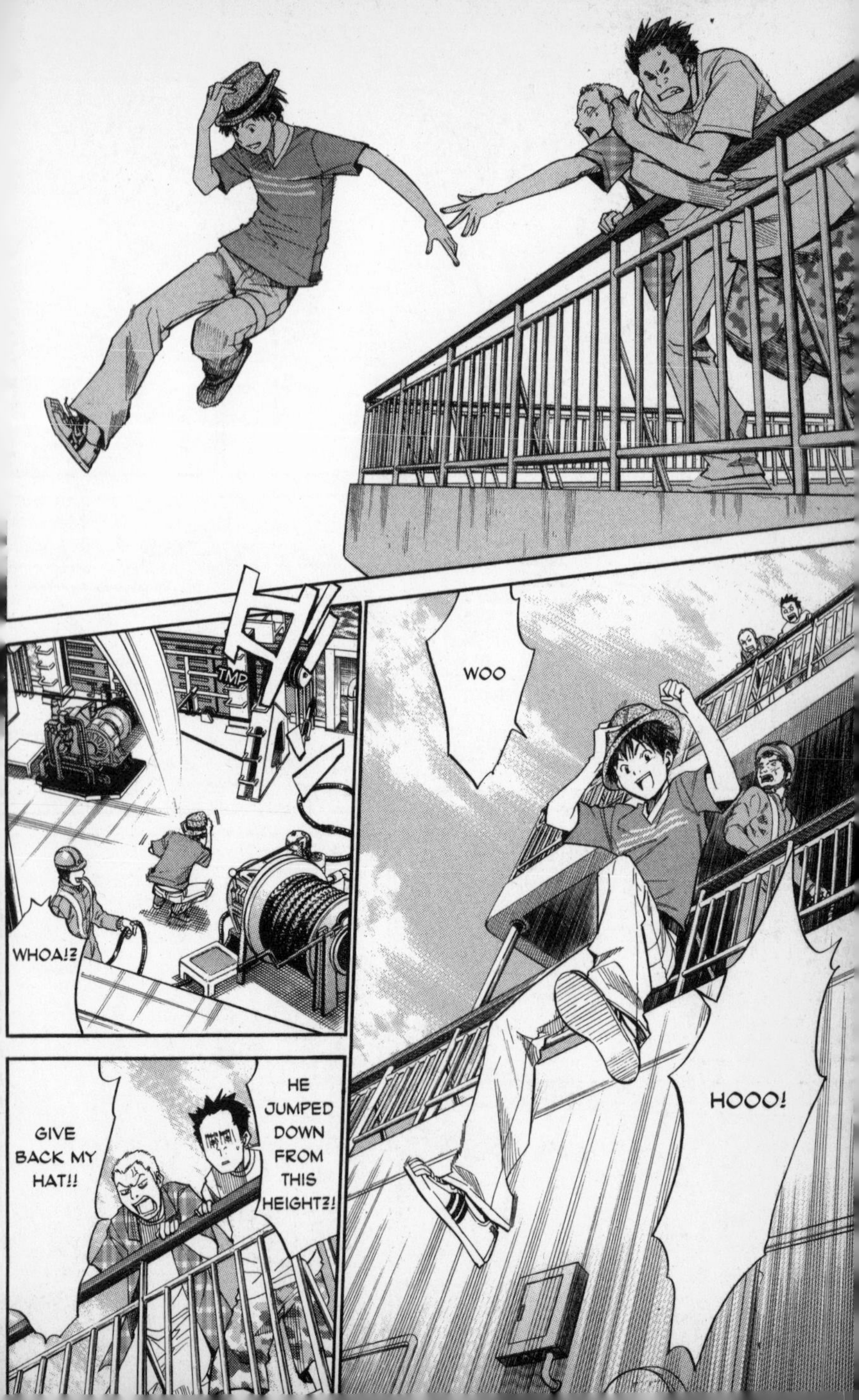
WOO
HOOO!
TMP
WHOA!?
HE JUMPED DOWN FROM THIS HEIGHT?!
GIVE BACK MY HAT!!

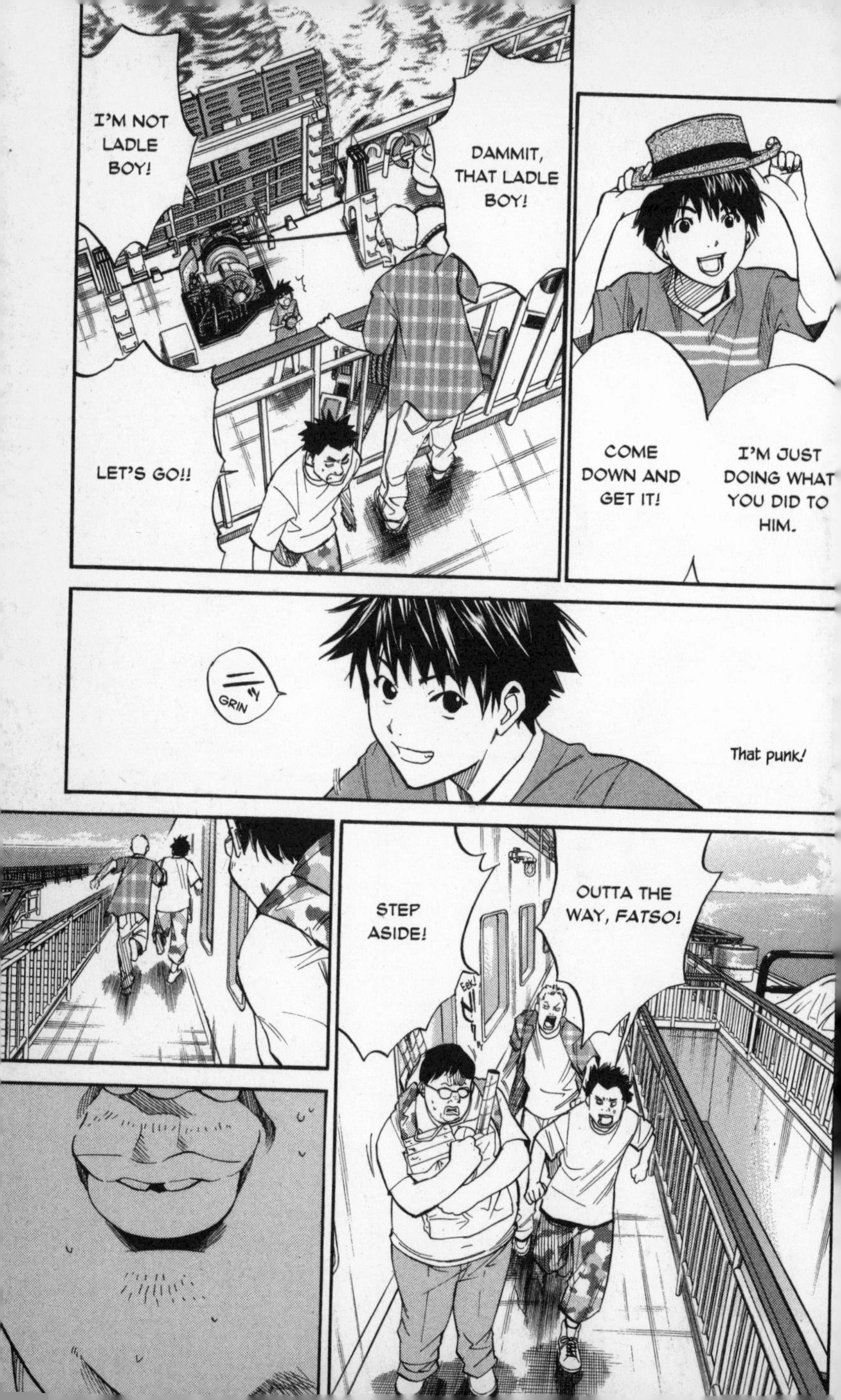
I'M JUST DOING WHAT YOU DID TO HIM.
COME DOWN AND GET IT!
DAMMIT, THAT LADLE BOY!
I'M NOT LADLE BOY!
LET'S GO!!
That punk!
GRIN
OUTTA THE WAY, FATSO!
STEP ASIDE!
Eek!

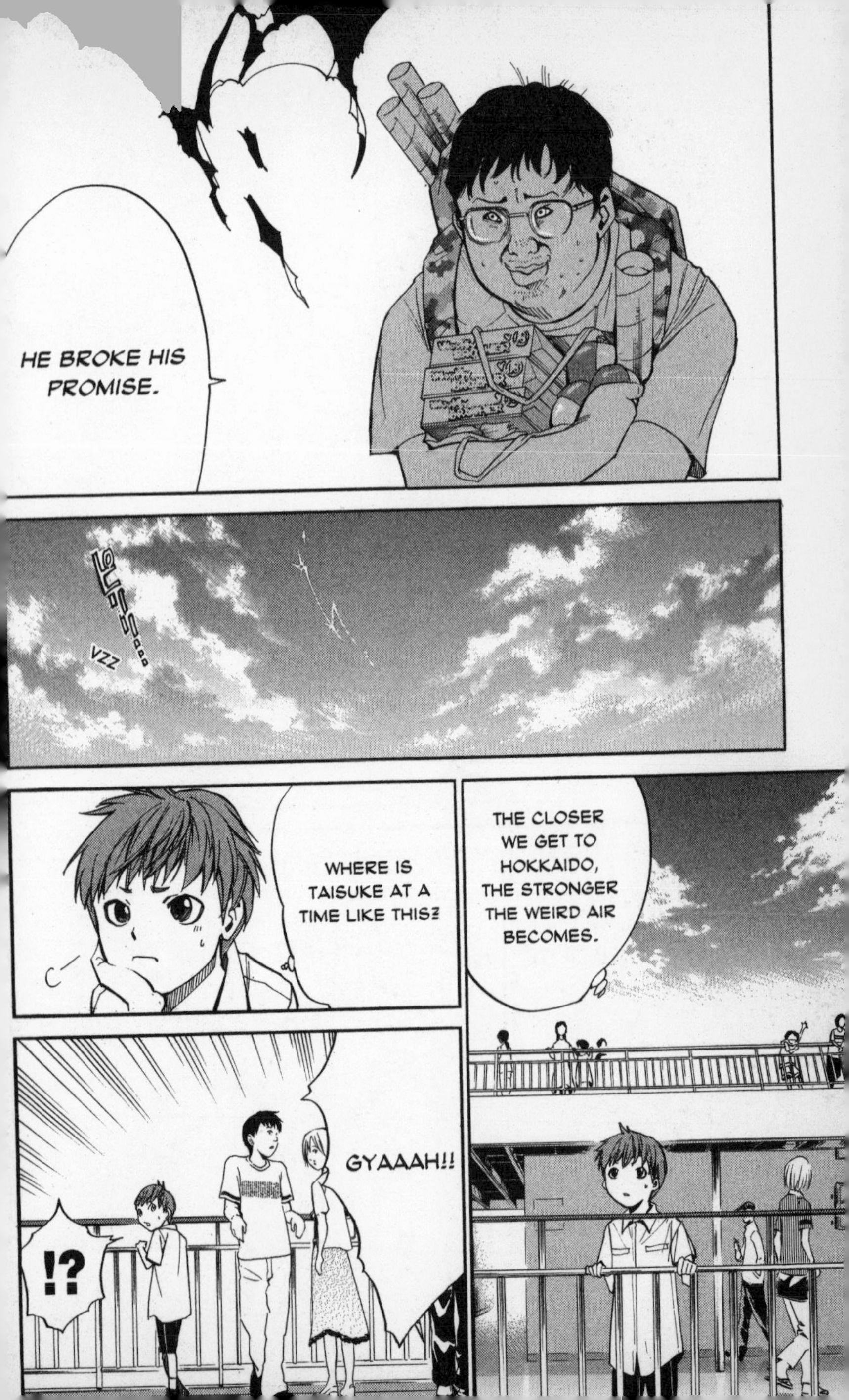
HE BROKE HIS PROMISE.
VZZ
THE CLOSER WE GET TO HOKKAIDO, THE STRONGER THE WEIRD AIR BECOMES.
WHERE IS TAISUKE AT A TIME LIKE THIS?
GYAAAH!!
!?

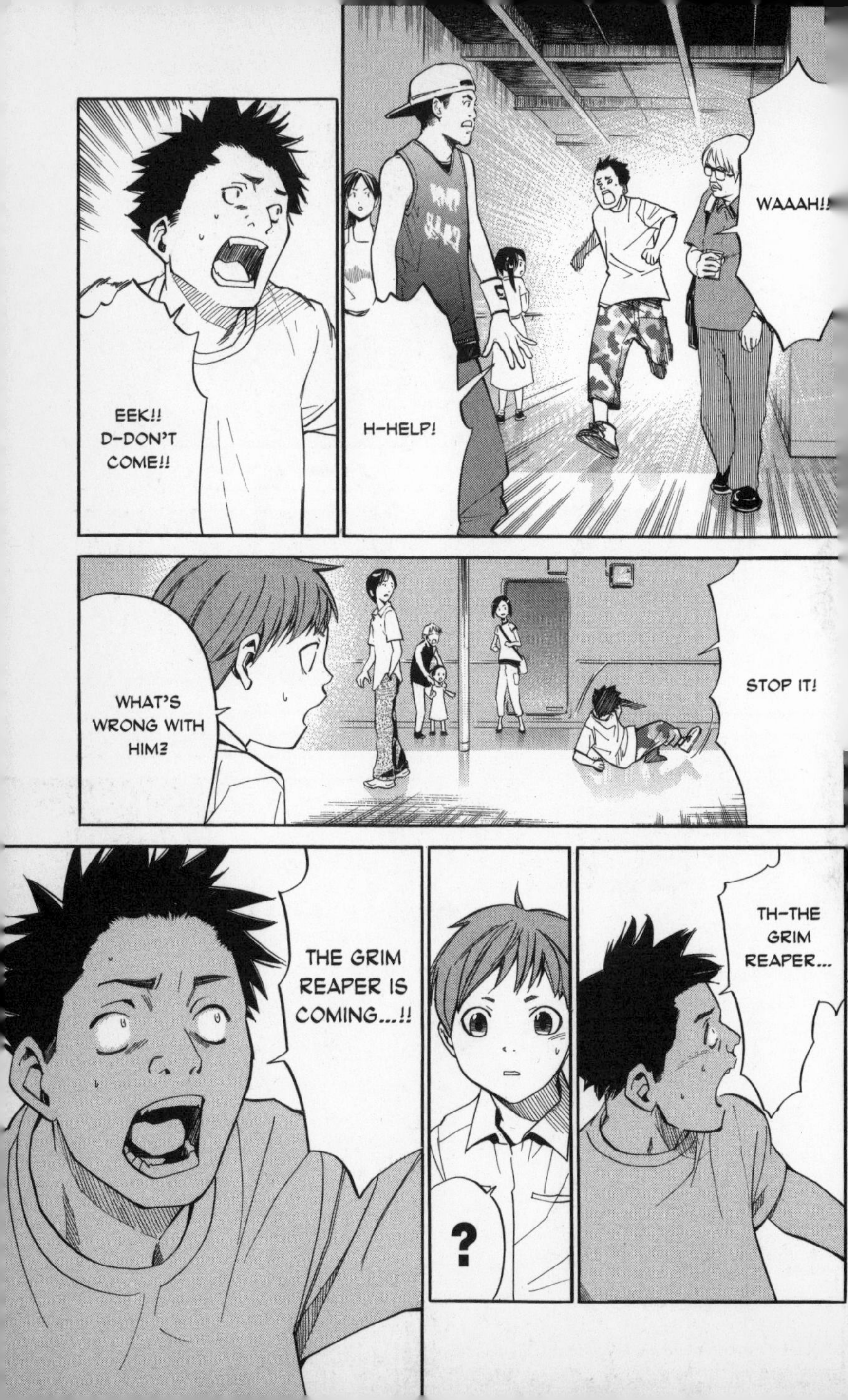
WAAAH!!
H-HELP!
EEK!! D-DON'T COME!!
STOP IT!
WHAT'S WRONG WITH HIM?
TH-THE GRIM REAPER...
?
THE GRIM REAPER IS COMING...!!

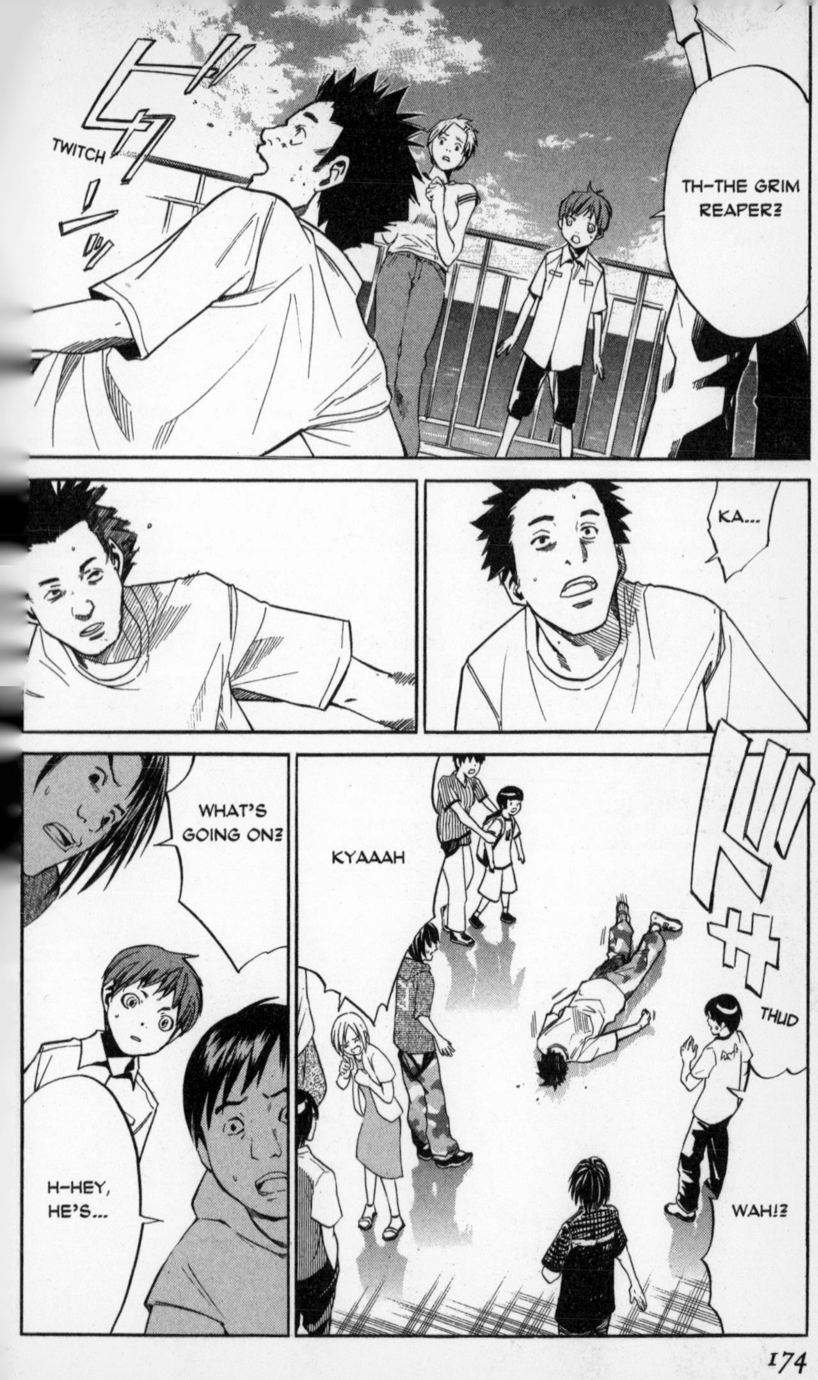
TH-THE GRIM REAPER!?
TWITCH
KA...
THUD
KYAAAH
WAH!?
WHAT'S GOING ON!?
H-HEY, HE'S...

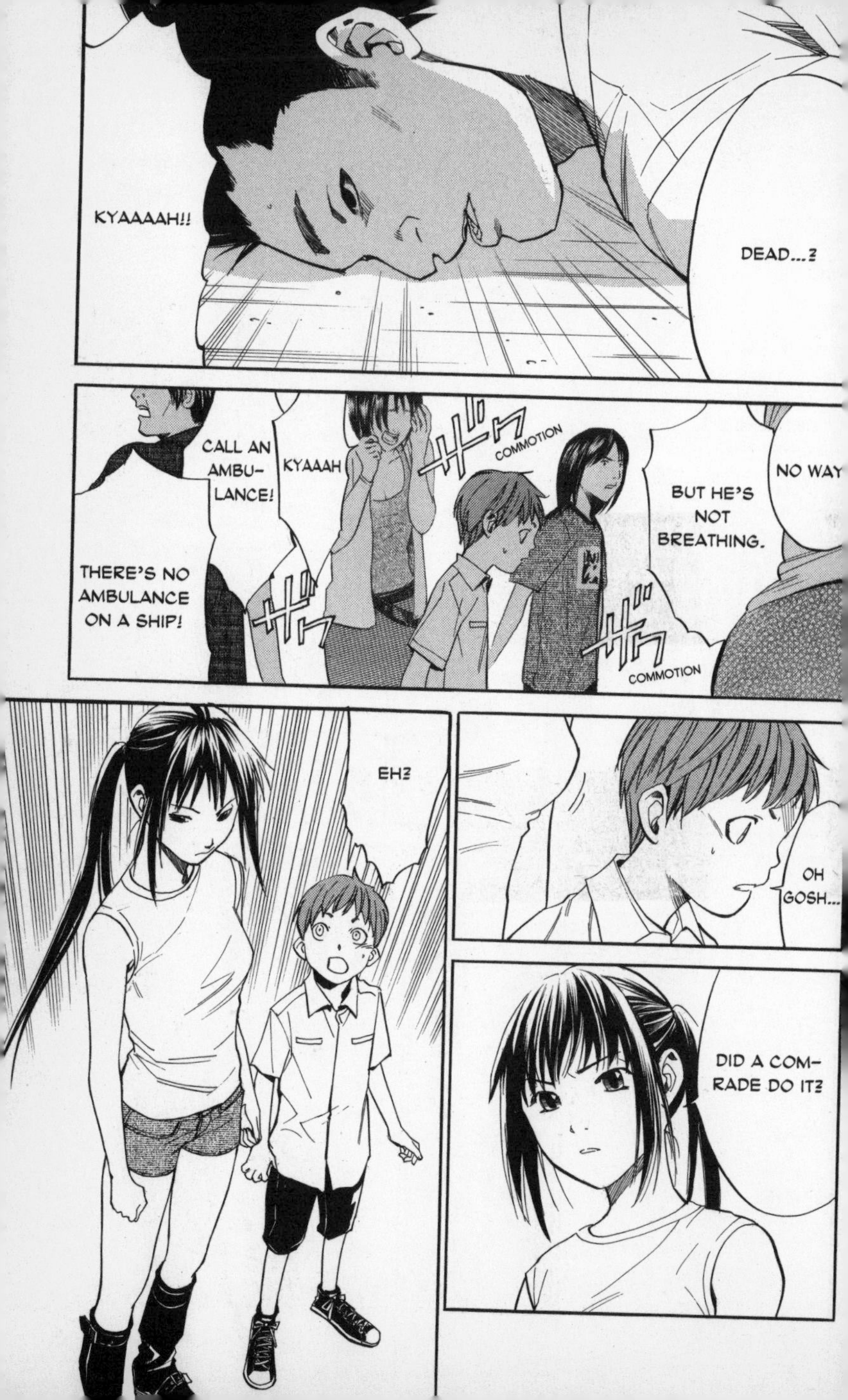
DEAD...?
KYAAAAH!!
NO WAY
BUT HE'S NOT BREATHING.
COMMOTION
COMMOTION
KYAAAH
CALL AN AMBU-LANCE!
THERE'S NO AMBULANCE ON A SHIP!
OH GOSH...
DID A COM-RADE DO IT?
EH?

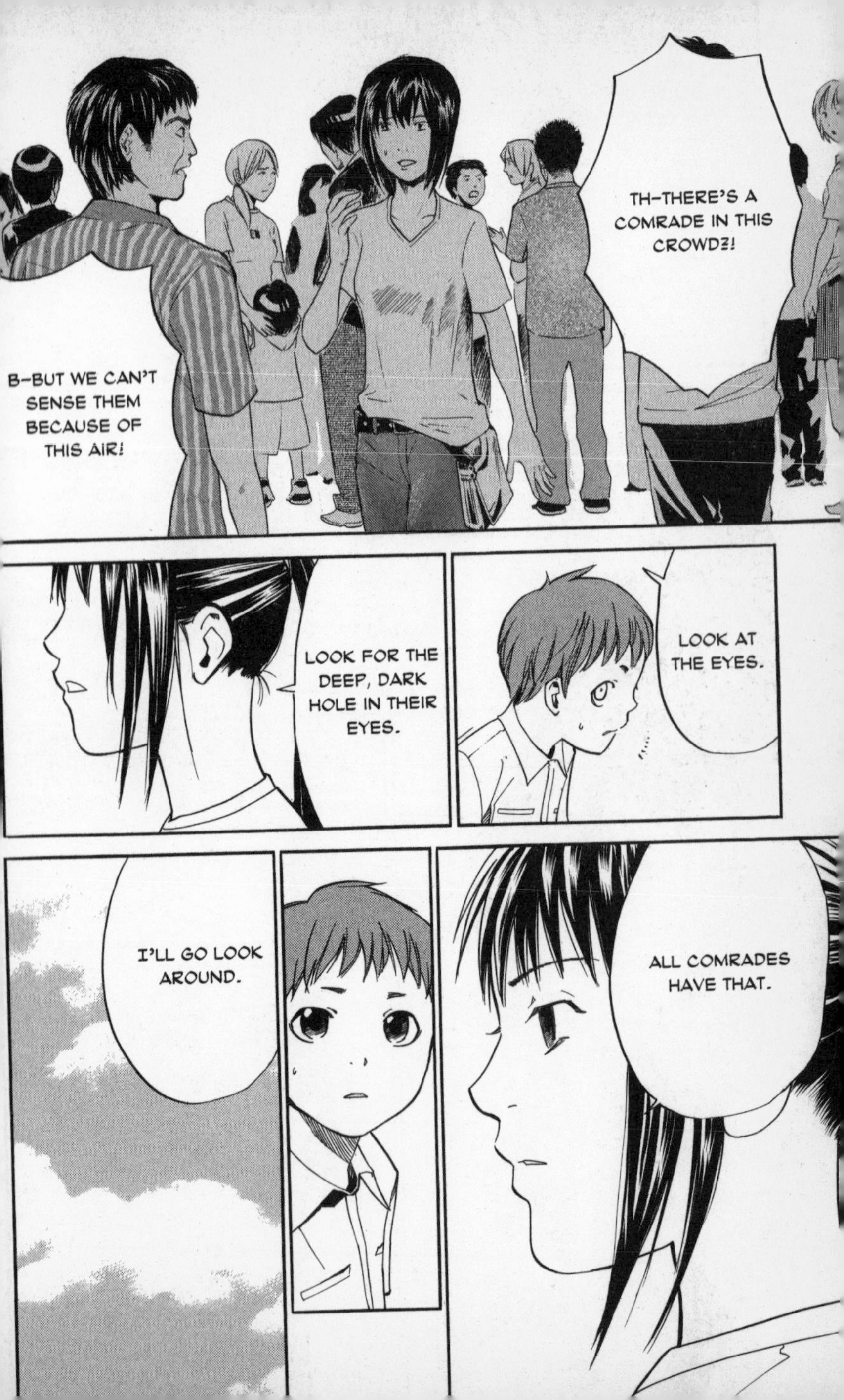
TH-THERE'S A COMRADE IN THIS CROWD?!
B-BUT WE CAN'T SENSE THEM BECAUSE OF THIS AIR!
LOOK AT THE EYES.
LOOK FOR THE DEEP, DARK HOLE IN THEIR EYES.
ALL COMRADES HAVE THAT.
I'LL GO LOOK AROUND.

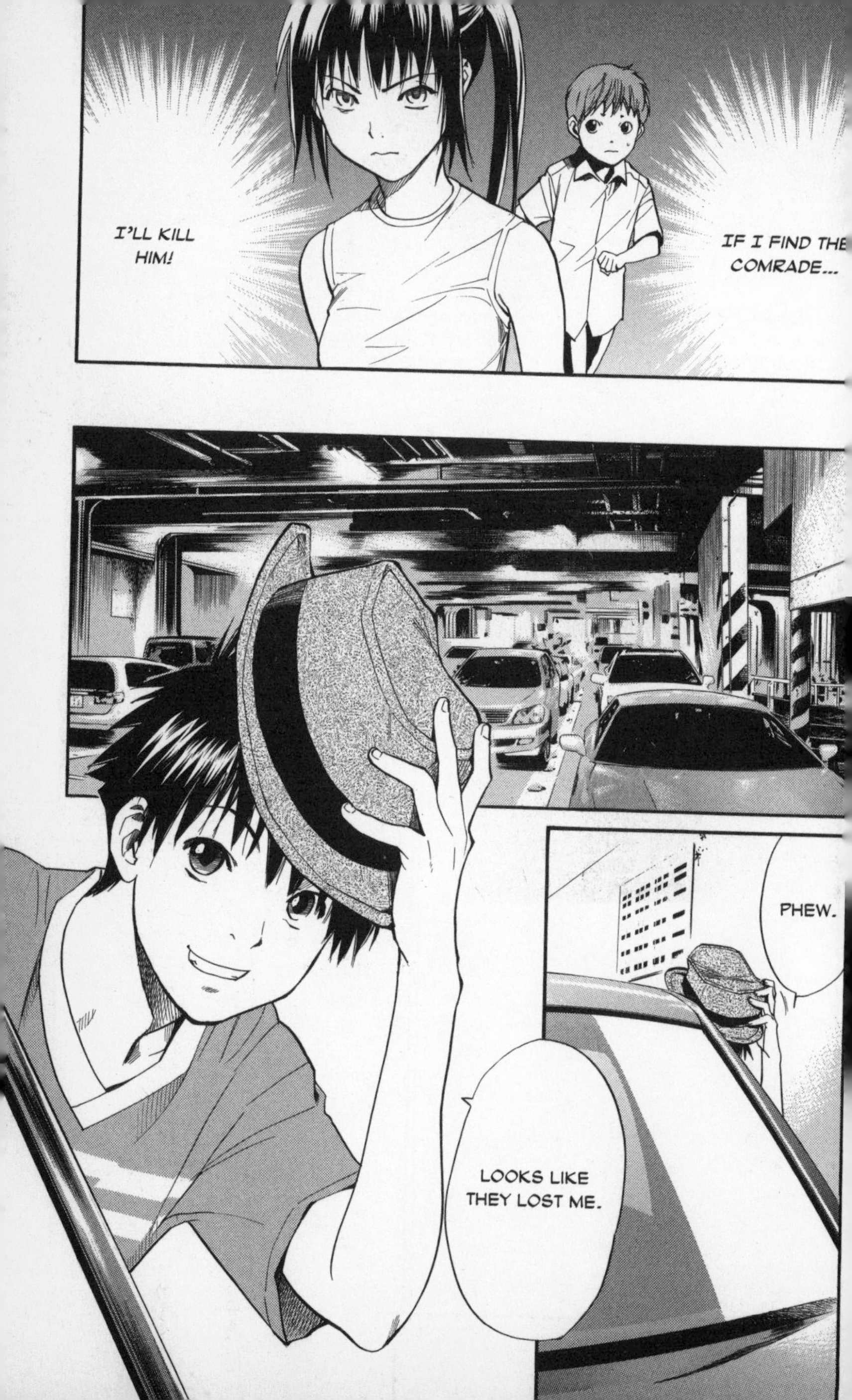
IF I FIND THE COMRADE...
I'LL KILL HIM!
PHEW.
LOOKS LIKE THEY LOST ME.

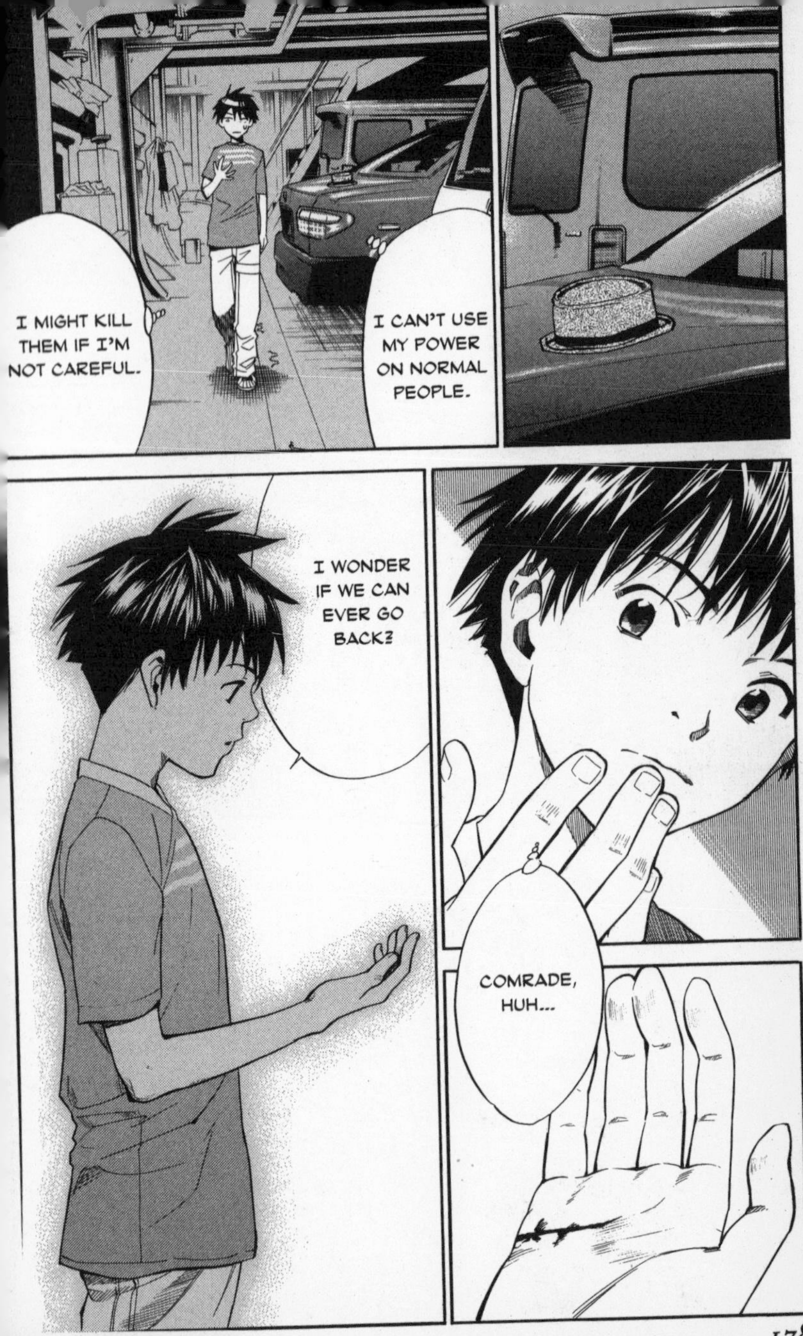
I CAN'T USE MY POWER ON NORMAL PEOPLE.
I MIGHT KILL THEM IF I'M NOT CAREFUL.
COMRADE, HUH...
I WONDER IF WE CAN EVER GO BACK?

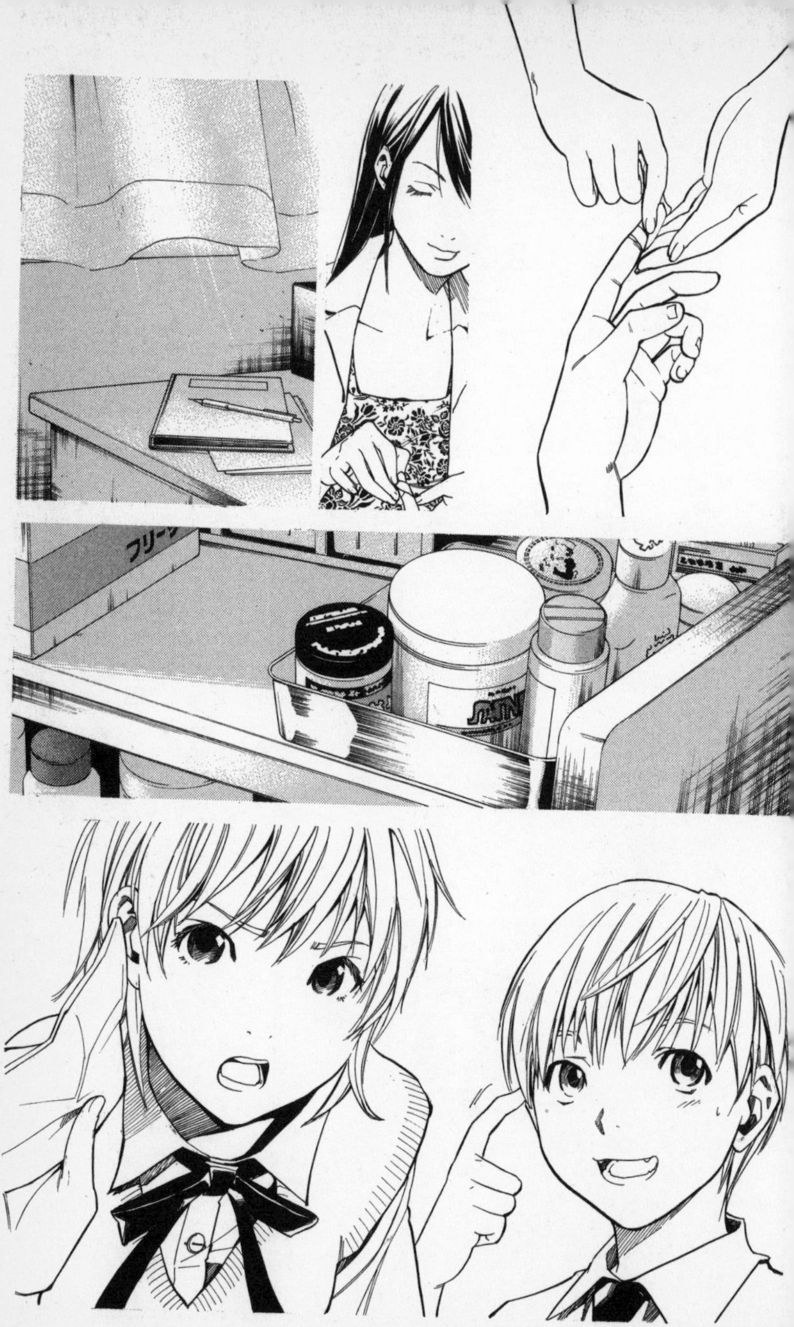

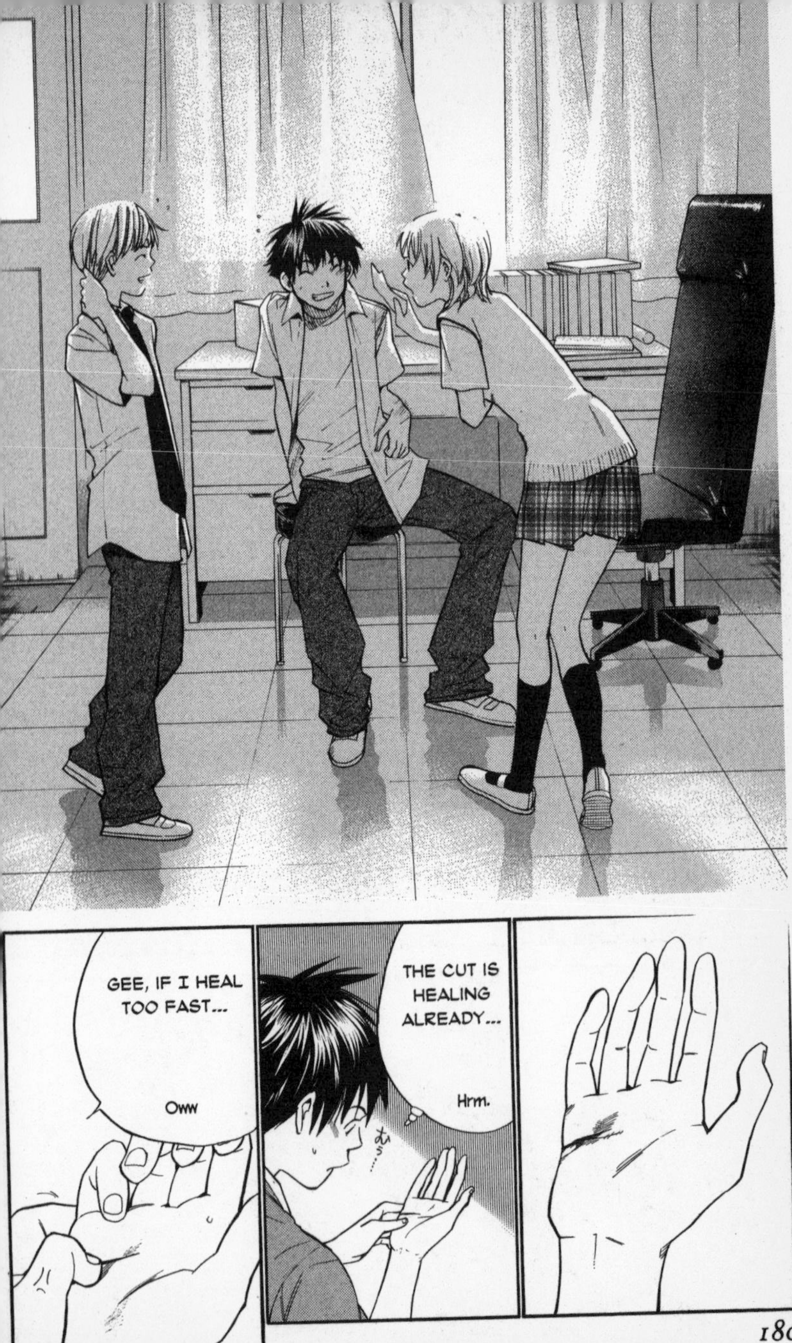
THE CUT IS HEALING ALREADY...
Hrm.
GEE, IF I HEAL TOO FAST...
Oww

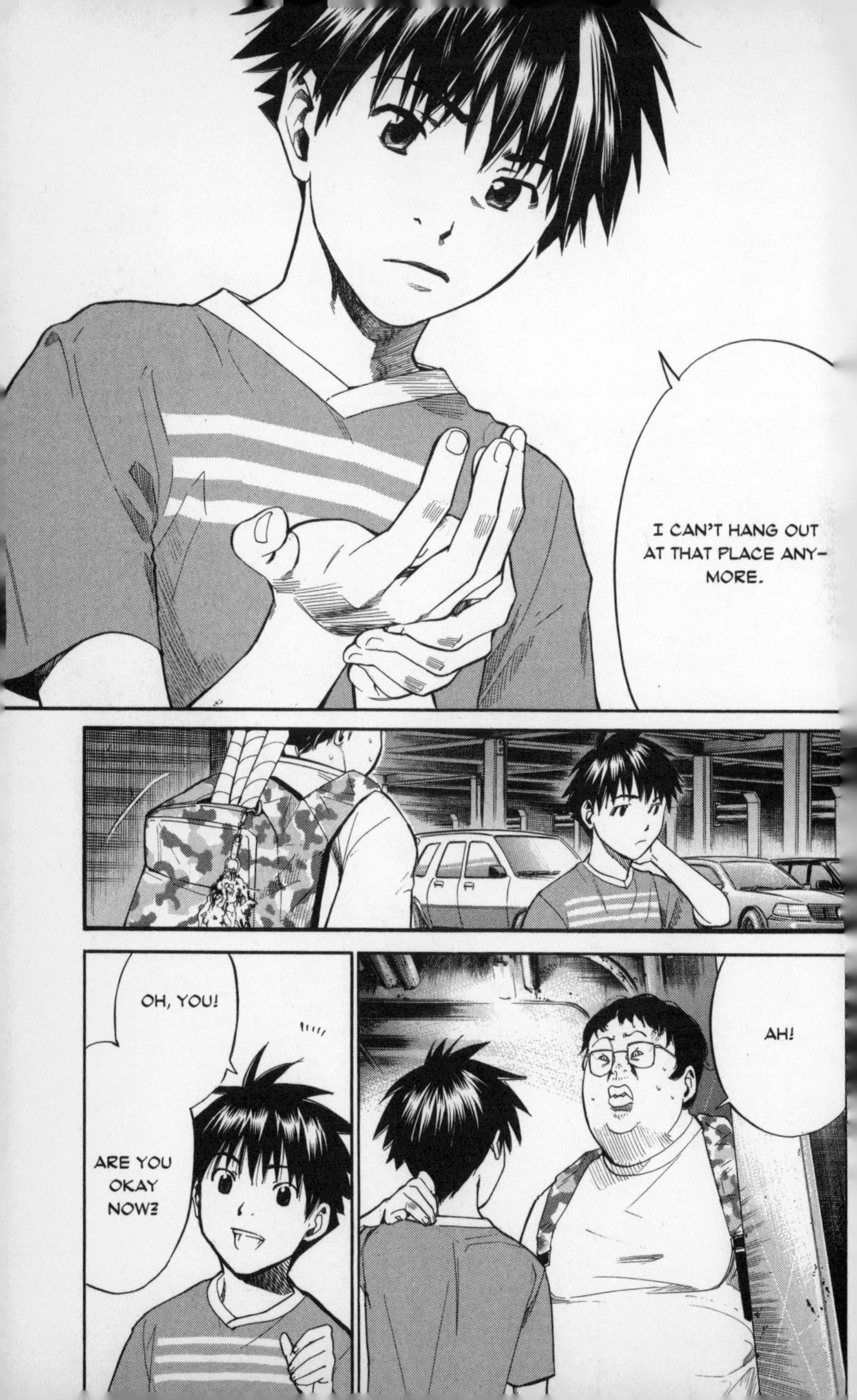
I CAN'T HANG OUT AT THAT PLACE ANY-MORE.
AH!
OH, YOU!
ARE YOU OKAY NOW?

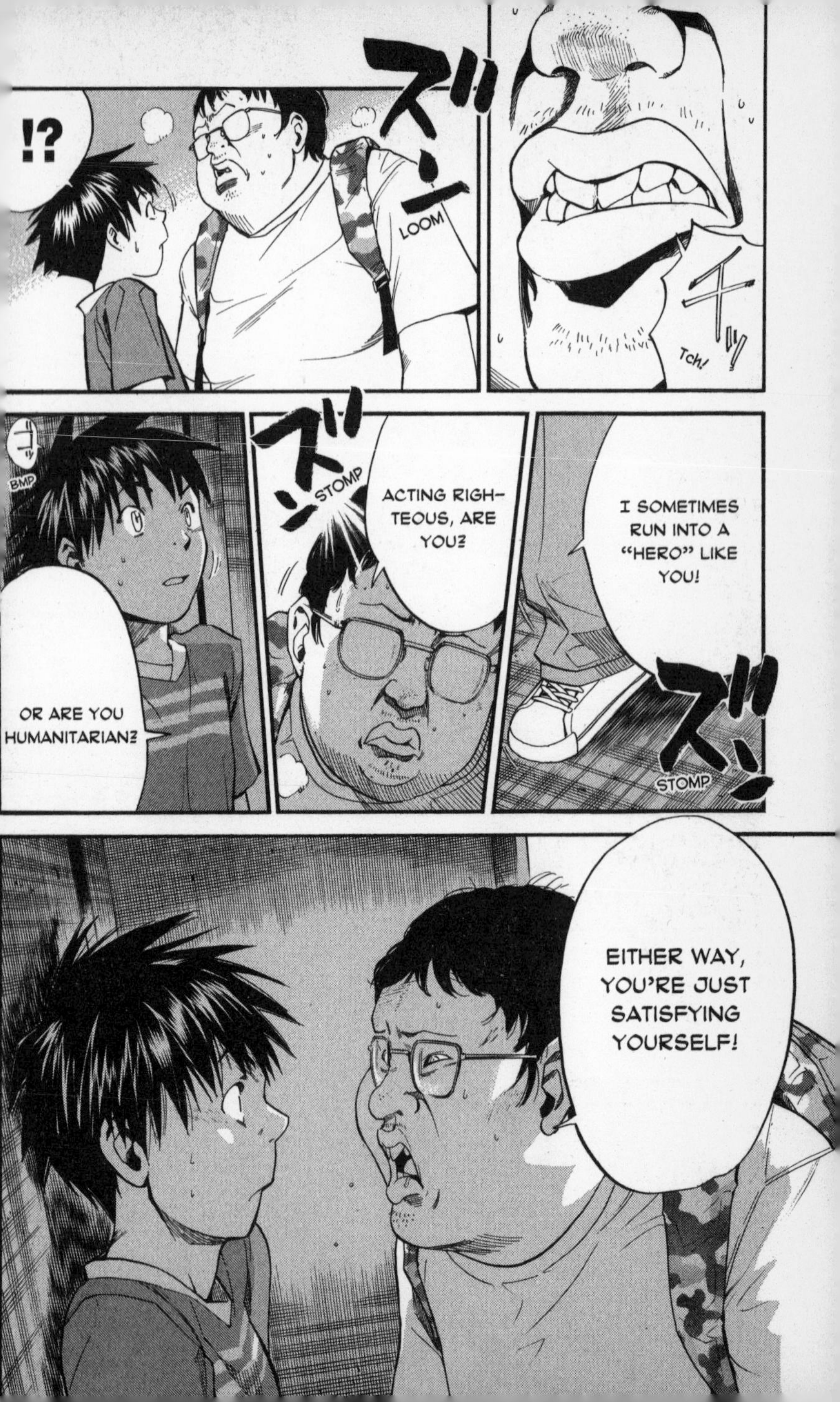
Tch!
LOOM
!?
I SOMETIMES RUN INTO A "HERO" LIKE YOU!
STOMP
STOMP
ACTING RIGHTEOUS, ARE YOU?
BMP
OR ARE YOU HUMANITARIAN?
EITHER WAY, YOU'RE JUST SATISFYING YOURSELF!

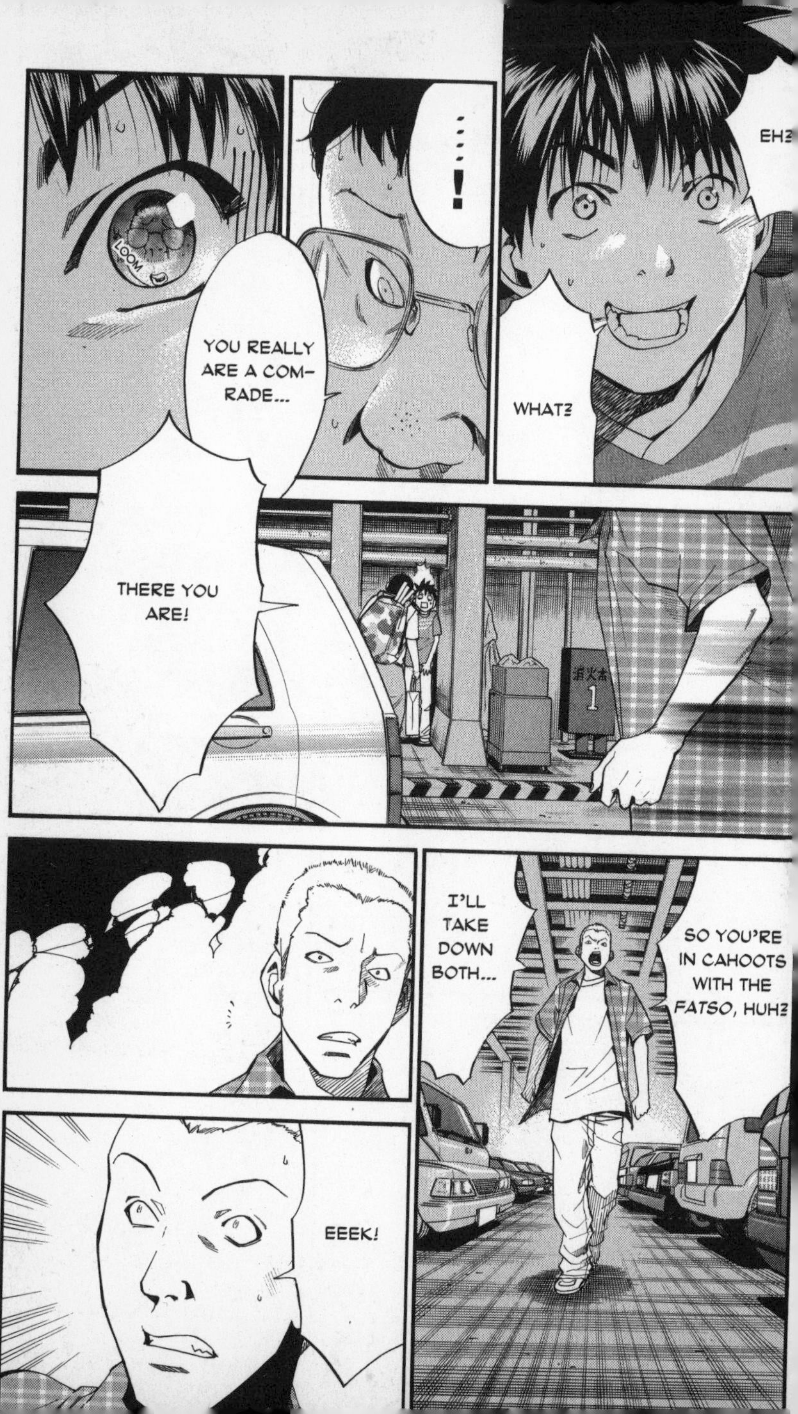
EH?
WHAT?
......!
YOU REALLY ARE A COM-RADE...
LOOM
THERE YOU ARE!
SO YOU'RE IN CAHOOTS WITH THE FATSO, HUH?
I'LL TAKE DOWN BOTH...
EEEK!

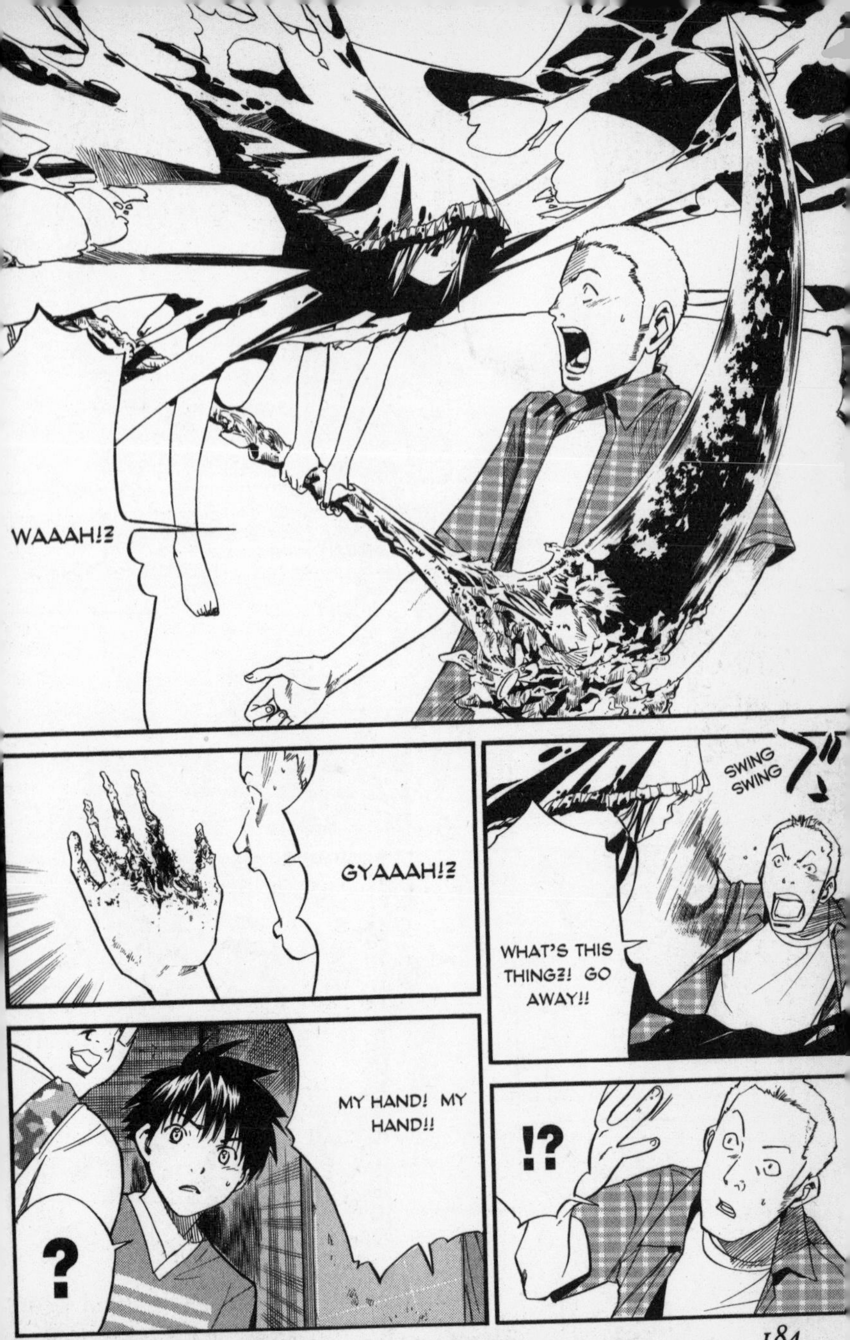

WAAAH!?
SWING SWING
WHAT'S THIS THING?! GO AWAY!!
GYAAAH!?
!?
MY HAND! MY HAND!!
?

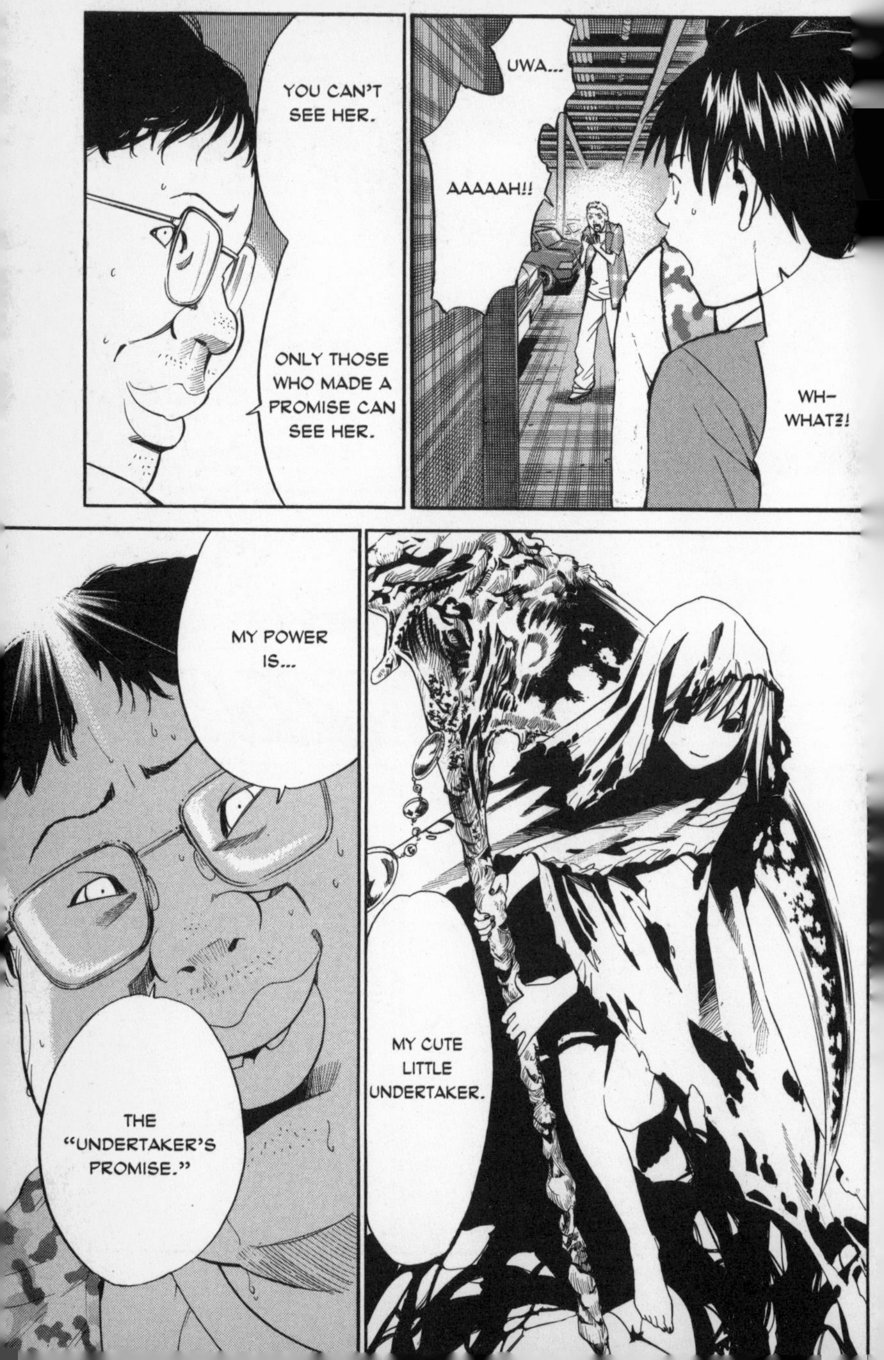

UWA...
AAAAAH!!
WH- WHAT?!
YOU CAN'T SEE HER.
ONLY THOSE WHO MADE A PROMISE CAN SEE HER.
MY CUTE LITTLE UNDERTAKER.
MY POWER IS...
THE "UNDERTAKER'S PROMISE."

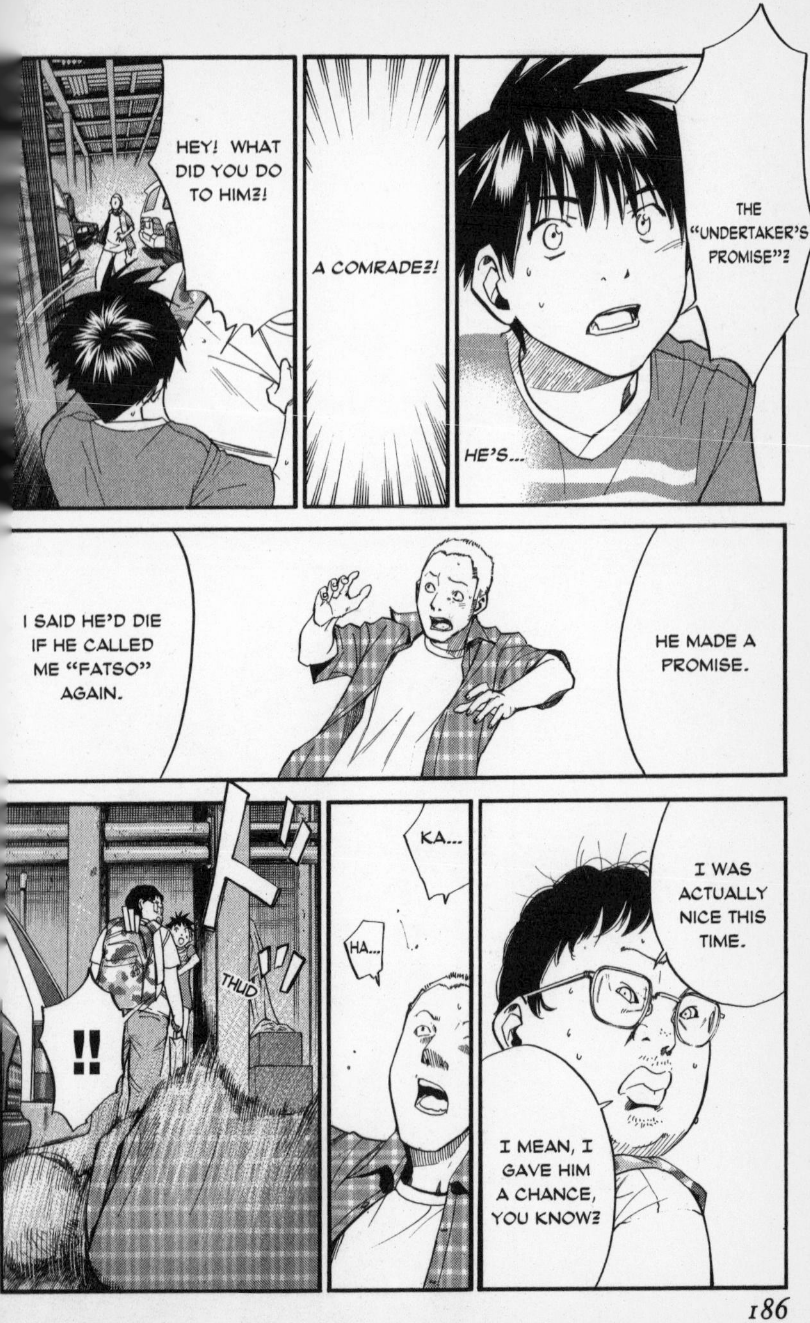
THE "UNDERTAKER'S PROMISE"?
HE'S...
A COMRADE?!
HEY! WHAT DID YOU DO TO HIM?!
HE MADE A PROMISE.
I SAID HE'D DIE IF HE CALLED ME "FATSO" AGAIN.
I WAS ACTUALLY NICE THIS TIME.
I MEAN, I GAVE HIM A CHANCE, YOU KNOW?
KA...
HA...
THUD
!!

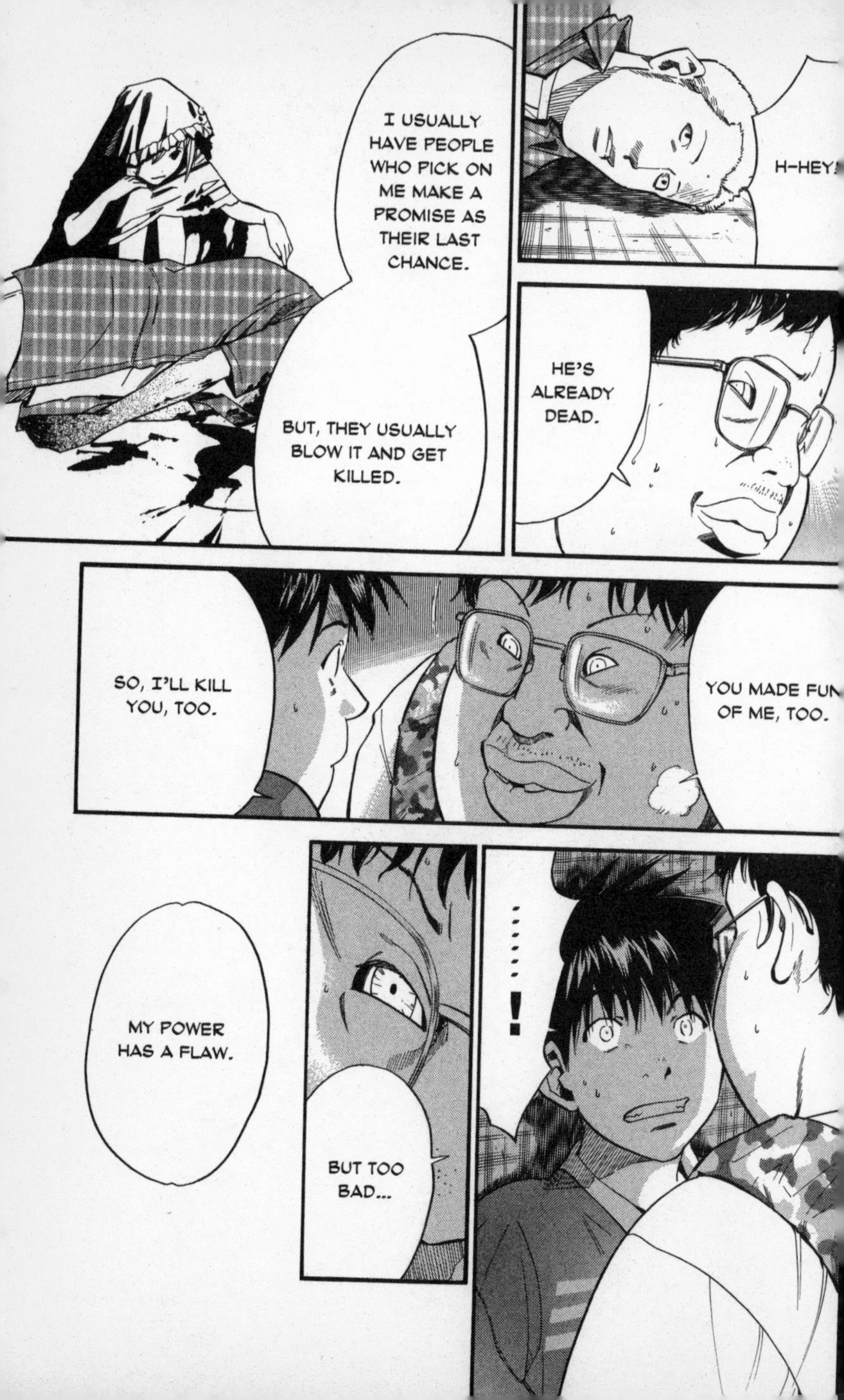
H-HEY!
HE'S ALREADY DEAD.
I USUALLY HAVE PEOPLE WHO PICK ON ME MAKE A PROMISE AS THEIR LAST CHANCE.
BUT, THEY USUALLY BLOW IT AND GET KILLED.
YOU MADE FUN OF ME, TOO.
SO, I'LL KILL YOU, TOO.
......!
BUT TOO BAD...
MY POWER HAS A FLAW.

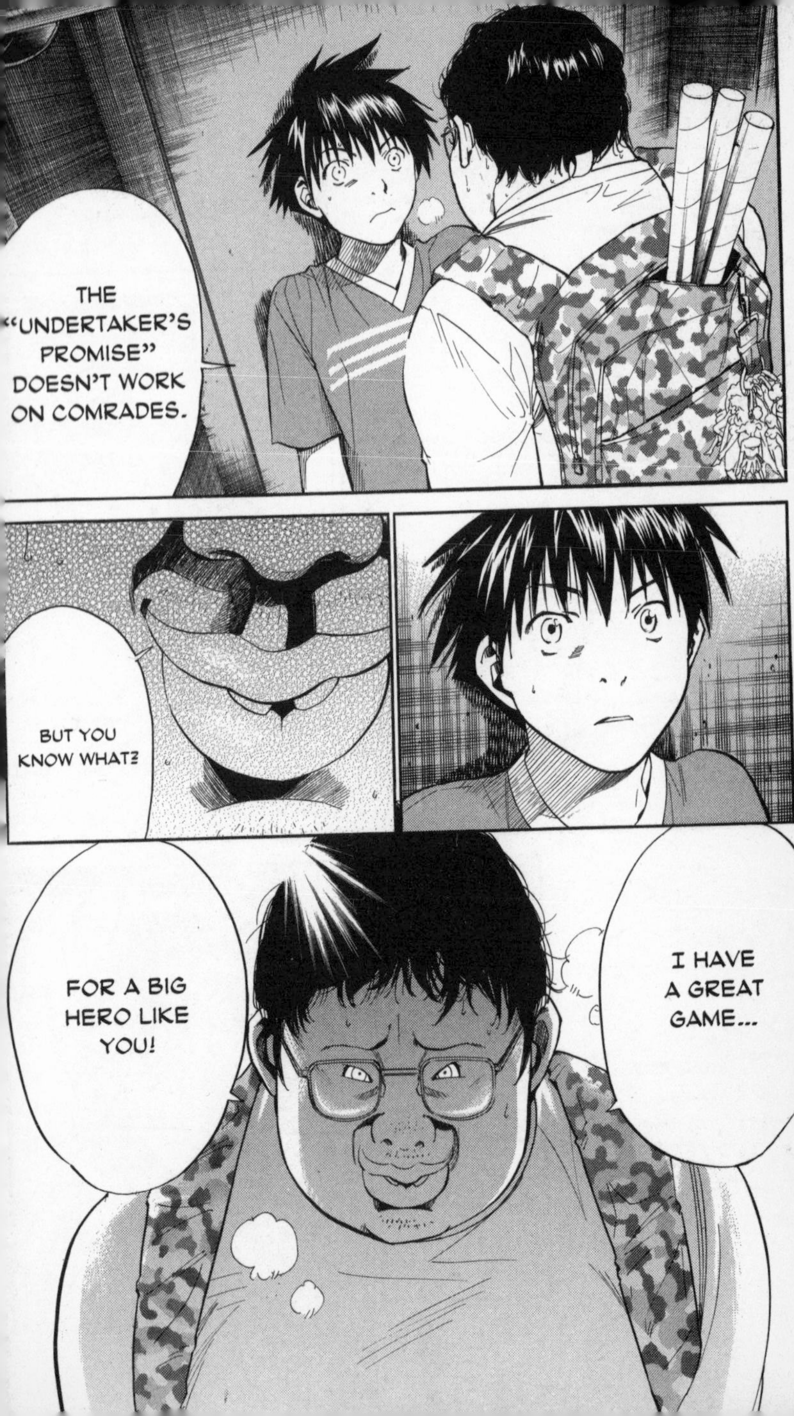
THE "UNDERTAKER'S PROMISE" DOESN'T WORK ON COMRADES.
BUT YOU KNOW WHAT?
I HAVE A GREAT GAME...
FOR A BIG HERO LIKE YOU!

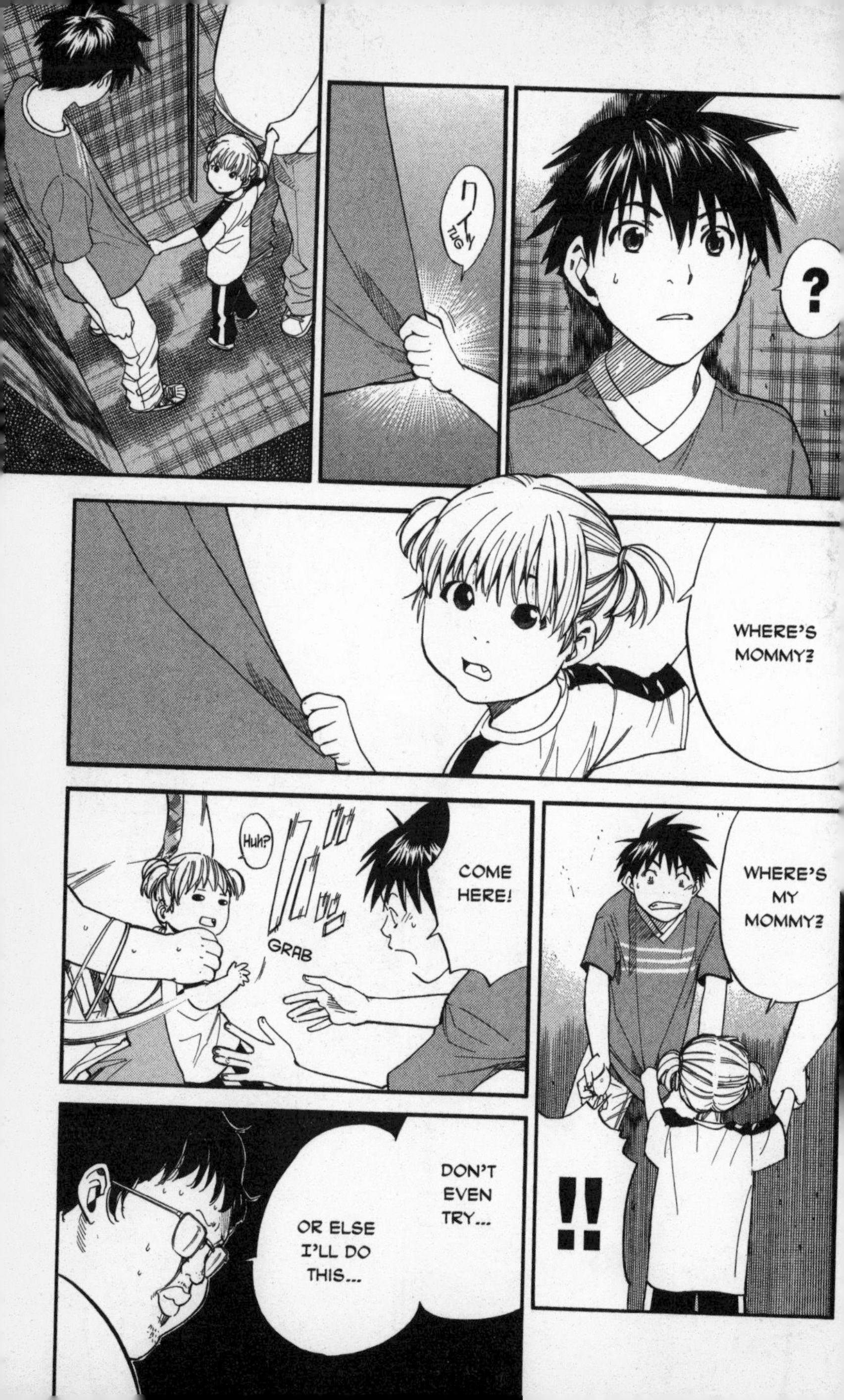
?
クイッ
TUG
WHERE'S MOMMY?
WHERE'S MY MOMMY?
!!
COME HERE!
Huh?
GRAB
DON'T EVEN TRY...
OR ELSE I'LL DO THIS...

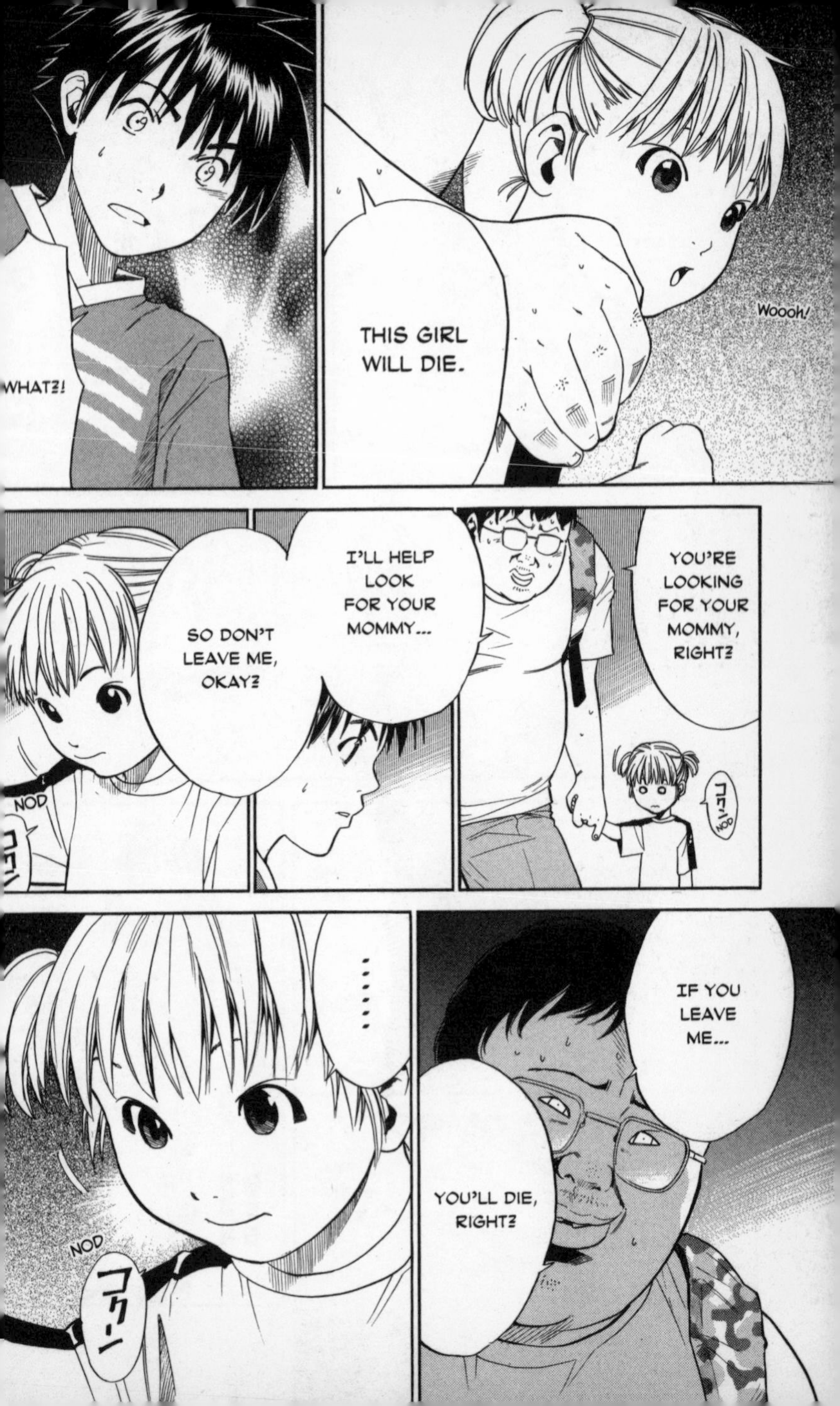
THIS GIRL WILL DIE.
Woooh!
WHAT?!
YOU'RE LOOKING FOR YOUR MOMMY, RIGHT?
NOD
I'LL HELP LOOK FOR YOUR MOMMY...
SO DON'T LEAVE ME, OKAY?
NOD
IF YOU LEAVE ME...
YOU'LL DIE, RIGHT?
......
NOD
コクーン

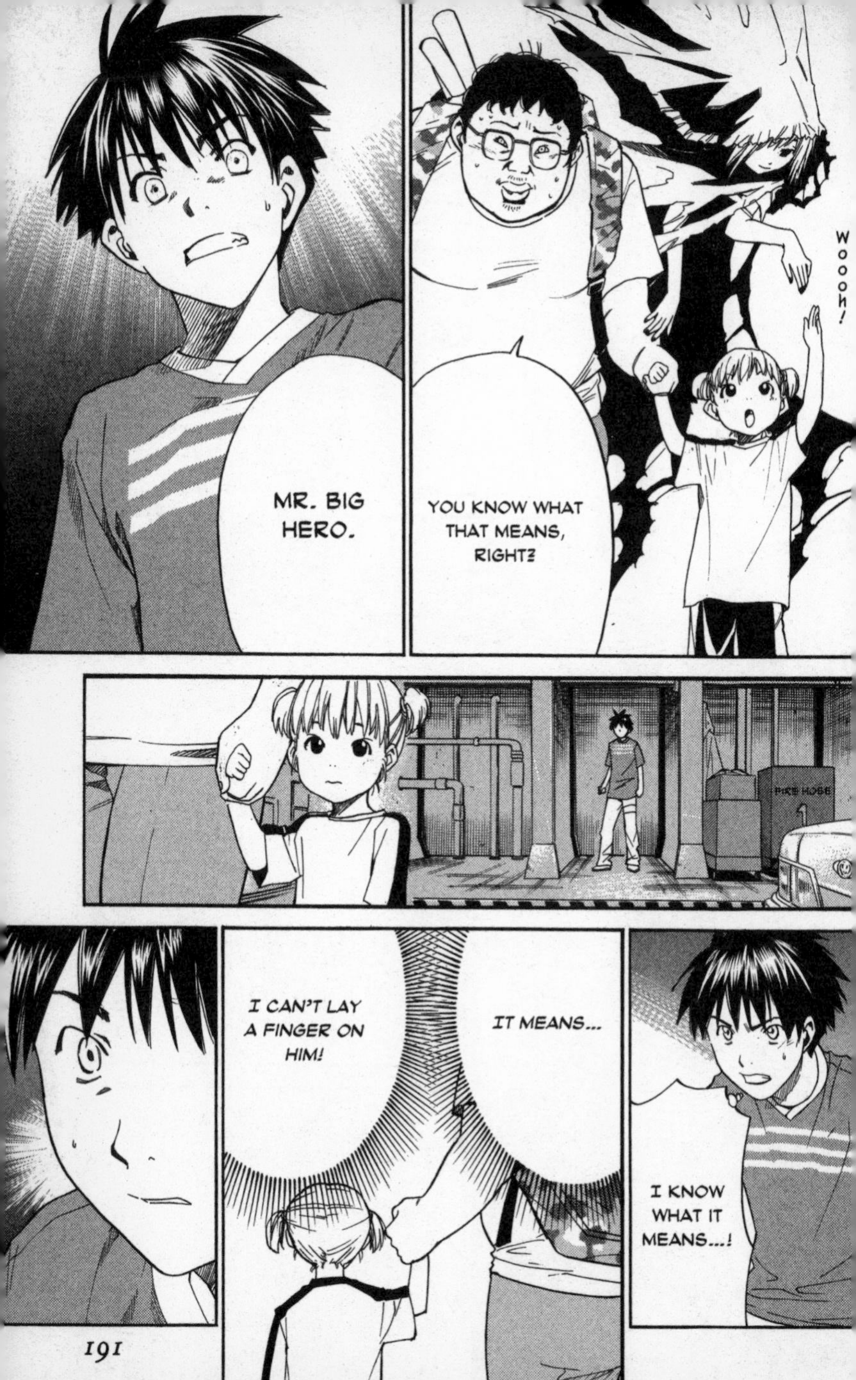
Woooh!
YOU KNOW WHAT THAT MEANS, RIGHT?
MR. BIG HERO.
I KNOW WHAT IT MEANS...!
IT MEANS...
I CAN'T LAY A FINGER ON HIM!

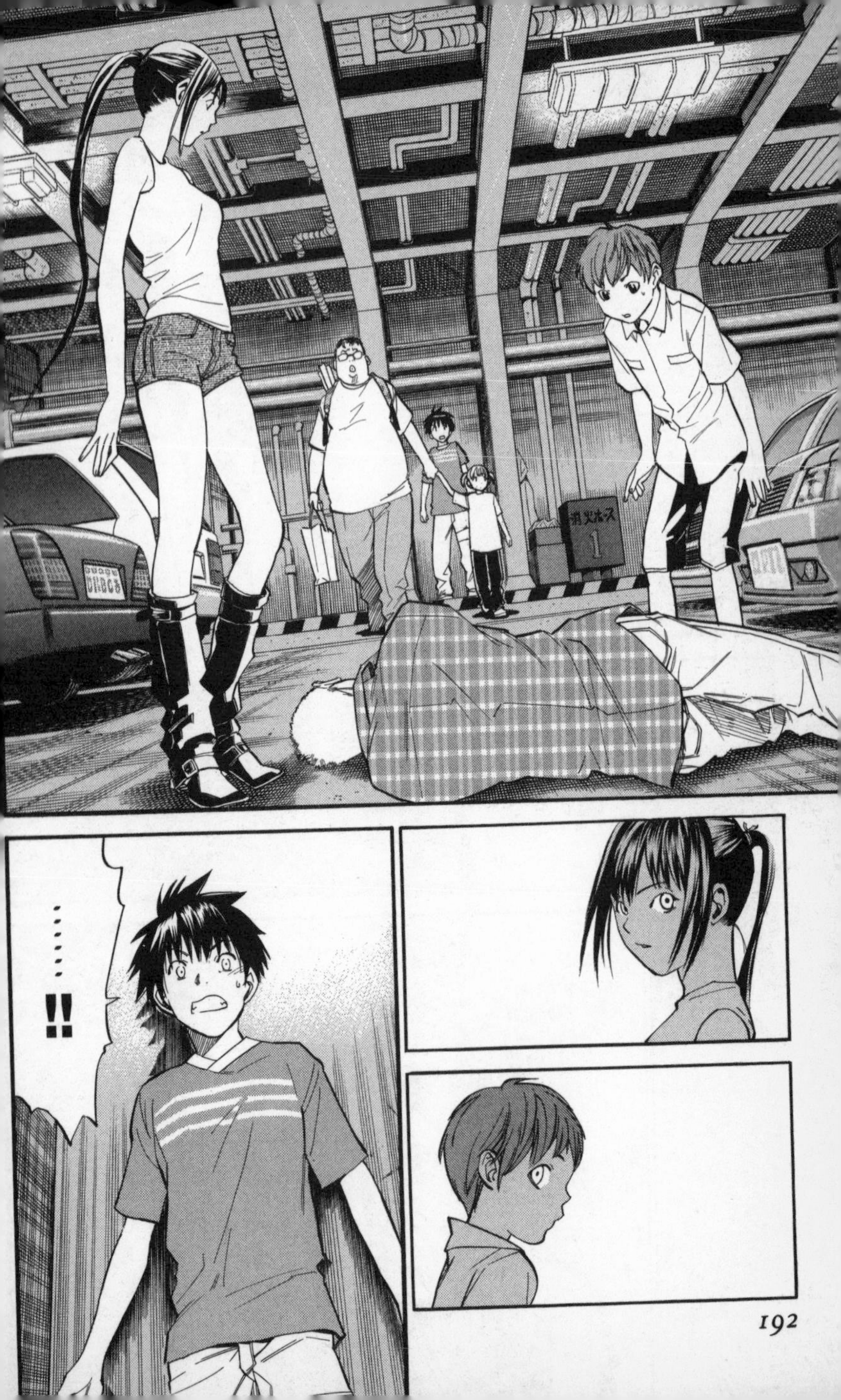
消火ホース
1
......!!

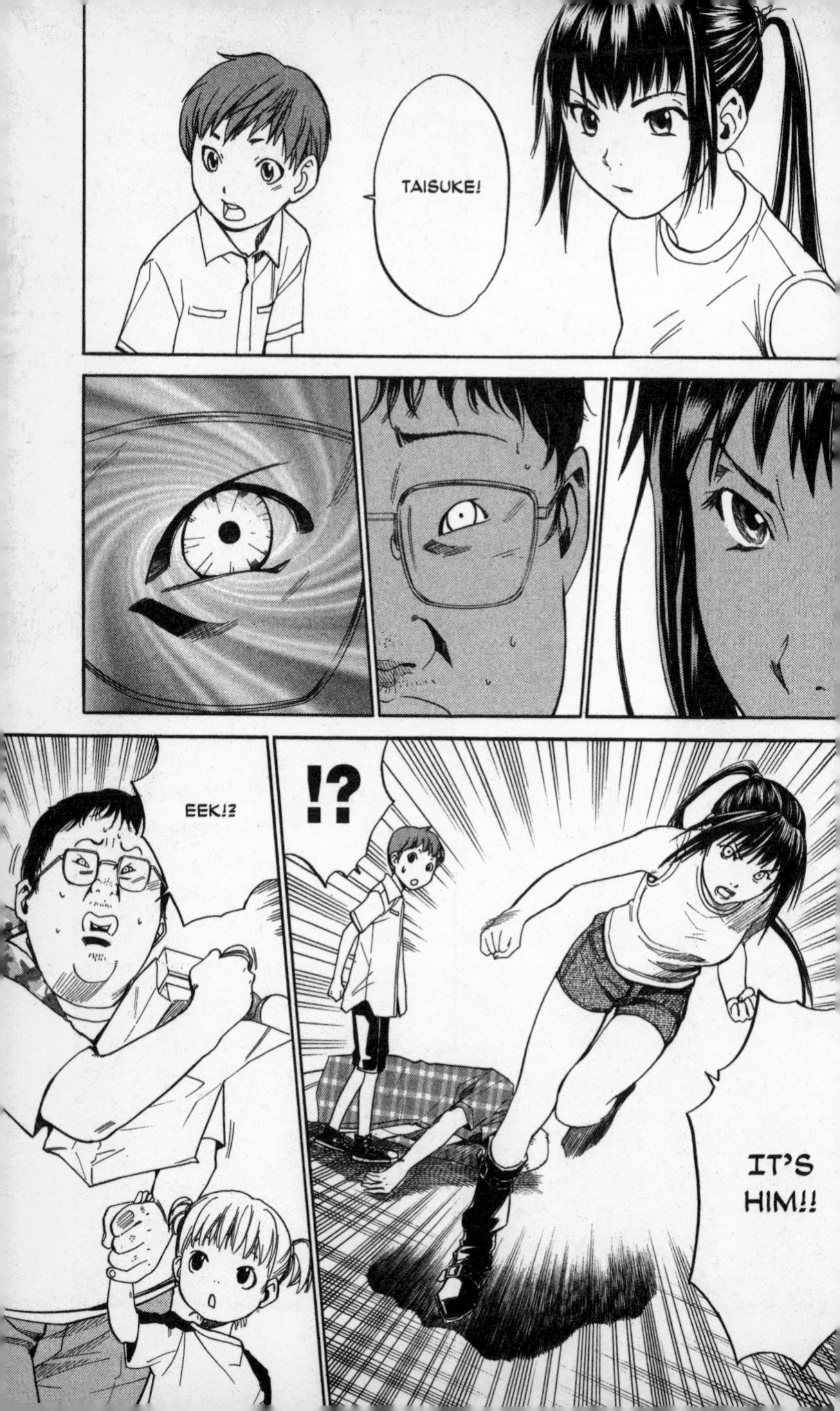
TAISUKE!
IT'S HIM!!
!?
EEK!?

NAMI,
DON'T!!

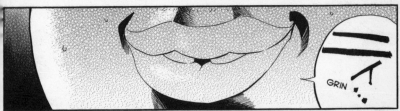

GRIN

ISN'T THIS A
GREAT GAME ♡

**Continued in Volume 5**

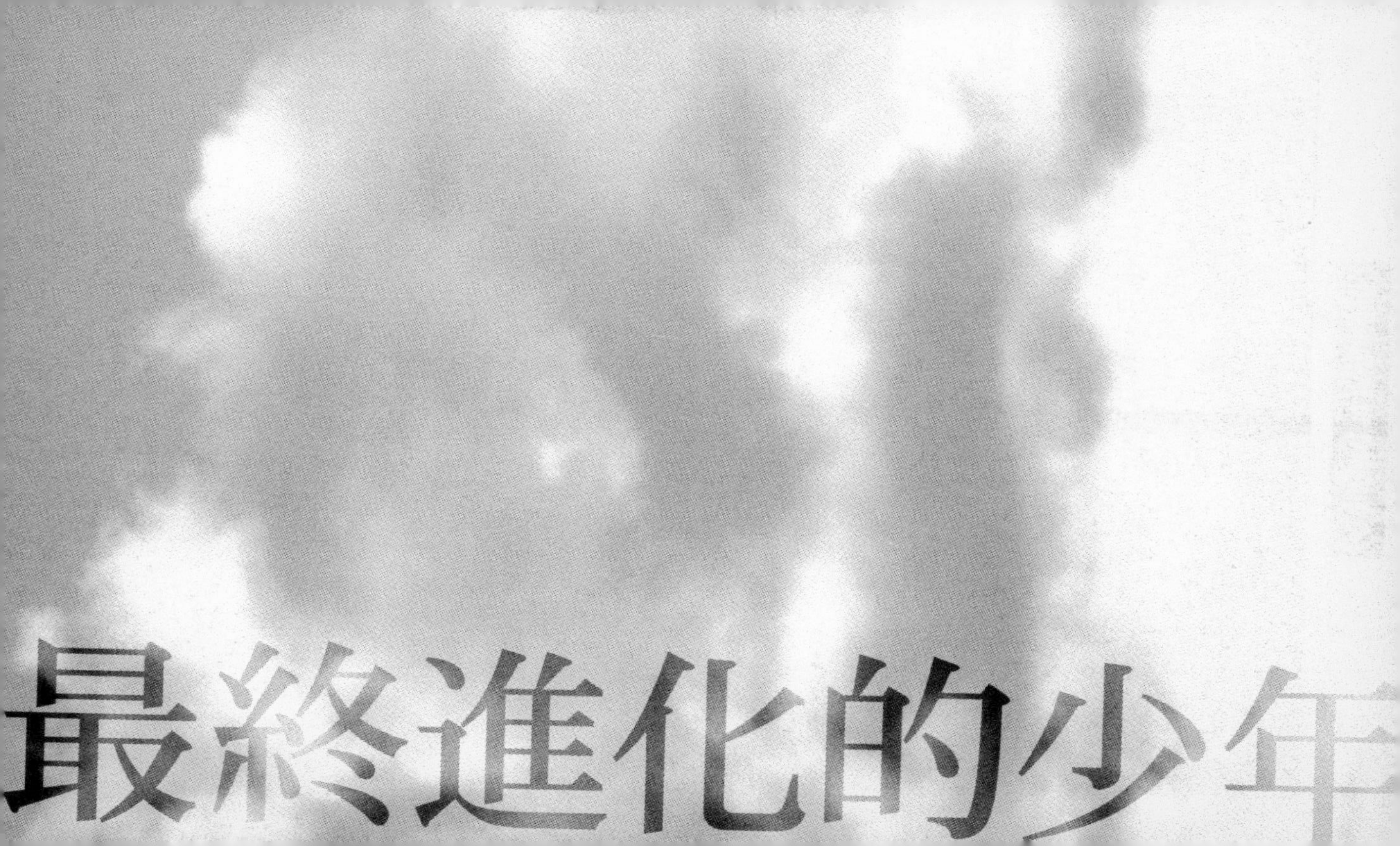
最終進化的少年

# Light Visual Manga 4

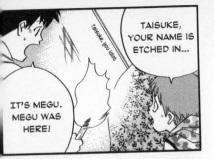

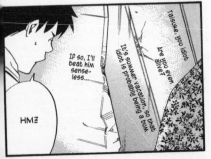

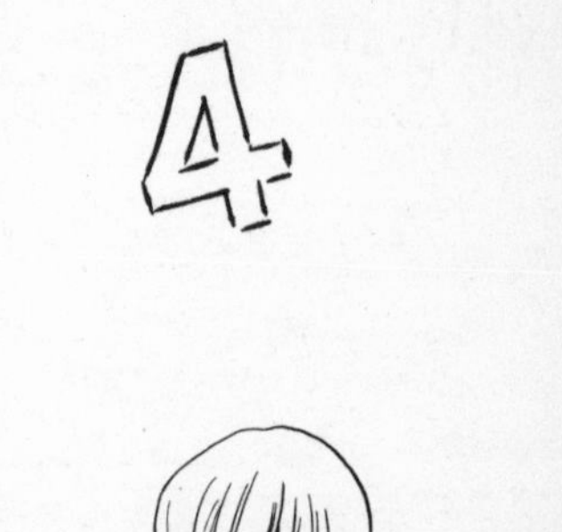

4
I'm bored.
ETCH
ETCH

TAISUKE, YOUR NAME IS ETCHED IN...
Taisuke, you idiot
IT'S MEGU. MEGU WAS HERE!
Taisuke, you idiot
Are you even alive?
It's summer vacation, so that idiot is probably being a bum
If so, I'll beat him senseless...
HM?
I'll make him regret that he was alive.
I'll stick my hand in...and make him shake so hard he won't go out in public.
I'll run away.
SISTER, I'M BACK...
TAISUKE!!
Morioka delicacy - cold noodles
I'm so scared!

ALIVE END

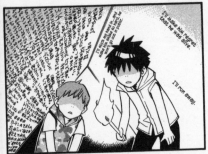

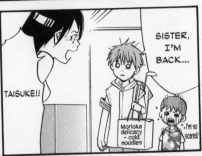

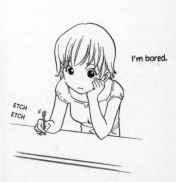

GROPER

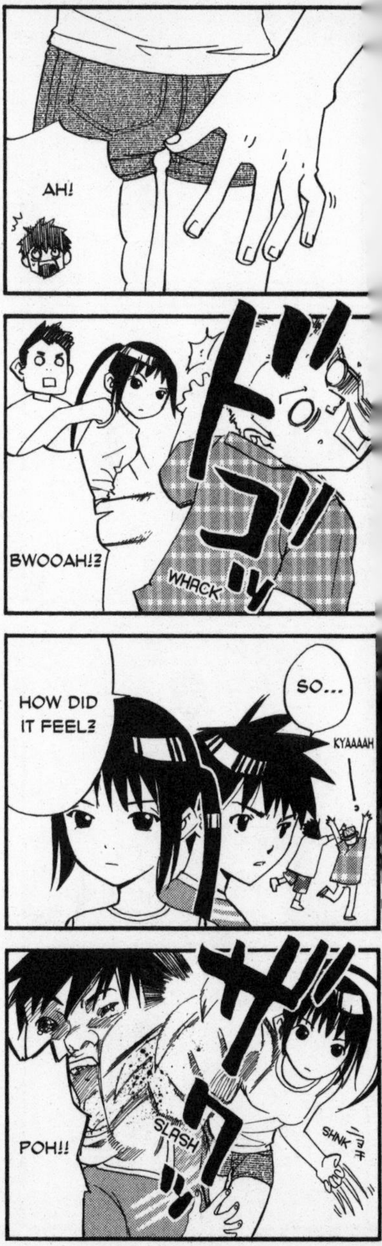
AH!
BWOOAH!?
WHACK
SO...
KYAAAAH
HOW DID IT FEEL?
SHNK
SLASH
POH!!

CATCHPHRASES FOR EVERYONE

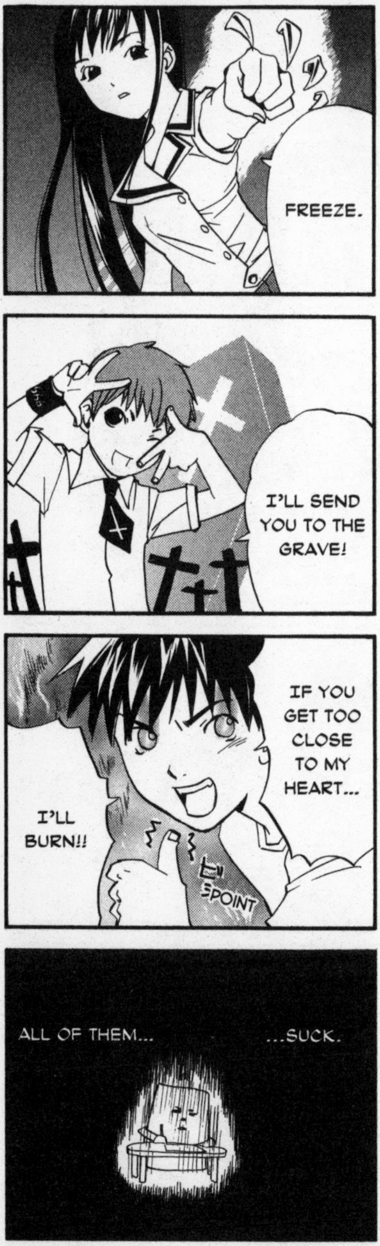
FREEZE.
I'LL SEND YOU TO THE GRAVE!
IF YOU GET TOO CLOSE TO MY HEART...
I'LL BURN!!
POINT
ALL OF THEM...
...SUCK.

## IT'S NAMI'S MOM, AFTER ALL

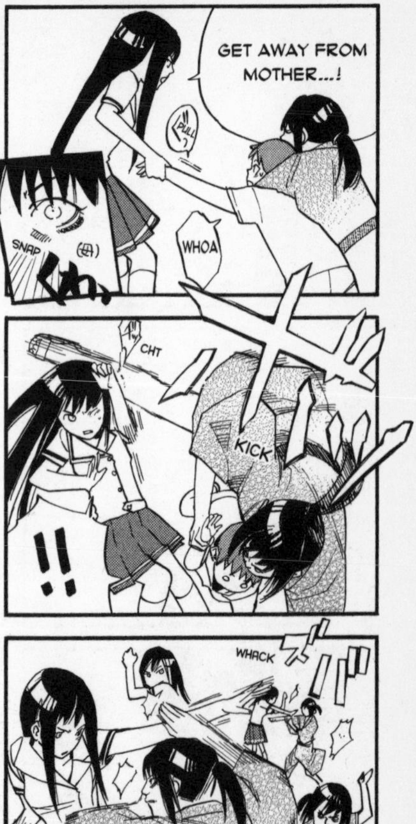
GET AWAY FROM MOTHER...!
PULL
WHOA
SNAP
CHT
KICK
!!
WHACK
PUNCH
KICK
MOTHER, HE IS NOT SATORU!
Haiii!
KICK
PUNCH
AWA-WA-WA-WA-WAHHH
IT'S SATORU! HAAAH!!
TREMBLE
TREMBLE

## ORIGINS OF THE ENERGY PULSES

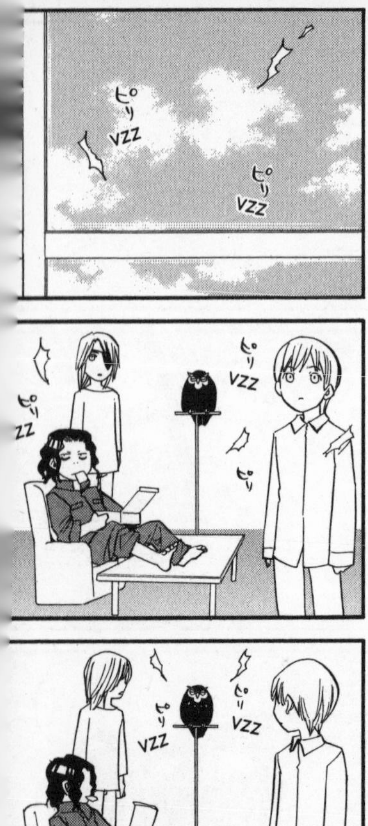
ピリ
VZZ
ピリ
VZZ
ピリ
VZZ
ピリ
ZZ
ピリ
VZZ
ピリ
VZZ
FUZZY FUZZY
HOOT
It's so relaxing...
Yeaaaahh...
ALPHA WAVES COMING FROM THE OWL...!!
THERE'S A LOT OF...
I'm sleepy...

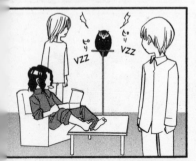

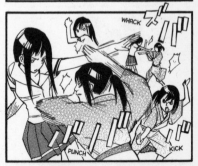

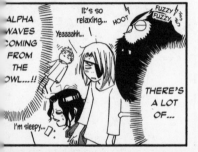

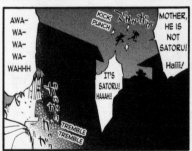

BECAUSE MEGU WAS TOO BORED

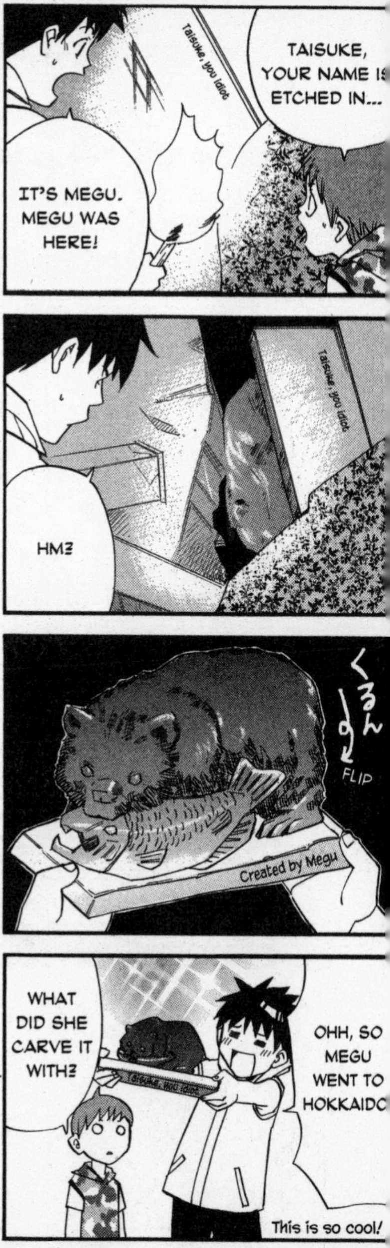
TAISUKE, YOUR NAME IS ETCHED IN...
Taisuke, you idiot
IT'S MEGU. MEGU WAS HERE!
Taisuke, you idiot
HM?
くるん
FLIP
Created by Megu
OHH, SO MEGU WENT TO HOKKAIDO
WHAT DID SHE CARVE IT WITH?
Taisuke, you idiot
This is so cool!

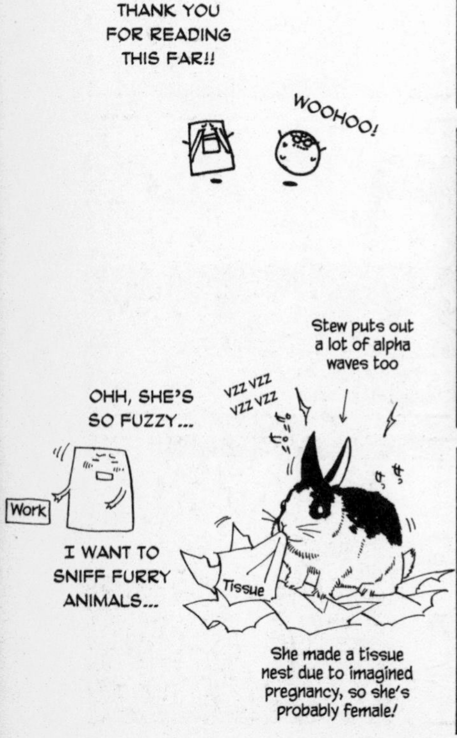
THANK YOU FOR READING THIS FAR!!
WOOHOO!
OHH, SHE'S SO FUZZY...
Stew puts out a lot of alpha waves too
VZZ VZZ VZZ VZZ
Work
I WANT TO SNIFF FURRY ANIMALS...
Tissue
She made a tissue nest due to imagined pregnancy, so she's probably female!

# Translation Notes

Japanese is a tricky language for most Westerners, and translation is often more art than science. For your edification and reading pleasure, here are notes on some of the places where we could have gone in a different direction with our translation of the work, or where a Japanese cultural reference is used.

### *Kamaitachi*, page 3

*Kamaitachi* was a mythical phenomenon in which winds would mysteriously cut or slice people and objects like a *kama* (sickle). It was thought to be caused by an *itachi* (weasel), so the term *kamaitachi* (sickle weasel) came about.

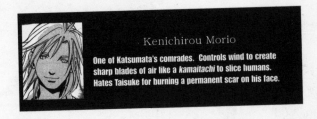

Kenichirou Morio

One of Katsumata's comrades. Controls wind to create sharp blades of air like a *kamaitachi* to slice humans. Hates Taisuke for burning a permanent scar on his face.

**Kattsun, page 10**

Kattsun is a nickname Yura made up for Katsumata.

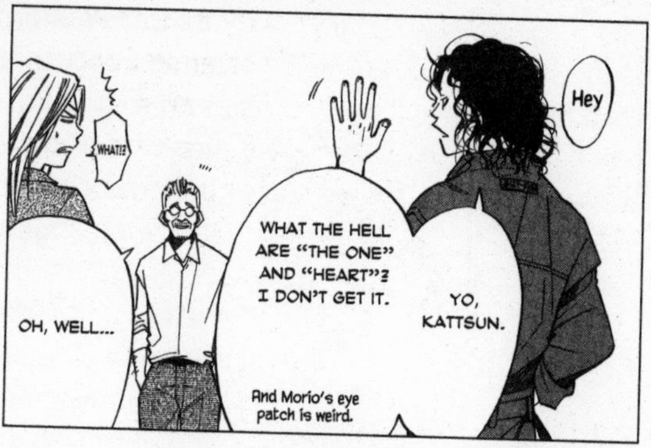
Hey
YO, KATTSUN.
WHAT THE HELL ARE "THE ONE" AND "HEART"? I DON'T GET IT.
And Morio's eye patch is weird.
WHAT!?
OH, WELL...

**Mutsu*ro-san, page 12**

Mutsu*ro-san is actually "Mutsugoro-san" (with a syllable blacked out on purpose by the artist). Mutsugoro-san was a famous expert on animals who appeared on many animal TV shows.

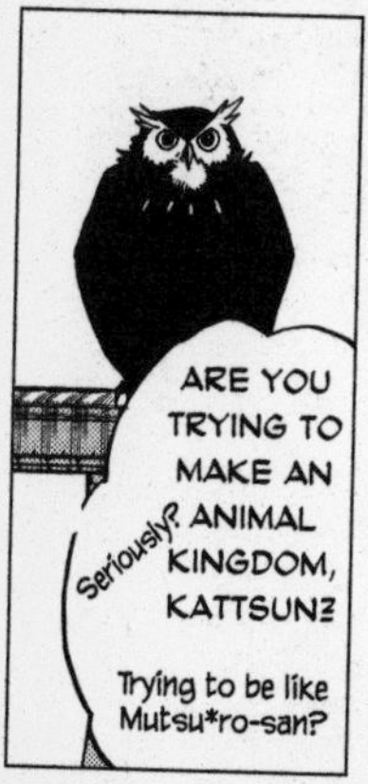
ARE YOU TRYING TO MAKE AN ANIMAL KINGDOM, KATTSUN?
Seriously?
Trying to be like Mutsu*ro-san?

Mutsugoro-san was well-known for his hands-on approach of interacting with animals, playfully wrestling bears and tigers – a Japanese version of the Crocodile Hunter, so to speak. There was an animal TV show called "Mutsugoro and his Delightful Friends," where his ranch full of animals was nicknamed "Mutsugoro's Animal Kingdom."

HEY, YUTA? SORRY, I REVERTED TO MY OLD DAYS...
NO, NOTHING'S WRONG...
I shouldn't do that anymore

## "Reverted to my old days," pages 25 and 28

Ryo was a former *yankee* (nickname for members of the *bousouzoku*, a Japanese racing gang) back in her schoolgirl days, or "old days." *Bousouzoku* members did not follow traffic rules much, and tangled with the police often and fought other gangs over territories. There were both all-female (Ladies' groups) and all-male (Tokkoutai groups) *bousouzoku*. Ryo talked about "revert(ing) to my old days," meaning that she picked fights or stared people down out of habit. A lot of *bousouzoku* came from blue-collar families, and often ended up being blue collar too, such as Ryo becoming a truck driver.

SQUEAK
RYO SOUNDED KINDA WEIRD TODAY...
"Reverted to her old days"?

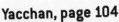

## Yacchan, page 104

Yacchan is a nickname for "Yakuza," or the Japanese mafia. This juice can is a parody of a real orange juice called "Nacchan."

Yacchan
Yacchan

### *Hidebu* and "I'm already dead," page 108

*Hidebu* was a term used in the manga/anime *Hokuto no Ken* (*Fist of the North Star*). *Hidebu* was the typical dying cry of any minor character that got killed by the protagonist, Kenshiro. In this case, Yuta probably punched or kicked Taisuke in his sleep, which made Taisuke yelp *hidebu* and also murmur the phrase "I'm already dead"—which was a parody of what Kenshiro used to say to the dying characters: "You're already dead."

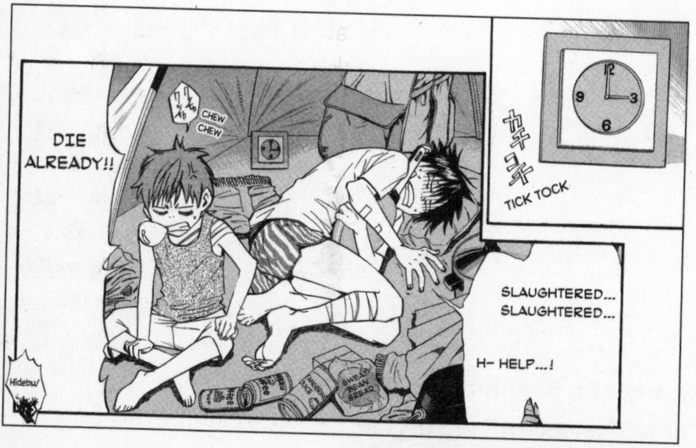
TICK TOCK
SLAUGHTERED... SLAUGHTERED...
H- HELP...!
CHEW CHEW
DIE ALREADY!!
Hidebu/

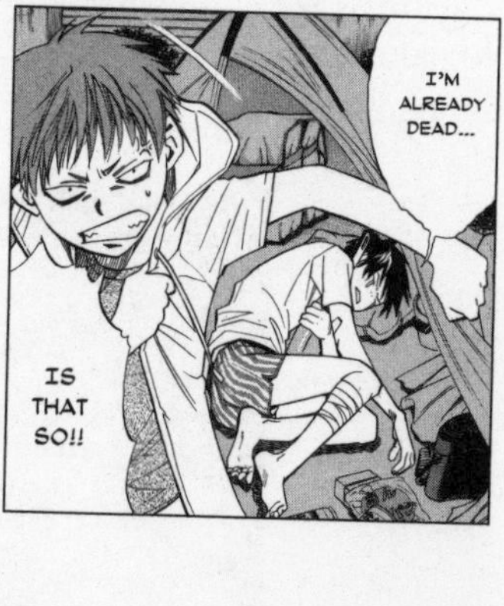
I'M ALREADY DEAD...
IS THAT SO!!

**Takuboku Ishikawa, page 129**

Takuboku Ishikawa was a famous naturalist poet known for writing *tanka* (an older form of haiku using a 5-7-5-7-7 mora pattern) and modern/free style poems.

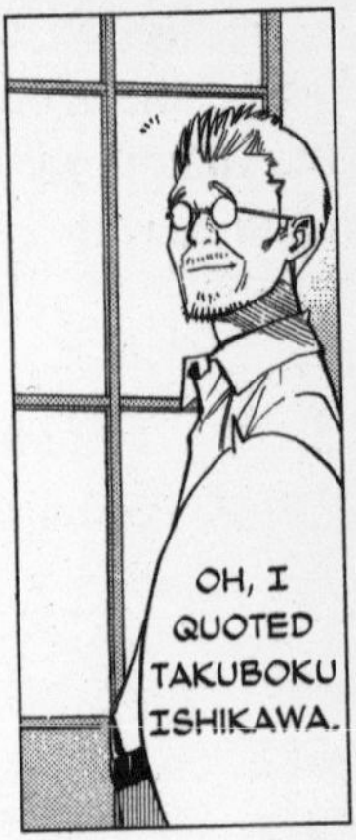
OH, I QUOTED TAKUBOKU ISHIKAWA.

**Statue of a bear biting a salmon, page 199**

One of Hokkaido's famous gifts is a wood carving of a bear biting into a salmon. To a Japanese person, this statue means Hokkaido, just as the Statue of Liberty means New York City to Americans.

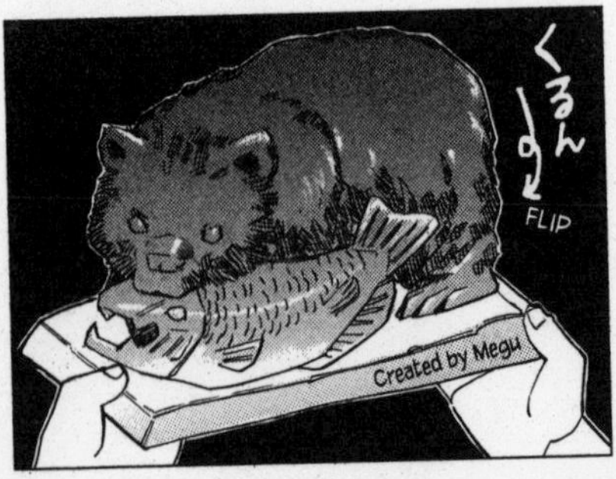
くるん
FLIP
Created by Megu

We're pleased to present you a preview from *Alive* volume 5. Please check our website (www.delreymanga.com) to see when this volume will be available in English. For now you'll have to make do with Japanese!

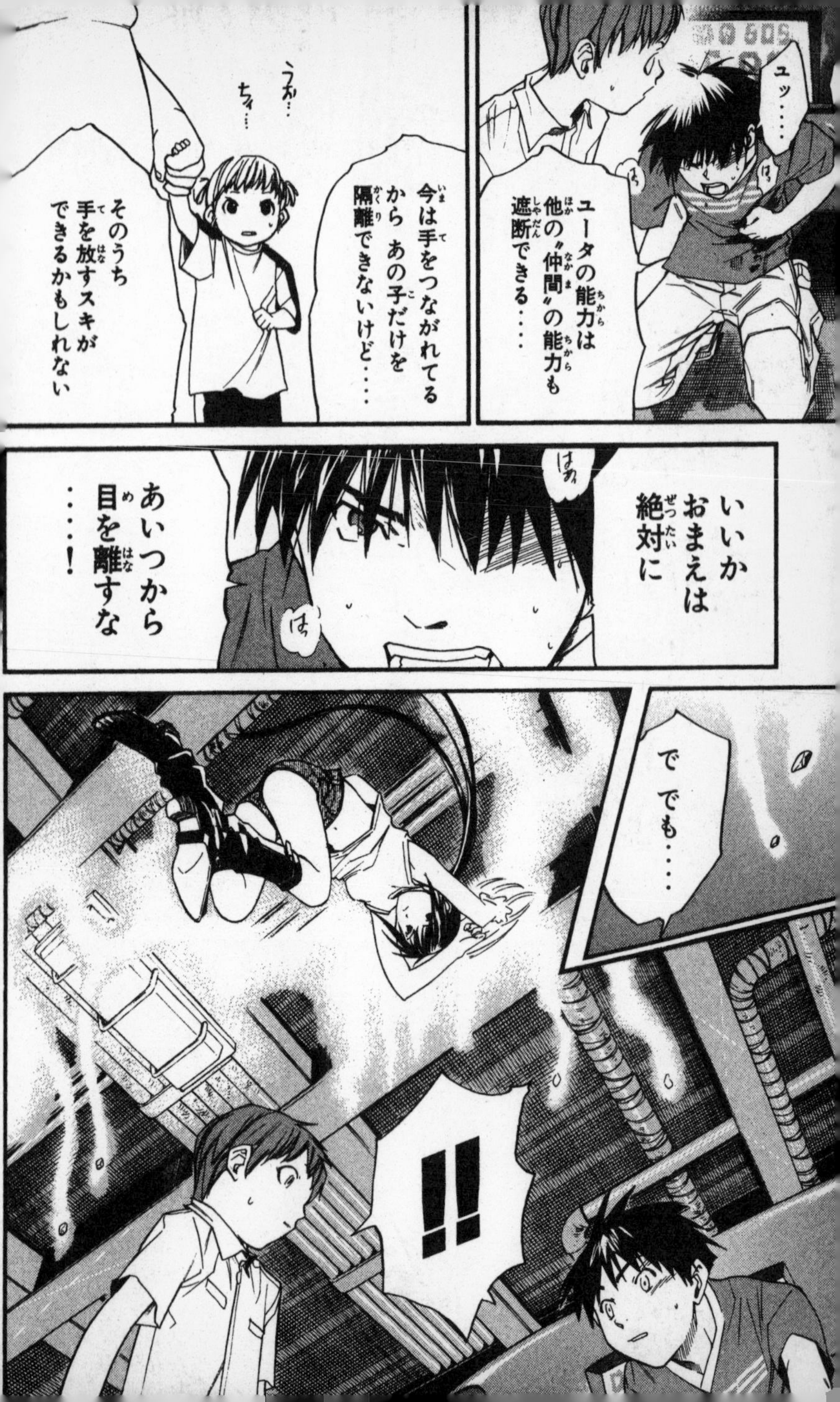
ユッ‥‥
はっ
はっ
ユータの能力は他の〝仲間〟の能力も遮断できる‥‥
今は手をつながれてるから あの子だけを隔離できないけど‥‥
うお…
ちィ…
そのうち手を放すスキができるかもしれない
いいか おまえは絶対に
はぁ
はっ
あいつから目を離すな‥‥！
で でも‥‥
!!

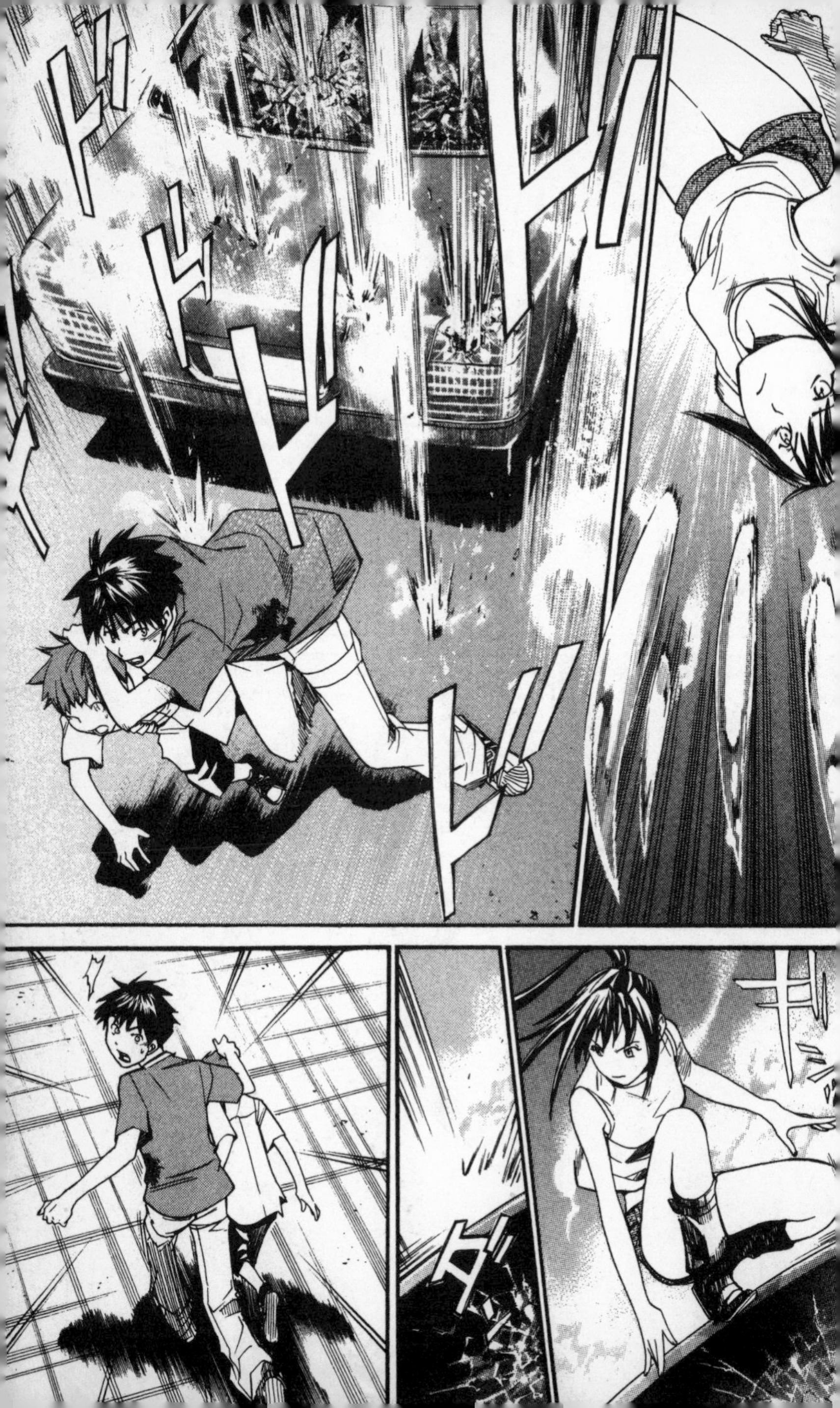

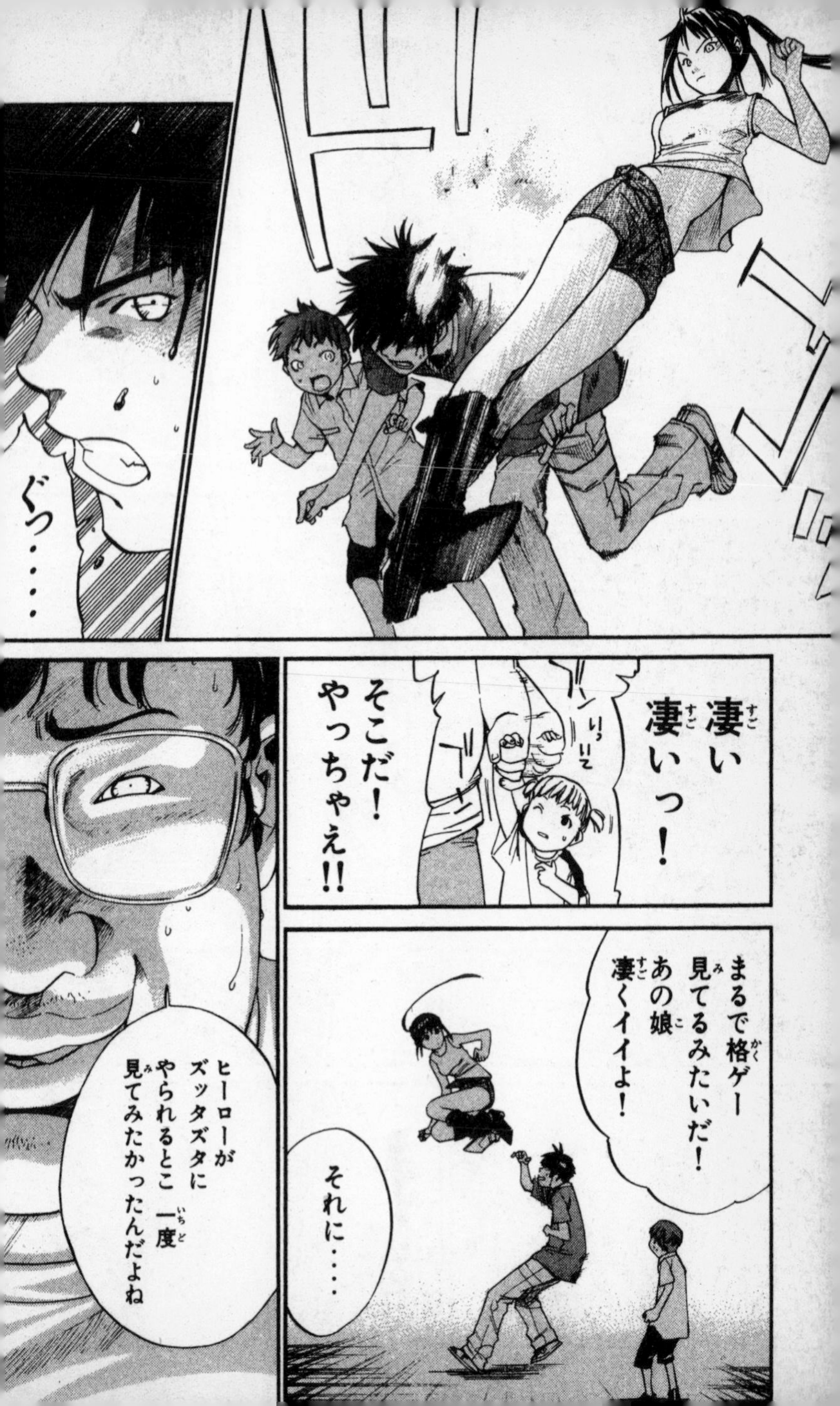
ぐっ・・・・
凄い凄いっ！
そこだ！やっちゃえ!!
まるで格ゲー見てるみたいだ！
あの娘凄くイイよ！
それに・・・・
ヒーローがズッタズタにやられるとこ一度見てみたかったんだよね

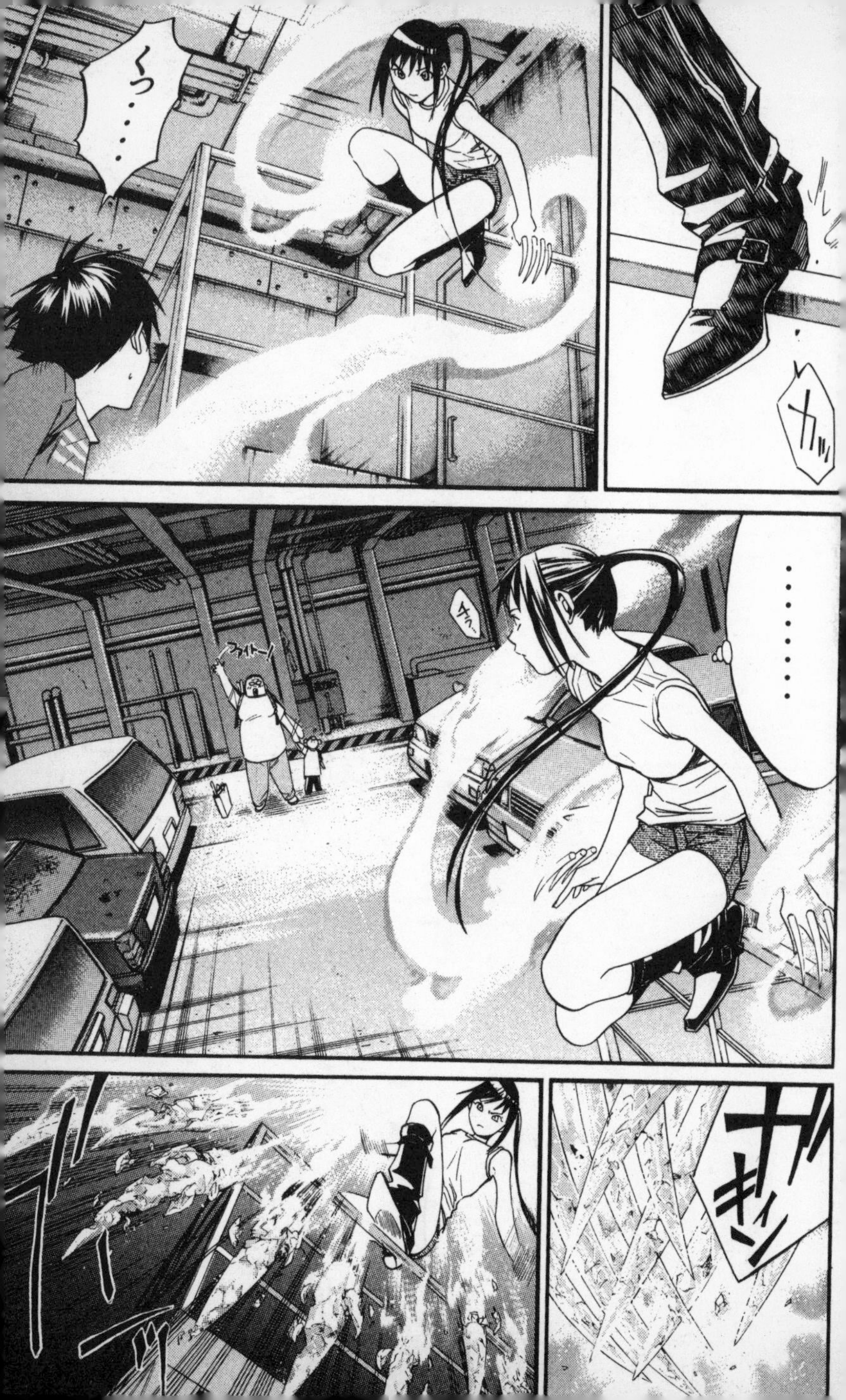
カッ
くっ……
……
チラ…
ファイトー!
ガキィン

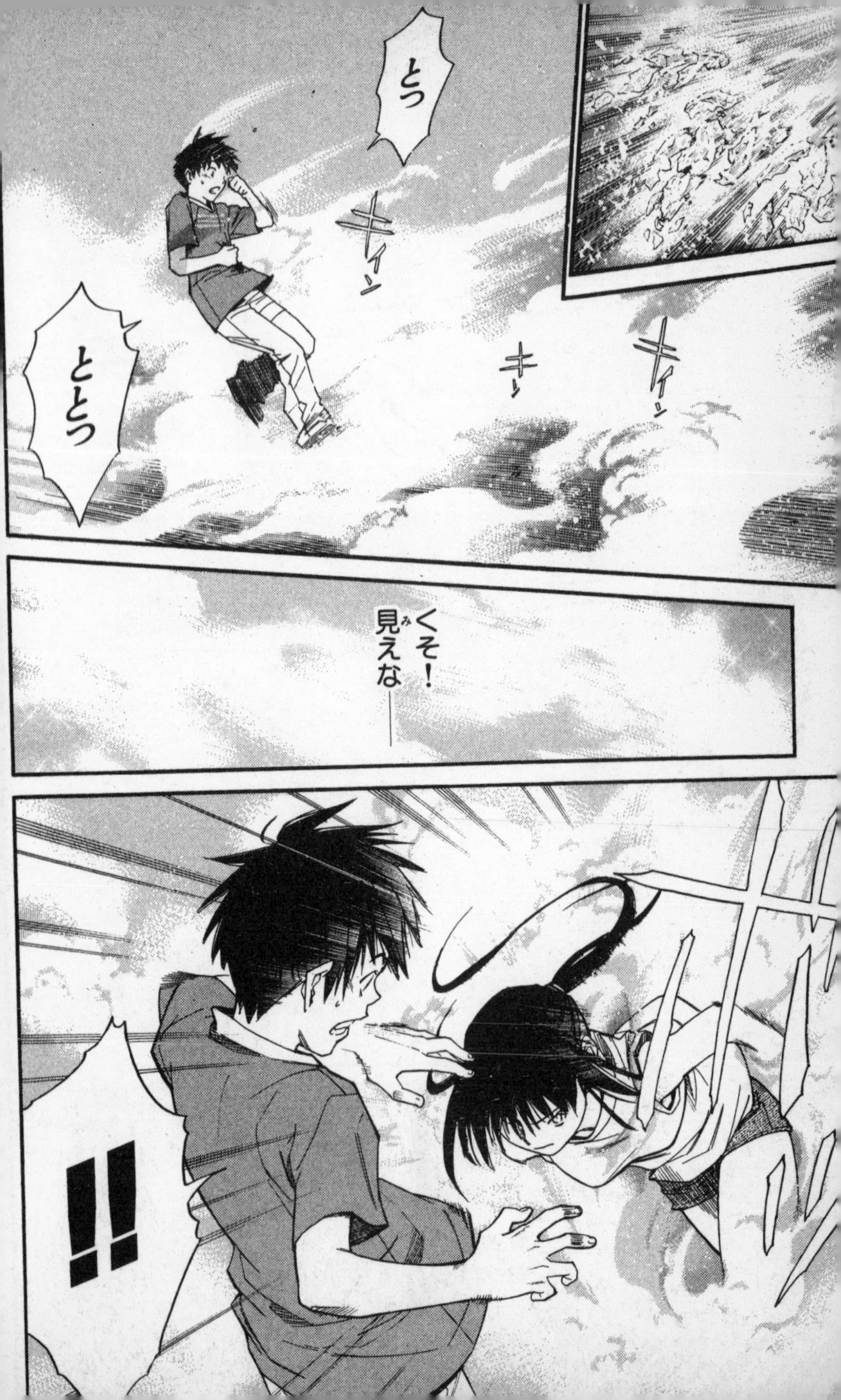

とっ
キィン
キィン
キン
ととっ
くそ！
見えな――
!!

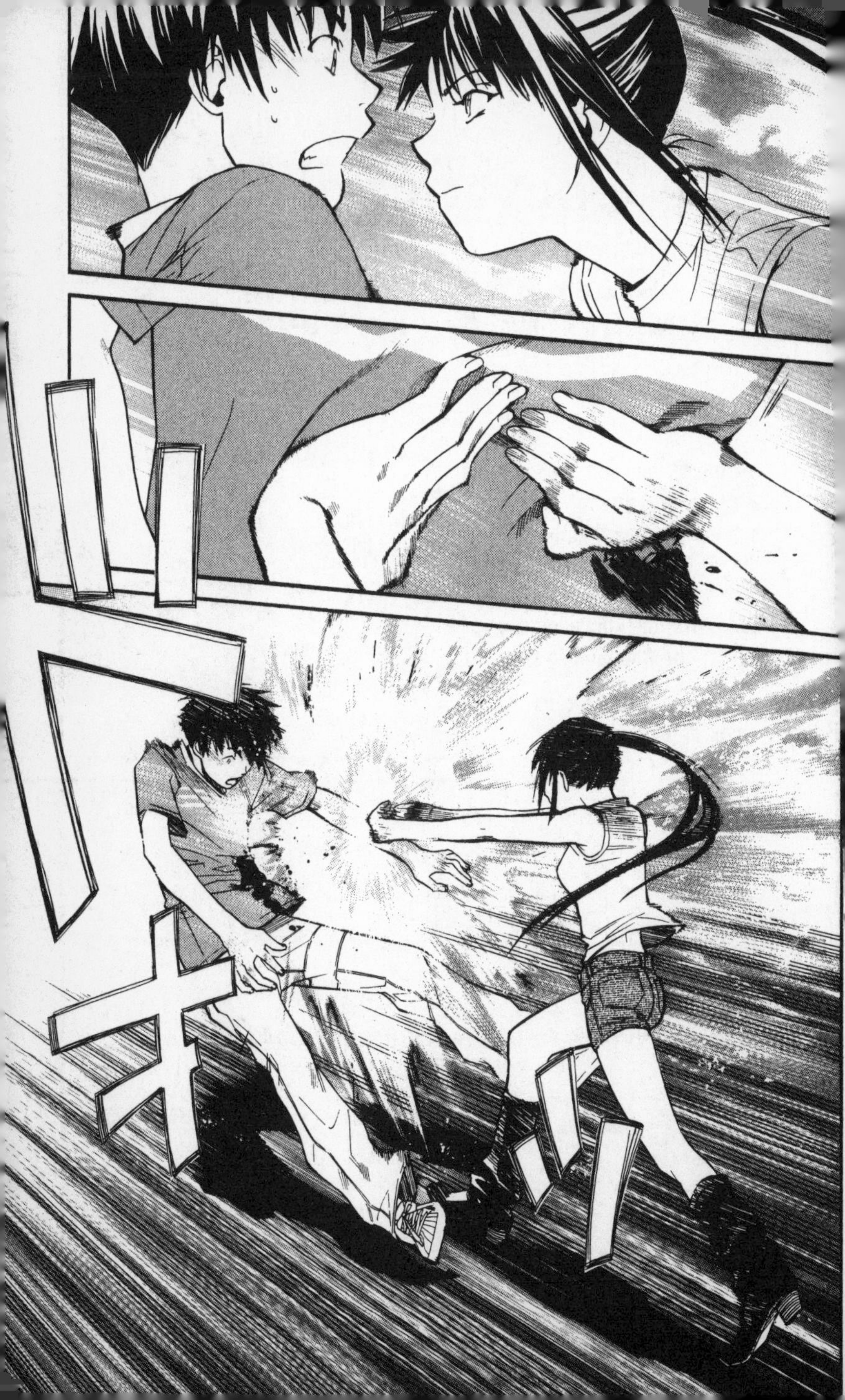

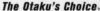

# PARASYTE

## BY HITOSHI IWAAKI

### THEY DESCEND FROM THE SKIES.
### THEY HAVE A HUNGER FOR HUMAN FLESH.

They are parasites and they are everywhere. They must take control of a human host to survive, and once they do, they can assume any deadly form they choose.

But they haven't taken over everyone! High school student Shin is resisting the invasion—battling for control of his own body against an alien parasite committed to thwart his plans to warn humanity of the horrors to come.

- *Now published in authentic right-to-left format!*
- *Featuring an all-new translation!*

## *Special extras in each volume! Read them all!*

# Psycho Busters

**MANGA BY AKINARI NAO**
**STORY BY YUYA AOKI**

## PSYCHIC TEENS ON THE RUN!

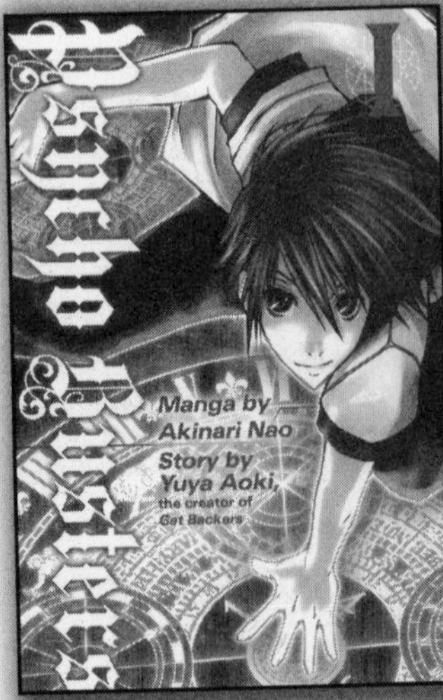

Manga by
Akinari Nao
Story by
Yuya Aoki,
the creator of
Get Backers


**Out of the blue, a beautiful girl asks Kakeru to run away with her. This could be any boy's dream come true, but there's something strange afoot.**

**It turns out that this girl is on the run from a shadowy government organization intent on using her psychic abilities for its own nefarious ends. But why does she need Kakeru's help? Could it be that he has secret powers, too?**

- **Story by Yuya Aoki, creator of *Get Backers***

***Special extras in each volume! Read them all!***

**VISIT WWW.DELREYMANGA.COM TO:**

- Read sample pages
- View release date calendars for upcoming volumes
- Sign up for Del Rey's free manga e-newsletter
- Find out the latest about new Del Rey Manga series

RATING T AGES 13+

DEL REY MANGA デルレイ

*The Otaku's Choice*™

# SHIKI TSUKAI

## MANGA BY TORU ZEKU
## ART BY YUNA TAKANAGI

### DEFENDING THE NATURAL ORDER OF THE UNIVERSE!

The *shiki tsukai* are "Keepers
of the Seasons"—magical
warriors pledged to defend the
planet's natural order against
those who would threaten it.
    When 14-year-old Akira Kizuki
joins the *shiki tsukai*, he knows
that it'll be a difficult life. But with
his new friends and mentors,
he's up to the challenge!

*Special extras in each volume! Read them all!*

# DRAGON EYE

## BY KAIRI FUJIYAMA

### HUMANITY'S SECRET WEAPON

Dracules—bloodthirsty, infectious monsters—have hunted human beings to the brink of extinction. Only the elite warriors of the VIUS Squad stand as humanity's last best hope.

Young Leila Mikami is one of the squad's most promising recruits, but she's not only training to battle the Dracules, she's determined to find the magical Dragon Eye, a weapon that will make her the most powerful warrior in the world.

*Special extras in each volume! Read them all!*